D0965889

# THE BOOK OF

# JEWISH
# VALUES

ALSO BY RABBI JOSEPH TELUSHKIN

NONFICTION

*The Nine Questions People Ask About Judaism* (with Dennis Prager)

*Why the Jews?: The Reason for Antisemitism* (with Dennis Prager)

*Jewish Literacy: The Most Important Things to Know About
the Jewish Religion, Its People, and Its History*

*Jewish Humor: What the Best Jewish Jokes Say About the Jews*

*Jewish Wisdom: Ethical, Spiritual, and Historical Lessons
from the Great Works and Thinkers*

*Words That Hurt, Words That Heal: How to Use Words Wisely and Well*

*Biblical Literacy: The Most Important People, Events,
and Ideas of the Hebrew Bible*

FICTION

*The Unorthodox Murder of Rabbi Wahl*

*The Final Analysis of Dr. Stark*

*An Eye for an Eye*

# THE BOOK OF
# JEWISH
# VALUES

## A DAY-BY-DAY GUIDE
## TO ETHICAL LIVING

## RABBI JOSEPH TELUSHKIN

BELL TOWER

NEW YORK

Acknowledgment for permission to reprint previously published material
is found on page 512.

Published by Bell Tower,
New York, New York.
Member of the Crown Publishing Group.

Random House, Inc. New York, Toronto, London, Sydney, Auckland
www.randomhouse.com

Bell Tower and colophon are registered trademarks of Random House, Inc.

Printed in the United States of America

Design by Meryl Sussman Levavi, Digitext

Library of Congress Cataloging-in-Publication Data
Telushkin, Joseph, 1948–
The book of Jewish values : a day-by-day guide to ethical living/
Joseph Telushkin.—1st ed.
1. Ethics, Jewish.   2. Conduct of life.   3. Jewish way of life.
I. Title.
BJ1285.T45   2000

296.3'6—dc21                                    99-34021

ISBN 0-609-60330-2

9   10

*For my beloved wife and children*

*Dvorah,*

*Rebecca, Naomi, Shira, and Benjamin.*

# Acknowledgments

❧

Several friends and colleagues generously gave of their time to read drafts of this book. Along with providing encouragement and stylistic and editorial advice, they also critiqued entries that they felt were not working, which led me to rework many chapters, expand others, and drop some. I feel blessed by God to have such devoted and intelligent friends, and am particularly pleased to acknowledge publicly the contributions of Rabbi Irwin Kula, Daniel Taub, Dr. Stephen Marmer, Rabbi David Woznica, Rabbi Hanoch Teller, Allen Estrin, Rabbi Leonid Feldman, Larry Gellman, and my beloved wife and fellow writer, Dvorah Telushkin. I would also like to thank Rabbi Israel Stein for reviewing and verifying the many hundreds of sources cited and David Wade Smith for his excellent job of copyediting.

Rabbi Dr. Michael Berger of Emory University, a friend and a Jewish scholar of wide-ranging knowledge, read *The Book of Jewish Values* in its entirety. He challenged my thinking and my conclusions when he thought they were wrong or overstated, and suggested sources I had overlooked. I am deeply grateful to him for enriching this manuscript, as he has done with several of my earlier books.

David Szonyi has edited my last six books. Each time I entrust him with manuscript pages, I am taken aback and humbled by how many stylistic and editorial improvements he makes. As I have noted before, David is a blessing to any writer.

About two dozen of the more than three hundred short chapters in *The Book of Jewish Values* draw heavily on the works of other writers, several of whom are dear friends. I acknowledge with thanks Dennis Prager, Rabbi Abraham Twerski, M.D., Yitta Halberstam Mandelbaum, Rabbi Hanoch Teller, and Rabbi Jack Riemer for granting me permission to quote from their books—works that have profoundly affected me and which I hope, in turn, will so affect you. I am also grateful to the other writers and publishers who granted me permission to quote from their writings.

I am particularly grateful to David Zerner for his belief in this project and his generous support of it and of an additional project I am undertaking in further developing the study of Jewish ethics and its applicability to daily behavior. David is a man of great ethical integrity, committed to Judaism and the Jewish community, and to the importance of Jewish study. I am honored to have known him now for the past twenty years. I wish to thank as well for their support his wife, Lillian, his daughters, Donna, and Sandra Zerner, Rabbi Tirzah Firestone, and David Friedman.

I am grateful as well to my congregation, the Synagogue for the Performing Arts in Los Angeles, whose beloved members and wonderful, supportive leadership have given me the forum to develop many of the ideas in this book, and to CLAL, the National Jewish Center for Learning and Leadership, where I have served as an Associate since 1987. I am particularly happy to acknowledge two of the organization's professional leaders, Rabbi Irwin Kula, its president, and Donna Rosenthal, its executive vice-chairman, for their friendship and support. For over two decades, CLAL (founded by Rabbi Yitz Greenberg) and its extraordinary faculty and staff have played a major role in educating many of American Jewry's lay leadership in Jewish values. I believe that the impact of this organization, in raising the intellectual and moral quality of American Jewry, will continue to expand even more in the coming years.

Richard Pine has been my agent now for almost two decades, and my respect, admiration, and affection for him grow from year to year and book to book.

This is the first book on which I have worked with Toinette Lippe, my editor at Bell Tower, and the experience has been joyous. A woman of great literary and editorial discernment, she has made her enthusiasm for this project apparent since when she first read my proposal. As every writer knows, there are few things as inspirational and motivational to a writer as having an editor who believes in you and in the significance of your project.

The writing of *The Book of Jewish Values* has been particularly important to me. Most of my previous books have been devoted to explaining Judaism and its ideas to Jews and non-Jews. Although I always write as a strong believer in Judaism, my earlier books were largely descriptive, whereas this work is entirely devoted to advocacy, to presenting people with hundreds of lessons drawn from Jewish sources and scholars that teach one how to be a better person. In the course of writing this book, I know that I was often transformed and, I hope, elevated. The writing of *The Book of Jewish Values* became for me a holy act, an attempt to bring about a little of the "perfection of the world under the rule of God" for which Jews pray daily. If some of the lessons contained here influence you to practice goodness and kindness more actively and more imaginatively, I will feel more than amply compensated. Indeed, I thank you for reading this book.

# Contents

⚭

ACKNOWLEDGMENTS                                                    VII
INTRODUCTION                                                        1

## WEEK 1

DAY   1   On Hearing a Siren                                        3
DAY   2   "Let Your Fellow's Money Be as Precious to You as Your Own"   4
DAY   3   The Purchase That Is Always Forbidden                    6
DAY   4   "What Would God Want Me to Do?"                          8
DAY   5   Be Generous Even When Your Instincts Are Lazy            9
DAY   6   When You're Tempted to Cheat                            10
DAY   7   Shabbat                                                 11

## WEEK 2

DAY   8   Give Cheerfully                                         11
DAY   9   When a Person Says "I'm Hungry"                         13
DAY  10   Don't Play Favorites                                    14
DAY  11   Don't Make Your Family Afraid of You                    15
DAY  12   Support Political Asylum                                17
DAY  13   Bless Your Children                                     18
DAY  14   Shabbat                                                 20

## WEEK 3

DAY  15   Don't Waste Time                                        21
DAY  16   "Stay Away from a Bad Neighbor"                         23
DAY  17   The First Trait to Look for in a Spouse                 25
DAY  18   "Love Your Wife as Yourself"                            26
DAY  19   Respect Your In-Laws                                    27
DAY  20   Don't Speak Unless You Have Something to Say            29
DAY  21   Shabbat                                                 30

## WEEK 4

DAY  22   If You Have a Bad Temper (1)                            31
DAY  23   If You Have a Bad Temper (2)                            33
DAY  24   Find Excuses for Behavior That Seems Unkind             34

DAY 25   *"Judge the Whole of a Person Favorably"*                          36
DAY 26   *Return Lost Objects*                                              37
DAY 27   *"As Long as the Candle Is Burning…"*                              39
DAY 28   *Shabbat*                                                          40

## WEEK 5

DAY 29   *Don't "Steal" Another Person's Mind*                              40
DAY 30   *Who Is Wise?*                                                     42
DAY 31   *The Special Obligation to Visit and Help People,*
         *Particularly Poor People, Who Are Sick*                           44
DAY 32   *Visiting the Sick: Seven Suggestions*                             45
DAY 33   *A Gynecologist from New Jersey, a Lawyer from Brooklyn*           48
DAY 34   *Sharing Helpful News*                                            49
DAY 35   *Shabbat*                                                          51

## WEEK 6

DAY 36   *Is a Jew Permitted to Smoke?*                                     51
DAY 37   *When Not Giving Charity Is the Highest Charity*                   54
DAY 38   *Give Money When Times Are Hard*                                   56
DAY 39   *Acting Cheerfully Is Not a Choice*                                57
DAY 40   *One Must Always Greet Another Person*                             59
DAY 41   *Should a Recovering Alcoholic Drink Wine on Shabbat*
         *and at the Seder?*                                                61
DAY 42   *Shabbat*                                                          63

## WEEK 7

DAY 43   *The Jewish Ethics of Speech: What Is* Lashon Hara?                64
DAY 44   *Don't Pass on Negative Comments*                                  65
DAY 45   *The Sin That No One Ever Acknowledges Committing*                 67
DAY 46   *When Confrontation Is Desirable*                                  68
DAY 47   *"You Shall Not Ill-Treat Any…Orphan"*                             70
DAY 48   *Why Refraining from Gossiping Is an Important Challenge*          72
DAY 49   *Shabbat*                                                          73

## WEEK 8

DAY 50   *Tzedaka Is More Than Charity*                                     74
DAY 51   *Fight Fairly*                                                     76
DAY 52   *A Day Without Rumors; How About a Week?*                          78
DAY 53   *When Is It Appropriate to Pass On a Rumor?*                       79
DAY 54   *Some Thoughts for a Bar Mitzvah or Bat Mitzvah*                   80
DAY 55   *Learning from the Bad to Do Good*                                 82
DAY 56   *Shabbat*                                                          84

WEEK 9

| DAY 57 | Love the Stranger | 84 |
| DAY 58 | The Torah on the Blind and the Deaf | 86 |
| DAY 59 | Standing Up for Justice | 87 |
| DAY 60 | Don't Buy Products Produced by Exploited Workers | 88 |
| DAY 61 | Everybody Deserves a "Tenk You" | 89 |
| DAY 62 | The Need for Moral Imagination | 90 |
| DAY 63 | Shabbat | 91 |

WEEK 10

| DAY 64 | "One Who Learns from His Companion a Single Chapter" | 92 |
| DAY 65 | Cite Your Sources | 93 |
| DAY 66 | Who Is Rich? | 94 |
| DAY 67 | Enjoy, Enjoy | 95 |
| DAY 68 | "Keep Far Away from Falsehood" | 97 |
| DAY 69 | "What Good Thing Happened to Me This Week?" | 98 |
| DAY 70 | Shabbat | 99 |

WEEK 11

| DAY 71 | When, If Ever, Is It Permitted to Lie? (1): When Life Is at Stake | 100 |
| DAY 72 | When, If Ever, Is It Permitted to Lie? (2): Judaism and White Lies | 102 |
| DAY 73 | When, If Ever, Is It Permitted to Lie? (3): Lies Told for Reasons of Humility, Privacy, and Not to Harm Another | 104 |
| DAY 74 | Declaring a "Complaining Fast" | 106 |
| DAY 75 | The Most Unusual of Blessings | 107 |
| DAY 76 | Treating People Who Are Retarded with Respect | 109 |
| DAY 77 | Shabbat | 110 |

WEEK 12

| DAY 78 | Don't Charge Interest | 111 |
| DAY 79 | Help Someone Laugh | 113 |
| DAY 80 | For Whom Was I Named? | 114 |
| DAY 81 | A Lifesaving Bribe | 115 |
| DAY 82 | The Little Indecencies That Reveal Character | 116 |
| DAY 83 | "The Most Beautiful Etrog I Have Ever Seen" | 118 |
| DAY 84 | Shabbat | 120 |

WEEK 13

| DAY 85 | "Do Not Stand by While Your Neighbor's Blood Is Shed": The Requirement to Intervene | 120 |
| DAY 86 | When You Suspect Child Abuse | 122 |
| DAY 87 | Untamed Anger and the Death Of Love | 124 |
| DAY 88 | Be Fair to Your Enemy | 126 |

DAY   89  Don't Make People Tell You Lies                                          127
DAY   90  "He Who Saves a Single Life It Is as If He Saved an Entire World"  128
DAY   91  Shabbat                                                                    130

## WEEK 14

DAY   92  Spend a Week Following Your Heart                                   130
DAY   93  Don't Make Unrealistic Demands of People                          131
DAY   94  A Jewish View of Hunting                                              133
DAY   95  Feed Your Animals Before Yourself                                   135
DAY   96  Don't Spread Negative, but Irrelevant, Information
          About Someone You Dislike                                             136
DAY   97  Don't Humiliate an Enemy                                             137
DAY   98  Shabbat                                                                138

## WEEK 15

DAY   99  Pray for Someone Else Today                                        139
DAY  100  Raising Your Child to Be a Mensch                                 140
DAY  101  The Questions All Parents Should Ask Themselves               142
DAY  102  "Just as Theft of Money Is Theft, So Is Theft of Time"         143
DAY  103  What It Means to Sanctify God's Name                            145
DAY  104  The Special Obligation of Religious Jews to Sanctify God's Name  147
DAY  105  Shabbat                                                              148

## WEEK 16

DAY  106  When Is the Best Time to Repent?                                 149
DAY  107  Acknowledge Your Sin and Accept Responsibility                151
DAY  108  Ask for Forgiveness Even When You're Not Fully in the Wrong  152
DAY  109  Tipping Even Those Whose Faces You Don't See                  153
DAY  110  What If You Could Read Your Obituary Today?                    154
DAY  111  The Infinite Ways of Doing Good                                   155
DAY  112  Shabbat                                                              157

## WEEK 17

DAY  113  "You Shall Not Place a Stumbling Block"                         157
DAY  114  The Nameless Person Behind the Counter                         160
DAY  115  Acts of Kindness (1): Looking Backward                         163
DAY  116  Acts of Kindness (2): Looking Ahead                            164
DAY  117  Acts of Kindness (3): Looking Ahead                            166
DAY  118  The Least Time to Spare, the Most Time to Give                168
DAY  119  Shabbat                                                              169

## WEEK 18

DAY  120  God's Four Questions                                              170
DAY  121  Do You Scream When You Should?                                 172

DAY 122  *Paying a Laborer's Wages Promptly*                                    173
DAY 123  *What a Worker Owes His Employer*                                      174
DAY 124  *What We Owe Our Siblings*                                             177
DAY 125  *Anger: Three Thoughts Before You Explode*                            178
DAY 126  *Shabbat*                                                             179

## WEEK 19

DAY 127  *What Does It Mean to Honor and Revere Your Parents?*                 180
DAY 128  *What You Don't Owe Your Parents*                                     182
DAY 129  *Escort Your Guests*                                                  184
DAY 130  *Two Pieces of Paper*                                                 185
DAY 131  *Read and Listen to Points of View with Which You Disagree*           186
DAY 132  *It's Not Only What You Do for Your Parents That Counts—*
         *It's Your Attitude*                                                  188
DAY 133  *Shabbat*                                                            189

## WEEK 20

DAY 134  *"Educate a Child According to His Way"*                              190
DAY 135  *Don't Threaten Your Children with Physical Punishment*               192
DAY 136  *Enter a Mourner's Home with Silence*                                 193
DAY 137  *"Don't Take My Grief from Me"*                                       195
DAY 138  *"You Shall Not Carry God's Name in Vain": An Unforgivable Sin*       197
DAY 139  *When It's Good to Be a Fool*                                         199
DAY 140  *Shabbat*                                                            200

## WEEK 21

DAY 141  *Helping Non-Jews*                                                    201
DAY 142  *Schedule Kindness into Your Day*                                     203
DAY 143  *Don't Be a Pious Fool*                                               204
DAY 144  *Don't Serve Liquor with an Overly Generous Hand*                     206
DAY 145  *True Hospitality: Did You Ask Your Wife?*                            207
DAY 146  *Don't Embarrass Your Guest, Don't Embarrass Your Children*          208
DAY 147  *Shabbat*                                                            209

## WEEK 22

DAY 148  *When You Suspect Spousal Abuse*                                      210
DAY 149  *An Abused Spouse: How You Can Help*                                  213
DAY 150  *Maimonides' Advice: How to Change Negative Behavior*                 215
DAY 151  *The Unending Obligation to Be Kind*                                  217
DAY 152  *"What's Hateful Unto You..."*                                        218
DAY 153  *Not Everything That Is Thought Should Be Said*                       219
DAY 154  *Shabbat*                                                            220

## Week 23

| | | |
|---|---|---:|
| DAY 155 | *A Day of Kind Deeds* | 221 |
| DAY 156 | *An Expensive Technique for Overcoming Anger* | 222 |
| DAY 157 | *When You're Angry at Your Spouse: Putting Things into Perspective* | 224 |
| DAY 158 | *Treating Your Employees with Respect* | 225 |
| DAY 159 | *Abraham, the Model of Hospitality* | 226 |
| DAY 160 | *There Is No Such Thing as a Free Lunch* | 228 |
| DAY 161 | *Shabbat* | 229 |

## Week 24

| | | |
|---|---|---:|
| DAY 162 | *How Fear of God Can Make You a Better Person (1)* | 230 |
| DAY 163 | *How Fear of God Can Make You a Better Person (2)* | 231 |
| DAY 164 | *Express Gratitude to Your Parents* | 233 |
| DAY 165 | *When Your Mate and Your Parents Are in Conflict* | 234 |
| DAY 166 | *"From a Child Is Beautiful, Anything"* | 236 |
| DAY 167 | *"This Is the Most Delicious Muffin I Have Ever Tasted"* | 237 |
| DAY 168 | *Shabbat* | 239 |

## Week 25

| | | |
|---|---|---:|
| DAY 169 | *When You Hear That Someone's Taking a Long Trip, Make Sure They Take Along Some Extra Money* | 240 |
| DAY 170 | *Steady Giving* | 241 |
| DAY 171 | *Prevention of Cruelty to Animals: What the Torah Says* | 243 |
| DAY 172 | *Can Veal Be Kosher?* | 244 |
| DAY 173 | *Should a Jew Wear Fur?* | 246 |
| DAY 174 | *When Giving Enough Is Not Enough* | 248 |
| DAY 175 | *Shabbat* | 249 |

## Week 26

| | | |
|---|---|---:|
| DAY 176 | *What Does the Sick Person Need?* | 250 |
| DAY 177 | *Should a Doctor or a Close Family Member Tell the Truth to a Person Who Is Dying?* | 252 |
| DAY 178 | *Is Your Work Sacred?* | 255 |
| DAY 179 | *Is Abortion Murder? Should a Woman's Right to Abortion Be Absolute?* | 257 |
| DAY 180 | *Should a Woman Have the Right to Do What She Wants with Her Body?* | 260 |
| DAY 181 | *Rabbi Aryeh Levine and the Mitzvah to Visit the Sick* | 261 |
| DAY 182 | *Shabbat* | 263 |

## Week 27

| | | |
|---|---|---:|
| DAY 183 | *Help Someone to Find a Spouse, Help Someone to Find Work* | 264 |
| DAY 184 | *Do Good...Now* | 265 |

DAY 185   Teach Your Child Torah                                           266
DAY 186   Teach Your Child the Value of Human Life                         268
DAY 187   A Pragmatic Reason for Forgiving Others                          270
DAY 188   Charity Is Not Enough                                            271
DAY 189   Shabbat                                                          272

## WEEK 28

DAY 190   Find Work for the Developmentally Disabled                       273
DAY 191   An Employer Must Know How His Employees Live                     274
DAY 192   Confession and Your Neighbor's Soul                              275
DAY 193   How Can One Repent Who Has Committed the Ultimate
          and Unforgivable Sin?                                            277
DAY 194   When a Jew Acts Dishonestly Toward a Non-Jew                     278
DAY 195   One Boss in a Million                                            280
DAY 196   Shabbat                                                          281

## WEEK 29

DAY 197   Have You Written an Ethical Will?                                282
DAY 198   Three Traits That Reveal Your Character                          285
DAY 199   "Until the Day of One's Death"                                   286
DAY 200   When the Old Become Frail                                        288
DAY 201   Beyond the Letter of the Law                                     289
DAY 202   Consult with Your Spouse, Consult with Your Friends             291
DAY 203   Shabbat                                                          292

## WEEK 30

DAY 204   "The Dust of Forbidden Speech"                                   293
DAY 205   A Twenty-Four-Hour Experiment                                    294
DAY 206   Don't Bear a Grudge                                              295
DAY 207   Picking Up Stumbling Blocks                                      297
DAY 208   The Limits of Self-Sacrifice                                     298
DAY 209   "Go and Gather the Feathers"                                     299
DAY 210   Shabbat                                                          300

## WEEK 31

DAY 211   Make Sure You Have a Friend Who Can Criticize You               301
DAY 212   Bar Mitzvahs and Bat Mitzvahs, and the Need for a
          New Kind of Hero                                                 302
DAY 213   Start Your Day with Gratitude                                    303
DAY 214   If You Have a Tendency to Complain About Others                  305
DAY 215   Respect Your Family's Privacy                                    306
DAY 216   "What Does a Good Guest Say?"                                    307
DAY 217   Shabbat                                                          308

## WEEK 32

| | | |
|---|---|---|
| DAY 218 | Question to Ask Yourself Before You Criticize Another | 309 |
| DAY 219 | Knowing When to Step Aside | 311 |
| DAY 220 | When You've Judged Another Unfairly | 313 |
| DAY 221 | "Therefore Was Man Created Singly" | 315 |
| DAY 222 | "If Someone Wishes to Kill You, Get Up Early and Kill Him First" | 317 |
| DAY 223 | Be Conscious of the Goodness and Sweetness in Others | 318 |
| DAY 224 | Shabbat | 320 |

## WEEK 33

| | | |
|---|---|---|
| DAY 225 | The Good That You Do Lives On | 321 |
| DAY 226 | When It's Right to Be Early | 322 |
| DAY 227 | "His Mercy Is Upon All His Works" | 323 |
| DAY 228 | Be Kind to Your Enemy's Animal | 325 |
| DAY 229 | "Seek Peace and Pursue It" | 327 |
| DAY 230 | On Loving Yourself | 328 |
| DAY 231 | Shabbat | 329 |

## WEEK 34

| | | |
|---|---|---|
| DAY 232 | "There Is No Messenger in a Case of Sin" | 329 |
| DAY 233 | The Power of Goodness | 331 |
| DAY 234 | Teach Your Child a Profession | 333 |
| DAY 235 | Teach Your Child That What Matters Most to God Is Goodness | 334 |
| DAY 236 | Don't Give Away Too Much | 336 |
| DAY 237 | Can a Religious Person Be Cruel? | 338 |
| DAY 238 | Shabbat | 339 |

## WEEK 35

| | | |
|---|---|---|
| DAY 239 | The Antidote to Arrogance | 340 |
| DAY 240 | Don't Pretend to Virtues You Don't Have | 341 |
| DAY 241 | "Love Your Neighbor": What Is the Neighbor's Responsibility? | 343 |
| DAY 242 | "Honor Your Father and Mother": The Surprising Wording of the Biblical Commandment | 345 |
| DAY 243 | If Parents Become Senile | 346 |
| DAY 244 | How to Learn Empathy | 347 |
| DAY 245 | Shabbat | 349 |

## WEEK 36

| | | |
|---|---|---|
| DAY 246 | Don't Snap at Your Spouse | 349 |
| DAY 247 | Are You in an Abusive Relationship? | 351 |
| DAY 248 | Don't Be an Elitist | 352 |
| DAY 249 | Don't Encourage Your Children to Date Wealthy People | 354 |
| DAY 250 | The Painful, Challenging, Question Parents Must Ask Children | 355 |

DAY 251 *Marriage Is Also Supposed to Be Fun* 356
DAY 252 *Shabbat* 357

## WEEK 37

DAY 253 *Rabbenu Gershom and the Prohibition Against Being a Snoop* 358
DAY 254 *Be Generous with Power* 359
DAY 255 *When Silence Is Golden* 361
DAY 256 *Learn Even from Those with Whom You Disagree* 362
DAY 257 *Revenge and the Command to Love Your Neighbor* 363
DAY 258 *Who Is a Hero? A Jewish Perspective* 365
DAY 259 *Shabbat* 366

## WEEK 38

DAY 260 *Accidents Do Happen* 367
DAY 261 *When an Accident Is No Accident* 368
DAY 262 *Don't Be a Mitzvah Hero at Someone Else's Expense* 369
DAY 263 *Speak Truth to Power* 370
DAY 264 *Just How Much Are You Supposed to Fear God?* 372
DAY 265 *Don't Mouth Pious Platitudes* 373
DAY 266 *Shabbat* 374

## WEEK 39

DAY 267 *Do a Favor...for Your Enemy* 375
DAY 268 *Maimonides, Art Buchwald, and the Importance of Every Deed* 376
DAY 269 *When You Have Been Sinned Against: Your Obligation* 378
DAY 270 *A Nightly Prayer Before Going to Sleep* 380
DAY 271 *Don't Let Your Child Humiliate Another Child* 382
DAY 272 *What the Fifth Commandment Demands of Parents* 383
DAY 273 *Shabbat* 384

## WEEK 40

DAY 274 *Make Your Celebration a Cause for Everyone to Celebrate* 385
DAY 275 *On Not Embarrassing the Recipient* 386
DAY 276 *Is There Someone You're Ignoring Whom You Should Ask for Forgiveness?* 388
DAY 277 *Don't Forgive on Other People's Behalf* 389
DAY 278 *The Punishment of One Who Humiliates Another* 391
DAY 279 *When You Can't Give Money* 393
DAY 280 *Shabbat* 394

## WEEK 41

DAY 281 *How to Avoid Giving in to Temptation* 394
DAY 282 *When You're Tempted to Do Something Wrong* 395

DAY 283  *When There Is No Shalom Bayit in Your Bayit*                          397
DAY 284  *When Jewish Law Permits a Person to Be Publicly Shamed*              398
DAY 285  *The Limits of God's Forgiveness*                                      400
DAY 286  *It's Not Enough to Be Nice, Timing Also Matters*                      401
DAY 287  *Shabbat*                                                              402

## WEEK 42

DAY 288  *Help Non-Jews as Well as Jews*                                        402
DAY 289  *The Final Words a Jew Should Speak*                                    403
DAY 290  *Should a Jew Donate His Organs?*                                       405
DAY 291  *Listen...Really Listen*                                               407
DAY 292  *How Not to Teach Torah*                                               408
DAY 293  *Charity, Idolatry, and Deafness*                                       409
DAY 294  *Shabbat*                                                              410

## WEEK 43

DAY 295  *Sanctifying the Secular*                                              411
DAY 296  *Don't Be a Racist*                                                    412
DAY 297  *Never Practice Ingratitude*                                           413
DAY 298  *Raising Truthful Children*                                            414
DAY 299  *Empathy Is Not Natural*                                              416
DAY 300  *Express Your Gratitude to the People Nearest to You...Now*            418
DAY 301  *Shabbat*                                                              419

## WEEK 44

DAY 302  *Learning to Say "I Need"*                                             420
DAY 303  *When Anonymous Giving Is Important, and When It Is Not*               421
DAY 304  *When Silence Is Criminal*                                             422
DAY 305  *If You Learn That Someone Is Intending to Hurt Another*               423
DAY 306  *"You Are Not as Good as You Think You Are, and the World
         Is Not as Bad as You Think It Is"*                                     424
DAY 307  *When Pious Words Are Irreligious*                                     426
DAY 308  *Shabbat*                                                              427

## WEEK 45

DAY 309  *When a Half-Truth Becomes a Whole Lie*                               427
DAY 310  *Is Your Blood Redder?*                                               429
DAY 311  *Should There Be a Limit to Parental Love?*                           430
DAY 312  *Teach Your Child Survival Skills*                                     431
DAY 313  *The Most Perfect Act of Kindness*                                     432
DAY 314  *A Ritual Way to Make Each of Your Children Feel Special*             433
DAY 315  *Shabbat*                                                             434

## WEEK 46

| | | |
|---|---|---|
| DAY 316 | A Time for Silence | 435 |
| DAY 317 | When Praising Someone Is the Wrong Thing to Do | 436 |
| DAY 318 | You and Your Ex | 437 |
| DAY 319 | Solomon's Sword: How to Determine a Child's Best Interests | 438 |
| DAY 320 | The Special Obligation of Adoptive Parents | 440 |
| DAY 321 | Don't Speak Lashon Hara About Yourself | 441 |
| DAY 322 | Shabbat | 442 |

## WEEK 47

| | | |
|---|---|---|
| DAY 323 | Learning to Keep Your Envy in Check | 443 |
| DAY 324 | Don't Get Used to Other People's Suffering | 445 |
| DAY 325 | What's Wrong with Your Life? What's Right? | 446 |
| DAY 326 | Shiva, the Final Act of Gratitude | 447 |
| DAY 327 | Repentance Is Good—Overrepentance Is Not | 448 |
| DAY 328 | Don't Stereotype Groups | 450 |
| DAY 329 | Shabbat | 451 |

## WEEK 48

| | | |
|---|---|---|
| DAY 330 | Raising Your Children to Love Both Themselves and Others | 452 |
| DAY 331 | Watch Your…Compliments | 453 |
| DAY 332 | When Legal Doesn't Equal Moral | 454 |
| DAY 333 | Using Your Evil Urge to Do Good | 455 |
| DAY 334 | Let Your Word, Not Your Oath, Be Your Bond | 457 |
| DAY 335 | Never Insult Another | 458 |
| DAY 336 | Shabbat | 460 |

## WEEK 49

| | | |
|---|---|---|
| DAY 337 | When Is It Permitted to Pass On Negative Information About Another? | 461 |
| DAY 338 | Passing On Negative Information When a Couple Are Dating: The Four Guidelines of the Chaffetz Chayyim | 462 |
| DAY 339 | Telling Your Children "I'm Sorry" | 464 |
| DAY 340 | Make Time for Your Children | 466 |
| DAY 341 | "You Must Not Remain Indifferent" | 467 |
| DAY 342 | When You Learn Torah, Use It | 468 |
| DAY 343 | Shabbat | 470 |

## WEEK 50

| | | |
|---|---|---|
| DAY 344 | One Who Calls Another Person by a Cruel Nickname | 471 |
| DAY 345 | When Anonymous Giving Is Not Good | 472 |
| DAY 346 | Do You Owe Your Children an Inheritance? | 474 |
| DAY 347 | "One Who Is Bashful Will Never Learn" | 476 |

DAY 348  *Study Judaism Fifteen Minutes a Day…Starting Now*          478
DAY 349  *Random Acts of Kindness*          479
DAY 350  *Shabbat*          480

WEEK 51

DAY 351  *A Particularly Evil Form of Stealing*          481
DAY 352  *A Husband's Obligations to His Wife*          482
DAY 353  *Don't Insult Your Spouse*          483
DAY 354  *Jews Shouldn't Be Cheap; Jewish Funerals Should Be*          484
DAY 355  *A Law That Needs to Be Changed*          486
DAY 356  *The Holiness of Laughter*          489
DAY 357  *Shabbat*          490

WEEK 52

DAY 358  *Unfair Competition*          491
DAY 359  *Would Jewish Ethics Permit a Jew to Own a Gun Store?*          492
DAY 360  *Wronging with Words*          493
DAY 361  *The Telephone as an Instrument for Good*          495
DAY 362  *Torah Study and the Importance of Review*          497
DAY 363  *A Week of Kindness, a Week of* Gemilut Chesed          498
DAY 364  *Shabbat*          500
DAY 365  *Your First Check for the New Year*          500

TOPICAL INDEX          502
GLOSSARY OF HEBREW TEXTS CITED          504
BIBLIOGRAPHY          506
INDEX          513

*Hillel used to say: If I am not for myself, who will be for me?*
*And if I am only for myself, what am I? And if not now, when?*
    —Ethics of the Fathers 1:14

# Introduction

One of the preeminent figures of the Talmud and of all Jewish history is Rabbi Akiva, the second-century C.E. shepherd who became the foremost scholar, leader, and martyr of his age. Unlike many of the other sages, Rabbi Akiva did not come from a family of scholars; the Talmud informs us that well into middle age he was still illiterate.

A rabbinic tale describes the process by which Akiva became *Rabbi* Akiva: "He was forty years old and had not yet learned a thing. Once, he stood at the mouth of a well and asked, 'Who hollowed this stone?' He was told, 'Is it not the water which constantly falls on it day after day?' Rabbi Akiva immediately reasoned, 'If soft water can wear away hard stone, how much more can the words of the Torah, which are as hard as iron, carve a way into my heart, which is of flesh and blood?'" (*The Fathers According to Rabbi Nathan* 6:2).

In the nineteenth century, Rabbi Israel Salanter pointed out that study must be consistent to be truly effective and transformative: "The waters carved the stone only because it fell drop after drop, year after year, without a pause. Had the accumulated water all poured down at once in a powerful stream, it would have slipped off the rock without leaving a trace."

All of us might find ourselves inspired to try to spiritually and morally elevate ourselves for a moment, an hour, or even a week. But for ethical teachings to carve a way into our hearts, we must study and practice them, as Rabbi Akiva did, day after day after day. It was this philosophy that inspired the writing of *The Book of Jewish Values*. The goal of this book is to transform and elevate its readers (and its author) one day at a time. Its teachings cover the whole gamut of human activities and concerns, including:

- how to raise truthful children (Day 298);
- the first trait to look for in a spouse (Day 17);
- why acting cheerfully is an obligation, not a choice (Day 39);
- how to change negative patterns of behavior (Day 150);
- an effective though expensive technique for overcoming anger (Day 156);
- a twenty-four-hour experiment that can change forever the way you speak (Day 205).

Read and practice the exercises offered here one day at a time, review and discuss the teachings on the Sabbath, and you will quickly find that how you act toward others, and how you understand your own purpose in life, will be changed, perhaps permanently.

On occasion, when a rabbinic insight or quotation is relevant in more than one context, I have repeated it (as in Days 44 and 72), as I have done in one or two instances with a telling anecdote (Days 292 and 339).

Almost two hundred years ago, Rabbi Nachman of Bratslav offered a challenge to his followers, one with which I challenge you, and myself: "If you are not going to be better tomorrow than you were today, then what need have you for tomorrow?"

I wish you a good day today, and an even better tomorrow.

SUNDAY

# On Hearing a Siren

What is your reaction when you are talking with a friend and your conversation is suddenly interrupted by the piercing wail of an ambulance siren? Is it pure sympathy for the person inside—or about to be picked up by—the ambulance, or do you feel some measure of annoyance? Similarly, how do you react when you are awakened from a deep sleep by a series of clanging fire trucks or the wail of a police car?

I am embarrassed to admit that, along with many others, my initial reaction to such noises is often impatience and annoyance rather than empathy. My friend Rabbi Zalman Schachter-Shalomi, known through-out the Jewish world as "Reb Zalman," suggests that whenever we hear the sound of a passing ambulance we offer a prayer that the ambulance arrive in time. Similarly, whenever our sense of calm is interrupted by fire trucks, we should pray to God that the trucks arrive in time to save the endangered people and home. We should also pray that no fire-fighter be injured. And when we hear police sirens, we should implore God that the police respond in time to the emergency.

Reb Zalman's suggestion is profound. By accustoming ourselves to uttering a prayer at the very moment we feel unjustly annoyed, we become better, more loving people. The very act of praying motivates us to empathize with those who are suffering and in need of our prayers. Furthermore, imagine how encouraging it would be for those being rushed to a hospital to know that hundreds of people who hear the ambulance sirens are praying for their recovery.

Speaking to a Jewish group once in Baltimore, I shared Reb Zalman's suggestion. After my talk, several people commented on how moved they were by this idea, but one woman seemed particularly emotional when she spoke of this suggestion. When she was ten, she told me, she had been awakened from a deep sleep by passing fire trucks. It was almost one in the morning, and now, twenty-five years later, she still remembered her first response: it was so unfair that her sleep had been ruined.

The next morning she learned that her closest friend, a girl who lived only a few blocks away, had died in the fire. Ever since, she told me, whenever she hears fire trucks go by, she prays that they arrive at their destination in time.

Loving one's neighbor is usually carried out through tangible acts, by giving money or food to those in need, by stepping in and offering assistance to a neighbor who is ill, or by bringing guests into one's home. But sometimes loving is expressed through a prayer that connects us to our neighbor, even when we have no way of knowing just who our neighbor is.

DAY

2 MONDAY

# *"Let Your Fellow's Money Be as Precious to You as Your Own"*

*If one is honest in his business dealings and people esteem him, it is accounted to him as though he had fulfilled the whole Torah.*
—Mechilta, B'Shalach 1

Most Jews associate being religious with observing Judaism's rituals. Thus, if two people are talking about a third, and the question arises whether he or she is religious, the response invariably will be based on the person's level of ritual observance (for example, "She observes the Sabbath, she is religious," or "He doesn't keep kosher, he is not religious"). From these kinds of comments, common among Jews of all denominations, one could form the impression that, in Judaism, ethics are a fairly unimportant extracurricular activity.

How bracing it is, therefore, to learn that according to Jewish tradition, honesty in one's dealings with others is equated with observance of the whole Torah. A talmudic source powerfully reinforces this teaching: "In the hour when an individual is brought before the heavenly court for judgment, the person is asked: 'Did you conduct your business affairs honestly?'" (*Shabbat* 31a).

Having discussed this text before dozens of audiences, in synagogues and elsewhere, I know how surprised most people are to learn that the Talmud believes that the *first* question one will be asked by the heavenly court after one dies is not "Did you believe in God?" or "Did you observe the Jewish holidays?" but rather "Did you conduct your business affairs honestly?" (see Day 120, "God's Four Questions").

The Bible itself goes so far as to predicate Jewish national survival in Israel on merchants not defrauding their customers: "You must have completely honest weights and completely honest measures. If you do, you will long endure on the land that the Lord your God is giving you" (Deuteronomy 25:15).

*Ethics of the Fathers* (*Pirkei Avot*) comprises the favorite ethical aphorisms of rabbis, most of whom lived between the period from just before the Common Era until about 200 C.E. One prominent sage, Rabbi Yossi, offers a useful guideline concerning virtually any business situation in which you might find yourself: "Let your fellow's money be as precious to you as your own...." (*Ethics of the Fathers* 2:7).

Of course, the principle underlying Rabbi Yossi's comment is the Golden Rule, "Love your neighbor as yourself" (Leviticus 19:18). In the context of business ethics, such a criterion would, for example, forbid taking risks with another person's money that you would not take with your own (unless, of course, the money's owner has instructed you to take such risks).

Instructing people to observe the Golden Rule while trying to earn a living might strike some as utterly unrealistic, even naïve. Of course, that is precisely why many people prefer to assess religiosity on the basis of ritual observance and faith: by and large, it is easier to be punctilious about such matters than to act ethically in a consistent manner, particularly in financial areas.

Still, Jewish tradition insists on the primacy of ethical behavior. Commenting on the verse in Psalms (116:9), "I shall walk before the Lord in the lands of the living," the Rabbis* were struck by the odd phrase "the lands of the living." Explained Rabbi Judah, the leading scholar of his age, "that means the marketplaces" (Babylonian Talmud, *Yoma* 71a). Whether or not a person truly worships God can be determined even more by how he acts in the marketplace than in the synagogue. As Rabbi Tzvi Hirsch Koidonover (d. 1712), a scholar as well as a successful businessman, wrote in his ethical treatise *Kav Hayashar (An Honest Measure)*: "Only he who is reliable in money matters may be considered pious."

DAY

## 3

### TUESDAY

# *The Purchase That Is Always Forbidden*

*One may not buy wool, milk, or kids from shepherds. Nor may one buy wood or fruit from the watchmen of orchards.... [Even in instances where it is permitted to buy something], in all cases in which the seller asks that the goods be hidden, it is forbidden [to make such a purchase]....*
—Mishna, *Bava Kamma* 10:9

Common sense lies behind this ancient ruling. There is no way you can know for certain that the shepherds or watchmen have stolen the items from their employers, but common sense suggests that if they are offering for sale precisely those items they are paid to guard, they have probably acquired them illegally.

*Here and throughout this book, I have capitalized the word *Rabbis* when referring to the Rabbis of the Talmudic era (comprising the last centuries before the Common Era until about 500 C.E.).

In modern terms, imagine that the checkout man at your local supermarket meets you on the street and tells you he can deliver dairy goods to your house at half the price you pay at the supermarket that employs him. You can't be certain that he is acquiring the products illegally, but nonetheless, Jewish law says that in such a case you should regard the person as guilty until proven innocent, and refuse to purchase food from him.

Similarly, one sees on the streets of many American cities people selling videos of recently released movies for a fraction of what they cost in stores. Since reason suggests that such films have been "pirated" (illegally copied) or stolen—how else can one account for the cheap price at which they are being sold?—Jewish law would prohibit purchasing them.

As a rule, otherwise honest people who buy stolen merchandise continue to regard themselves as honest, and certainly see themselves as being on a higher moral rung than the people from whom they have purchased their goods. Maimonides makes it clear that Jewish law does not share this view: "It is prohibited to buy from a thief any property he has stolen, such buying being a great sin, since it encourages criminals and causes the thief to steal other property. For if a thief finds no buyer, he will not steal" (*Mishneh Torah*, "The Laws of Theft" 5:1).

An actual, if less obvious, instance of dealing in stolen goods, the insider stock-trading scandal, occurred in the late 1980s in the New York financial markets; in that case, a financier paid employees of law firms and financial institutions to inform him when companies with which they dealt were going to be bought out. Knowing that the stock prices in those companies would rise substantially, the man bought shares and, over a number of years, made tens of millions of dollars in profit. When his scheme eventually was exposed, he, along with the people who supplied him with the information, was sent to prison. From my understanding of Judaism's perspective, purchasing information that the seller has no right to market is yet another way in which a person traffics in stolen goods.

Very simply, if someone is trying to sell you something that is not his to sell—whether goods or information—you have no right to buy. As it is written in Proverbs (29:24), "He who shares with a thief is the enemy of his own soul."

# "What Would God Want Me to Do?"

A rabbinic teaching notes that the Torah begins and ends with divine acts of kindness (*gemilut chesed*). Thus, at Genesis' beginning, God provides clothes for Adam and Eve (Genesis 3:21), while the Torah's final chapter describes God's burial of Moses: "He buried [Moses] in the valley of Moab" (Deuteronomy 34:6). Yet another episode depicts God as visiting Abraham shortly after his circumcision, when the Patriarch presumably was still weak (Genesis 18:1).

As highly as the Jewish tradition esteems the giving of charity, it ranks performing acts of kindness even higher:

> Our Rabbis taught: Acts of kindness are greater than charity in three ways.
>
> Charity is done with one's money, while kindness may be done with one's money or with one's person [e.g., visiting a sick person; see, for example, Day 32];
>
> Charity is given only to the poor, while kindness may be done for both the poor and the rich [e.g., consoling mourners or those who are depressed; see Days 136 and 356];
>
> Charity is given only to the living, while kindness may be shown to both the living and the dead [e.g., arranging the burial of a person who died indigent; see Day 313].
>
> —Babylonian Talmud, *Sukkah* 49b

Jewish law attributes great significance to the performance of kind acts. Indeed, making the effort to perform such deeds is a real challenge, since, as we become older, many of us find it easier to be charitable with our money than with our time. Therefore, Jewish tradition teaches that offering one's time and one's heart represents the highest type of giving.

Starting today and for the rest of this week (and on a continuing basis), be on the alert for opportunities to perform deeds of kindness. Do you see a frail person in the street carrying a package that seems too heavy for the person to manage? Have you come across an acquaintance who seems upset and distracted, and is in need of someone to speak with? Do you spot a neighbor who is recuperating from an operation and needs a companion with whom to take daily walks to build up her strength? Your instinct in these cases might well be to continue doing whatever you are doing—I certainly often feel that way—but during this coming week, before you rush away, ask yourself the question, "What would God want me to do?"

DAY

5

THURSDAY

## *Be Generous Even When Your Instincts Are Lazy*

Ungenerous people are usually thought of as stingy, which is certainly an apt description of those who have the means but who refuse to donate to the poor. But in nonmonetary matters, the reason many people don't help others has less to do with stinginess than with laziness.

For example, the last time you went through your closets and removed clothing that you and other family members were no longer wearing, what did you do with it? Did you make a telephone call and arrange to have those items that were still in good condition picked up by an organization that distributes clothing to the poor? Did you make inquiries among friends and acquaintances to learn if anyone you know might need the clothes? (During several years when their children were small, a couple I know both received and gave away thousands of dollars' worth of children's clothing.) Or did you pack the clothing in large plastic bags and put it in the garbage?

Withholding good from others because of laziness is selfish. God knows, I have often been guilty of such behavior, but it is only when I think about it that I realize how wrong it is.

Rabbi Aharon Lichtenstein suggests another example of how people commonly refrain from showing consideration for others. People who have tickets for a play or concert and cannot attend frequently throw them away without trying to find a friend to whom they can give them.

Doing good for others can sometimes require special thought and effort. But what a worthwhile way to use your time!

FRIDAY

# When You're Tempted to Cheat

*Know what is above you: an eye that sees....*
—*Ethics of the Fathers* 2:1

Rabbi Israel Baal Shem Tov (circa 1700–1760), the founder of Chasidism, once hired a wagon driver to take him to a nearby town. The two men soon passed by a field filled with luscious produce.

The driver stopped the wagon, turned to the Baal Shem Tov—whose identity he did not know—and said, "I'm going to get us some good vegetables from that field. You be the lookout. Call out if you see anybody coming."

As the driver bent down to pick up some vegetables, the Baal Shem Tov screamed, "We're seen! We're seen!"

The frightened man ran back to the wagon and raced away. After traveling a short distance, he turned around and saw no one behind them.

"Why did you call out like that?" he angrily castigated the rabbi. "There was nobody watching."

The Baal Shem Tov pointed to the heavens. "God was watching. God is always watching."

May you have a Shabbat Shalom!

## S H A B B A T

During the course of this Shabbat, review the material from the preceding six days, and use some of the texts studied as the basis for discussion during the Shabbat meals:

Day 1.  When You Hear a Siren
Day 2.  "Let Your Fellow's Money Be as Precious to You as Your Own"
Day 3.  The Purchase That Is Always Forbidden
Day 4.  "What Would God Want Me to Do?"
Day 5.  Be Generous Even When Your Instincts Are Lazy
Day 6.  When You're Tempted to Cheat

Shabbat Shalom!

# WEEK 2

## S U N D A Y

# Give Cheerfully

The area of New York City in which my family and I live is filled with so many panhandlers that people often ignore their presence completely or place money in a beggar's palm and immediately walk away. Such was the case one day when my wife was strolling down Broadway with our daughter Naomi. "Mommy," the then-seven-year-old stopped her, "you didn't do a proper mitzvah."

"What should I have done?" Dvorah asked.

Naomi was prepared with the lesson she had learned at her Jewish day school. "You didn't look the person in the face and say, 'God bless you.' Because when you give *tzedaka* [charity], you have to give with a full heart."

My wife immediately went back, gave the beggar another dollar, looked him in the eye, and said, "God bless you!" Later she told me, "When I looked him in the eye, I saw a human being, not a beggar."

Naomi's words were not only a reflection of her and her schoolteacher's kind hearts, but also represent Judaism's view of the right attitude donors should show. Jewish law abhors giving with a mean expression and extols those who show kindness to the poor. As Moses Maimonides (known in Jewish life as *Rambam*) writes in the *Mishneh Torah*, his twelfth-century code of Jewish law:

> Whoever gives charity to a poor man ill-manneredly and with downcast looks has lost all the merit of his action even though he gives him a thousand gold pieces. He should give him with good grace and with joy and should sympathize with him in his plight.... He should speak to him words of consolation and sympathy....
>
> —Moses Maimonides, *Mishneh Torah*, "Laws of Gifts to the Poor," 10:4

Maimonides adds that even when you have nothing to give, you should at least speak to the poor person in a kind, encouraging manner (such as by saying "I hope your situation improves").

Of course, money is an important aspect of charity, but it is not the only important thing. As Anne Frank reminds us, in words written almost eight hundred years after Maimonides; "Give of yourself...you can always give something, even if it is only kindness." *

---

*Frank, *Diary,* March 1944.

9 | MONDAY

# When a Person Says "I'm Hungry"

One of the less pleasant aspects of life in large American cities is the presence of numerous beggars who solicit money from passing pedestrians. My wife and I once traveled to our Manhattan destination by subway and were approached by so many beggars that I remarked that "it would have been cheaper had we gone by taxi."

In offering guidance to officials who distribute communal charity, the Talmud provides helpful guidance to those of us who are approached by beggars: "When a man says, 'Provide me with clothes,' he should be investigated (lest he be found to be a cheat); when he says, 'Feed me,' he should not be investigated [but fed immediately, lest he starve to death during the investigation]" (*Bava Bathra* 9a).

My mother, Helen Telushkin, always gives generously to beggars who say, "I'm hungry." She has told me that when she is hungry, she finds the hunger pangs so hard to bear that it would be impossible for her to ignore the plea of one who claims to need food.

But what if you have no way of knowing whether the beggar is telling the truth? Perhaps he or she is faking, and will take the money you give and use it for illegal drugs or liquor.

Because we can rarely ascertain whether the one who solicits us is telling the truth, we should be guided by the obviously hyperbolic words of a Chasidic *rebbe*, Chaim of Sanz (d. 1786): "The merit of charity is so great that I am happy to give to one hundred beggars even if only one might actually be needy. Some people, however, act as if they are exempt from giving charity to one hundred beggars in the event that one might be a fraud."

# Don't Play Favorites

The patriarch Jacob had twelve sons, but he did not love them equally. He favored Joseph, the son of Rachel, his favorite wife. After she died giving birth to Benjamin, much of Jacob's love for Rachel was transferred to Joseph.

Jacob made no effort to conceal his favoritism. When he had clothing made for his sons, he gave Joseph a special coat of many colors, a garment far more beautiful than the ones prepared for his brothers. On other occasions he dispatched his sons to do physical labor, but kept Joseph home with him.

What effect did this undisguised favoritism have? As the Bible tells us, "and when his brothers saw that their father loved him more than any of his brothers, they hated him so that they could not speak a friendly word to him" (Genesis 37:4). Joseph's brothers bided their time; when the opportunity arose, they sold him to slave traders who were heading for Egypt.

When the rabbis of the Talmud studied Genesis 37, its ethical implications struck them as clear: "A man should never single out one of his children for favorable treatment, for because of the two extra coins' worth of silk [which Jacob had woven into Joseph's special coat], Joseph's brothers became jealous of him, and one thing led to another until our ancestors became slaves in Egypt" (*Shabbat* 10b).

In your heart, you, like Jacob, might favor a certain child. If you do, don't act as the Patriarch did, but keep your feelings in your heart. If you must speak about your feelings, do so with your spouse, a very close friend, clergy, or therapist. But make very sure you don't allow your feelings to become known to your children, or cause you to treat them in unequal ways (for example, by being highly critical of one's shortcomings, and lenient and tolerant of another's).

A parent has a moral obligation to make sure that his or her children feel equally treasured and appreciated. Rabbi Irwin Kula notes that "loving equally *does not* mean loving in precisely the same way. In fact, to have one's children experience that they are loved equally demands that one know how to love one's children differently. Therefore, to love one's children equally means to love them each uniquely" (see Day 134, "Educate a Child According to His Way"). Parents who convey their love unequally inflict lifelong damage on the less loved child. For with what greater disadvantage can a child go out into the world than with the feeling that even her own mother and father don't really love her as much as they do a brother or sister?

The Joseph story further reminds us that when parental love cannot be taken for granted, brother/sister love becomes endangered as well. Whether your children grow up to love and appreciate one another depends largely on their not feeling, as did Jacob's children, that they are in competition for a finite amount of parental love.

How much happier Jacob's family would have been had the biblical verse that informs us "Now [Jacob] loved Joseph best of all his sons" (Genesis 37:3) told us instead, "Now Jacob loved all his sons."

DAY

11    WEDNESDAY

## *Don't Make Your Family Afraid of You*

*Rabbi Judah said in the name of Rav: "If a man terrorizes his household, he will eventually commit [or be responsible for] three sins: unchastity, bloodshed, and desecration of the Sabbath."*

—Babylonian Talmud, *Gittin* 6b

Some adults with untamed tempers physically and verbally abuse their children, and sometimes their spouses. Such behavior is evil in and of itself, and frequently, as this talmudic text reminds us, it also causes other evils. Daniel Taub makes the point that reliance by a parent on his or her superior physical force also is a short-lived policy; the child eventually will be stronger than the parent, and the basis of the child's respect, fear, will disappear.

Uncontrolled rage can lead to the shedding of blood in at least two ways: A parent, who is much larger and stronger than a child, can beat a child and kill him or her. Newspapers routinely report such incidents; each year hundreds of children in the United States are beaten to death by their parents. In addition, fear of parental rage can cause a child to commit suicide (see Day 135).

What, however, is the connection between a parent's wicked temper and the violation of the Sabbath?

Jewish law has strict Sabbath regulations. For example, the Torah forbids igniting a fire on the Sabbath. Yet a wife or a child, fearful that a husband or father will be enraged if a meal was not prepared in advance of the holy day, may be tempted to ignite a fire and cook the food after the Sabbath has begun.

The Talmud cites an instance involving Rabbi Hanina ben Gamliel, whose bad temper caused him to be served unkosher food. A servant, afraid to inform him that no more meat was available, prepared unkosher meat for him. As the Talmud relates the story, it would seem that its sympathy lies with the servant, not the ill-tempered rabbi (*Gittin* 7a; see Rashi's gloss).

In similar fashion, parents who put excessive pressure on their children to succeed in school should be aware that they might well become the cause of a child cheating on examinations. A child, fearful of showing a parent a low test score, will be motivated to cheat. Similarly, parents who become unduly angry when their child misbehaves will cause their child to become a liar. Many children who are untruthful have learned from painful experience that the price paid for telling the truth is too high (as regards the harm that ensues when a parent lies to a child, see Day 298).

Finally, what is the possible connection between a man terrorizing his household and unchastity? Jewish law forbids a man from having sexual contact with his wife while she is menstruating and for seven days afterwards. The commentaries understand this passage as meaning that a woman who fears her husband's temper will be afraid to tell him that she is forbidden to him. Another explanation of this statement: A woman who feels browbeaten and unloved by her spouse may seek love with another man. While Jewish law condemns adultery, the person who brought terror into the relationship bears the larger measure of moral guilt when it occurs.

Although the Talmud seems to envision only a man as capable of inflicting such terror on his spouse, in today's world women can be equally guilty of the sort of abuse that demoralizes a partner and drives him away. Verbal cruelty can also terrorize a household; if you doubt it, speak to people who were raised in such a home.

If you find that often you cannot control your temper, then you are morally obligated to seek professional help. You owe it to your spouse and children and, as this talmudic teaching makes clear, you also owe it to God.

THURSDAY

# *Support Political Asylum*

In its insistence that there is one universal God who created and rules over the universe, and in its rejection of idolatry, the Torah was revolutionary. But when it comes to social policy and ethical issues, its approach often was evolutionary. For example, Torah law permitted a man to have more than one wife (Deuteronomy 21:15), although in its narrative portions every polygamous marriage it describes is unhappy. Later Jewish law, perhaps influenced by these descriptions, outlawed polygamy.

Similarly, in a world in which slavery was universally practiced, the Torah didn't outlaw it, but hedged it with restrictions. For example, unlike other cultures in the time of the ancient Israelites, and unlike the American South of the nineteenth century, the Torah ruled that a master who beat a slave to death was himself subject to execution (Exodus 21:20ff.), while a master who knocked out a slave's tooth or eye was obliged to free him (Exodus 21:26).

Most significantly, the Torah decreed that runaway slaves should not be sent back to their owners: "You shall not turn over to his master a slave who seeks refuge with you from his master. He shall live with you in any place he may choose among the settlements in your midst, wherever he pleases; you must not mistreat him" (Deuteronomy 23:16–17).

Today, slavery is almost universally outlawed. However, this prohibition is often honored more in the breach than in the observance. There are societies in which slavery is still practiced, countries in which young girls are sold into lives of prostitution, and authoritarian and totalitarian states in which human beings are, in effect, state property. When such a person succeeds in fleeing his captivity, this Torah law mandates that we give him or her political asylum. As the law instructs us, not only are we forbidden to return such people to their enslavers, but we also must permit them to live where they wish, and take special care not to wrong them. The Torah felt that people fleeing from captivity have suffered enough.

In detailing the Ten Plagues that God imposed upon the Egyptians for enslaving the Israelites, the Book of Exodus makes it clear that the Bible's ideal hope is for human beings to live in freedom. Nothing conveys this biblical teaching more powerfully than its insistence on codifying as one of its 613 commandments the obligation to help runaway slaves remain free.

DAY

13　　　FRIDAY

## *Bless Your Children*

It is customary among traditional Jewish parents (particularly fathers) to bless their children after the Shabbat candles are lit or at the dinner table before the Shabbat meal. The father, mother, or both place their lips on the child's forehead and hold the child while reciting to a son, "May God make you like Ephraim and Menashe" (the two sons of Joseph who are blessed by their grandfather Jacob; Genesis

48:20), and to a daughter, "May God make you like Sarah, Rebecca, Rachel, and Leah" (the four matriarchs), followed by the priestly benediction ("May the Lord bless and protect you! May the Lord deal kindly and graciously with you! May the Lord bestow His favor upon you and grant you peace"; Numbers 6:24–26).*After reciting the blessing, many parents add a special message for each child. One father I know told me that he likes to remind each of his children of something they did during the preceding week in which he took pride. Another father told me that he adds his own blessing to his children: "May God always be near to you, and may you enjoy many wonderful Shabbatot someday with children of your own, who will give you as much joy as you bring your mom and me."

Herbert Wiener, an American Reform rabbi who witnessed an elderly North African Jew reciting such a blessing in Safed, Israel, was moved to write: "I could not help but think of successful suburban fathers who had made comfortable provisions for their children, yet would never receive the honor and respect [from their children] that had fallen to the lot of the old North African father who could offer only blessings."

Parents also bestow the blessing for children before the major holidays. One Yom Kippur eve when I was in my late twenties and had just moved from New York to Los Angeles, I remember being disappointed at having arrived home too late to call my parents before the onset of the holiday (because of the time difference, Yom Kippur starts three hours earlier in New York than in California). When I arrived at my apartment, I was happy to hear a message my parents had left on my answering machine, including the blessing for sons that my father had added on for me.**

*As to why the blessing for boys speaks of the brothers Ephraim and Menashe and not the patriarchs (in the manner that the blessing for girls speaks of the matriarchs), Rabbi Shlomo Riskin has commented, "It's precisely because Ephraim and Menashe got along so well that they are mentioned, because most brothers in the Torah (Cain and Abel, Isaac and Ishmael, Jacob and Esau, Joseph and his brothers) didn't. So that in blessing their sons to be like Ephraim and Menashe, the parents are simultaneously expressing the hope that their sons will get along." (See Day 124, "What We Owe Our Siblings.")

**Now, when I'm away from home for Shabbat, I try to make sure to give a blessing to each of my children over the telephone. Because my normal procedure at home is to offer the blessing after kissing my children on the forehead, my wife told me that when my then six-year-old daughter Shira heard me recite the blessing, she would hold the receiver against her forehead.

People who practice the weekly custom of blessing their children often report unexpected dividends. I know of several families in which the children reciprocate the parents' blessings with their own.

Many years ago, a woman told me that neighbors who had witnessed this ritual asked her husband what gift the father had just promised his daughter. They assumed a gift had been promised because they saw the little girl's face light up after her father whispered something to her.

Though some important Jewish rituals are time-consuming or arduous to perform, blessing your children is pure pleasure for everyone.

May you have a Shabbat Shalom!

DAY

## 14     S H A B B A T

During the course of this Shabbat, try to review the material from the preceding six days, and use some of the texts studied as the basis for discussion during the Shabbat meals:

Day 8. Give Cheerfully

Day 9. When a Person Says "I'm Hungry"

Day 10. Don't Play Favorites

Day 11. Don't Make Your Family Afraid of You

Day 12. Support Political Asylum

Day 13. Bless Your Children

Shabbat Shalom!

# Week 3

## 15    Sunday

# Don't Waste Time

One of the most valuable life lessons I learned during the years I spent studying in yeshiva was the concept of *bittul Torah* (literally "waste of Torah"); this term refers to time that one squanders that could have been better spent learning Torah. Since Jewish tradition regards Torah learning as among the most pious and worthwhile acts in which a person can engage, it regards wasting one's time on unnecessary matters as wrong or even sinful.

When I was twenty, and spending a year at Yeshiva Kerem B'Yavneh in Israel, following the example of other students there, I started to take this concept very seriously. At one point I kept a notepad with me at all times in which I marked down any minutes, even if I was simply chatting with a friend, that I was not devoting to my studies. One day I felt very proud when I saw that, in addition to time spent praying, eating, sleeping, and relaxing with friends, I had devoted ten hours and forty-five minutes to study.

Now, as I reread the preceding sentences, I can imagine some readers regarding such behavior as obsessive. In truth, though, I remember my year at Kerem B'Yavneh as not only relaxed and extremely happy, but more. For there I learned not to dismiss the significance of one moment, let alone five or ten.

Many people who have a few minutes of spare time look for ways to kill it; they will turn on the television, or sit and do nothing. *But we don't kill time, it kills us.* And five minutes is sufficient time to pick up a book and read a few pages, or mentally review a concept and start to grapple with its implications.

A rabbinic head of a yeshiva once established a special five-minute study session. Even students who lived blocks away were expected to come back for this very short activity. As the rabbi explained, "I want you to learn that something can be accomplished in five minutes."

For years, my family has been treated by a dentist, Dr. Joseph Adler, who is a religious Jew. Between patients, he goes into his office and spends a few minutes studying Talmud. In the course of a day, these added minutes enable him to complete studying an entire two-sided page of Talmud, so that every seven and a half years he studies the entire Talmud.

Though I am sure that many of my older readers won't find my emphasis on utilizing time exceptional, younger readers might want to take note. I am grateful that I went to Kerem B'Yavneh when I was twenty, and learned this lesson relatively early in life.

Try today, and if you can tomorrow, and the day after, to make a special effort to fill those otherwise wasted moments of your life with content. Use a notebook if necessary to mark down the wasted moments, as well as the time well spent.

In Herman Wouk's World War II novel, *The Caine Mutiny*, Willie, the central character, is serving in the navy when he receives a letter from his father, who is about to die from cancer. Reflecting upon his life, one in which he achieved much less than he had expected to as a young man, he cautions his son, "Remember this, if you can: THERE'S NOTH-ING, NOTHING, NOTHING MORE PRECIOUS THAN TIME. You probably feel you have a measureless supply of it, but you haven't. Wasted hours destroy your life just as surely at the beginning as at the end, only at the end it's more obvious."

MONDAY

# "Stay Away from a Bad Neighbor"

*Stay away from a bad neighbor.*
—*Ethics of the Fathers* 1:7

The Bible informs us that Lot, Abraham's nephew, spent many years living near his uncle. Yet he subsequently moved to Sodom, a city the Bible regarded as epitomizing evil. While Lot never became as evil as his Sodomite neighbors, it seems that at least some of their baseness rubbed off on him. Thus, when the town's citizens demanded that Lot turn over his guests to be raped by them, he refused, but instead vilely offered them his two virgin daughters to be abused (see Genesis 19:4–8). Eventually, when God destroyed Sodom, He saved Lot—perhaps not because he was so righteous but because he was Abraham's nephew.

Judaism regards peers' influence as very powerful. In another biblical episode, Korach, a member of the tribe of Levi, entered into an alliance with 250 men from the tribe of Reuven to challenge and overthrow Moses. A number of Bible commentators speculate on how Korach and the Reubenites came to join forces. Rashi, the classic eleventh-century biblical exegete, explains that during the period when the Israelites marched through the desert, Korach and his family lived alongside the tribe of Reuben (Rashi on Numbers 16:1). Based on what we know of the episode, Korach, a powerful demagogue, probably influenced his neighbors to join him in rebellion. Shortly thereafter, Korach and the 250 rebels were killed by God. A Mishnaic text, writing in a different context, notes: "Woe unto the wicked, and woe unto his neighbor" (*Nega 'im* 12:6).

As a parent, you make repeated, important, decisions about your children's lives. None might be more important than choosing ·the neighborhood in which you will raise them, and the school to which you will send them. Of course, children are deeply influenced by parents, but once they reach their teen years (or even earlier), they are also profoundly affected by their peers (which is one reason why siblings raised in the same household and exposed to the same values sometimes turn out so differently). If you want to project what sort of people your children will grow up to be, consider carefully what kind of people you are exposing them to.*

As the biblical stories of Lot and Korach remind us, evil tends to be a more powerful influence than good. For example, it is easier for a "bad kid" to turn a "good kid" on to drugs, than for a "good kid" to influence a companion doing drugs to quit. Likewise with adults. While Lot apparently did not exert a morally uplifting influence on his neighbors in Sodom, they apparently left their mark on him.

Stay away from bad neighbors. Even more important, make certain that your children do.**

---

*A friend suggests that when you consider the school to which you will send your child, don't just look at the first grade; rather, go to some of the older classes to see what sort of character traits the school develops.

**A perceptive essay on the subject of "Peer Pressure" is found in Amsel, *The Jewish Encyclopedia of Moral and Ethical Issues*, 214–18; several of the examples in this entry are drawn from this book.

TUESDAY

# The First Trait to Look for in a Spouse

*When I was young, I admired clever people. Now that I am older, I admire kind people.*

—Rabbi Milton Steinberg

The Bible describes Eliezer, Abraham's trusted servant, as history's first matchmaker. When the Patriarch dispatches him on a mission to find a suitable wife for his son Isaac, he gives his servant only one guideline: the woman should come from the far-off area in which Abraham was raised.

Eliezer sets off on his journey, taking along ten camels. Some days later, upon arriving at his destination, the city of Nahor, he stops at the town's well at the time when the local women are coming out to draw water. Eliezer prays to God for a sign by which he can choose an appropriate bride for Isaac: "Let the maiden to whom I say, 'Please, lower your jar that I may drink,' and who replies, 'Drink, and I will also water your camels,' let her be the one whom You have decreed for Your servant Isaac" (Genesis 24:14).

Almost immediately, Rebecca arrives at the well, and fills her jar with water. When Eliezer asks for a sip, she lets him drink till his thirst is quenched, then says, "I will also draw for your camels, until they finish drinking." A few minutes later she invites Eliezer to stay at her family's home.

Before the evening is over, Eliezer has arranged with Rebecca and her family for her marriage to Isaac; she thus becomes Judaism's second matriarch.

This episode suggests several commendable traits in Rebecca. She is healthy and strong (it takes considerable strength to carry jar after jar of water for ten camels) as well as energetic and hospitable. But the trait that drives all the others is kindness. Seeing a thirsty man and thirsty animals, her immediate desire is to help relieve their plight, and to provide them with lodging.

Although our modern urban society hardly lends itself to the sort of test Eliezer devised for Isaac's future wife, his awareness of kindness as the supreme virtue in a spouse remains most relevant. Unfortunately, many people, both then and now, focus on other traits at a relationship's outset. But, as Dennis Prager suggests, "When you go out on a date, it is more important to see how your date treats the waitress than how he (or she) treats you. Since it is important at the relationship's beginning for your date to make a good impression on you, he will treat you well. But how he treats the waitress will reflect how he is going to treat you once he can take your love for granted."

Rebecca had no idea who Eliezer was. That is what makes her kindness to him so striking.

Obviously, there are many additional traits that matter in a spouse—shared values, sexual attraction and compatibility, humor, and intelligence, among others. But kindness, this biblical text teaches us, is in a class by itself. Its presence alone does not guarantee that a relationship will work. Its absence, however, should guarantee that it won't.

DAY

18

WEDNESDAY

# "Love Your Wife as Yourself"

*Love your wife as yourself*
—Babylonian Talmud, *Yevamot* 62b

An ancient Jewish teaching dictates that relatives and friends of a newly married couple host a festive meal for them during each of the seven days following the wedding. At one such celebration, held several days after our marriage, our friend Professor Reuven Kimelman, a well-known talmudic scholar, stood up to toast my wife and me.

"Why is it," he asked, "that the Talmud goes out of its way to apply the biblical law of 'love your neighbor as yourself' specifically to one's spouse? Isn't it obvious that this biblical law would include the person to whom you are married?"

He continued (because this happened many years ago, I am paraphrasing), "Sometimes, when a relationship is very close, we need a special reminder of how to fulfill the commandment of love. For example, at social gatherings, I have often heard men say things about their wives that they wouldn't say about their business partners if they intended to stay in business with them. Yet, if you challenge the man, he'll say, 'Oh, I can speak like that. I love her.' But," he added, "the proof of whether or not you have fulfilled the commandment to love your wife isn't that you feel you have acted with love, but that your wife feels she is loved."

In recent years, much attention has been focused on spouses who physically abuse one another; unfortunately, insufficient attention has been devoted to the sin of verbal cruelty, the kind that commonly occurs even between people who claim to love each other.

The next time you find yourself speaking critically about your wife or husband to another person, ask yourself two questions: "Why am I doing this?" and "Am I abiding by the law, 'Love your wife [or husband] as yourself'?"

DAY

19   THURSDAY

## Respect Your In-Laws

One day, while shepherding a flock for his father-in-law, Jethro, Moses saw a bush burning but not consumed. When he approached to examine this strange phenomenon, a heavenly voice called out to him. Moments later, God ordered Moses to return to Egypt and lead the Israelite slaves to freedom.

How remarkable for Moses to be personally addressed and commanded by God. Yet he did not immediately obey the Lord's command. As the Bible records, "Moses went back to his father-in-law Jethro and said to him, 'Let me go back to my kinsmen in Egypt and see how they are faring. And Jethro said to Moses, 'Go in peace.'" (Exodus 4:18).

Some years later, Moses was leading the Israelites in the desert when he was told that his father-in-law had come to visit him. Upon Jethro's arrival, "Moses went out to meet his father-in-law; he bowed low and kissed him; each asked after the other's welfare, and they went into the tent" (Exodus 18:7).

Throughout his father-in-law's visit, Moses was friendly, respectful, and very willing to learn from the older man's advice and experience. For example, the Bible informs us that the Israelites would approach Moses to adjudicate all kinds of disputes from morning till evening, so that he often was exhausted. Jethro stepped forward and reproved him: "The thing you are doing is not right; you will surely wear yourself out …the task is too heavy for you; you cannot do it alone" (Exodus 18:17). Heeding his father-in-law's advice, Moses established a judicial system. From that point on, Moses was only asked to rule on the most difficult cases.

Over the years, I have met people who ignore the Moses/Jethro model and who treat their in-laws like outlaws. One woman I know constantly criticizes her husband's parents, and tries to discourage him from spending time with them. An observant Jew, she justifies her contempt for her in-laws on the grounds that they are irreligious. Such a justification, however, totally negates the spirit of the Bible, for not only was Moses' father-in-law not a religious Jew, he was a Midianite priest (Exodus 3:16). Yet Moses lavished respect upon him.

On the other hand, does Jewish ethics' insistence that we respect and consult our spouse's parents apply to all in-laws? No. When parents-in-law are vicious and interfering, self-preservation requires that a son-in-law or daughter-in-law stay far away. But such cases are the exception.

If your marriage is good, but your in-laws have traits that are annoying or even obnoxious, remember that you still owe a great deal to them. They produced and helped mold the most significant person in your life: your spouse. That reason alone demands that we show them gratitude, honor, and respect.

# Don't Speak Unless You Have Something to Say

A new member of Parliament once solicited the advice of Benjamin Disraeli, the nineteenth-century British prime minister, on whether he should speak up on a controversial issue.

"Do you have anything to say that has not already been said?" Disraeli asked him.

"No," the man conceded. "I just want the people whom I represent and the members of Parliament to know that I participated in the debate."

Disraeli answered, "It is better to remain silent and have people say, 'I wonder what he's thinking,' than to speak up and have people say, 'I wonder why he spoke.'"

As Disraeli recognized, there are those who speak up only in order to make their presence felt. The *Malbim* (Rabbi Meir Loeb ben Yechiel Michael), the famous nineteenth-century Bible commentator and lecturer, once was present when a *maggid* (preacher) in Berlin gave a long and empty talk, devoid of insights and perspective. Annoyed that his time had been wasted, the *Malbim* commented (I assume without mentioning the name of the person about whom he was speaking): "Ecclesiastes gives us a list of twenty contrasts, such as 'a time to love and a time to hate' (3:8), or 'a time to weep and a time to laugh' (3:4). In all these contrasts, there is a middle ground. After all, one can be in a state where one neither loves nor hates, or when one is neither weeping nor laughing. There is one contrast in Ecclesiastes, though, that always puzzled me. That is the one that states, 'a time to remain silent and a time to speak' (3:7). Up to now, I could not understand where the middle ground between the two could be. After having heard this speaker, however, I see that it is possible for a person not to remain silent, and yet say nothing!"

This Shabbat, let us all try to speak up only when we have something to say that other people need to hear. But let us speak up then, and only then.

May you have a Shabbat Shalom!

S H A B B A T

During the course of this Shabbat, try to review the material from the preceding six days, and use some of the texts studied as the basis for discussion during the Shabbat meals:

Day 15. Don't Waste Time
Day 16. "Stay Away from a Bad Neighbor"
Day 17. The First Trait to Look for in a Spouse
Day 18. "Love Your Wife as Yourself"
Day 19. Respect Your In-Laws
Day 20. Don't Speak Unless You Have Something to Say

Shabbat Shalom!

# WEEK 4

SUNDAY

## If You Have a Bad Temper (1)

*There are four types of temperament:*
*He who is easily angered and easily appeased, his loss is canceled by his gain.*
*He whom it is hard to anger but hard to appease, his gain is canceled by his loss.*
*He whom it is hard to anger and easy to appease, this is a saintly temperament.*
*He whom it is easy to anger and hard to appease, this is a wicked temperament.*

—*Ethics of the Fathers* 5:14

As the quotation above makes clear, the Mishna, of which *Ethics of the Fathers* forms one book, takes it for granted that people sometimes become irritated and annoyed with others. Indeed, Maimonides was later to argue in his code of Jewish law, the *Mishneh Torah,* that it is wrong for a person never to feel annoyance, for such a person is akin to a corpse ("Laws of Character Development," 1:4).

The Mishna therefore distinguishes between healthy and unhealthy temperaments. Thus, the temperament toward which we should strive is that of the person it most extols, one who is hard to enrage and easy to appease.

Less good, but still desirable, is one whom it is easy to anger but easy to appease. The negative trait of being easily angered is overwhelmed by the positive trait of being easily pacified.

Two temperaments, however, are undesirable. The lesser but still serious one is a person who is hard to enrage but hard to appease. While it is good to be slow to anger, the negative effects of being difficult to pacify outweigh the good. Although there might be only a few people at whom such a person will become angry, once his or her anger is provoked, it is very hard to assuage.

Finally, the worst of all temperaments is one who is easy to antagonize and difficult to appease. I know a man like this, a very intelligent person; he is also an attractive, idealistic, and energetic individual. Yet, as long as I have known him, he has possessed an easily triggered temper. He is also cursed with the memory of an elephant; he remembers slights and resists efforts at reconciliation. People who have known him for as long as I, often comment on how much less he has achieved in life than was expected of him in his youth.

If you fall into this final category, how likely is it that you can transform yourself into one who is slow to anger and easy to appease? Not very, or at least not soon. But you should try to work on correcting, one at a time, both of these bad traits. Since an inability to be appeased is more destructive to one's relationships with others than being easily provoked, start by working on this trait first. For example, when you grow angry at someone, particularly a person with whom you were previously friendly, remind yourself of the good things that person has done, either for you or for others. If necessary, sit down with a pad and pen and write them down. If you have known the person a long time, it should not be difficult to summon up such memories. Also, force yourself to construct one or two positive scenarios that can explain why this individual might have acted as he or she did (see Day 24). Are you sure you are assessing him or her in accordance with the biblical command "In justice shall you judge your fellow"? (Leviticus 19:15; see, for example, Day 25).

Recalling the person's good deeds, and trying to put a "positive spin" on why he or she has now acted inappropriately, might stop you from rupturing a relationship over an issue that is not really significant.

Regarding the other faulty trait, that of becoming easily enraged, consider practicing the *one* suggestion in tomorrow's entry.

## MONDAY

# *If You Have a Bad Temper (2)*

Anger clouds judgment; rage destroys it. The Talmud teaches that when a wise man loses his temper, he also loses his wisdom (*Nedarim* 22b). For example, the book of Numbers describes an episode in which Moses, whom Jewish tradition regards as the greatest of all prophets, becomes enraged at the Israelites' constant whining about their lack of water. God directs Moses to speak to a large rock, which will then yield water. But Moses instead hits the rock, shouting, "Listen, you rebels, shall we get water for you out of this rock?" (Numbers 20:10).

When angry, we are apt to hit objects and to make extreme and foolish statements. And although Moses certainly did not intend it, his use of "we" implied that the authors of the miracle were he and his brother Aaron, who was standing alongside him. This comment could have misled the Israelites into believing that Moses and Aaron were themselves gods. Moses paid dearly for this angry outburst: God denied him entry into the Promised Land (Numbers 20:12).

Can you, like Moses, think of something you have said when angry that you now regret? If you can't, you probably just have a very poor memory.

When angry, we often attack the character and/or personality of the individual who has infuriated us in unfair ways. Many of us use words like "always" ("You always mess up everything you touch") and "never" ("You never care about anyone except yourself").

Such verbal assaults demoralize the person to whom they are addressed, and make it impossible for her to acknowledge a fault without simultaneously confessing to being an utter incompetent ("Yes, it's true, I always ruin everything") or totally self-centered ("Yes, you're correct, I am totally selfish, I only think of what's good for me").

Equally important, such attacks are unethical because they are lies.

Unless you have been cursed with knowing one of the most incompetent or evil human beings ever, it is unlikely that the person at whom you are raging is guilty of the charge you are making.

A guideline I have found very useful in trying to control my temper—and my tongue—is *Restrict the expression of your anger to the incident that provoked it.* Be as critical and annoyed as you like, but as long as your words remain focused on the incident that caused you to become angry, you are unlikely to say anything permanently damaging. But words like "always" and "never," or the tendency to summon up every action the other person has ever done that has hurt and enraged you, leads people to make comments that are difficult to forgive and impossible to forget.

Have I ever violated this principle and broadened my anger so as to make large accusations and attacks at the person at whom I am angry? On several occasions I have, and *every time* I have done so, I have regretted it. My behavior was unfair, cruel, and wrong.

If you have a quick and harsh temper, try to be guided by the wise counsel of the eleventh-century Jewish poet and philosopher Solomon ibn Gabirol: "I can retract what I did not say, but I cannot retract what I already have said."

DAY

24    TUESDAY
_____

## *Find Excuses for Behavior That Seems Unkind*

The rabbinic teaching that we should try to give people the benefit of the doubt is easier to fulfill in theory than in fact. Even those of us who say to ourselves when we are offended, "There must be a reason so-and-so acted in such a manner," often continue to nurse resentments against the person. Therefore, if you wish to try to seriously fulfill the biblical commandment "In justice you shall judge your neighbor" (Leviticus 19:15), don't content yourself with saying, "He (or she) must have a reason for his behavior"; instead, try to come up with possible exonerating excuses (particularly if you know the person to be an otherwise good human being; see next entry).

Rabbi Zelig Pliskin writes of a group in Jerusalem that meets on a regular basis and tries to formulate excuses for slights that members of the group have suffered. In Pliskin's book *Love Your Neighbor*, he cites several examples:

1. You didn't receive an invitation to a wedding.
   a. Perhaps the person was under the impression that he had already sent you an invitation.
   b. Perhaps he sent it to you and it was lost in the mail.
   c. Perhaps he can't afford to invite many people.
2. You are standing at a bus stop with a heavy load of packages, and a neighbor drives by in an empty car [sees you] and doesn't offer you a ride.
   a. Perhaps he was only going a short distance.
   b. Perhaps he has already committed himself to pick up some other people.
   c. Perhaps he had a problem that weighed on his mind so heavily that he couldn't think of anything else.
3. You were hoping that somebody would invite you to his house, but he failed to do so.
   a. Perhaps someone in his family is ill.
   b. Perhaps he was planning to be away from home.
   c. Perhaps he did not have enough food in his house.*

When you first start trying to formulate excuses for people who have offended you, it will be hard. But as you continue, it will become easier and, as Rabbi Pliskin writes, "By judging someone favorably, even if your assumption is wrong, you still fulfill a Torah commandment."

*Pliskin, *Love Your Neighbor*, 261.

# "Judge the Whole of a Person Favorably"

I f you are unfamiliar with the talmudic aphorism "Judge the whole of a person favorably" (*Ethics of the Fathers* 1:6), that is probably because it is usually translated inaccurately as "Judge everyone favorably," or paraphrased as "Give everyone the benefit of the doubt."

Such sentiments seem somewhat foolhardy. Are we supposed to judge favorably a thief who's applying to work as a bank teller? Is a woman supposed to give the benefit of the doubt to a man who wants to marry her, but whose last wife divorced him for beating her? Why should she?

In truth, the accurate translation of the rabbinic proverb is "Judge the whole of a person favorably." In other words, when you assess another, do not rely exclusively on one or two bad things you know about the person; be influenced by the good things you know as well, particularly if they are more significant. For example, I recently came across a largely critical assessment of Oskar Schindler in a magazine; the critique focused on Schindler's reputation as a womanizer. In addition, Schindler, prior to World War II, was an unscrupulous businessman.

While these unattractive qualities were all genuine facets of Oskar Schindler, he also repeatedly risked his life and used his extraordinary ingenuity to save some 1,150 Jews who otherwise would have been murdered by the Nazis. In assessing Oskar Schindler, this one big truth overwhelms the smaller truths in significance.

Jewish ethics also dictates that when you know a person to be largely good, and subsequently learn that he or she has done something wrong, you should not rush to condemn that individual. Rather, try to understand why the person acted as he did, and consider possible excuses for his behavior (see yesterday's entry for examples of how to find such excuses). If you cannot come up with a logical excuse, then your first reaction should be to judge the wrongful act as aberrant rather than view it as characteristic of the person.

Dennis Prager once noted that if you know any person intimately, you can cite five qualities that can make the person seem kind and extraordinary, and five more that can make him or her seem cruel or pathetic. Often we judge people unfairly; if we dislike them, we dismiss them by citing only the negative things we know.

Today, Abraham Lincoln is universally acknowledged as America's greatest president. In his lifetime, however, he was pilloried mercilessly. Were there indeed facets of Lincoln's personality that were unattractive? Undoubtedly there were, but those who focused on them are regarded today as cynics and fools; upon seeing a diamond, they searched only for its flaws.

So be balanced when judging another. Most of all, be fair.

DAY

26 THURSDAY

## *Return Lost Objects*

*If you see your fellow's ox or sheep gone astray, do not ignore it; you must take it back to your fellow...you shall do the same with his garment; and so too shall you do with any-thing that your fellow loses and you find; you must not remain indifferent.*

—Deuteronomy 22:1, 3

Some years ago, a woman I know was taking a long car trip. She stopped at a gasoline station and, while using the restroom, found a small change purse; inside was four hundred dollars in twenty-dollar bills.

She found herself in a quandary. If she left the money where it was, in the hope that the person who lost it would come back for it, another person might come first and take it. And if she left it with the gas station attendant, she feared that he might keep it. So she took the money, left behind a note in the washroom that said, "I have found a change purse here. If it is yours, please call me," and gave her phone number. She soon received a call from a woman who claimed to have lost the change purse and the money it contained. But when she asked the caller how much money she had lost and where the purse had been placed, it became immediately apparent that the woman was simply guessing. Then a man called, saying that the purse and money belonged to his mother. He told the woman that his mother had lost $400 in twenty-dollar bills. Later, when the son and mother came to retrieve the money, she learned that the woman was quite poor; the $400 was her social security money, and she was relieved and grateful to get her money back.

In picking up the lost object and setting about to return it to its rightful owner, my friend was fulfilling the Torah law cited at this entry's beginning. In Hebrew, this mitzvah is known as *hashavat aveidah* (returning a lost object). Because the finder has the obligation to restore the lost object to its rightful owner, it was appropriate for my friend not to hand the money over to the attendant or to anyone who simply called up and said it was his or hers. Jewish law imposes on the finder the obligation to announce what he has found (for example, in her note she indicated she had found a change purse), and to then ask claimants for specific signs (such as "How much money was in the purse? Where in the room did you leave it?") In an instance where an item has no specific signs (such as a dollar bill that has fallen onto a busy street), it may be assumed that the loser has given up hope of having it returned, and the finder is permitted to keep it.

Jewish ethics regards keeping a lost but potentially identifiable object as a particularly serious sin, for this is not only a form of thievery but a sin for which one can never fully repent. Even if one subsequently regrets one's dishonest behavior, it is very unlikely that he will be able to find the person to whom the item belongs; therefore the finder will have no way of undoing the evil he has committed (Maimonides, *Mishneh Torah*, "Laws of Repentance," 4:3).

Almost all of us at one time or another are going to find something valuable (either intrinsically valuable, such as money, or valuable to the person who lost it, such as a credit card or an item of sentimental significance). The Torah's words "you must take it back to your fellow" remind us that keeping an item we have found is not *like* stealing; it *is* stealing.

FRIDAY

# "As Long as the Candle Is Burning..."

The great rabbinic sage Rabbi Israel Salanter (1810–1883) was once spending the night at a shoemaker's home. Late at night, Salanter saw the man still working by the light of a flickering, almost extinguished candle.

Rabbi Salanter went over to the man: "Look how late it is; your candle is about to go out. Why are you still working?"

The shoemaker, undeterred by the rabbi's words, replied, "As long as the candle is burning, it is still possible to mend."

For weeks afterward, Rabbi Salanter was heard repeating the shoemaker's words: "As long as the candle is burning, it is still possible to mend."

As long as there is life—as long as the candle is burning—we can mend. We can reconcile with those from whom we've become estranged, help make peace within our families, give charity, aid a friend in financial straits to establish himself or herself in business, and work on learning to express our anger fairly.

In what two or three ways do you want to mend yourself? Identify them, then identify what you can do to start bringing that mending about.

As long as the candle is burning, we can mend our relationships, our world, and ourselves.

May you have a Shabbat Shalom!

S H A B B A T

During the course of this Shabbat, try to review the material from the preceding six days, and use some of the texts studied as the basis for discussion during the Shabbat meals:

    Day 22. If You Have a Bad Temper (1)
    Day 23. If You Have a Bad Temper (2)
    Day 24. Find Excuses for Behavior that Seems Unkind
    Day 25. "Judge the Whole of a Person Favorably"
    Day 26. Return Lost Objects
    Day 27. "As Long as the Candle Is Burning"

Shabbat Shalom!

# WEEK 5

D A Y

29     S U N D A Y

## Don't "Steal" Another Person's Mind

Some years ago, a woman I know attended a dinner hosted by a wealthy cousin at an exclusive restaurant. When the waiter brought the bill, her cousin blanched; the meal clearly had turned out to be far more expensive than he had anticipated. Noticing his unhappy reaction, the woman offered to split the meal's cost. The man smiled, and happily accepted the offer.

Yet, in reality, the woman, who had much more limited means than her cousin, was furious. Never having expected him to accept her offer, she felt betrayed when he did. Her son and daughter-in-law, the people who told me of the incident, agreed. As they explained, "She only made the offer to be polite. Somehow, she thought that it would make him feel better. It was wrong of him to accept it."

Their reasoning did not persuade me. According to the Talmud, the woman had only herself to blame for her predicament.

Jewish ethics opposes making offers that you have every reason to expect will be rejected. It condemns such behavior as *g'neivat da'at* (stealing the mind), attempting to deceive another person into thinking that you wish to do more for him or her than in fact you intend to. The Talmud offers several examples of this type of deception; for example: "Rabbi Meir used to say, 'A man should not urge his friend to eat with him if he knows very well that he won't. Nor should he offer him any gifts if he knows that he won't accept them'" (*Hullin* 94a).

If the point of your invitation is to mislead the invitee into believing that he is more beloved by you than he is, or that you are more gener- ous than you really are, you are guilty of trying to "steal another's mind."* The Talmud offers another example: One should not open a barrel (in modern terms, an expensive bottle) of wine, and tell the guest that you are doing so in his honor, if that is not the case.

On the other hand, Jewish ethics engages in a delicate balancing act between its desire not to deceive people and its wish to discourage tact- lessness. Thus, if a guest thanks you for opening the wine in her honor, you are not supposed to tell her that serving this good wine has nothing to do with her, that you were planning on opening it in any case. Jewish law regards the guest's misperception as an example of a person mis- leading herself. Correcting such a self-deception would hurt the per- son's feelings. Thus the Talmud tells of two rabbis, Safra and Rava, who were on the outskirts of a town when they came upon Mar Zutra, a distinguished colleague, approaching from the opposite direction. "Believing that the two had come to meet him, Mar Zutra asked, 'Why

---

*Such would not be the case if you invited hundreds of people to a wedding or other celebra- tion, and included invitations to people who you knew couldn't come. Where invitations are to a public event, withholding the invitations could be constructed as an insult. However, it would be inappropriate to send someone an invitation if you were almost certain they would not come and you were inviting them *only* to procure a gift.

did you take the trouble to come such a distance [to meet me]?' Rabbi Safra replied, 'We did not know that you were coming; had we known it, we would have come an even greater distance.' Later, Rava asked Rabbi Safra, 'Why did you tell him what really happened? Now you have embarrassed him.' Rabbi Safra said, 'But if I hadn't told him, we would have been deceiving him.' [Rava answered]: 'No, he would have deceived himself'" (*Hullin* 94b).

The bottom line is that our interactions with others should be tactful but honest. If you want to help someone pay a large bill, then offer to do so—but only if you mean it. And, if you care for someone and wish to extend them hospitality, then invite them to your house—but only if you have reason to believe that they can come.

·

DAY

30    MONDAY

## *Who Is Wise?*

*Who is wise? One who foresees the future consequences of his acts.*

—Babylonian Talmud, *Tamid* 32a

As the many accounts of his life indicate, Mahatma Gandhi was a saint who performed numerous extraordinary idealistic acts of self-sacrifice. But a public letter that he wrote in 1942 calls into question whether, from an ethical perspective, he was always wise.

In the middle of World War II, at a time when it was far from clear whether the Allies or the Nazis would emerge triumphant, Gandhi wrote an open letter to the people of England, offering them the following advice:

I would like you to lay down the arms you have as being useless for saving you or humanity. You will invite Herr Hitler and Signor

Mussolini to take what they want of the countries you call your possessions....If these gentlemen choose to occupy your homes you will vacate them. If they do not give you free passage out, you will allow yourselves, man, woman, and child, to be slaughtered, but you will refuse to owe allegiance to them.

Had the Allied soldiers laid down their arms and their people followed the advice of Gandhi, the Nazis would have defeated the world's democracies, murdered virtually every Jew alive, and ruled the world.

The rabbinic understanding that one of wisdom's main components is the ability to anticipate the implications of one's words and acts applies to the individual as well as the national level. Thus, the Torah mandates: "When you build a new house, you shall make a parapet for your roof, so that you do not bring bloodguilt on your house if anyone should fall from it" (Deuteronomy 22:8). The rationale for this law suggests that one must anticipate any damages that might be caused by you or your property and that might bring about another's death or injury. Thus, basing itself on this verse, the Talmud ruled that "a person should not raise a vicious dog or keep a rickety ladder in his house" (Babylonian Talmud, *Ketubot* 41b). The sixteenth-century *Shulchan Aruch* (the standard code of Jewish law) ruled that if you dig a pit or well on your property, you have to make a railing around it or cover it so that no one falls in (*Choshen Mishpat* 427:7).

A large part of being wise is anticipating the evil that might result from one's words (as I believe Gandhi failed to do in this case) * or from one's deeds (as in the case of one who keeps a vicious dog on his or her property). When it comes to morality, good intentions are not enough; wisdom is equally important.

---

* Alternatively, Gandhi's error was that he believed pacifism to be so absolute a value that he preferred to see the Nazis conquer the world than have their opponents go to war against them.

# The Special Obligation to Visit and Help People, Particularly Poor People, Who Are Sick

*It once happened that one of Rabbi Akiva's students became sick, but none of the sages went to visit him. Rabbi Akiva, however, went to visit him. Because he swept and cleaned the floor for him, the student recovered. The student said to him, "Rabbi you have revived me!" Rabbi Akiva came out and taught, "Those who do not visit a sick person might just as well have spilled his blood."*
—Babylonian Talmud, *Nedarim* 40a

A man I know was talking to an elderly friend who was suffering from intense back pains. At first he thought that there was simply nothing the physicians could do to alleviate the man's distress, but then he learned that there was medicine that could help him, only his friend could not afford it. Fortunately, he was able to help him acquire the medicine.

What a happy solution to an otherwise heartwrenching problem. In *Ahavat Chesed (Love of Kindness)*, the Chaffetz Chayyim, the great Eastern European sage and ethicist (1838–1933), emphasizes that the commandment to visit the sick applies with particular force to poor people: "If the poor person is not visited, his very life may be jeopardized. Usually he cannot afford the food he needs to eat. He has no one to consult with concerning his condition. Sometimes he cannot even afford to call a doctor or buy medicine....His worries increase when he realizes that he has lain in bed for several days, and no one has opened the door to care for him or to revive him."

This is the power of the Talmud's story about Rabbi Akiva. The sick student whom he visited might well not have been able to afford to hire someone to nurse him, or even to clean his dwelling. By cleaning his environment, Rabbi Akiva might literally have saved the person's life. Such was certainly true in the past, when many sick people lived in poor, and often dirty, homes.

Rabbi Akiva's visit undoubtedly helped the sick person in another way: Because he was so preeminent a sage, others would have noticed the care he lavished on the sick man, and taken care to visit the man as well. Thus, a prominent person can accomplish additional good by visiting a poor or unknown person who is ill; others may well be inspired to emulate him.

In addition to helping take care of the material needs of the impoverished ill (for example, by making sure they have money for medicine), one should go to the supermarket and shop for them. In many Jewish communities there are *Bikur Cholim* societies which visit not only those who are in hospitals but also shut-ins, those whose illnesses are apt to be ignored by the general community. These societies make sure that such people have visitors and a daily hot meal, and are taken to and from their medical appointments. While affluent people can hire others to shop for them and accompany them to medical appointments, poor people cannot. If such aid is not extended, they might stay in their homes and die.

As Jewish law reminds us, visiting the sick is done not only to sustain the ill person emotionally; sometimes it can save the person's life.

DAY

32

WEDNESDAY

# Visiting the Sick: Seven Suggestions

Rabbi Bradley Artson, author of *It's a Mitzvah!*, has combined traditional Jewish writings, common sense, and lessons learned from his pulpit experiences, to identify several activities through which we can all help the sick:

♦ When you hear that someone is hospitalized—particularly if the treatment will extend beyond a day or two—send a card. Rabbi Artson notes that when he visits sick people to whom such notes have been sent, they invariably are taped to the hospital wall, where they serve as a constant reminder to the sick person that others care.

♦ If you are planning to visit an ill person, call him or her first, so that in addition to your visit itself, the person, who might well be feeling lonely, will have the pleasure of anticipating it. And if by chance the person does not wish visitors that day, he or she can tell you that.

♦ Before entering a hospital room, knock and request permission to enter. As a rule, hospital patients are passive, their privacy routinely invaded by nurses and physicians. Asking permission to enter shows respect, and provides the patient a measure of control over his or her environment.

♦ If the patient wants to talk, sit and listen. Sick people often experience anxiety, and need to have the opportunity to express their worries.

♦ Offer to pray with the patient. For example, recite a psalm together, such as Psalm 23, which has comforted Jews and Christians alike for thousands of years:

The Lord is my shepherd; I shall not want.
He makes me lie down in green pastures;
He leads me beside still waters.
He renews my life; He guides me in right paths,
For His name's sake.
Though I walk through the valley of the shadow of death,
I will fear no evil, for You are with me;
Your rod and Your staff—they comfort me.
You spread a table for me in full view of my enemies;
You anoint my head with oil; my cup overflows.
Only goodness and steadfast love shall pursue me all the days
    of my life,
and I shall dwell in the house of the Lord forever.

Another appropriate prayer is Psalm 130, which begins, "Out of the depths I call You, O Lord. O Lord, listen to my cry, let Your ears be attentive to my plea for mercy"; as well as Psalm 121, which begins, "I turn my eyes to the mountains; from where will my help come? My help comes from the Lord, maker of heaven and earth."

◆ If you cannot visit a hospitalized person on a holiday, then visit just before. As Artson suggests, "On a Friday, consider bringing two small *challah* rolls and a little wine or grape juice (depending on what the patient is allowed to drink). Before Purim, bring some hamentashen; provide honey and apples before Rosh Hashanah, or matzoh and a haggadah for Passover. Linking your visits to the Jewish holidays is an effective way to combat the disorienting quality of being sick, and reconnect the suffering individual to what other Jews are experiencing beyond the walls of the sickroom."

◆ Arrange to have a prayer said for the sick person in the synagogue. (The standard prayer for the sick, known as *mi sheh-beirach*, is recited during the Torah reading; the person for whom it is being said is mentioned by his or her Hebrew name and the Hebrew name of his or her mother, for example, Avraham ben Sarah.) Even people who are not particularly religious often feel more vulnerable when ill, and may be reassured by the thought that a special prayer is being said for them in the synagogue.*

The prayer can be recited at a hospital bed as well. As Rabbi Artson relates: "One woman spoke in almost scientific objectivity about her illness until I took her hand and started to recite a *mi sheh-beirach*....Tears welled in her eyes, and by the end of the short prayer she was sobbing beyond control. Moved beyond words by the power of prayer, she was finally open to feel and to share, a process more healing than all the analysis and discussion that had come before."

Often, when we hear that someone is sick, particularly if the illness is serious or the injury irreversible, we feel impotent. The Jewish tradition of *bikur cholim* reminds us that there are almost always things we can do to help.

---

* Artson, *It's a Mitzvah!*, 62–73.

THURSDAY

# A Gynecologist from New Jersey, a Lawyer from Brooklyn

My friend Rabbi Irwin Kula, President of CLAL, the National Jewish Center for Learning and Leadership, was speaking to a doctor from New Jersey. Their talk ranged over Jewish and medical issues; because the doctor was not particularly interested in Jewish matters, the latter issues predominated.

At one point, Rabbi Kula explained to the physician the talmudic teaching that the lesson to be learned from God having started humanity with Adam, a single human being, is that each person is regarded as a whole world, and each individual possesses infinite value (Mishna, *Sanhedrin* 4:5; see Day 221). "What would it mean," Rabbi Kula asked the doctor, "if a physician treated each patient with a sense of modesty and with the sense that he or she possessed infinite value?"

Three weeks later, Rabbi Kula received a phone call from the doctor. A woman whom he had just treated said to him, "I've never been examined this way before." The doctor explained that since his conversation with the rabbi, he had made some changes in how he treated his patients. For example, it used to be common practice at his office for women who were to be examined to remove most of their clothing. Now, conscious of the talmudic teaching about the value and dignity of each person, the doctor no longer asked the women he was examining to undress completely. Instead, he asked them to remove only the clothing that covered the particular part of the body he needed to examine.*

---

*A famous talmudic passage tells of a spiritual ancestor of this New Jersey doctor: "Abba the surgeon would receive greetings from a heavenly voice each day, while Abbaye [a great rabbinic sage, would receive such greetings] each Friday, and Rava [another great rabbinic sage] each Yom Kippur Eve. Abbaye felt distressed because of Abba the surgeon [and wondered why he was not deemed worthy to receive such greetings daily also]. Abbaye was told: 'You are not able to perform deeds such as his.' And what were the [special] deeds of Abba the

In every profession, opportunities arise to treat human beings in light of this talmudic teaching. My uncle Bernie Resnick was a lawyer in Brooklyn. On one occasion my grandfather, Rabbi Nissen Telushkin, asked of him a favor: to meet with a poor woman who had a legal problem. My uncle agreed, and when the woman arrived, he took her straight into his office, ahead of two paying clients who were waiting.

That night the woman told my grandfather with astonishment what my uncle had done. Later, Bernie explained, "The paying customers would assume that a genuine emergency had arisen in an important case, and would not feel slighted. But if I had made the woman wait, she would assume that I regarded her as a charity case, and a bit of a nuisance. She would have felt humiliated, and I didn't want her to feel humiliated."

Whatever work we do, we are all given many opportunities to treat human beings in light of the Talmud's remarkable teaching that each human being we meet possesses infinite value, and is therefore entitled to infinite respect and concern.

FRIDAY

## Sharing Helpful News

Recently, over a period of several months, I met with three couples whose marriage ceremonies I would soon be performing. During our discussions, it came out that each couple had met through some sort of dating service (in one case, through a Jewish singles service on the Internet; in another, through the personal ads of a newspaper; and

---

surgeon? When he would perform the procedure of letting blood...he had a garment which had a cupping horn [attached to it]....When a woman would come to him, he would have her put it on, so that he would not look at her exposed body" (Babylonian Talmud, *Ta'anit* 21b). As the ArtScroll translation of the Talmud explains: "The patient would put on a large, loose garment that had a slit in it. Abba would insert the lancet through this slit to make the incision into the vein. Then the garment would be adjusted so that the cupping horn sewn into the garment could be moved over the incision and the blood could then be drawn through the horn, all without the patient's having to expose any part of her body."

in the third, through an office-based dating service). Happy as they were with the experience, two of the couples told me that their parents were anxious that they not tell others how they had met. Believing that meeting through a service was embarrassing, they suggested that their children make up a presumably more flattering account of how they and their intended mates had gotten together.

I was impressed that all three couples did not share their parents' trepidations; they were very willing to tell me and others, particularly their unmarried friends, how they met. One couple even wanted me to mention in my remarks under the wedding canopy how they had come together. All six people felt that they had found something good in their lives, and wanted to share this news, in the hope that this information might also help their friends to find a spouse.

This willingness to share good news, even news that some would find embarrassing to reveal, is an important hallmark of a good person. Not long ago, a new drug, Viagra, was introduced, a drug that helps most men who take it overcome problems of impotence. There is probably no ailment more humiliating for a man to acknowledge than impotence. It was impressive, then, when, a short time after the drug's introduction, Bob Dole, the former senator and Republican nominee for president, announced in a public speech that he had used Viagra and that it had worked.

It was courageous for these couples and for Dole to speak up. Obviously, many of us would like to project the image that we are able to find boyfriends and girlfriends, and spouses, easily, simply because people are so drawn to our charm and looks. Obviously, most men would like others to assume that they are experienced and very successful lovers (indeed, it was only after Viagra's introduction that it became widely known that impotence affects tens of millions of American men). How commendable are those who can overcome the natural tendency to worry about what other people are thinking, and instead to offer information that can bring happiness and healing to other people's lives.

May you have a Shabbat Shalom!

S H A B B A T

During the course of this Shabbat, try to review the material from the preceding six days, and use some of the texts studied as the basis for discussion during the Shabbat meals:

Day 29. Don't "Steal" Another Person's Mind
Day 30. Who Is Wise?
Day 31. The Special Obligation to Visit and Help People, Particularly Poor People, Who Are Sick
Day 32. Visiting the Sick: Seven Suggestions
Day 33. A Gynecologist from New Jersey, a Lawyer from Brooklyn
Day 34. Sharing Helpful News

Shabbat Shalom!

# WEEK 6

S U N D A Y

# *Is a Jew Permitted to Smoke?*

"Responsa" is the term used to describe writings containing rabbinic answers to specific questions concerning Jewish law (in Hebrew, such writings are known as *she'elot ve-teshuvot,* questions and answers). In making a legal ruling, the responsa's author takes into account principles and precedents enunciated in the Bible, the Talmud, Jewish legal codes, and previous responsa, along with common sense and contemporary scientific knowledge.

Therefore, it should come as no surprise to learn that the small body of centuries-old rabbinic responsa about smoking, which were written when tobacco first started to be used, were almost uniformly permissive. Certainly there was no text in the Bible, the Talmud, or the legal codes to suggest tobacco's prohibition. Perhaps part of the reason for this is that when smoking first became popular, it was widely perceived as not only pleasurable but also as medically beneficial. The illustrious rabbinical scholar Rabbi Jacob Emden (1697–1776), responding to a query about whether smoking tobacco was permitted, wrote:

> Tobacco is a healthful substance for the body…its natural action is important in helping to digest food, cleanse the mouth…and help the movement of essential functions and blood circulation which are the root of health….It is indeed beneficial to every healthy man, not only because of the pleasure and enjoyment it affords, but because it preserves one's health and medical fitness.

Strange as Rabbi Emden's words sound today (anyone who has ever been subjected to a smoker's "tobacco breath" must surely wonder at the rabbi's suggestion that tobacco "cleanses the mouth"), they were based on prevailing eighteenth-century medical notions of tobacco's positive health benefits.

We know better now. An estimated 400,000 Americans die annually from smoking-related diseases. In any given year, all smokers have a higher risk of death than nonsmokers. In addition, pregnant women who smoke have far higher incidences of miscarriages, premature births, children born with defects, and lower-than-normal birth weights.

As the increasing evidence of tobacco's unhealthful effects have emerged, contemporary rabbinic scholars are often asked a question quite different from the one posed to Rabbi Emden: "Given that smoking endangers life, is it forbidden for a Jew to smoke?"

The late Rabbi Moshe Feinstein, of blessed memory, the leading author of twentieth-century responsa, was reluctant to draw this conclusion. Reasoning that many past and present religious Jews, including great rabbinic scholars, smoked, he did not feel comfortable declaring such people in violation of the Torah verse, "You shall carefully preserve your lives" (Deuteronomy 4:15), which has long been understood as prohibiting any activity that needlessly endangers one's life.* As Maimonides rules in his code of Jewish law: "Our Sages forbade many matters because they involve a threat to life. And one who transgresses [these guidelines], saying, 'I will risk my life, what does this matter to others?' or 'I am not careful about these things,' should be punished by lashes for rebelliousness" (*Mishneh Torah*, "The Laws of Murder and the Protection of Human Life," 11:5).

Other rabbinic writers have taken issue with Rabbi Feinstein. In essence, they argue that religious scholars in the past who smoked did so without knowing that it was addictive and dangerous to their health. Thus, the question a writer of responsa needs to address is not "How can we declare smoking to be prohibited when many great religious scholars have smoked?" but rather, "Would rabbis of the past, men such as Jacob Emden, have permitted smoking if they knew of the great harm it could cause?"

Phrased in this manner, the question seems to virtually answer itself. Earlier rabbis, relying on medical information of the time, permitted smoking because they perceived it as pleasurable and beneficial. Unfortunately, while they were right about smoking being pleasurable, they were tragically wrong about its being beneficial.

At the very least, Jewish ethics today would, I believe, mandate prohibiting one who does not smoke from starting this dangerous habit, and would similarly prohibit a pregnant woman from smoking. It would also prohibit an adult from helping or encouraging a young person or other nonsmoker to smoke (for example, by giving a young person cigarettes or by participating in an advertising campaign targeting young people or nonsmokers).

Regarding those who already smoke, if it is possible for them to break their addiction, they should; if they cannot, then let them at least try to smoke less.

Some Jewish sages advocate a more aggressive stance. Thus, Rabbi Haim David Halevi, the Sephardic chief rabbi of Tel Aviv, when asked by a young man how he should act when his father sent him out to buy a

---

*Rabbi Feinstein did, however, write that for one who did not yet smoke, it was proper not to begin to do so.

pack of cigarettes, responded: "In view of the fact that physicians have universally warned against the great danger of smoking to human health, and since, in my opinion, it is forbidden by the Torah, which commands, 'You shall carefully preserve your lives' [Deuteronomy 4:15], you are not permitted to buy him cigarettes."

Dr. Fred Rosner, an Orthodox physician and leading contemporary scholar of Jewish medical ethics, has devoted considerable efforts to influencing Orthodox rabbis to join with Orthodox scholars such as Rabbi Halevi (and Rabbis Eliezer Waldenberg, Moses Aberbach, and Nathan Drazin) to ban smoking. Reform rabbis W. Gunther Plaut and Mark Washofsky write in their book, *Teshuvot* [Responsa] *for the Nineties,* "According to *halacha* (Jewish law), we have stewardship rather than ownership of the body given to us by our Creator, and therefore may not jeopardize our life." *

DAY

37

MONDAY

# *When Not Giving Charity Is the Highest Charity*

*There are eight degrees of charity, each one higher than the next. The highest degree, exceeded by none, is that of the person who assists a poor Jew by providing him with a gift or a loan, or by entering into a partnership with him, or helping*

---

*Plaut and Washofsky, *Teshuvot for the Nineties,* 334; I have also found several important sources, including the comments by both Rabbis Emden and Halevi in this book, pages 331–35 and 312. The citation from Rabbi Halevi is found in his Hebrew volume, *Responsa Aseh Lecha Rav,* volume 6, number 59. His original prohibition of smoking, published in 1978, is found in volume 2, 9–13. Fred Rosner has written an important overview of "Cigarette and Marijuana Smoking" in his *Modern Medicine and Jewish Ethics,* 391–403; the data on smoking's negative effects is found on pages 393 and 397.

*him find work; in a word, by putting him in a position where*
*he can dispense with other people's aid.*

—Moses Maimonides, *Mishneh Torah,*
"Laws Concerning Gifts to the Poor," 10:7

Many people assume that this famous teaching of Maimonides concerning the highest level of charity was entirely his innovation. In fact, the Talmud understood that the most important imperative in the laws of *tzedaka* is to save a person from needing it, or from requiring it for more than a short period of time. "Rabbi Abba said in the name of Rabbi Shimon ben Lakish: 'He who lends money [to a poor person] is greater than he who gives charity; and he who throws money into a common purse [to form a partnership with a poor man] is greater than either" (*Shabbat* 63a).

The Jewish understanding that the most desirable type of charity is to help the recipient become self-sufficient is rooted in a verse in the Torah, and a rabbinic commentary on it: "When your brother Israelite is reduced to poverty and cannot support himself in the community [literally, 'and his hand fails'], you shall uphold him as you would a resident stranger" (Leviticus 25:35).

"And you shall uphold him": This may be explained with an analogy to a heavy load on a donkey; as long as the donkey is standing up, one person may grab him [to keep him from falling] and keep him standing upright. Once he has fallen, five men cannot make him stand up again. (*Sifra,* Leviticus)

Some years ago, during a recession in the United States, I was invited to speak to a group of Reform rabbis on Long Island. During the informal discussion that preceded my talk, I learned that many of the rabbis present were spending considerable time trying to find work for unemployed congregants. I was moved and profoundly impressed by how committed these rabbis were to practicing Judaism's highest level of charity. Unlike some other religious traditions, Judaism has never esteemed poverty: "If all the sufferings and pain in the world were gathered [on one side of a scale] and poverty was on the other side, poverty would outweigh them all" (*Exodus Rabbah* 31:14).

Give money and aid to those who are poor, and you have done a very good thing. But if you help a poor person to get a job or acquire a skill that can raise him or her out of poverty, then you have done a *great* thing.

TUESDAY

# Give Money When Times Are Hard

I know a woman, a freelance writer, whose earnings vary from year to year. She told me that when her income falls, the first expenses she eliminates in their entirety are her charitable contributions.

This woman's attitude may be extreme, but many people whose earnings decline cut their donations by a percentage far larger than the decline in their income. Thus, if your income falls by 15 percent, it makes sense to give 15 percent less to charity; it does not make *moral* sense to give 80 percent less.

Even regarding poor people, Jewish law imposes an obligation upon them to donate something. The Talmud rules: "Even a poor man who himself survives on charity should give charity" (*Gittin* 7b). It is likely that the Rabbis did not want poor people to see themselves solely as beggars or as living off the public dole, but rather as individuals who, like other human beings, are capable of helping others. Also, demanding of the poor that they make donations helps protect them from becoming self-pitying, for the obligation to give to others reminds them that there are people in equally bad or even worse circumstances than they are. The Talmud tells of a time when Rabbi Akiva and his wife were so poor that they had no beds, and so slept on straw. In the morning, as Akiva picked the straw from his wife's hair, he said to her, "If I could only afford it, I would give you a Jerusalem of Gold" (a golden tiara with "Jerusalem" engraved on it). Suddenly the prophet Elijah, disguised as a mortal, came and cried out at the door, "Please give me a bit of straw; my wife is about to give birth, and I have nothing for her to lie on." After he gave the man straw, Rabbi Akiva said to his wife, "Look at this man, he does not even have the straw that we have" (*Nedarim* 50a).

When necessity imposes upon us the financial need to cut back on expenses, we should make sure that we don't stop giving charity. As the Talmud teaches: "If a man sees that his livelihood is barely sufficient for him, he should [still] give charity from it" (*Gittin* 7a). Why such insistence on this particular mitzvah? Because "Charity is equal in importance to all the other commandments combined" (*Bava Bathra* 9a).

WEDNESDAY

# Acting Cheerfully Is Not a Choice

*Shammai said: "Receive all people with a cheerful expression."*
—*Ethics of the Fathers* 1:15

Do Rabbi Shammai's words mean that you are expected to receive someone cheerfully when you yourself are in a bad mood?* The Talmud's answer is yes (obviously, in those instances when you are unhappy because of something awful happening in your life, you are not expected to walk around with a phony smile). The fact that you are feeling unhappy does not entitle you to inflict your bad mood on others.

---

*My friend David Zerner suggests that rather than focus on a person's obligation to be cheerful, it would be wiser, and perhaps more accurate, to translate Shammai's dictum as "Receive all people cordially."

True, at any given moment you might be unable to control what you are *feeling*, but that does not mean that you cannot control how you *act*. And just as you would prefer to be greeted by someone in a cheerful, pleasant manner, so should you greet others.

I remember once reading of a rabbi who was informed by a student that he had become engaged. Joyous as the news was, the student transmitted this information with a most serious and grave expression on his face. After congratulating the young man, the rabbi instructed him to practice standing in front of a mirror and smiling, "because if you speak to your fiancée with the same expression on your face with which you spoke to me, she will worry that you are upset with her."

The rabbi intuited an important point, and one that is seldom mentioned: Cheerlessness and moodiness are not victimless "crimes." Those who are around moody people often feel that they are somehow responsible for the moody person's unhappiness. And while such individuals might deny that they are responsible for anyone else feeling unhappy, they know in their hearts that it is unpleasant to be with a depressed person. That is why most depressed people, like most upbeat ones, prefer to be around cheerful people.*

The rabbi's admonition to the young man reminds us that Shammai's exhortation to receive people cheerfully should not be restricted to acquaintances and people we meet in the street; it is particularly important that we practice such behavior in our homes. I once heard a middle-aged man describe how his father's eyes lit up when his older brother walked into the room, but never when he did. Years of living in a home where he seldom experienced his father's "cheerful expression" left this man feeling unloved, and unworthy of being loved.

Dennis Prager, author of *Happiness Is a Serious Problem*, likes to say, "We have a moral obligation to be as happy as we can be." A talmudic passage reinforces this and Shammai's teaching by quoting an ancient Jewish proverb: "The man who shows his teeth to his friend in a smile is better than one who gives him milk to drink" (*Ketubot* 111b). Smiles, this text teaches, are a powerful form of nourishment.

---

*Some people's moodiness is beyond their control, a result of chemical and hormonal imbalances. I believe that such people have a moral obligation to those around them to seek out the psychological and drug treatments that can redress these imbalances.

THURSDAY

# One Must Always Greet Another Person

*It was said of Rabbi Yochanan ben Zakkai that no person ever greeted him first.*

—Babylonian Talmud, *Berachot* 17a

A foremost proponent of this teaching was Rabbi Shlomo Carlebach, the twentieth-century troubadour who composed hundreds of melodies that are still sung in synagogues, and at Sabbath tables and Jewish weddings. Though "Reb Shlomo" was best known for his great musical gifts, he was no less a genius in fulfilling the commandment to "Love your neighbor as yourself."

One man who spent time with him recalled driving Reb Shlomo to a concert engagement in Pennsylvania. The drive was long, and after several minutes of conversation, Carlebach asked the man if it was okay if he sat quietly and studied the Talmud. As Yitta Halberstam Mandelbaum recorded the story in her book *Holy Brother,* a collection of anecdotes told by Reb Shlomo's friends and acquaintances:

It was clear from his apologetic manner that he was fearful of offending me and appearing discourteous. Knowing how hectic his life was and how rare the opportunity for private study must be, I assured him that I didn't mind at all, and he should please go ahead. He opened the Talmud with an enraptured look and was quickly immersed in its study, intent on the words and oblivious to our surroundings....However, each time we pulled up to one of the many tollbooths we passed that day, he would snap out of his reverie, close the Talmud, look up at the tollbooth attendant, smile broadly, wave a greeting, and exchange a few words of friendship. No matter how ill-tempered or brusque the attendants appeared at the start, by the time Reb Shlomo had finished waving, smiling, and joking, they were transformed. After we passed each booth, Reb Shlomo would return to his Talmud, closing it again as we approached the next tollbooth. Despite his complete immersion in the text, he didn't miss a single station or attendant. Reb Shlomo's light touched and blessed them all.

Reb Shlomo did not, of course, just greet tollbooth attendants. Throughout his life, he extended a warm greeting to beggars on the street, and made everyone who came to his synagogue in Manhattan feel special. "Holy Sister Yitta," Yitta Halberstam Mandelbaum recalls Shlomo greeting her whenever they met. "You're the sweetest. The holiest." And, as Mandelbaum goes on to note, "It didn't matter that I had just heard him utter the exact same greeting to three hundred people before me. His luminous countenance radiated unmistakable sincerity and I felt suffused with the warmth of his unconditional love and acceptance."*

Greeting people you pass, particularly on a regular basis, with a warm "Hello" or "Good morning" establishes a human connection between those who otherwise might have no link at all. Yaffa Eliach's remarkable *Hasidic Tales of the Holocaust* tells the story of a Hasidic rabbi who lived in Danzig in the 1930s. Each morning he used to take a stroll; taking care to fulfill Rabbi Yochanan's dictum, he would greet every man, woman, and child "with a warm smile and a cordial 'Good morning.' Over the years, the rabbi became acquainted with many of his fellow townspeople...and would always greet them by their proper title and name." In the fields near the town, there was a farmer whom he used to pass. "Good morning, Herr Muller," he would greet him. "Good morning, Herr Rabbiner," the man would respond.

When World War II erupted, the rabbi's walks stopped, while Herr Muller left his fields and joined the SS. After losing his family at the Treblinka death camp, the rabbi himself was deported to Auschwitz. One day a selection occurred during which all the Jewish inmates had to pass in front of a Nazi officer, who signaled some people to go to the left, to the gas chambers, and others to the right, to a life of slave labor. By this

*Mandelbaum, *Holy Brother*, 27–28.

time the rabbi, who had long suffered from starvation and disease, already looked like a "walking skeleton."

As the line moved forward, the voice directing people to the right and to the left started to sound familiar. Soon the rabbi could see the face of the man who was sending people to life or death. As he stood in front of the officer, he heard himself saying, "Good morning, Herr Muller."

"Good morning, Herr Rabbiner!" the man responded. "What are you doing here?"

Saying nothing, the rabbi smiled faintly; seconds later, Herr Muller lifted his baton and signaled the rabbi to go to the right, to life. A day later he was transferred to a safer camp, and survived the war.

The rabbi, Yaffa Eliach reports, "now in his eighties, told me in his gentle voice, 'This is the power of a good-morning greeting. A man must always greet his fellow man.'" *

FRIDAY

# Should a Recovering Alcoholic Drink Wine on Shabbat and at the Seder?

Jewish law assigns an important place to wine. Twice each Shabbat, it is blessed and consumed at the family table, while on Passover, one is obliged to drink four cups of wine at the Seder.

When I was growing up, it was popularly assumed that no harm could result from these rituals. Jews, and many gentiles, assumed that there were very few alcoholics or problem drinkers in the Jewish com-

* Eliach, *Hasidic Tales of the Holocaust*, 109–10.

munity. But we now know that though alcoholism rates are lower among Jews than in the general population, the Jewish community, too, has many people who suffer from alcohol addiction or dependence.

What, then, should a recovering alcoholic do on Shabbat and Passover? Should he recite the *kiddush,* drink the wine, and trust in God that all will be well? Or should he refrain from saying *kiddush* on Shabbat and drinking the four cups at the Seder, in line with the biblical verse, "You shall carefully preserve your lives" (Deuteronomy 4:15)?

Fortunately, Jewish law provides an intermediate solution. The specific blessing recited over wine, "Blessed are You, Lord our God, King of the universe, who has created the fruit of the vine," is also recited over grape juice. Therefore, a Jew who should not drink alcoholic beverages should still recite the same blessing as all other Jews, and drink grape juice.*

In *Do Unto Others* Rabbi Abraham Twerski, a psychiatrist, tells of the happy result that ensued when he shared this Jewish legal ruling with a prominent Catholic official. Twerski was treating a thirty-four-year-old priest who had been admitted to St. Francis's Hospital in Pittsburgh for alcohol addiction. While he was being treated at the hospital, the priest couldn't obtain liquor, but Twerski learned that he had asked for a large number of bottles of mouthwash.

He confronted the priest, who acknowledged that he had been drinking the mouthwash for its alcohol content. Twerski told the priest that the only hope for keeping him away from liquor in the future would be to give him Antabuse, a medication that in combination with liquor makes one deathly ill:

> "Can I take a sip of wine at Mass?" Father asked.
> "No way," I said.
> "Then I can't take Antabuse."
> "Yes, you can," I said. "Just use grape juice and you'll be able to say Mass."
> "We can't use grape juice," Father said. "It must be wine."
> I called my friend Cardinal Wright at the Vatican. "Cardinal," I

---

*A recovering alcoholic who insists on drinking wine on Shabbat and Passover is regarded by Jewish law as a sinner for endangering his health and the health of those who interact with him.

said, "You must help me. This young priest is going to die. Please get him a dispensation to use grape juice for Mass."

"I will personally take this request to the Holy Father," Cardinal Wright replied.

"Tell the Pope I said he will have a mitzvah," I said.

Two days later, Cardinal Wright called me. The Pope had instructed all alcoholic priests to use grape juice in the Mass.

Dr. Twerski concludes:

The Pope had a mitzvah.
The cardinal had a mitzvah.
I had a mitzvah.
And to this day, those priests in danger of relapse to alcohol addiction because of the Mass are saved.*

May you have a Shabbat Shalom!

DAY

42    SHABBAT

During the course of this Shabbat, try to review the material from the preceding six days, and use some of the texts studied as the basis for discussion during the Shabbat meals:

Day 36. Is a Jew Permitted to Smoke?
Day 37. When Not Giving Charity Is the Highest Charity
Day 38. Give Money When Times Are Hard
Day 39. Acting Cheerfully Is Not a Choice
Day 40. One Must Always Greet Another Person

---

*Twerski, Do Unto Others: How Good Deeds Can Change Your Life, 138–39.

Day 41.  Should a Recovering Alcoholic Drink Wine on Shabbat and
at the Seder?

Shabbat Shalom!

# WEEK 7

## *The Jewish Ethics of Speech: What Is* Lashon Hara?

While libel and slander, which involve the transmission of untrue statements, are universally regarded as immoral and generally illegal, most people regard a negative but true statement made about another as morally permissible.

Jewish law opposes this view. The fact that something is true doesn't mean it is anybody else's business. The Hebrew term for forbidden speech about others, *lashon hara* (literally "bad tongue"), refers to any statement that is true, but that lowers the status of the person about whom it is said.* Thus, sharing with your friends the news that so-and-so eats like a pig, is sexually promiscuous, or is regarded by her co-workers as lazy, is forbidden, even if true.

Admittedly, this standard is sometimes difficult to observe: The Talmud itself concedes that virtually everyone will violate the laws of ethical speech at least once a day (*Bava Bathra* 164b–165a). Nonetheless, those who make an effort to practice these regulations will find that they soon start speaking about others in a far fairer manner.

When it comes to gossip, most of us routinely violate the Golden

---

*The Hebrew term that encompasses libel and slander is *motzi shem ra* (giving another a bad name), and constitutes the most grievous violation of the Jewish laws of ethical speech.

Rule, "Do unto others as you would have others do unto you." For example, if you were about to enter a room and heard the people inside talking about you, what you probably would least like to hear them talking about are your character flaws or the intimate details of your social life. Yet, when we speak of others, these are the things we generally find most interesting to discuss.

There *are* times when it is permitted to relate detrimental information about another (see Days 337 and 338), but they are relatively rare. While the fact that something negative is true might serve as a defense against a charge of libel or slander in a court of law, it is an invalid defense against the charge that you have violated an important Jewish ethical law.

M O N D A Y

# Don't Pass on Negative Comments

A woman I know, whose father had died, had long planned to have her older brother escort her down the aisle at her wedding. However, a short time before the event, her sister informed her of something she had heard the brother say: "Carol's a very sweet girl, but David is much more accomplished than she is. I'm afraid he's going to get bored with her." Devastated by these words, Carol refused to walk down the aisle with her brother; now, years later, their relationship is almost nonexistent.

Some time later I ran into the sister, and asked her about the incident. She told me that she had been talking with her sister, and the comment just "slipped out"; she thought her sister was entitled to know just what her brother thought of her.

The sister's response, a standard justification offered by those who pass on hurtful comments, sounds logical: Shouldn't we know if people who act warmly when they are with us say unkind things when we are not present?

But the brother's one comment did not express his full opinion of his sister. And her sister certainly had never bothered to pass on all the complimentary things he had said about her. While his comment may have been unkind, in truth almost all of us have said insensitive things about people we love. As Blaise Pascal, the great seventeenth-century French philosopher, wrote: "I lay it down as a fact that if all men knew what others say of them, there would not be four friends in the world."

Mark Twain highlighted the pain caused by people who pass on hurtful comments: "It takes your enemy and your friend, working together, to hurt you to the quick; the one to slander you and the other to get the news to you."

The Torah teaches how wrong it is to pass on hurtful comments, and the one who refrains from doing so is God Himself. Genesis 18 tells of three angels who came to Abraham's house to inform him that Sarah, his elderly wife, would give birth to her first child a year later. Standing some distance from the angels, Sarah heard their comment and laughed to herself, saying, "Now that I am withered, am I to have [the] enjoyment [of having a child], with my husband so old?"

A verse later, God appears to Abraham and says to him, "Why did Sarah laugh, saying, 'Shall I in truth bear a child, old as I am?'"

The Rabbis of the Talmud were struck by what God said—and did not say. In transmitting the substance of Sarah's statement, He left out her final words, "with my husband so old." Abraham in fact was old, but God apparently feared that he would resent Sarah saying so, in a manner that he might have regarded as dismissive.

The Talmud concludes from this incident, "Great is peace, seeing that for its sake even God modified the truth" (Yevamot 65b).

Of course, there are instances in which it is important to pass on negative comments. Let's say you hear someone accuse a person you know to be honest of acting dishonestly. Not only should you publicly dispute the accusation, but you should also warn the person who is being slandered. But such cases are relatively rare; unless there is a constructive reason to pass on a negative comment, you should not do so.

While Jewish ethics normally forbids lying, you are permitted to be less than fully honest when someone asks you, "What did so-and-so say about me?" When you know the response will provoke hurt or animosity, you are permitted to speak as God spoke to Abraham, relating some details and omitting others. If you are pressed for more information, Jewish ethics teaches that you can answer that the person said nothing critical. In short, when no constructive purpose is served by being truthful, peace is valued more highly than truth.

# The Sin That No One Ever Acknowledges Committing

*Why was the first Temple destroyed [in 586 B.C.E.]? Because of the three offenses committed [by the Jews of that period]: idolatry, sexual immorality, and murder....But why then was the second Temple destroyed [in 70 C.E.], given that the Jews of that time studied Torah, kept the Commandments, and performed acts of charity? Because groundless hatred was prevalent. This teaches us that the offense of groundless hatred is the equivalent of the three sins of idolatry, sexual immorality, and murder.*

—Babylonian Talmud, *Yoma* 9b

Many years ago, I heard Rabbi Aaron Kreiser, a professor of Talmud at Yeshiva University, pose the following question: Why is it that the first Temple, which was destroyed for the most serious of sins, was rebuilt within seventy years, while the second Temple, destroyed for the seemingly smaller offense of groundless hatred, has still not been rebuilt? He suggested the following answer: When people commit terrible offenses, and severe suffering befalls them, they sometimes step back, realize the evil they have done, and repent. Such was the case with many members of the Jewish community in the aftermath of the first Temple's destruction. But people guilty of "groundless hatred" never repent because they never acknowledge their sin. Even at the very moment they might be quoting to you this talmudic statement condemning "groundless hatred," they will still justify their own personal hatreds, and can explain to you why their adversaries are worthy of being hated. Thus, although the sin of "groundless hatred" might seem to be less serious than sins such as murder and idolatry, no one repents of its commission, or roots it out of his or her heart. And that is why we are still not worthy of having the Temple rebuilt.

In an effort to remove "groundless hatred" from your heart, think of someone whom you dislike. Even if you can justify your dislike for this person, consider whether your negativism is disproportionate to the evil this person has committed. If it is, then that means that at least some of your hatred is groundless.

Another method for rooting out groundless hatred: Try to learn something good about somebody you otherwise dislike, and let this knowledge inform your feelings. Force yourself to think of that good trait whenever you think of the person.*

Who knows how much good may be achieved by such an attitudinal change? Rabbi Abraham Isaac Kook (1865–1935), the Ashkenazic Chief Rabbi of Palestine, used to say, "The Talmud teaches that the Second Temple was destroyed because of causeless hatred. Perhaps the Third Temple will be built because of causeless love."

DAY

46    WEDNESDAY

## *When Confrontation Is Desirable*

Leviticus 19:17 decrees, "Do not hate your brother in your heart."

---

*This is not easy for most of us to do. I know a woman who finally reached the level where she was willing to acknowledge good deeds done by people she disliked; nonetheless, whenever she heard such deeds spoken about, she couldn't resist mentioning those aspects of the person that still annoyed her.

Why does the Torah choose this odd phraseology? Why not simply command, "You shall not hate your brother"?

The reason, I suspect, has much to do with the Torah's insight into human nature. People often dislike others, sometimes with good reason, and categorically prohibiting such dislike would not end it, but would just drive the enmity underground—into the heart.

This, then, is the hatred the Torah forbids. If you dislike somebody, don't keep it in your heart, where it will fester. The Torah tells us that Joseph's brothers "so hated him that they could not speak a friendly word to him" (Genesis 37:4). The hatred grew and grew, and eventually Joseph's brothers sold him into slavery.

If you are angry at another, don't just nurse the grievance in your heart, but raise the issue with the person who has enraged you, and make it known how he or she has hurt you. (Don't, however, confront the person when you are most angry, which is when you are apt to say unfair things.) Few people do this. Most either nurse their anger in sullen silence, or speak of it incessantly to their friends. Psychologist Carol Tavris reminds us how unhelpful such behavior is:

> If you are angry at Ludwig, all the discussions in the world with your best friend will not solve the problem. Unless the discussions result in your changing your perception of Ludwig ("Oh, I hadn't realized he didn't mean to insult me"), it is likely to reinforce your own interpretation, with the result that you rehearse your anger rather than rid yourself of it. If you displace your anger by punching pillows, conjuring up vengeful scenarios, telling nasty jokes, or hitting your child, your anger will not be diminished nor will the displacement be cathartic. This is because the cause of your anger remains unchanged.*

True, even after you speak with the person at whom you are angry, your anger might remain. This is unfortunate, but at least you will have satisfied the Torah's requirement of not hating your brother in your heart.

One final thought: The Torah's words "Do not hate your brother in

*Tavris, *Anger*, 152.

your heart" serve to remind us that the person we hate is not a stranger; even at the moment when our anger may be great, he or she is still our brother or sister.

THURSDAY

# "You Shall Not Ill-Treat Any... Orphan"

I f a notion akin to affirmative action can be found in Jewish sources, it applies to orphans and widows. Jewish law, going back to the Torah, codifies with great precision and passion the need to treat such people with tenderness, compassion, and an additional measure of fairness. Because they lack parental and spousal protectors and are easily exploited, the Torah promises that God will personally avenge one who takes advantage of such people: "You shall not ill-treat any widow or orphan. If you do mistreat them, I will heed their outcry as they cry out to Me, and My anger shall blaze forth. And I will put you to the sword, and your own wives shall become widows and your children orphans" (Exodus 22:21–23).

In an unusually poetic passage, Maimonides expands on the Torah and Talmud's laws:

A person must be especially heedful of his behavior toward widows and orphans because their souls are deeply depressed and their spirits low. Even if they are wealthy, even if they are the widows and orphans of a king, we are warned concerning them, "You shall not ill-treat any widow or orphan." How are we to conduct ourselves toward them?

One must always speak to them tenderly.

One must show them unwavering courtesy; not hurt them physically with hard toil, or wound their feelings with harsh speech.

One must take greater care of their property and money than of one's own. Whoever irritates them, provokes them to anger, pains them, tyrannizes over them, or causes them loss of money, is guilty of a transgression.

—Moses Maimonides, *Mishneh Torah,* "Laws of Character Development," 6:10

While the term *orphan* technically refers to one who has lost both parents, in biblical times it included children who had lost fathers, but whose mothers were still living. In patriarchal societies, such as prevailed throughout most of history, a child without a father was weak and vulnerable. In later Jewish writings, the term *orphan* referred to a child who had lost a mother, a father, or both parents.

Today, as a result of longer life expectancy, there are probably proportionately fewer orphans than at any other time in human history. But because of today's high levels of divorce, many children see little of their fathers. Much data recently has emerged to indicate that boys raised without fathers are far more prone to drug addiction, low levels of education, unemployment, and violent crime; girls from such backgrounds suffer much social maladjustment as well. Therefore, the biblical directive to take special care of orphans might also mandate serving, if possible, as a "big brother" or "big sister" to a boy or girl who has no contact with a biological father. Though technically not an orphan, in psychosocial terms such a child is one.

The Bible identifies God as "the father of orphans" (Psalms 68:6). Therefore, in regularly and significantly trying to help orphans, we become, in at least one way, like God.

FRIDAY

# Why Refraining from Gossiping Is an Important Challenge

I know a woman who loved shrimp. When she married a religiously observant Jew, she gave up eating this biblically forbidden shellfish, and became an observant Jew. Several years later she commented to her husband that she felt irreligious because she still craved shrimp. "On the contrary," he told her, "the fact that you want to eat shrimp, but refrain from doing so because it's prohibited, is proof of your religiosity. The Rabbis teach that one should not say, 'I loathe eating pig,' but rather, 'I do desire it, yet what can I do, since my Father in heaven has forbidden it?'" (*Sifre*, Numbers 20:26).

Rabbi Abraham Twerski, a psychiatrist, wisely observes that this rabbinic dictum no longer applies to Jews who were raised in ritually observant households. For example, the woman's husband never expressed a desire to eat shrimp. Had he done so, he would probably have become nauseous. The prohibition against eating forbidden foods has become so internalized among observant Jews that refraining from such foods no longer requires any self-sacrifice.

But there is one commandment that almost all observant—and non-observant—Jews are tempted to violate: the ban against speaking negatively of others (*lashon hara*; see Day 43). Many otherwise observant Jews frequently violate this biblical prohibition. They would do well to update the rabbinic quote to read, "One should not say, 'I do not like to gossip,' but rather, 'I really enjoy talking about and listening to the intimate details of other people's lives, and discussing other people's character flaws, but what can I do, since my Heavenly Father has forbidden it?'"

Adopting this attitude will not only lead to a diminution in gossiping, it will also, as Twerski argues, offer a powerful lesson of true religiosity to one's children. He advocates cutting short a discussion at the dinner table because it is becoming gossipy, and explaining to your children that you are tempted to continue the discussion, but that such conversations are forbidden by God. By doing that, you can demonstrate to your children "by living example the negation of [your] will to that of a higher Authority. It may well be one of the few lessons they'll never forget." *

May you have a Shabbat Shalom!

DAY

## 49    SHABBAT

During the course of this Shabbat, try to review the material from the preceding six days, and use some of the texts studied as the basis for discussion during the Shabbat meals:

Day 43. The Jewish Ethics of Speech: What Is *Lashon Hara*?
Day 44. Don't Pass on Negative Comments
Day 45. The Sin That No One Ever Acknowledges Committing
Day 46. When Confrontation Is Desirable
Day 47. "You Shall Not Ill-Treat Any...Orphan"
Day 48. Why Refraining from Gossiping Is an Important Challenge

Shabbat Shalom!

* Twerski, "Be a Living Example," *Jewish Action,* Fall 1998, 99.

# WEEK 8

SUNDAY

# Tzedaka *Is More Than Charity*

American folklore has it that when the taciturn Calvin Coolidge once came home from church, his wife asked him, "What did the minister speak about?"

"Sin," he responded.

"And what did he say?"

"He was against it."

You might think that anyone writing about *tzedaka* would run into the same difficulty as Coolidge's minister. After all, once you say that donating *tzedaka* is a good thing, is there really all that much more to be said?

A look at Jewish sources reveals that in fact there is a great deal more to be said. Above all, *tzedaka* is more than charity, which comes from the Latin word *caritas,* meaning "from the heart," and implies a voluntary donation. One who gives a gift is "charitable," and one who doesn't is "uncharitable"—an ugly epithet to be sure, but certainly unactionable. The word *tzedaka,* on the other hand, derives from *tzedek* (Hebrew for "justice"). Performing deeds of justice is among the most important obligations Judaism imposes on the Jew. "*Tzedek, tzedek* you shall pursue," the Torah instructs us (Deuteronomy 16:20). Hundreds of years later, the Talmud taught, "*Tzedaka* is equal to all the other commandments combined" (*Bava Bathra* 9a).

Thus, from Judaism's perspective, one who gives *tzedaka* is acting justly, while one who doesn't is acting unjustly, which is why Jewish law regards withholding *tzedaka* as not only ugly but also illegal. Throughout

Jewish history, when Jewish communities were self-governing, Jews were assessed *tzedaka,* as today people are assessed taxes.*

The giving of *tzedaka* was first legislated in the Torah. Deuteronomy (26:12) ordained that Jews give ten percent of their earnings to the poor every third year, and an additional unspecified percentage of their harvest annually (Leviticus 19:9–10). The Torah also tried to encourage a generosity of spirit: "If, however, there is a needy person among you...do not harden your heart and shut your hand against your needy kinsman. Rather, you must open your hand..." (Deuteronomy 15:7–8). Lest one become tired of the recurring demands made by the poor, the Torah reminds us, "For there will never cease to be needy people in your land, which is why I command you: open your hand to the poor and needy" (Deuteronomy 15:11).

After the Temple was destroyed, and the annual ten percent tax Jews were required to pay for the support of the priests and Levites became inoperable, Jewish law eventually decreed ten percent as the minimum percentage of net income it expected Jews to donate to the needy (see Maimonides, *Mishneh Torah,* "Laws Concerning Gifts for the Poor," 7:5).**

Why is Jewish law so insistent on requiring one to donate a set percentage of his or her income to charity? Perhaps because it intuits that if no percentage is specified, people will give much less than is needed. Indeed, tens of millions of Americans donate less than three percent of their earnings to charity; many give almost nothing at all. And while Jewish law would love people to give charity from their hearts, it understands that waiting for people's hearts to motivate them to give ten percent of their income might require a very long wait. Therefore, as Dennis

---

*Ample historical evidence documents that the idea of *tzedaka* was not only preached in Jewish books, but was also widely practiced. To cite one example, in seventeenth-century Rome, a Jewish community numbering only several thousand maintained seven charitable societies that provided clothes, shoes, beds, and food for the poor. There was a special organization to aid families struck by sudden death, and another responsible for visiting the sick. One society collected charity for Jews in Israel, and eleven raised money for various Jewish educational and religious activities.

**"All authorities are agreed that direct taxes on earnings like income or capital gains tax should be deducted before *maaser* (a tithe) is taken. In the words of Rabbi Moshe Feinstein (*Igrot Moshe, Yoreh De'ah,* number 143), income of this kind can be considered as if it was never earned" (Domb, *Maaser Kesafim,* 79).

Prager observes, "Judaism says, 'Give ten percent.' And if your heart catches up, terrific. In the meantime, good has been done."

A suggestion: If you currently donate less than ten percent of your income to charity, perhaps a lot less, try to increase your donations during this coming year by one percent (for example, if you currently contribute four percent of your income, give five). While this may feel like a financial "stretch," you will gain the satisfaction of having done significantly more good.*

## MONDAY

# *Fight Fairly*

One of the saddest stories in the Talmud tells of a bitter quarrel that destroyed the lives of Rabbis Yochanan and Resh Lakish, two men who were once best friends.

Rabbi Yochanan was already a recognized scholar when he first met Resh Lakish, then a gladiator and bandit. Struck by Resh Lakish's impressive physical appearance and imposing intellect, Rabbi Yochanan prevailed upon him to repent and become an observant Jew. Soon, Resh Lakish became both a great scholar and Rabbi Yochanan's brother-in-law. But one day, during an argument in Rabbi Yochanan's yeshiva over a matter of Jewish law concerning the ritual status of swords, knives, and daggers, Resh Lakish dissented from Rabbi Yochanan's view, and the latter became outraged. While arguing against the validity of his opponent's dissenting view, Yochanan made a cruel reference to Resh Lakish's unsavory past: "A robber understands his trade."

The anguished Resh Lakish responded: "What good, then, have you done me by influencing me to give up my life as a bandit? Among the gladiators I was called 'Master,' and here too I am called 'Master.'"

*For this entry, I have drawn on several examples cited in my book *Jewish Literacy*, pages 511–14.

Rabbi Yochanan, in turn, expressed great pain that Resh Lakish so casually dismissed the good that he had done him by influencing him to become an observant Jew.

Almost immediately thereafter, Resh Lakish became gravely ill. When his wife, Rabbi Yochanan's sister, pleaded with her brother to go see him, Rabbi Yochanan refused; he made it clear that he did not care in the slightest what happened to Resh Lakish. "I will support you if your husband dies," was all he would say.

Resh Lakish did die, and Rabbi Yochanan, perhaps to his own amazement, fell into a depression so deep that he lost his mind. The Rabbis prayed that God might take mercy on him, and a short time later he died (see Babylonian Talmud, *Bava Mezia* 84a).*

Of course, this incident represents an extreme example of what can occur when people who are fighting lose all perspective and all control of their tongues. Yet its lesson applies to all of us. No matter how outraged you become during an argument, keep your words focused exclusively on the issue over which you are quarreling. Never use damaging personal information to invalidate your adversary and, by implication, his contentions.** This rule is simple, but breaking it is what so often transforms moderate arguments into furious quarrels, the kind that lead to permanent ruptures between friends or family members.

You inevitably will have arguments with others, sometimes with people with whom you are close. If you watch your words when you fight, the issue can usually be resolved. But if you use words not to advance your argument but to hurt your adversary, he or she will find ways to wound you in return. This is what happened between Rabbi Yochanan and Resh Lakish. The only way to avoid such bitterness in your life is to learn how to fight—fairly.

---

*Alluding to the fact that Resh Lakish had once been a robber in no way advanced Rabbi Yochanan's argument.

**In my book *Words That Hurt, Words That Heal*, pages 84–89, there is a more detailed description and discussion of this talmudic tale.

# A Day Without Rumors; How About a Week?

While all moral people would agree that spreading a malicious and untrue story about another person is vile, almost every reader of this book, including me, has done so—most, many times.

When? When we routinely pass on rumors.

Most rumors are not positive and complimentary ("Hey, did you hear that so-and-so is really a wonderful person?"). Rather, many, if not most, rumors are negative and often untrue as well. If you pass on a rumor that turns out to be both ("I heard that Michael was fired from his last job because he was caught embezzling"), you have helped cause serious damage to another person's reputation, and inflicted possibly irrevocable damage. Jewish law categorizes such behavior as *motzi shem ra* (giving another [literally "spreading"] a bad name), and regards it as a particularly vicious offense.

People who transmit reputation-destroying rumors often defend themselves by claiming, "But I didn't do it on purpose. When I spread the rumor, I thought it was true." Such a defense is analogous to a drunk driver who has caused a fatal accident saying, "But I didn't intend to kill anyone." Of course he or she didn't, but so what? That a person was killed because of negligence, and not on purpose, is scant consolation to the victim's family. Similarly, the fact that the person who passes on an ugly rumor thinks that it is true in no way minimizes the harm inflicted on the rumor's object.

Therefore, how careful should we be to verify a rumor's truthfulness before we transmit it as fact? The Talmud suggests the following guideline: "If the information is as clear to you as the fact that your sister is forbidden to you as a sexual mate, [only] then say it" (*Shabbat* 145b).

How hard is it to comply with such a standard? Very; the one consolation is that offered by the sage Ben Sira: "Have you heard something? Let it die with you. Be strong; it will not burst you" (Apocrypha, Ben Sira 19:10).

*Regarding those instances when rumors should be transmitted, see tomorrow's entry.*

WEDNESDAY

# When Is It Appropriate to Pass On a Rumor?

As noted yesterday, Jewish law generally forbids transmitting rumors.

But is such a standard too restrictive? For example, what if a friend tells you that he is going to invest money with someone whom you have *heard* has a poor track record as a financial manager? Or if you have *heard* that your friend's job is at risk? Or if you learn that an acquaintance is consulting a physician whom you have *heard* is incompetent?

Some might argue that since you do not know for a fact that the negative details you have heard are true, you should say nothing. Others, myself included, feel that saying nothing does not seem morally right. After all, does your lack of definitive knowledge require you to stand by and wait for your friend to lose money, or to become a victim of malpractice?

There is an intermediate moral position, one that neither permits the random spreading of rumors nor categorically forbids passing on rumors you don't definitively know to be true: to warn your friend of what you have heard, but not claim that what you are telling him or her is established fact. For example, in the case of the money manager, say to your friend something like this: "Before you invest money with so-and-so, make sure that you check with several others who've invested with him. I've heard that his track record is spotty. I don't know this for a fact, but it would be naïve to dismiss out of hand what one has heard people say." *

By emphasizing that what you have heard is hearsay, and that your friend should first investigate the matter, you protect the potential investor while avoiding, to the extent possible, damaging the reputation of the person being discussed.

What Jewish tradition teaches us is that even when it comes to passing on a rumor, there is an ethical—and an unethical—way to act.

# Some Thoughts for a Bar Mitzvah or Bat Mitzvah

According to Jewish tradition, a girl turns bat mitzvah at twelve, a boy bar mitzvah at thirteen. The words *bar mitzvah* or *bat mitzvah* mean "responsible for keeping the commandments" (literally, "son [daughter] of the commandments"). Some of the commandments and rituals you are expected to keep will be observed on the day of your bar mitzvah or bat mitzvah. For example, that is the first time when, according to Jewish tradition, you can be called up to the Torah for an *aliyah.*** In addition to blessing the Torah, you will be expected to chant from it and from the Haftorah, and to study your Torah portion and speak about it to the members of your congregation.

---

* Professor Michael Berger, who is also an ordained rabbi, is not fully comfortable with the solution I've proposed: "In my view, making the sort of comment you suggest is appropriate only if the other person will do due diligence and check out the person. But if your friend's reaction to your 'warning' is 'I don't need this headache,' and just dumps the person, then, if you have heard these rumors from a possible slanderer, you become complicit in ruining the financial manager's livelihood. It seems to me that the right thing to do is to insist that your friend check the person out because it's the *prudent* thing to do—and not because of something you have heard."

** Orthodox Jews do not call up women to the Torah, although some modern Orthodox Jews do so at special services attended by women only.

But obviously, Judaism would be a pretty pathetic religion were the performance of these synagogue rituals all that it expected from those who have become "responsible for the commandments." Therefore, in order to make the year preceding and following your bar mitzvah significant, Rabbi Jeffrey Salkin has developed a wide-ranging list of *mitzvot* (commandments) that, in his words, "make Jewish values real." * Start to observe some of these commandments, and you will not only emerge from your bar mitzvah or bat mitzvah as an adult, but you will actually feel like one:

♦ Visit someone who has lost a loved one. This fulfills the commandment of comforting mourners (*nichum aveilum;* see, for example, Days 136 and 137). You might never have done so before, since many parents shield children from death and so don't take them to funerals or cemeteries, or to visit mourners who have suffered a recent loss.

♦ Visit or call on someone who is ill. This fulfills the commandment of visiting the sick (*bikur cholim:* see Days 31, 32, and 176).

♦ Arrange to have leftover food from your bar mitzvah or bat mitzvah celebration taken to a soup kitchen or pantry that feeds the homeless and the hungry (see Day 274).

♦ Take *chametz* (leavened food products that Jewish law forbids eating during Passover) from your home to a local food pantry, and encourage relatives and friends to do so as well.

♦ Devote some time to a communal issue or cause. For example, write to an elected official about a significant social or political issue. The Torah commands us, "*Tzedek, tzedek tirdoff*—Justice, justice you shall pursue" (Deuteronomy 16:20). As Rabbi Salkin suggests, "Use a Jewish idea in the letter."

♦ Donate three percent of the cost of your bar or bat mitzvah celebration to Mazon (the Hebrew word for sustenance; see the note regarding Mazon at the end of Day 170), a Jewish organization that distributes money to food banks and for hunger relief throughout the world.

---

* Salkin, *For Kids Putting God on Your Guest List: How to Claim the Spiritual Meaning of Your Bar/Bat Mitzvah,* 55–72.

- Keep a *tzedaka* (charity) box in your house, and put some money in it, along with other members of your family, every Friday night before Shabbat. Then, when a significant sum is collected, sit down with your family and decide where the money should be donated.
- Jewish tradition puts great emphasis on the mitzvah of showing respect for elderly people (Leviticus 19:32 rules, "You shall honor the old"). If you are willing to carry out this mitzvah regularly, there is much you can do. For example, help nursing home residents conduct Shabbat or holiday services; take flowers to nursing home residents on Friday afternoon; "adopt" an old person, and visit him or her every week or every month.
- Don't wait for your grandparents to call you; act like an adult, and call them on your own.
- As suggested on Day 80, ask your parents for whom you were named. What special Jewish and general qualities did that person have, and why did your parents choose to name you for that person?

And, of course, let me wish you *mazal tov.*

FRIDAY

## Learning from the Bad to Do Good

I remember once reading of a British king who made his own family, particularly his sons, afraid of him. A friend suggested that he be gentler with his children, but the king rebuffed this advice: "My father made me afraid of him, and I want my sons to be afraid of me."

When I read this, I had pity and contempt for the king, but I pitied his sons, and their sons, far more. Having been bullied as a child, this man had learned only how to be a bully.

The Torah wants Jews to learn precisely the opposite lesson from suffering. When one has been oppressed and bullied, one should learn how horrible it is to suffer, and to make sure to refrain from inflicting pain on others. Hence, the Torah commands the Jews who have just been released from Egyptian slavery, "You shall not wrong a stranger [a non-Israelite, the most vulnerable member of society] or oppress him, for you were strangers in the land of Egypt" (Exodus 22:20).

The Israelites could have learned other lessons from their slave experience; for example, "Do unto others as they did unto you, and do it first," or the lesson learned by this British king, that people who have power should use it to tyrannize those who are weaker than themselves. Throughout history, these are two lessons many people who have suffered have learned. How often have we heard historians explain the widespread German support of Nazism as an angry reaction on their part to the severe terms imposed upon them by the Allies after World War I? Similarly, we know that the parents most likely to abuse their children are those who were themselves abused when young. As a rule, suffering is not an ennobling teacher.

The Torah wants us, all of us, individuals and nations, to break this pattern. If you have been hurt—and who of us has not?—learn how *not* to hurt. Were you taunted with an ugly nickname as a child? Were you mocked because of your lack of athletic ability? Have you ever lost out on a job opening because of discrimination? Were you pained because someone spread a malicious rumor about you? Think of how you have suffered, and how you can ensure that those who have contact with you don't suffer in a similar way.

We all suffer in life. The *only* good that can come from this suffering is to learn from it to *do* good.

May you have a Shabbat Shalom!

## 56     SHABBAT

During the course of this Shabbat, try to review the material from the preceding six days, and use some of the texts studied as the basis for discussion during the Shabbat meals:

Day 50. *Tzedaka* Is More Than Charity
Day 51. Fight Fairly
Day 52. A Day Without Rumors; How About a Week?
Day 53. When Is It Appropriate to Pass On a Rumor?
Day 54. Some Thoughts for a Bar Mitzvah or Bat Mitzvah
Day 55. Learning from the Bad to Do Good

Shabbat Shalom!

# WEEK 9

## 57     SUNDAY

## *Love the Stranger*

Many people are aware of two of the three Torah laws that command love: "Love your neighbor as yourself" (Leviticus 19:18) and "You shall love the Lord your God with all your heart" (Deuteronomy 6:5). Far fewer recall that the same biblical chapter that enjoins us to love our neighbor also mandates that we love the stranger: "When a stranger resides with you in your land, you shall not wrong him. The stranger who resides with you shall be to you as one of your citizens; you shall love him as yourself, for you were strangers in the land of Egypt: I am the Lord your God" (Leviticus 19:33–34).

A century ago, the German-Jewish philosopher Hermann Cohen (1842–1918) contended that in the injunction to love the stranger we find the beginning of true religion: "The stranger was to be protected, although he was not a member of one's family, clan, religion, community, or people, simply because he was a human being. In the stranger, therefore, man discovered the idea of humanity."

In today's world, to whom does this law apply? In both Israel and the Diaspora, this law applies to all those non-Jewish residents who wish to live in peace with their Jewish neighbors.*

This law applies with particular force to poor, and politically weak, non-Jews; as the Torah reminds us, "for you were strangers in the land of Egypt." In reminding us how difficult it was to live as strangers and slaves in Egypt, the Torah is urging us to act fairly and mercifully to those who today occupy society's most disadvantaged positions.

Thus, it is our responsibility to try to ensure that such people are treated equally before the law. As the Torah commands in the verse quoted earlier, "The stranger who resides with you shall be to you as one of your citizens" (Leviticus 19:34; see Exodus 12:49).

It seems to me that an additional corollary of this law would prohibit referring to people who reside in the United States peaceably, but without government permission, as "illegal aliens." I once heard Elie Wiesel point out that it is offensive to describe a person as illegal—how could a human being be illegal?—and A. M. Rosenthal, the former editor of, and now columnist for, *The New York Times*, has observed that to call a human being an alien is to deny that person's very humanity, and make him seem like a creature from another planet.

In biblical tradition, strangers have a unique distinction; they, in addition to the Patriarchs (Deuteronomy 4:37) are the only category of human beings whom God is identified as loving: "And God loves the stranger" (Deuteronomy 10:18).**

---

*Torah law, which is rooted in both morality and common sense, doesn't command Israeli Jews to love those non-Jewish neighbors who wish to destroy them.

**The biblical word for "stranger" is *ger*. Hundreds of years after the Torah was written, that word came to denote "convert," a usage it still retains in modern Hebrew. Consequently, starting with the Talmud, many Jews started to assume that the biblical injunction to love the *ger* and to treat him or her equally referred to a Jew by choice. Yet, unquestionably, the Torah's intent in this law was to protect the stranger, not the convert, from mistreatment. For if the Torah, in using *ger*, was referring to the convert, the verse would read, "You shall not wrong a convert or oppress him, for you were *converts* in the land of Egypt" (Exodus

MONDAY

# The Torah on the Blind and the Deaf

*You shall not curse the deaf and you shall not place a stumbling block before the blind. You shall fear your God.*
—Leviticus 19:14

Why would anyone trip a blind person? A cruel person might actually be inclined to trip other people as well, but fear to do so lest the injured party see who harmed him. But in the case of a blind person, no such fear applies. He won't know who hurt him (and might not even realize that he was the victim of premeditated cruelty and not an accident), just as the deaf person will not "hear" the curse directed against her. That, indeed, is why the verse concludes with the admonition "You shall fear your God." Remember, the Torah is warning all sadists, even if no human witnesses see what you have done, God sees.

Later rabbis, convinced that no Jew would be so cruel as to cause a blind person to fall on purpose, interpreted this verse figuratively. For example, they explained the verse as applying to one who deliberately gives disadvantageous advice to another (such as taking advantage of another's "blindness" in the matter at hand; see Day 113).

Yet we cannot ignore the verse's literal meaning. The Torah realized that throughout history, the pain of disabled people has derived from both the disability itself and the cruelty others have practiced against the handicapped. Addressing the First National Conference for Jewish Spe-

---

22:20–21). The implication of such an understanding would be that our ancestors had converted to the Egyptian religion; such a reading is, of course, absurd.

One final point: Dr. Stephen Marmer, a psychiatrist, notes that the commandment to "love the stranger" is the "critical antidote to religious intolerance. It is the singular ingredient which makes it possible to be enthusiastic about your own faith, and your own nation, yet be forbidden to impose your way on, or otherwise mistreat, those who are of another faith or nation."

cial Educational Professionals in 1979, Dr. Morton Siegel noted that "in ancient traditions, those who were physically impaired were not uncommonly viewed as 'cursed of God,' and if 'cursed of God,' why not cursed of man? Do you pass legislation telling people not to do something unless they have been doing it? Obviously, they *have* been doing it."

Daniel Taub notes that this commandment also has broader social applications. Thus, planning city developments without taking into consideration the needs of the disabled (ramps for wheelchairs, traffic lights with beepers for the blind) could literally be creating a "stumbling block."

Blind and deaf people function in the world of the sighted and the hearing with two strikes against them. Be very sure that you don't— through cruelty, negligence, or indifference—deliver the third.

DAY

59

TUESDAY

## Standing Up for Justice

Moses was reared as a young prince in the palace of Egypt's Pharaoh. Yet somehow—the Bible doesn't tell us how—he learned that he was not an Egyptian but an Israelite. And so he went out one day from the palace to see how his fellow Israelites, all of whom were slaves, were faring. And he saw an Egyptian overseer brutally whipping an Israelite. Overcome with anger, Moses intervened. He hit the Egyptian overseer so hard that the man died.

The following day, Moses witnessed two Israelites fighting, and tried to make peace between them. The men rebuffed his efforts, and one asked if he was going to kill them the way he had killed the Egyptian. Realizing that his action of the previous day had been witnessed, and would be regarded by Egyptian authorities as a crime, Moses fled to Midian. One could well imagine that at this point all he wanted was peace, but immediately upon his arrival in Midian, he saw several male shepherds mistreating a group of female shepherds. He rose to the young women's defense and watered their flocks.

Moses' behavior has much to teach us. First, you should stand up when you see an injustice being committed. Second, you should involve yourself in fighting injustice, whether it is a fellow Jew who is being hurt (as in the case of the Israelite slave being beaten), or whether it is non-Jews who are being oppressed (as in the case of the Midianite women). Third, in fighting injustice, don't rely on one strategy, but use whatever strategy is appropriate. Thus, Moses used physical force to stop the man who was whipping the Israelite slave, he used words to try to reconcile the two men who were fighting, and he stood up and identified himself with the unfairly treated Midianite women. Perhaps in this last instance, Moses sensed that physical force would be unnecessary. In any case, his behavior teaches us that one strategy doesn't fit all situations.*

The Jewish tradition regards Moses as the greatest of all prophets. That the three incidents the Bible reveals about him prior to God choosing him to be a leader of the Jewish people all deal with one theme, fighting injustice, is perhaps the strongest proof that Judaism forbids us to stand by indifferent or silent when an injustice is committed. The Torah enjoins, "Justice, justice you shall pursue" (Deuteronomy 16:20). Like Moses, we, too, are commanded to stand up for justice.

DAY

60    WEDNESDAY

## Don't Buy Products Produced by Exploited Workers

When you do business with people who exploit their employees, you help guarantee that they will continue to oppress their workers. Only if you, and enough others, stop buying their products might they be motivated to improve their workers' living conditions.

*My understanding of these episodes in Moses' life has been deeply influenced by Nechama Leibowitz's *Studies in Shemot*, 39–48.

This problem is both contemporary (it would seem to me that one should not buy products produced by exploited laborers in China, or by child workers throughout the world), and has been with us for a long time. In 1913, the great American Jewish labor leader Samuel Gompers, president of the American Federation of Labor, criticized the moral apathy of most consumers:

> Did the public concern itself about the sanitary conditions under which garments were produced? About the grievously long hours which the toilers were compelled to labor? About the little children deprived of the right to play and grow, and even to live? Did this public busy itself to trying to right these wrongs and accord justice to those misused? On the contrary, this disinterested "just" public continued its search for bargains, cheap clothing, and gave little thought to the…waste and loss of human life.

As noted, Jewish law strictly forbids buying goods one has reason to believe have been stolen (see Day 3). Buying goods produced by exploited workers or child laborers deprived of a decent childhood is nothing more than trafficking in a form of stolen goods.

When confronted by such a situation, the question to ask yourself is not only, "Is this a good bargain?" but "What would God want me to do?"

DAY

61   THURSDAY

## *Everybody Deserves a "Tenk You"*

I often cringe when I see people complain rudely to a waiter about a food item they disliked, or when, at a wedding or bar mitzvah celebration, I see guests treat a waiter or waitress like a robot, not acknowledging the server when he or she sets a plate of food in front of them or clears it away.

Rabbi Berel Wein recalls that he was once driving with the great rabbinical scholar Rabbi Jacob Kamenetzky. When the two men had to wait a long time at a tollbooth, Wein grew exasperated. Finally, when they arrived at the booth, Wein handed the toll collector the money and drove on. The European-born Rabbi Kamenetzky reproved him, "You didn't say 'Tenk you.'"

Everybody deserves a thank-you: the waitress who serves you, the bank teller who completes your transaction, and the taxi driver who delivers you to your destination. We might be in a hurry, but saying "thank you" won't delay us. Like a payment or a tip, it is part of the debt we owe to whoever treats us courteously and performs a service for us.

DAY

62     FRIDAY

## *The Need for Moral Imagination*

Rabbi Raphael Benjamin Levine, the son of the revered Jerusalem saint, Rabbi Aryeh Levine, once asked his father why, when the students came to the Etz Chayim yeshiva where he taught in the morning, Reb Aryeh would study each child who passed.

"I'll tell you what," Reb Aryeh answered. "You come and stand with me and take a close look at them. What do you see? What do you observe?"

The following morning, the son stood with his father and soon thought he understood the reason for his father's behavior. "It is quite interesting to watch them going in. You can see how eager they are to study the Torah. There I saw a boy pushing ahead of another. He has a zest for learning. That one over there, though, is not at all anxious to enter. His mind is still on the games he was playing."

Responded Reb Aryeh, "Yet I look at different things altogether. That child's trousers are torn. This one's shoes are quite tattered and worn. That boy over there is definitely hungry, how will he ever be able to study?"

As Reb Aryeh's son told Simcha Raz: "More than once, my father would take money from his pocket and give it to children so that they could ride home on the bus in the cold winter nights and not have to trudge through the wet, muddy, unpaved streets." *

May you have a Shabbat Shalom!

## 63      S H A B B A T

$$D$$uring the course of this Shabbat, try to review the material from the preceding six days, and use some of the texts studied as the basis for discussion during the Shabbat meals:

Day 57. Love the Stranger
Day 58. The Torah on the Blind and the Deaf
Day 59. Standing Up for Justice
Day 60. Don't Buy Products Produced by Exploited Workers
Day 61. Everybody Deserves a "Tenk You"
Day 62. The Need for Moral Imagination

Shabbat Shalom!

---

* There is a book chronicling hundreds of tales of Reb Aryeh's goodness, *A Tzaddik in Our Time* by Simcha Raz, which I reread each year before the High Holidays. The story in this entry is found on page 319 of that book.

## 64    SUNDAY

# "One Who Learns from His Companion a Single Chapter"

An elderly rabbi whom I know has inspired hundreds, perhaps thousands, of people to lead lives of greater Jewish commitment. The overwhelming majority remain deeply grateful to him, but he once told me of an experience that shook him. He was attending a conference where he came across a former student of his, a young man who had been an assimilated Jew when they had first met. The student had since gone on to lead a much more rigorously observant lifestyle than that led by his former teacher. When they saw each other at the conference, he sneered at the rabbi, "You have no right to call yourself a rabbi or to be a teacher of Judaism! You're not a good Jew! You're a faker!"

The student's words stunned and deeply pained the rabbi ("I think he was a kinder person when he was assimilated," he confided to me). Indeed, the young man, although he might have thought that he was acting as a religious Jew, was violating one of Judaism's deepest ethical principles. For just as Jewish ethics praises a person for practicing *hakarat hatov*, being grateful, so does it condemn those guilty of being *kafui tova*, ingrates. This student would have been better off, both as a person and in God's eyes, had he tried to incorporate the Mishna's teaching cited in *Ethics of the Fathers:* "One who learns from his companion a single chapter, a single law, a single verse, a single expression, or even a single letter, should accord him respect" (6:3).

The fact that a student feels he has moved beyond his teacher in certain ways does not free him from according that teacher respect and gratitude for the things he did learn. The Palestinian Talmud (*Bava Mezia*

2:11) records that when the rabbinic sage Shmuel heard that one of his early teachers had died, he tore his garment as a sign of mourning. Shmuel's childhood teacher might well have been the person who taught him to read, and Shmuel had clearly matured into a far greater scholar than that teacher, but he recognized that what he had accomplished in life would have been impossible had he been illiterate, or lacked the basic knowledge which this teacher had provided him.

You don't have to learn very much from another person or ideology for Jewish ethics to impose upon you the obligation of gratitude; it is enough that you learn a "single chapter...a single verse [or] a single expression." Even if that is all you learn, you owe the person who taught it to you gratitude and respect.

MONDAY

## Cite Your Sources

*Whoever repeats a statement in the name of the one who said it brings redemption to the world.*
—Ethics of the Fathers 6:6

A friend of mine publishes a newsletter that contains his reflections on contemporary issues, and to which several thousand people subscribe. When he publishes a particularly insightful or provocative piece, he receives many phone calls and letters from readers. What particularly amazes him, though, is that some people will tell him, without shame, "Your piece was great, and I stole from it"; they proceed to explain how they based a whole talk they had given on an article he wrote, without crediting him. In short, they presented his ideas as their own.

Unless someone gives you permission to do so, you are morally obligated to credit the person from whom you learned something. Not to do so constitutes a sort of double thievery: You steal the credit due to the person who first enunciated the idea, and then you engage in what Jewish ethics calls *g'neivat da'at* ("stealing the mind"): you deceive your listeners into thinking that you are smarter or more knowledgeable and insightful than you really are.

But why do the Rabbis credit the act of acknowledging someone else as "bringing redemption to the world"?

As a rule, a person involved in a discussion has two possible motives for interjecting a new fact or insight: to help bring the participants to a deeper understanding of the issue under discussion, and/or to impress everyone present with his or her intelligence. If a person presents as her own an intelligent observation that she learned from another, then it would seem that she did so only to impress everyone with how "bright" she is. But if she cites the source from whom she learned this information, then it would seem that her motive was to deepen everyone's understanding. And a world in which people share information and insights to advance understanding, and not just to advance themselves, is one well on its way to redemption.

So remember, if you have learned something from someone else that can be helpful to others, don't keep it to yourself, but share it—as long as you do so in the name of the person from whom you learned it.

DAY

66    TUESDAY

## Who Is Rich?

W hen I was growing up in the 1950s and 1960s, anyone who had a million dollars or more was regarded as very wealthy.

By the late 1990s, after decades of inflation, most people I know had redefined "rich" to mean possessing over $5 million.

Almost two thousand years ago, the Talmud, too, asked this question: "Who is rich?"

Rabbi Tarfon, a sage of the second century C.E., and something of a literalist, answered, "He who possesses a hundred vineyards, a hundred fields, and a hundred slaves working in them" (Babylonian Talmud, *Shabbat* 25b).

But Rabbi Ben Zoma, a young colleague of Rabbi Tarfon, offered this response: "One who is happy with what he has" (*Ethics of the Fathers* 4:1).

The profundity of Ben Zoma's answer is suggested by Dennis Prager's observation that there are plenty of objectively "wealthy" people who still feel financially unsatisfied: "I recall reading that an actor who receives millions of dollars for every film was unhappy because Arnold Schwarzenegger was making a few million dollars more. Had this actor compared his salary with that of, let us say, any of his high school classmates, he would have been deliriously happy at his extraordinary good fortune. Instead he chose to compare his income with that of one of the few actors in the world who makes more than he does."

Ben Zoma's words remind us that not all questions should be answered literally. A question that seems to be about money turns out to be about something far deeper. After all, if a person has $100 million but still feels constantly driven to make more, is he or she wealthy?

So what about you—are you rich?

# Enjoy, Enjoy

Is it fair to enjoy the pleasures of this world while others are suffering?

If you believe that it isn't, then you will never know enjoyment, for the world is *always* filled with suffering. As the Torah reminds us, "For there will never cease to be needy people in your land, which is why I command you: open your hand to the poor and needy" (Deuteronomy 15:11). Furthermore, even if the suffering caused by poverty were eliminated, the pain caused by illness and human cruelty would persist.

So, should one feel free to experience pleasure while many others are suffering?

Judaism's answer is yes. As long as you act morally and generously, you have a right to enjoy life's delights.

I am convinced that Judaism's concern that people enjoy life without feeling guilty is one reason Jewish law specifies a percentage of income one should donate to charity (between ten and twenty percent). Had no such percentage been designated, a moral person would always feel he or she hadn't done enough. However, once you've given ten percent, you should feel free to spend the rest of your money as you please.

Judaism believes that the pursuit of pleasure, if done in moderation, is good. The Talmud teaches, "In the future world, a man will have to give an accounting for every good thing his eyes saw, but of which he did not eat" (Palestinian Talmud, *Kiddushin* 4:12). It relates that Rabbi Elazar "paid particular attention to this statement, setting aside money so that he could eat every kind of food at least once a year."

Anyone who has ever attended a lavish Jewish wedding or a bar or bat mitzvah party might assume that Jews were particularly conscious only of the pleasures of eating, but that is hardly the case. Samson Raphael Hirsch, the great leader of nineteenth-century German Orthodoxy, surprised his followers one day by announcing his intention to travel to Switzerland. "When I stand shortly before the Almighty," he explained, "I will be held accountable to many questions....But what will I say when...and I'm sure to be asked, 'Shimshon, did you see my Alps?'" *

Many people associate piety with asceticism. In Catholicism and Buddhism, monks and nuns take vows of poverty, as do many Hindu holy men. And while individual Jewish scholars have lived and encouraged lives of asceticism, the more normative Jewish view is that taught by Maimonides: "No one should, by vows and oaths, forbid to himself the use of things otherwise permitted" (*Mishneh Torah*, "Laws of Character Development," 3:1).

So, as the Jewish writer and raconteur Harry Golden, a native of New York's Lower East Side, remembers his mother constantly saying, "Enjoy, enjoy."

*This story is found in Martin Gordon, *Journal of Jewish Thought*, 1985, 123.

# "Keep Far Away from Falsehood"

Why does the Torah not content itself with the command "Do not lie," but also ordains, "Keep far away from falsehood" (Exodus 23:7).

Apparently this verse is intended not only to prohibit lying but also to warn people against statements that could lead to lies, such as exaggerations. Many people, particularly raconteurs or those who are anxious to "prove" a point, feel the need to "help" the truth along, which can easily turn into an untruth. A Yiddish proverb teaches, "A half-truth is a whole lie" (see Day 309). The biblical verse's phrasing suggests that the Torah wants people to be precise, so as to avoid entering the realm of lies by staying "far away from falsehood."

Jewish law particularly opposes lies that are told to secure a personal advantage. Thus, a storekeeper who tells a customer that a product is better than it actually is, is guilty not only of lying but also of thievery; he is unjustly taking money that the customer would not have handed over had he known the whole truth about the product.

The connection between lying and stealing is underscored in another biblical law: "Do not steal, do not deceive, and do not lie to one another" (Leviticus 19:11). A lie told by a salesperson invalidates the sale, and the salesperson is responsible for returning the money to the buyer.

The Talmud warns parents not to lie to children: "One shouldn't promise a child something and then not give it to him, because as a result the child will learn to lie" (*Sukkah* 46b). In other words, if you promise a child a toy or a special trip, you are morally obligated to keep your word. Failure to do so is not only unfair, but also might cause the child to conclude that in the real world one isn't obligated to carry out one's promise.

Parents also should not encourage children to tell lies to others (such as having your child say to a phone caller, "Mommy's not home," when you are there; see Day 298). A child who's taught to lie when it is to the *parent's* advantage will soon learn to lie when it is in his or her own interest.

Sometimes we lie because we want others to think we are more knowledgeable than we are. The Talmud suggests an antidote to such behavior: "Teach your tongue to say, 'I do not know,' lest you be led to lie" (*Berachot* 4a).

While there are occasional instances in which Jewish law permits one to deviate from the truth (see Days 71–73), the general guideline is "Keep far away from falsehood." In practical terms, this means don't lie or exaggerate, and avoid the company of people who don't speak truthfully.

DAY

69   FRIDAY

## *"What Good Thing Happened to Me This Week?"*

Some years ago, I attended a Shabbat service conducted by my friend Rabbi Leonid Feldman of Temple Emanu-El in Palm Beach, Florida. Before the service began, he wished everyone "Shabbat Shalom," and asked if anyone in the congregation had good news that had occurred over the preceding week which he or she wished to share with others. People stood up and announced engagements, anniversaries, the first words spoken by a child or grandchild, a book's publication, the visit by a family member or friend whom they hadn't seen in many years, the completion of a degree, and more.

I was moved. Rabbi Feldman's question motivated people to start their Shabbat with a remembrance of the good things that were going on in their lives. Ever since, I have started every Friday-night service with my congregation, the Synagogue for the Performing Arts in Los Angeles, by asking the same question.

My wife decided to bring this ritual into our home. At the beginning of the Friday-night Shabbat meal, she asks family members and guests to share something good or memorable that happened to them during the week.

Usually everyone, even those who have had difficult weeks, can think of at least one pleasurable moment that occurred during the preceding week. In the rare instance when someone cannot summon up even one positive recollection, family members or friends generally remember something good that the other person has forgotten.

Even during hard times, we all have experiences or interactions for which we are grateful. It is important to focus on those happy memories even—perhaps particularly—during hard times.

How fitting, therefore, to start your Shabbat by asking and answering the question Rabbi Feldman posed before his congregation: "What good thing happened to me this week?"

May you have a Shabbat Shalom!

DAY

## 70      SHABBAT

During the course of this Shabbat, try to review the material from the preceding six days, and use some of the texts studied as the basis for discussion during the Shabbat meals:

Day 64. "One Who Learns from His Companion a Single Chapter"
Day 65. Cite Your Sources
Day 66. Who Is Rich?
Day 67. Enjoy, Enjoy
Day 68. "Keep Far Away from Falsehood"
Day 69. "What Good Thing Happened to Me This Week?"

Shabbat Shalom!

SUNDAY

# *When, If Ever, Is It Permitted to Lie? (1): When Life Is at Stake*

Some of the greatest figures in Christian theology and Western thought have argued that lying is always wrong, even when life is at stake.

Saint Augustine, the great fourth-century Church Father, argued that lying bars one from eternal life; hence, it makes no sense to give up one's place in the next world to save another life if it means having to lie: "Does he not speak most perversely who says that one person ought to die spiritually, so another may live?...Since, then, eternal life is lost by lying, a lie may never be told for the preservation of the temporal life of another."*

Some fifteen hundred years after Saint Augustine, Immanuel Kant, in an effort to establish a universally binding secular ethic, also condemned all lying, whatever the circumstances. Thus, Kant taught that if a man fleeing for his life is hiding in our house, and the would-be murderer asks whether "our friend who is pursued by him has taken refuge in our house," we are forbidden to lie or mislead him.**

In Judaism's view, one who would tell a truth that would enable a would-be murderer to kill an innocent person would bear a grave moral responsibility. Kant had a low regard for Judaism and so had no interest in what it taught. However, he was a German, and his thinking made a particularly deep and enduring impact in his native country. As philoso-

---

*Saint Augustine, "On Lying," in Defarrari, *Treatises on Various Subjects.*
**Kant, *Critique of Practical Reason,* 346–50.

pher Sissela Bok notes, a German ship captain who was hiding Jews from the Nazis, and was confronted by a Nazi vessel whose commander demanded to know if any Jews were aboard, would have been forbidden, by Kant's reasoning, from lying to the Nazis.*

Truth, as Judaism teaches, is a high value (see Day 68) but not an absolute one.

The first chapter of Exodus describes the effort by Pharaoh to eliminate the Israelites by drowning their newborn male babies in the Nile. He appoints Shifra and Puah, two midwives, to carry out this task. But the midwives fear God and, instead of killing the babies, help save them.

Pharaoh, distressed to learn that his murderous campaign is being thwarted, summons the midwives and demands to know why they have disobeyed his order. The Bible tells us that the two women tell Pharaoh a lie: "The Hebrew women are not like the Egyptian women: they are vigorous. Before the midwives can come to them, they have given birth" (Exodus 1:19).

Did the Bible feel the midwives' response was cowardly, and dislike the fact that they lied?

Not at all. The subsequent verses tell us that God "dealt well" with the midwives, and established "households" (large families) for them. In other words, the midwives were right for saving the Israelite infants and for lying to Pharaoh.

In a later incident, God Himself is depicted as instructing a prophet to save himself by telling a lie. Thus, when God tells the prophet Samuel to anoint David as king in lieu of Saul, Samuel is horrified. If Saul learns of what he is doing, the king will have him executed. God instructs Samuel to tell Saul a lie, that he is making his trip to offer a special sacrifice to God, and not to mention his real purpose (see I Samuel 16).

Of course, God could have told Samuel to tell Saul the truth, and assure the prophet that He would protect him, but instead He tells him to lie. From this, we learn that we should also lie to thwart would-be killers, and not tell them the truth and rely on God to save us.

There are rare instances in which Judaism instructs one to be a martyr. For example, if you can save your life only by killing an innocent person, you are forbidden to do so, and should allow yourself to be

*Bok, *Lying,* 44.

killed rather than kill (see Day 310). However, Jewish law condemns as foolish and immoral both telling the truth to an evil person and thereby enabling him to go on doing evil, or telling the truth to an evil person that leads to your murder.

Truth is a high value; the saving of innocent life is a higher one.

MONDAY

# When, If Ever, Is It Permitted to Lie? (2): Judaism and White Lies

The Talmud records an unusual debate between the houses of Hillel and Shammai concerning the words celebrants should sing when dancing in front of a newly married woman. According to the House of Hillel, the dancers should chant the same words in front of all brides: "What a beautiful and graceful bride!" Their opponents, the House of Shammai, disagree. "If she is lame or blind, are you going to say of her, 'What a beautiful and graceful bride?' Does not the Torah command, 'Stay far away from falsehood?'" (Exodus 23:7). They thus oppose reciting a standard formula; rather, each bride should be described "as she is" (see *Ketubot* 17a).

Hillel's position is accepted as Jewish law. One praises the beauty of all brides and, in any case, the bride is likely to appear beautiful in the eyes of her groom.*

---

*Rabbi Irwin Kula notes that the weakness in Shammai's reasoning is that he thought there was always one objective truth: either the bride was beautiful or was not. Hillel understood that truth is multiple and contextual; true, *he*, Hillel, might not find the bride beautiful, but that is simply his opinion. Thus, to speak of the bride as Shammai advocates not only causes hurt feelings but to a certain degree is also not fully truthful because, from the human perspective, there is not always one truth, certainly not when the subject is a bride's beauty. Kula goes on to note that "it is now clear why Hillel and his disciples taught Shammai's opinions in their academy; it was not simply because Hillel was good-natured and tolerant, but

Elsewhere, the Talmud teaches that a person should modify his or her words so as not to hurt another's feelings gratuitously. Thus, as mentioned earlier, the Rabbis note that the Torah depicts God as modifying the truth so as not to create enmity between Abraham and Sarah. In Genesis 18, three angels visit the ninety-nine-year-old Abraham to inform him that his eighty-nine-year-old wife, Sarah, will give birth to a child in a year. Standing in a nearby tent, Sarah overhears the comment and laughs to herself, saying, "Now that I am withered, am I to have enjoyment, with my husband so old?" A verse later, God appears to Abraham and says, "Why did Sarah laugh, saying, 'Shall I in truth bear a child, old as I am?'" (Genesis 18:12–13).

God repeated only part of Sarah's original comment, omitting the words in which she spoke of Abraham as being "so old." That comment could have hurt Abraham, or made him angry at Sarah. On the basis of this biblical story, the Talmud concludes, "Great is peace, seeing that for its sake, even God modified the truth" (*Yevamot* 65b).

According to Jewish law, one also should not go about telling people critical comments you hear made about them. Indeed, if somebody asks you what another person said about him, you should leave out the negative comments by the other person (except in the instance where a person slanders another, and the victim needs to be warned of the damage being done to his or her name; see Day 44).

When it comes to trying to reconcile feuding parties, Jewish law is remarkably tolerant of "white lies." Of Aaron, Moses' brother and Israel's first high priest, the Rabbis relate that he would utilize untruthful means to make peace between people who had fought. He would go to one, telling him how sad his adversary was about the dispute, and how ashamed and disheartened he felt. Then he would go to the other and tell him the same thing. As the Midrash concludes, "Later, when the two met, they would embrace and kiss each other" (*The Fathers According to Rabbi Nathan* 12:3).

A friend of mine told me that he utilized this technique once, and had unhappy results. When the two parties met, one said to the other, "I'm happy you now realize that you acted unfairly," and my friend's

---

because he believed that the other, opposing, opinion contained some truth and therefore needed to be taught." (For further discussion of this point, see Day 131.)

white lie was quickly exposed. Still, the fact that Jewish tradition endorses Aaron's behavior means that in instances of personal feuding, when truth and peace conflict, peace usually should take precedence.

It is also worth modifying the truth when it can only inflict hurt without any benefit. Thus, if, before going to a party, your spouse or a friend asks you if he or she looks good, and you think they look awful or are dressed inappropriately, you should tell them the truth. Doing so in as tactful a manner as possible will spare them from embarrassment. But if somebody at a party asks you how they look, and you think they don't look well at all, a blunt statement of what you feel may cause the person terrible discomfort, and accomplish no good whatsoever.

Before you tell a truth that can cause only pain and inflict gratuitous hurt, ask yourself *why* you should tell it. There are indeed times when a pretty lie is preferable to an ugly truth.

DAY

73    TUESDAY

## *When, If Ever, Is It Permitted to Lie? (3): Lies Told for Reasons of Humility, Privacy, and Not to Harm Another*

The story is told that Frank Lloyd Wright once served as a witness in a court case during which he referred to himself as "the greatest living architect."

When his wife later reproved him for making so immodest a comment in public, Wright responded, "I had no choice. I was under oath."

While Jewish law imposes extremely strict standards of truth on those testifying in court (the Ninth Commandment prohibits perjury), a remarkable talmudic passage notes that Jewish law permits even religious scholars to deviate from the truth in certain situations, and when they are not under oath: "In the following three matters, learned men do conceal the truth: In matters of tractate, bed, and hospitality" (Babylonian Talmud, *Bava Mezia* 23b–24a).

As the commentaries explain: If someone asks a scholar if he is conversant with a certain talmudic tractate, he is permitted to say no, even if he is, so as not to appear to be bragging. And if somebody asks a scholar (or any person) intrusive questions about his or her sexual life (such as "Did you refrain from coming to the study hall yesterday because you had been sleeping with your wife?"), he is permitted to safeguard his private affairs by lying. The *Tosafot,* a standard medieval commentary on the Talmud, suggests that one may respond to such inappropriate questions by saying one was sick, or that some emergency had come up. The Talmud understood that the details of one's intimate life were no one else's business.

The third area in which lying is permitted, "hospitality," is surprising, but eminently sensible. If a scholar has been treated with exemplary graciousness and generosity by his hosts, and is then asked by other people how he was received, he is permitted to downplay, or even lie about, the extent of the hosts' hospitality if he has reason to suspect that speaking the truth will cause people to descend upon the hosts and exploit them.

The Talmud asks, "What is the point of telling us that religious scholars are permitted to lie in these three areas?"

Rabbi Mar Zutra answers that if you have found a lost item and a religious scholar comes and says that it is his, you are permitted to give it to him without further questions if you know that he is a person who lies only in these three areas but in no other (in other words, lying for these reasons is not an indication of unreliability). But if you know that he lies about other matters as well, then you should not return the lost item to him without further proof.

So, when can a religious scholar—and, by implication, any Jew—lie?

To appear humble, to safeguard his private life, and not to cause harm to another. Otherwise, he—and you—should tell the truth.

# Declaring a "Complaining Fast"

The Hebrew term *ta'anit dibur* means "speech fast"; some of Judaism's greatest sages would periodically engage in such fasts both to avoid inappropriate speech (see, for example, Days 43 and 44), and to keep their minds focused on more spiritual concerns. It is told of the great scholar and moralist Rabbi Israel Salanter that for forty days before Yom Kippur he would refrain as much as possible from all speech.

A speech fast is arduous, and I know of few people who engage in them today. My wife and I, however, periodically try to engage in a "complaining fast." For a week at a time, we try to refrain from all whining and complaining.

What generally motivates us to initiate such a fast is a spate of constant grumbling. It frequently happens that one of us will start complaining about what a hard week or month we have been having. More often than not, such complaints at first evoke sympathy, but soon prompt the other spouse to start recalling every difficulty he or she has been having that week or month.

Often, such conversations quickly escalate into a delineation of all the difficulties each of us is experiencing. By the time the discussion is finished, we are aware of everything in our lives that is not going well, and we are both miserable.

Dennis Prager likes to make the point that many people are unhappy unless they have a reason to be happy; it would be far better, he argues, for people to be happy unless there is a reason to be unhappy—and complaining gives people reasons to be unhappy.

One way to achieve more happiness is to declare a temporary moratorium on complaining. Doing so makes it easier to become conscious of the things that are going well in your life. As an old American proverb teaches, "If you can't be grateful for all the things you don't have and want, be grateful for all the things you don't have and don't want."

A household that goes for a day or a week without complaining will be a pleasanter place in which to live. By declaring a "complaining fast," people will have the space to focus on those aspects of their lives for which they are grateful.

T H U R S D A Y

# The Most Unusual of Blessings

In Judaism, a blessing (*bracha*), always starts with the formula, "Blessed are You, Lord our God, Sovereign of the Universe...." Because of the invocation of God's name, Jews generally associate blessings with holiness. Observant Jews recite dozens of blessings during the three daily prayer services, and many more before and after eating, a total of at least one hundred blessings daily.

Many Jews, however, are unaware of a blessing that is supposed to be recited after every trip to the bathroom:

> Blessed are You, Lord our God, Sovereign of the Universe, Who has formed man in wisdom, and created within him many openings and many cavities. It is obvious and known before Your throne of glory that if one of them were to be ruptured or one of them blocked, it would be impossible to survive and to stand before You. Blessed are You, God, Who heals all flesh and does wonders.

Dr. Kenneth Prager of Columbia Presbyterian Hospital, an Orthodox Jew, recalls that this blessing was posted outside the bathroom of the Jewish day school he attended as a child. Unfortunately, but perhaps understandably, it provoked much laughter among him and his young friends: "For grade school children, there could be nothing more strange or ridiculous than to link the acts of [urination] and defecation with holy words that mentioned God's name."

Only in his second year of medical school did Prager start to appreciate the blessing's profundity: "Pathophysiology brought home to me the terrible consequences of even minor aberrations in the structure and function of the human body. At the very least, I began no longer to take for granted the normalcy of my trips to the bathroom. Instead, I started to realize how many things had to operate just right for these minor interruptions of my daily routine to run smoothly....After seeing patients whose lives revolved around their dialysis machines, and others with colostomies and urinary catheters, I realized how wise Rabbi Abbaye [the composer of this blessing] had been."

Reciting this blessing (known as *asher yatzar*), which is also recited during the morning prayer service, offers each of us an opportunity to express gratitude to God for more than just the proper functioning of our excretory organs, but also for our overall good health.

Dr. Prager has written of this ancient blessing in an unlikely place, the *Journal of the American Medical Association.* He concludes his article with the story of twenty-year-old Josh, a young man who had suffered catastrophic injuries in a car crash. During many months of intensive physical therapy, the young man improved day by day:

> But Josh continued to require intermittent catheterization. I knew only too well the problems and perils this young man would face for the rest of his life because of a neurogenic bladder. The urologists were very pessimistic about his chances for not requiring catheterization. They had not seen this occur after a spinal cord injury of this severity.
>
> Then the impossible happened. I was there the day Josh no longer required a urinary catheter. I thought of Abbaye's *asher yatzar* prayer. Pointing out that I could not imagine a more meaningful scenario for its recitation, I suggested to Josh, who was also a yeshiva graduate, that he say the prayer. He agreed. As he recited the ancient *bracha,* tears welled in my eyes.
>
> Josh is my son.*

*Prager, "For Everything a Blessing"; Abbaye's blessing is found in the Talmud, *Berachot* 60b, and in the ArtScroll prayerbook on page 14.

FRIDAY

# Treating People Who Are Retarded with Respect

Rabbi Shlomo Zalman Auerbach (1910–1995) was one of the great rabbinic scholars of the twentieth century. A lifelong resident of Jerusalem, he was famous for the compassion and consideration he showed orphans, widows, and others whom society often neglects and ignores.

In *And From Jerusalem, His Word,* Rabbi Hanoch Teller's biography of Rabbi Auerbach, he recounts the story behind the most unusual rabbinical ordination (*semicha*) this great sage ever bestowed:

The concerned parents of a retarded child once came to Reb Shlomo Zalman to consult him on the choice of an institution for their son. They were considering two alternative facilities, each one having certain advantages over the other. Reb Shlomo Zalman listened carefully to their description and then asked, "Where is the boy? What does he say about all this?"

The parents looked at one another in astonishment. They conceded that it had never occurred to them to discuss the matter with their son. "And frankly," the father added, "I don't see much point in discussing it. This is not something he can grasp."

Reb Shlomo Zalman was irate: "You are committing a sin against the soul of this child!" he cried. "You intend to evict him from his home and consign him to a strange place with a regimented atmosphere. He must be encouraged and not allowed to feel that he is being betrayed." The parents were speechless.

"Where is the boy?" Reb Shlomo Zalman demanded. "I would like to see him and discuss the matter with him personally."

The couple hurriedly honored Reb Zalman's request and brought their son before the sage.

"What is your name, my boy?" the Gaon [great sage, a genius] asked.

"Akiva," the child replied.

"How do you do, Akiva. My name is Shlomo Zalman. I am the *Gadol Hador,* the greatest Torah authority of this generation,* and everyone listens to me. You are going to enter a special school now, and I would like you to represent me and look after all of the religious matters in your new home."

The boy's eyes were riveted to the Gaon's face, and the awestruck parents sat with their mouths agape as the Rav continued. "I shall now give you *semicha,* which makes you a rabbi, and I want you to use this honor wisely."

Reb Shlomo Zalman gently stroked the child's cheek and saw that he was as eager as could be to fulfill his part of the agreement. Over the years, on numerous occasions when this youngster was to spend a Shabbat at home, he refused to leave the institution, insisting that as the local rabbi he had a responsibility to his constituents. After all, he had been charged with this responsibility by none other than the *Gadol Hador!***

May you have a Shabbat Shalom!

DAY

## 77     S H A B B A T

During the course of this Shabbat, try to review the material from the preceding six days, and use some of the texts studied as the basis for discussion during the Shabbat meals:

Day 71. When, If Ever, Is It Permitted to Lie?
(1): When Life Is at Stake

---

*Reb Shlomo Zalman was exceptionally humble, and normally never referred or permitted others to refer to him by such a title.
**Teller, *And From Jerusalem, His Word,* 120–22.

Day 72. When, If Ever, Is It Permitted to Lie? (2): Judaism and
       White Lies

Day 73. When, If Ever, Is It Permitted to Lie? (3): Lies Told for
       Reasons of Humility, Privacy, and Not to Harm Another

Day 74. Declaring a "Complaining Fast"

Day 75. The Most Unusual of Blessings

Day 76. Treating People Who Are Retarded with Respect

Shabbat Shalom!

# WEEK 12

DAY

78      SUNDAY

## *Don't Charge Interest*

One of the most widely known negative images of Jews is as usurers. For example, the most famous usurer in literature is Shylock, the Jewish villain in Shakespeare's *The Merchant of Venice.* To this day, many people believe that medieval antisemitism was largely prompted by Jews charging their Christian neighbors high rates of interest.*

The Torah forbids Israelites from charging interest to fellow Israelites. It does permit doing so to other groups, who, we know, also charged the Israelites interest: "You shall not deduct interest from loans to your countrymen, whether in money or food or anything else that can be deducted as interest, but you may deduct interest from loans to foreigners" (Deuteronomy 23:20–21).

The Torah's prohibition on charging interest to fellow Israelites is categorical. Written at a time when most Jews earned their living

---

*Jewish money-lending was, of course, not the cause of antisemitism. Hatred of the Jews came first; that is why Jews were forbidden to practice almost all other professions and forced to become moneylenders; once they did so, this exacerbated, but did not cause, antisemitism.

through farming, the ban made a great deal of moral sense, since people working in agriculture usually needed to borrow only in emergencies.

As the economies in which Jews lived grew more sophisticated, and people wanted to borrow money to finance the opening or expansion of a business, the Torah ban on interest threatened to retard economic growth. Why would a borrower loan someone money to establish or expand a business when he or she earned nothing by doing so? To allow for economic expansion, later Jewish law developed a legal fiction, still used by Orthodox Jews, known as a *heter iska* (literally, "permission to do business"). Under this legal allowance, one who loans money is guaranteed a set percentage of the "profits," corresponding to a reasonable rate of interest, whether or not there is in fact a profit.

But while a *heter iska* is permitted for a business loan, Jewish law forbids using such a device when a loan is made for necessities. If someone needs money for food, clothing, rent, school tuition, or other necessities, you should extend the full loan, or whatever part you can afford, interest-free. Common sense suggests that you should loan a sum of money that if not repaid, will not cause you significant damage.*

Jewish communities throughout the world have free loan societies, some of which extend loans to hundreds of people; most report exceptionally high rates of repayment.

Lending money interest-free to one who is having serious financial difficulties is regarded in the Jewish tradition as the highest kind of *gemilut chesed*, an act of kindness par excellence.

---

*When a loan is extended for necessities and is not repaid, the lender may regard the lost money as part of his or her annual charity donations, although obviously no tax deduction is allowed for such "loans"/contributions.

# *Help Someone Laugh*

The Talmud tells of a certain Rabbi Beroka, who found himself in the marketplace of the Persian city of Be Lefet. Suddenly the prophet Elijah appeared to him. The rabbi asked him, "Is there anyone in this marketplace who deserves a place in the World-to-Come?" Elijah answered, "No."

A short time later, two men walked by and Elijah told the rabbi, "These men deserve a place in the World-to-Come."

Rabbi Beroka went over to them and asked them their occupation. "We are comedians," they told him, "and we cheer up those who are depressed. In addition, whenever we see two people involved in a quarrel, we work hard to make peace between them" (*Ta'anit* 22a).

As these comedians understood, true kindness consists in doing whatever the person with whom you are interacting most needs; thus, a depressed person focused only on that which is paining him might desperately need to laugh, and thereby recall that life is not just anguish. Speaking through Elijah, God so approves of the comedians' attitude that He holds them out as examples of the sort of people who most merit eternal reward.

Some fifteen hundred years after the incident with Rabbi Beroka, some disciples of Rabbi Israel Salanter once observed him standing and engaging in a lengthy and lighthearted conversation with an acquaintance. The disciples were amazed, as Rabbi Salanter was known to disapprove of wasting one's time in frivolous speech. Later, when one of the disciples commented on his behavior, Rabbi Salanter answered, "This man was feeling extremely bitter and depressed, and it was a great act of kindness to cheer him and to make him forget his troubles and his worries. Could I have done this by lecturing him about fear of God or the need for moral improvement? Surely, this could only be done by cheerful speech about down-to-earth matters" (*Or Yisra'el,* page 112).

The biblical book of Ecclesiastes reminds us that there is a time to weep and a time to laugh (3:4). And sometimes there is a time to make others laugh.

TUESDAY

# For Whom Was I Named?

I often officiate at services in which a Jewish child is given a Hebrew name (according to traditional Jewish law, a girl is named at the first Torah reading following her birth, a boy at his circumcision). Since the large majority of children are named for someone, I always speak with the parents before the naming and ask them what it was about the deceased* that motivated them to name a child for him or her. Usually, one parent will start to describe the dead person in loving detail. I then ask what specific traits of the deceased they particularly hope their newborn child will have. Later, at the naming ceremony, I mention these characteristics.

However, as children grow up, most parents don't tell them much about the person for whom they were named. Rabbi Jack Riemer has noted that this is unfortunate, since "if we don't tell our children our stories and the stories of those from whom we come, no one else ever will. The stories will disappear and our kids will be deprived. I have learned this truth from the meetings that I have had with the children in my synagogue who are going to be bar or bat mitzvah. One of the questions that I always ask them is, 'What is your Hebrew name?'... Then I ask them, 'Who are you named for?' They have some vague idea that it was for a great uncle so-and-so or for some great aunt such-and-such. And then I ask them: 'What was that person like? What qualities did that person have that were so important that your parents saw fit to name you for him or her?' And so their first home-

---

* Among Ashkenazim (Jews of European origin), children are named for a deceased ancestor. Among many Sephardim (Jews whose ancestors come from Spain or the Arab world), children are often named for people who are still living, particularly for grandparents, but not for parents.

work assignment from me is to go home and interview their parents and anyone else they can find who knew that person, so that they can find out who he or she was, what he or she stood for and lived through, and what it means to be named for them."

Fortunately, when I was being raised, my mother often spoke to me of her uncle, Rabbi Joseph Adler, for whom I was named. He was a great Talmud scholar who founded a yeshiva (Mesivtah Tiferet Yerushalayim) and helped bring to the United States Rabbi Moshe Feinstein, one of the great figures of twentieth-century Orthodox Jewish life, to head it. For many years, he and his wife earned their income from a small store they had established, since he did not wish to earn his living from teaching Torah.

He was also an exceptionally loving uncle to my mother. She often had Shabbat meals at his house, and he loved to play and laugh with her. Later, during the Depression, when my grandfather lost almost all his money, Rabbi Adler lent her the funds to finish her B.A. at New York University.

After you tell your children about the people for whom they were named, pick up the phone, call your parents, aunts and uncles, and others, and start finding out more about the person for whom *you* were named.

DAY

81

WEDNESDAY

## A Lifesaving Bribe

One-third of people who smoke die prematurely, and by an average of seven years. Obviously, parents should try to do what's possible to discourage their children from starting this self-destructive habit.

As noted, Jewish law prohibits one from engaging in self-destructive behavior (see, for example, Day 36). Rabbi Akiva summarized the Jewish position: "A person is not permitted to harm himself or herself" (Mishna, *Bava Kamma* 8:6).

Hence the following suggestion: Make a contract with your children, something like, "If you reach the age of twenty-one without smoking [or insert a maximum permissible number of cigarettes, e.g., twenty], I will give you one thousand dollars on your twenty-first birthday."

The sum of money to be paid should be discussed and agreed upon, and the contract effected with some ritual; certainly the parents should sign the document. Similar contracts can be made concerning the intake of illegal drugs and hard liquor.

Will such contracts work? For many children, no, but for a certain percentage, yes. And if one does not become addicted to cigarettes, drugs, or liquor prior to turning twenty-one, the chances of his or her subsequently becoming addicted are greatly reduced.

May God bless you that you have to pay off on all your contracts.

DAY

82    THURSDAY

## The Little Indecencies That Reveal Character

I was boarding a plane recently when a man, accompanied by a child of about seven, pushed ahead of me and other passengers so that he could board the flight a little more quickly. He did not say "Excuse me" as he walked by, or offer any explanation for his rude behavior.

The first thought that went through my head? I would never enter into a business deal with this man; whatever happened, he would find a way to protect his interests at the expense of mine. I had the same thought a few days later when I was waiting in the rain with my wife and three of our children for a taxi. Finally a taxi came, but a man who had arrived after us, and had seen us waiting, jumped in. My wife went over to say something to him, but he closed the door, and the taxi departed.

Maybe I am being unfair in assuming that both of these men would be selfish, and perhaps dishonest, in business dealings. The biblical verse "and in righteousness you shall judge your neighbor" (Leviticus 19:15) is usually understood as requiring one to be very cautious before condemning another, and obliges one to try and find possible justification for the other person's behavior (see Day 24). Yet both men's decision not even to say "Excuse me" made their behavior seem inexcusable. And given that the first man was serving as a role model for his young daughter, his lack of manners was even more disconcerting.

Rabbi Israel Meir Kagan, known in Jewish life as the Chaffetz Chayyim (see Day 321), was once present at a bathhouse when he witnessed a man cleaning himself with someone else's brush. When the brush's owner came out of the bathroom, it immediately became apparent that he hadn't given the older man permission to use it. Later the Chaffetz Chayyim walked over to the man who had misappropriated the brush and told him, "A person who uses another's brush without permission ends up dirtier than before he used it."

The biblical verses "Do what is right and good in the sight of the Lord" (Deuteronomy 6:18) and "Her ways [the ways of Torah] are pleasant" (Proverbs 3:17) mandate a level of fairness and courtesy in all our dealings with others. True, all of us, either out of haste or anxiety, act impolitely on occasion. But if you do so more often, this suggests that you regard other people as being of less value than yourself, and that you believe you are justified in taking advantage of them. Given that one of Judaism's most important concepts is that each human being is created "in God's image," bad manners is not a minor matter; it reveals that you don't really accept this fundamental Jewish belief (see also Day 310).

# "The Most Beautiful Etrog I Have Ever Seen"

Almost all entries in this book focus on specific acts through which one can lead a more ethical life. However, sometimes a story is so poignant and inspiring that it alone can motivate a person to practice virtuous deeds. Such is the case with a story S. Y. Agnon, the Israeli Nobel Prize laureate, told about, of all things, an *etrog*.

Jewish law ordains that a Jew acquire an *etrog*, or citron, before the holiday of Sukkot, and recite a blessing over it each day of the festival (except on the Sabbath). Early on, a still-observed tradition developed among pious Jews to spend a good deal of money to acquire a particularly beautiful *etrog*, one devoid of any defects. Purchasers take care to ensure that the citron's skin is unblemished and, most important, that the fruit's tip is erect; if it is broken, the *etrog* is forbidden for ritual use.

Agnon related that shortly before Sukkot in his Jerusalem neighborhood of Talpiot, he ran into one of his neighbors, an elderly rabbi from Russia, at a store selling *etrogim*. The rabbi told Agnon that he regarded it as particularly important to acquire a very beautiful, aesthetically perfect *etrog*. Although he had limited means, he was willing to spend a large sum to acquire this ritual object.

How surprised Agnon was, a day or two later, when the holiday began and the rabbi did not take out his *etrog* during the synagogue service. Perplexed, he asked the man where the *etrog* was. The rabbi told him the following incident:

> I awoke early, as is my habit, and prepared to recite the blessing over the *etrog* in my *Sukkah* [the special hut Jews build during this holiday] on my balcony. As you know, we have a neighbor with a large family, and our balconies adjoin. As you also know, our neighbor, the father of all these children next door, is a man of

short temper. Many times he shouts at them or even hits them for violating his rules and wishes. I have spoken to him many times about his harshness but to little avail.

As I stood in the *Sukkah* on my balcony, about to recite the blessing for the *etrog,* I heard a child's weeping coming from the next balcony. It was a little girl crying, one of the children of our neighbor. I walked over to find out what was wrong. She told me that she, too, had awakened early and had gone out on her balcony to examine her father's *etrog,* whose delightful appearance and fragrance fascinated her. Against her father's instructions, she removed the *etrog* from its protective box to look at it. She unfortunately dropped the *etrog* on the stone floor, irreparably damaging it and rendering it unacceptable for ritual use. She knew that her father would be enraged and would punish her severely, perhaps even violently. Hence the frightened tears and wails of apprehension. I comforted her, and I then took my *etrog* and placed it in her father's box, taking the damaged *etrog* to my premises. I told her to tell her father that his neighbor insisted that he accept the gift of the beautiful *etrog,* and that he would be honoring me and the holiday by so doing.*

Agnon concludes: "My rabbinic neighbor's damaged, bruised, ritually unusable *etrog* was the most beautiful *etrog* I have ever seen in my lifetime."

May you have a Shabbat Shalom!

---

*I haven't found the original Agnon story, but it is beautifully retold in Rabbi Berel Wein, *Second Thoughts,* 64–65.

## 84     S H A B B A T

During the course of this Shabbat, try and review the material from the preceding six days, and use some of the texts studied as the basis for discussion during the Shabbat meals:

Day 78. Don't Charge Interest
Day 79. Help Someone Laugh
Day 80. For Whom Was I Named?
Day 81. A Lifesaving Bribe
Day 82. The Little Indecencies That Reveal Character
Day 83. "The Most Beautiful *Etrog* I Have Ever Seen"

Shabbat Shalom!

# WEEK 13

## 85     S U N D A Y

## "Do Not Stand by While Your Neighbor's Blood Is Shed": The Requirement to Intervene

*Do not stand by while your neighbor's blood is shed.*
—Leviticus 19:16

*How do we know that if one sees someone drowning, being mauled by beasts, or being attacked by robbers, one is oblig-*

*ated to save him? From the verse, "Do not stand by while your neighbor's blood is shed."*

—Babylonian Talmud, *Sanhedrin* 73a

Jewish law focuses on obligations, American jurisprudence on rights. Thus there is no obligation in American law to rescue an endangered person. Troubled by the lack of such a requirement, Harvard law professor Mary Ann Glendon suggests the following hypothetical case: "An Olympic swimmer out for a stroll walks by a swimming pool and sees an adorable toddler drowning in the shallow end. He could easily save her with no risk to himself, but instead he pulls up a chair and looks on as she perishes. [This athlete has violated no law.] There is no peg in our legal system on which to hang a duty to rescue another person in danger." *

In contrast, Torah law makes it clear that one who can intervene when another's life is at stake and does not is a grievous sinner and in violation of an important law.

Jewish law does not, however, oblige one to put his or her own life at risk to save another. Thus, if you see a criminal threatening to kill someone, you are not required to try to tackle the man with the gun. Similarly, if you cannot swim, or if you swim poorly, there's no obligation to jump into deep water to save a person who is drowning. But you would still be required to try to reach the person with a rope or do whatever you could to summon aid.

When the risk to you is low, however, you are obliged to do all that you can to save the endangered person. Thus, if you witness a person accosted by criminals, at the very least you must immediately call the police. Perhaps this seems obvious, but in 1964, New York City was rocked by a case in which *thirty-eight witnesses* watched from apartment windows as Kitty Genovese, a twenty-eight-year-old woman, was stabbed to death. Although the knifing occurred over a period of thirty-five minutes, no one called the police until after the woman was dead and the murderer had fled. The police learned of the witnesses' exis-

* Glendon, *Rights Talk,* 78–80.

tence only when they interviewed the building's residents the following day.* They said they didn't want to get involved.

From Judaism's perspective, people who stand by, silent and indifferent, while another's life is at stake identify with Cain, the murderer who asked God, "Am I my brother's keeper?" (Genesis 4:9). Indeed, the law "Do not stand by while your neighbor's blood is shed" seems to come as a response to Cain's question: "Yes," the Torah is telling us, "you *are* your brother's and your sister's keeper."

DAY

## 86     M O N D A Y

# *When You Suspect Child Abuse*

There are many areas in which Jews generally have a positive self-image. For example, most Jews are shocked when they hear of a family where the parents don't care whether or not their children continue their education after high school. Obviously such families exist, but the Jewish self-image is of a people deeply devoted to their children's education. Similarly, most Jews, when they hear of a man who divorces his wife and never again has contact with his children, are also shocked. Such men exist, but Jewish fathers are expected to be devoted to their children.

The same applies to instances of child abuse, both physical and sexual; many Jews are loath to believe that it occurs in the Jewish community. Unfortunately, such stereotypical thinking can cause permanent psychological and physical damage, even death. Sufficient data has now emerged to indicate many instances of parental abuse of children within the Jewish community, spanning the spectrum from Orthodox to secular.

---

*See A. M. Rosenthal's book-length account, *Thirty-eight Witnesses*, and Kirschenbaum, "The 'Good Samaritan' and Jewish Law," in *Dine Israel: An Annual of Jewish Law*, 7–8.

Most people are reluctant to intervene when they suspect child abuse among their neighbors or relatives. Particularly among religious Jews, there is long-standing opposition to informing gentile authorities of crimes committed by fellow Jews. It is important to note, however, that the regulations prohibiting such informing arose in societies where Jews were subjected to unfair treatment before non-Jewish courts (comparable to the mistreatment of African-Americans in American courts in the nineteenth and much of the twentieth century). In such a society, to inform on a fellow Jew was regarded, often justifiably, as an evil act. The same does not apply to democratic societies in which Jews have equal rights.

Certainly, in cases involving a Jew who is committing a violent crime, no such hesitation about involving gentile authorities should apply. Rabbi Joseph Karo, the definitive Jewish legal expert and author of the standard code, the sixteenth-century *Shulchan Aruch*, ruled that if a man abused his wife (and by extension his children) "he should be excommunicated, and let him be forced by gentile [authorities] to give her a writ of divorce" (*Beit Yosef* to the *Arba'ah Turim, Even Ha-Ezer* 154:15). Rabbi Karo's contemporary, Rabbi Moses Isserles, the preeminent legal authority for European Jews, wrote, "A person who attacks others should be punished. If the Jewish authorities do not have the power to punish him, he must be punished by civil authorities" (*Choshen Mishpat* 388:7).

If you have good reason to suspect that a child is being abused, your primary concern must be the young person's well-being, while issues of "informing" and potentially defaming another's reputation become secondary.

One also must bear in mind that abuse is not committed only by mean-spirited parents with untamed tempers; sometimes it results from parental adherence to absurd ideologies. For example, a nurse recently told a rabbi I know of an ethical dilemma she had confronted. She was working at a Jewish school and a young child came to her with an ear infection that, it was clear to her practiced eye, had been present for a long time. The child was in real danger of losing his hearing, and needed to be put on a careful regimen of antibiotics. But the child's mother told the nurse that her husband, who was fanatically committed to alternative healing, opposed all use of antibiotics. A call to the father revealed this to be the case. Knowing the parents, the nurse had been reluctant to call a child services agency. When she asked the rabbi what Jewish law's attitude would be in such a case, he told her that there is no source in Jewish law that permits a parent to stand by and allow his or her child to become deaf. Therefore, whatever outside source can help guarantee that the child receives adequate medical care should be summoned (obviously, if a less dramatic step, such as involving the couple's rabbi, could bring about the desired result, that should be pursued first).*

Just as Jewish ethics hold liable those who watch a person drowning but do nothing to rescue the person (see yesterday's entry), so does it condemn those who can help a suffering and vulnerable child but don't. In line with the biblical verse, "Do not stand by while your brother's blood is shed" (Leviticus 19:16), Judaism sees passive bystanders as acquiescing to mistreatment and murder.

DAY

## 87       TUESDAY

# Untamed Anger and the Death of Love

The Bible generally describes romantic love from the male's perspective. We are told that Isaac loved Rebecca, Jacob loved Rachel, and Samson, to his regret, loved Delilah. However, there is only one woman whose love for a man is recorded: we are told twice that Michal, the daughter of King Saul, loved David, the hero of her father's army (I Samuel 18:20, 28).

Michal and David soon wed, but their marriage ultimately became miserably unhappy. Perhaps the main reason was that Michal and David both suffered from the same character flaw; each possessed a sharp tongue, which they refused to control when angry.

*In cases of physical or sexual abuse, it is very unlikely that intervention of the clergy could adequately and immediately address the problem.

The incident that led to the marriage's death happened just over three thousand years ago, in the aftermath of King David's capture of Jerusalem. He immediately established Jerusalem as the nation's capital, and brought to it the Ark of the Lord (the holiest object in ancient Jewish life, it contained the original Ten Commandments). The day the Ark arrived was the happiest day in his kingship, and so he danced wildly with his subjects. Herself a king's daughter, Michal watched David's dancing from a palace window and was annoyed; perhaps she thought it lowered the king's dignity to carry on with his subjects in so unrestrained a manner.

Throughout the day, Michal's anger grew, so that when David started back toward the palace, she met him outside and greeted him with cold sarcasm: "Didn't the king of Israel do himself honor today— exposing himself...as one of the riffraff might expose himself?" (II Samuel 6:20).

Confronted by this insult, David had several options: he could have responded to the substance of Michal's attack, remained silent, or walked away and taken a stroll around the palace. Instead, he did what many of us do when attacked. Michal had hurt him, so he wished to hurt her back. He responded, "It was before the Lord who chose me instead of your father and all his family [that I danced]." His utterance came just a short time after Michal's father and three of her brothers had been killed in battle against the Philistines.

The next verse records: "So to her dying day, Michal, daughter of Saul, had no children." Why is the fact of Michal's childlessness recorded here? I suspect that after so brutal an exchange—and probably there were other such fights—Michal and David were never again intimate.

The Bible's point is as clear today as it was in 1000 B.C.E.: If a husband and wife (or two siblings or two friends) do not restrain their words when angry, love is unlikely to survive, no matter how deeply the two people once cared for each other. The ability to control what we say when angry is a prerequisite for a lasting relationship.

Of course, this should not be understood as meaning that a couple should never fight. Human beings have a right to disagree and to argue. What they don't have a right to do is act as Michal and David did. Michal did not confront David with a cogent or fair argument; instead she insulted him, dismissing him as "riffraff." And David was unfair in utilizing his knowledge of the most painful event in Michal's life to score points in an argument.

Their errors, hurling insults and dredging up hurtful episodes from the past, remain two of the commonest types of cruelties committed by couples who fight. Whenever you are tempted to insult your spouse or summon up a painful memory from his or her past, remember what happened to David and Michal. A relationship that started with love and longing ended in contempt and loneliness. If you don't learn to control your tongue and to fight fairly (see Day 51), you may lose the person you love the most.*

DAY

## 88

WEDNESDAY

# *Be Fair to Your Enemy*

One of the most famous teachings attributed to Jesus in the New Testament is the admonition: "Love your enemies and pray for those who persecute you...for if you love those who love you, what right have you to claim any credit?" (Matthew 5:44, 46). Because this New Testament admonition was understood as being innovative and opposed to Jewish teachings, many Christians, and even some Jews, assume that Jewish law enjoins its adherents to hate their enemies and to treat them cruelly.** In truth, although the Torah does not command Jews to love their enemies, it does demand that they act fairly toward them: "When you encounter your enemy's ox or donkey wandering, you must take it back to him" (Exodus 23:4).*** The Bible is reminding us that even

---

*This entry draws in large measure on my earlier book, *Words That Hurt, Words That Heal*, 69–79.

**Matthew 5:43 attributes to Jesus the statement, "You have heard that it was said, 'Love your neighbor and hate your enemy.'" There is, however, no such Jewish teaching.

***Another Torah law legislates that if you see your enemy's animal struggling under a burden, you must help him release the burden (Exodus 23:5). This law, however, might well have less to do with helping your enemy than with helping your enemy's animal; in other words, the Torah is reminding us that just because you dislike somebody, don't take it out on his animal; don't take it out on his family, either.

when dealing with someone we despise, perhaps justifiably, we must still act justly. Thus, if you find something lost by someone you hate, you still must return it to him. Elsewhere, the Book of Proverbs teaches, "If your enemy is hungry, give him bread to eat; if he is thirsty, give him water to drink" (25:21). The notion here is the same. Jewish law instructs us to give food to one who is hungry (see Day 9); that the person who is famished is your enemy does not free you from this obligation.

We are not commanded to love our enemies, we are commanded to be fair toward them.

T H U R S D A Y

## Don't Make People Tell You Lies

"Keep far away from falsehood," the Torah teaches (Exodus 23:7; see Day 68). The thirteenth-century Rabbi Judah the Chasid understood the Bible's prohibition of lying as encompassing more than just not telling a lie; one must also take care not to cause other people to lie. He said, "If you see people whispering to each other, and you want to know what they are saying, [control your curiosity and] don't ask them, lest you make liars out of them. If they wanted you to know, they would have told you. Since it is clear that they don't want to share their secret with you, they will lie to you" (*Sefer Chasidim*, paragraph 1062).

The same logic dictates that one should not ask people questions, the answers to which one has no right to know. Many people, out of fear or politeness, will be reluctant to tell a curious questioner, "It's none of your business." Therefore, if you press a person to share with you information that was transmitted to her in confidence, you will likely force her to violate a confidence or lie to you. It is wrong to put someone in such a position.

Curiosity about how the world works has fueled all important scientific and other intellectual discoveries. But when it comes to intrusive curiosity about other people's private lives or secrets, one is best guided by the words of the ancient Jewish sage Ben Sira: "What is committed to you to do, attend to; for what is hidden is not your concern" (Apocrypha, Ben Sira 3:21).

FRIDAY

# "He Who Saves a Single Life It Is as If He Saved an Entire World" *

A famous talmudic text teaches that there are those who acquire their place in heaven in an instant (*Avodah Zara* 10b). This teaching applies to people who do heroic (sometimes self-sacrificial) acts and perform lifesaving deeds for another. Until the moment of their great act, such people may have been ordinary; they may even have committed some serious sins and suffered from ethical lapses. But the act of goodness they did outweighed all the previous misdeeds they had committed.

In Rabbi Lawrence Kushner's *Invisible Lines of Connection,* he tells the story of one such man, a stranger on a bus:

> A light snow was falling and the streets were crowded with people. It was Munich in Nazi Germany. One of my rabbinic students, Shifra Penzias, told me her great-aunt, Sussie, had been riding a city bus home from work when SS storm troopers suddenly stopped the coach and began examining the identification papers of the passengers. Most were annoyed, but a few were terrified.

* Mishna, *Sanhedrin* 4:5.

Jews were being told to leave the bus and get into a truck around the corner.

My student's great-aunt watched from her seat in the rear as the soldiers systematically worked their way down the aisle. She began to tremble, tears streaming down her face. When the man next to her noticed that she was crying, he politely asked her why.

"I don't have the papers you have. I am a Jew. They're going to take me."

The man exploded with disgust. He began to curse and scream at her.

"You stupid bitch," he roared. "I can't stand being near you."

The SS men asked what all the yelling was about.

"Damn her," the man shouted angrily. "My wife has forgotten her papers again! I'm so fed up. She always does this!"

The soldiers laughed and moved on.

My student said that her great-aunt never saw the man again. She never even knew his name.

Conversely, an act of cowardice, indifference, or cruelty when another's life is at stake can guarantee a person a hellish existence on this earth. In Albert Camus's novel *The Fall*, a man witnesses a girl drowning in a river. He can save her, but instead he walks away. He is overwhelmed by guilt, and his life quickly deteriorates. By the novel's end, he is praying, "O young woman, throw yourself into the water again so that I may a second time have the chance of saving both of us."

"Both of us." We are all creatures in God's image, connected through our relationship to God. As Kushner concludes, "The more we comprehend our mutual interdependence, the more we fathom the implications of our most trivial acts. We find ourselves within a luminous organism of sacred responsibility. Even on a bus in Munich."

May you have a Shabbat Shalom!

During the course of this Shabbat, try to review the material from the preceding six days, and use some of the texts studied as the basis for discussion during the Shabbat meals.

Day 85. "Do Not Stand by While Your Neighbor's Blood Is Shed": The Requirement to Intervene
Day 86. When You Suspect Child Abuse
Day 87. Untamed Anger and the Death of Love
Day 88. Be Fair to Your Enemy
Day 89. Don't Make People Tell You Lies
Day 90. "He Who Saves a Single Life It Is as If He Saved an Entire World"

Shabbat Shalom!

# WEEK 14

DAY

92     SUNDAY

## *Spend a Week Following Your Heart*

More than fifteen hundred years ago, Rabbi Safra, a talmudic sage, had a donkey for sale. One morning while he was praying, a buyer approached. Oblivious to what the rabbi was doing, the man called out an offer for the animal.

Rabbi Safra was in the middle of a prayer during which Jewish tradition forbids speaking, and said nothing. Interpreting this silence as rejection, the would-be purchaser upped his bid once, then did so again.

A few minutes later the rabbi finished his prayer. He turned toward the man and accepted—his first bid. As he explained, "Since I knew when I heard you call out your offer that it was acceptable to me, it would be dishonest for me to accept your higher bid" (see Rashi on *Bava Bathra* 88a).

To the Rabbis, Rabbi Safra epitomizes a virtue described in the Psalms, "one who speaks the truth in his heart" (Psalms 15:2). This refers to one who follows the truth even when it is known only to him (and to God), and yet is disadvantageous in practical terms.

I don't know how many of us can live like Rabbi Safra all the time. But we should try periodically to live as he did, and follow our hearts' most noble dictates. For example, if you hear of a friend who is ill and think, "I really must go see her," do so, even if later on you are concerned that you are running late, or the visit seems inconvenient. Similarly, if during a charity appeal your heart is touched and your instinct is to give a larger sum than you normally would, donate it, even if later on, during a more calculating moment, you want to give less.

Over the coming week, emulate Rabbi Safra. Become "one who speaks the truth in his heart."

DAY

93          MONDAY

# Don't Make Unrealistic Demands of People

*[Rabbi Joshua taught]: "…we are forbidden to impose a decree on the community that the majority will find unbearable."*
—Babylonian Talmud, *Bava Bathra* 60b

$S$ome years ago I was present when an astute American businessman heard that Israeli tax rates could, and often did, exceed seventy percent. He commented, "It's very unwise for a country to adopt a policy like that. All that is accomplished by imposing such high tax rates is that you turn your citizens into cheats."

As this man observed, legislating unrealistic demands on people causes dishonesty and often leads to a lack of compliance. This applies on the personal as well as the national level. Several years ago, I wrote a book, *Words That Hurt, Words That Heal,* about the ethics of speech. In a chapter on anger, I noted that many people delude themselves into believing that they have no control over their tempers. I maintained that unless a person suffers from certain forms of brain damage or is on certain mind-altering medications, he can almost always control his temper. As proof, I suggested that people who believe they cannot do so ask themselves, "If you were told that you would receive two million dollars if you would *never* lose your temper over the next six months, would you find a way to control your anger?"

Dr. Stephen Marmer, a professor of psychiatry at UCLA Medical School, read my book in manuscript and strongly—and correctly—suggested that I reword the question: "If you were told that you would receive two million dollars if you would cut down on your loss of temper *by seventy-five percent* over the next six months, would you find a way to control your anger?"

As Dr. Marmer commented: "Seventy-five percent is feasible, doable, and therefore a fair request to make. But if you demand one-hundred-percent compliance, all you will guarantee is failure."

It is told of a noted rabbi that his congregants followed whatever he demanded of them. "How do you achieve such compliance?" a colleague asked.

"Because I only ask of them that of which they are capable."

You have a right to demand improvement from those who have failed you or hurt you—but you must be realistic. Don't demand of others a perfection you cannot achieve in yourself.

T U E S D A Y

# A Jewish View of Hunting

In *Climbing the Mountain: My Search for Meaning,* Kirk Douglas writes of the one wild-game hunt in which he participated. Outfitted with a high-powered rifle, he traveled to Kenya and, over several days, succeeded in shooting a leopard, a gazelle, an oryx, and a zebra. He acquired a new nickname, Killer Douglas. When he arrived back in Beverly Hills, he mounted the trophies of his killings on the walls of his house.

Years later, when Douglas was in his seventies, he started to study the Torah and Jewish ethics. He writes, "I learned that as a Jew I had committed a sin. It is against my religion to hunt and kill wild animals, let alone eat them." *

Given that Judaism doesn't insist on vegetarianism, what accounts for its opposition to hunting? Kashrut, the dietary laws that regulate which foods are permitted and which forbidden, mandates that even those animals that one is permitted to eat must be killed with a single stroke to the neck, one quick and powerful enough to cause instantaneous unconsciousness and death. If the slaughterer (*shochet*) in any way prolongs the animal's death, the meat is rendered forbidden (*treyf*). Thus, the slaughterer has an economic as well as an ethical and halachic (Jewish legal) incentive to ensure that the animal dies quickly.

In contrast to ritual slaughter, the deaths of hunted animals, although sometimes immediate, are often prolonged and painful. From the perspective of Jewish law, Jews are forbidden to eat animals killed by hunting. This prohibition has become so ingrained in the Jewish psyche that even among Jews who have long since stopped keeping kosher, one finds few Jews who hunt.

Over two centuries ago, a newly affluent Jew with a large estate consisting of villages and forests addressed a question to Rabbi Ezekiel

---

*Douglas, *Climbing the Mountain,* 57–58.

Landau (1713–1793) of Prague: Was it permissible for him to hunt for sport wild animals provided he did not eat of the forbidden meat? Rabbi Landau's response has long been considered the normative Jewish position on hunting:

> How can a Jew kill a living thing without any benefit to anyone and engage in hunting merely to satisfy "the enjoyable use of his time"? For according to the Talmud, it is permitted to slay wild animals only when they invade human settlements, but to pursue them in the woods, their own dwelling place, when they are not invading human habitations, is prohibited. Such pursuit simply means following the desires of one's heart.
>
> In the case of one who needs to do this and who derives his livelihood from hunting (e.g., one who deals with furs and skins), we would not say that hunting is necessarily cruel, as we slaughter cattle and birds and fish for the needs of man....But for one whose hunting has nothing to do with earning his livelihood, this is sheer cruelty.
>
> —Responsa *Nodeh B'Yehuda,* on *Yoreh Deah* 2:10*

While Rabbi Landau articulated the legal/ethical rationale for Judaism's opposition to hunting, Heinrich Heine (1797–1856), the great Jewish-born German writer, suggested that the Jewish aversion to such sport had much to do with the Jews' unhappy history: "My ancestors did not belong to the hunters as much as to the hunted, and the idea of attacking the descendants of those who were our comrades in misery goes against my grain." In other words, when a Jew sees an animal fleeing from a hunter wielding a gun, with whom do you think the Jew identifies?

*Freehof, *A Treasury of Responsa,* 216–19.

W E D N E S D A Y

## Feed Your Animals Before Yourself

*A man is forbidden to eat before he has given food to his animals.*
—Babylonian Talmud, *Berachot* 40a

A[s every parent knows, the main reason hungry infants cry so bitterly is that they don't know until the moment they are fed that food will be available for them. As the child gets a little older, he or she generally starts to develop a higher degree of patience.

We have reason to believe that hungry animals suffer in the way infants do. While an adult generally knows that he can satisfy his hunger within a few minutes, an animal has no such knowledge. It is perhaps for this reason that Jewish law rules that an animal must be fed first in the morning, even before one partakes of one's own breakfast. Quite simply, the animal's suffering from hunger, like that of an infant, is greater than that of adults.

This talmudic regulation, which originated at a time when most Jews were farmers, remains applicable today, when one's animals are usually pets. Each morning when we rise, my wife, our children, or I feed our two cats before eating our own breakfast. In addition to guaranteeing a humane attitude toward animals, this law teaches two important lessons to children: kindness to all of God's creatures, and the importance of delayed gratification. As Rabbi David Woznica puts it, "It's very beautiful for a child to see his parents feeding the helpless before themselves." And for a child to learn to delay his or her own eating to feed an animal helps that child become accustomed to doing the right thing, even when it might cause him or her a slightly uncomfortable delay.

Feeding your animal first, a lesson reinforced 365 times a year (remember, you have to feed your animal on Yom Kippur, even when you yourself are fasting), becomes one of Jewish law's unexpected daily teachings of goodness.

DAY

96 THURSDAY

## Don't Spread Negative, but Irrelevant, Information About Someone You Dislike

At workshops I have conducted on "The Ethics of Speech," I ask people whether they can think of at least one incident in their lives that would embarrass them if it became known to the other people present. Almost every hand goes up, except, as I note, for those "who've led very boring lives, have poor memories, or are lying."

The truth is that the incident of which the people are thinking is almost definitely a lot less serious than robbing a bank. Yet because it is also likely to be somewhat scandalous, it would humiliate them if others learned of it.

The Talmud cites several instances of how people utilize "inside information" to hurt another, and forbids doing so. For example, "If someone who had previously sinned becomes religious, it is forbidden to say to him, 'Remember how you used to act'" (Mishna, *Bava Mezia* 4:10).

Often, when we fight with, or simply dislike, someone, we are tempted to spread embarrassing but irrelevant information about that person to others. Because most of us don't want to admit that what we are doing is wrong, we sometimes devise brilliant rationalizations to justify why spreading this information is relevant.

If you are tempted to do so, resist the temptation. Fight with another if you have to, but fight fairly.

FRIDAY

# Don't Humiliate an Enemy

Almost all of us can think of people whom we dislike. During moments of intense anger, most of us have fantasized cruel things we would like to do to them. I know a woman who concocted a scheme (she never carried it out) to hide giant red ants all over the home of a man who had mistreated her. I also once came across a book about revenge in which the authors suggested dozens of ways to avenge those who have earned our enmity.

One of the Talmud's most famous stories concerns a man who had an enemy, and who was unexpectedly offered the opportunity either to reconcile with, or avenge himself on, this man. He chose revenge, and consequently the whole Jewish people suffered:

> A certain man had a friend named Kamtza and an enemy named Bar Kamtza. He once made a party and said to his servant, "Go and bring Kamtza." The servant went and brought Bar Kamtza. When the host saw Bar Kamtza at his party, he said to him, "...What are you doing here? Get out." Bar Kamtza said, "Since I am already here, let me stay, and I will pay you for whatever I eat and drink."
>
> The host answered: "I won't let you stay."
>
> Bar Kamtza said: "Then let me reimburse you for half the cost of the party."
>
> "No," said the host.
>
> Bar Kamtza said: "Then let me pay for the whole party."
>
> The host still said no; he took Bar Kamtza by the hand and had him expelled.
>
> Said Bar Kamtza [to himself], "Since there were prominent rabbis sitting there and they did not stop him, this shows that they agreed with how he behaved. I will go and inform against them to the government."
>
> —*Gittin* 55b–56a

The Talmud goes on to explain how this Bar Kamtza, an influential man, contacted the Roman emperor and convinced him that the Jews in Judea were plotting a rebellion against him. Because the emperor believed the man, a whole chain of events were set in motion that culminated in the destruction of the Jerusalem Temple and the Jewish state.

Who was most at fault? Obviously, Bar Kamtza; it was he who committed the act of treason that inflamed the emperor. But had the nameless host not humiliated him in front of Jerusalem's most notable figures, the whole tragedy might well have been averted. Did this host have the right to hate Bar Kamtza? Maybe yes, maybe no; the text does not tell us enough about what had earlier transpired between them to make a determination. However, it does make it clear that although the provocation might have been severe, it was wrong of the host to expel Bar Kamtza from his house publicly. And it was wrong of the sages to stand by and not stop him from doing so.

Revenge might be sweet in fantasy, as we imagine how we will so totally vanquish our foe that we never need to consider the possibility of his or her making a comeback. In practice, however, the Jewish way is not to be vengeful. The Torah legislates, "Do not take revenge...against a member of your people" (Leviticus 19:18). How much better if the host in this story had followed the Torah, and not the anger in his heart.

May you have a Shabbat Shalom!

DAY

## 98     SHABBAT

During the course of this Shabbat, try to review the material from the preceding six days, and use some of the texts studied as the basis for discussion during the Shabbat meals:

Day 92. Spend a Week Following Your Heart
Day 93. Don't Make Unrealistic Demands of People
Day 94. A Jewish View of Hunting
Day 95. Feed Your Animals Before Yourself

Day 96. Don't Spread Negative, but Irrelevant, Information About
        Someone You Dislike
Day 97. Don't Humiliate an Enemy

Shabbat Shalom!

# WEEK 15

DAY

## 99

### SUNDAY

# *Pray for Someone Else Today*

A talmudic text praises Jethro (in Hebrew, Yitro), Moses' Midianite father-in-law, for offering a prayer of thanksgiving to God. After Moses tells his father-in-law about how God freed the Israelites from slavery and helped them in the desert, Jethro responds, "Blessed be the Lord who delivered you from the Egyptians and from Pharaoh and who delivered the people from under the hand of the Egyptians" (Exodus 18:10). The text, which praises Jethro by implication, criticizes Moses and the Israelites for not having offered a similar prayer (*Sanhedrin* 94a).

This talmudic criticism seems strange. The Rabbis were well aware that when the Jews crossed over the Red Sea, Moses led them in offering God a wonderful prayer of gratitude; Exodus 15 is a long ode of thanksgiving to God. Why, then, were they critical of Moses for not having offered a prayer similar to Jethro's?

Rabbi Jacob J. Schacter provides an insightful answer. True, Moses and the Israelites had offered God a prayer of thanksgiving earlier, but unlike Jethro, they thanked God only for what He had done for *them;* Jethro thanked God for what He had done for someone else.

The prayers in the *siddur,* the Jewish prayer book, are usually phrased in the plural; they are prayers for the community, not for oneself. Nonetheless, many people (myself included) offer private prayers during which they speak personally and directly to God.

At some point today, offer a prayer to God not only on your, or your family's, behalf, but for someone else. I would advise you to pray not only on behalf of someone whom you know to be sick. Prayers for a sick person already are part of the Jewish liturgy, recited during the Torah reading; more important, I suspect it will probably be more of an achievement for you to compose a prayer *not* having to do with someone else's ill health. After all, it is easy to be generous when praying that a sick person will recover, but less easy when you are struggling to make a living and you pray that someone else might have professional success or luck in finding a job. It is also less easy to be generous when you are romantically uninvolved or unhappy and you pray that someone else will find a partner and achieve great joy.

It is important to have an honest relationship with God, one in which you feel comfortable asking God for whatever *you* need. But it is also good to expand the concerns of your heart and pray to God to grant someone else's wishes and needs. Learn from Jethro, the remarkable priest of Midian, to pray to God on someone else's behalf.

DAY

100     MONDAY

## *Raising Your Child to Be a Mensch\**

If children were born generous, you might enter a house and find a mother yelling at her three-year-old son, "Johnny, stop giving all your toys away to the other children in the neighborhood!" In truth, most children are born with a healthy streak of selfishness, and have to be taught and trained to share.

---

*This is the title of Rabbi Neil Kurshan's book on how parents can influence their children's moral development.

This training works most effectively when the teaching and practice of giving money or possessions away to those who need them is consistent. As an influential sixteenth-century work of Jewish ethics teaches, "A person who gives a thousand gold pieces to a worthy person is not as generous as one who gives a thousand gold pieces on a thousand different occasions, each to a worthy cause" (Anonymous, *Orchot Tzaddikim* [*The Ways of the Righteous*]).

One technique used by some parents to train their children to give is to keep a *tzedaka* (charity) box in the house, and insert coins in it just before lighting the Shabbat candles. Since Jewish tradition prohibits the use of money on the Sabbath, it is a powerful lesson to children that one's last use of funds before the holy day is for charity.

As children get older, their training in *tzedaka* should intensify. It is a wonderful idea to encourage children celebrating a bar mitzvah or bat mitzvah to give ten percent of the money they receive in gifts to charity. Given that the bar mitzvah and bat mitzvah symbolize a child's joining the adult Jewish community, what better way to begin this process than by encouraging him or her to choose a personal cause or causes to which the money should be donated.*

Follow these suggestions, and your child's bar or bat mitzvah—and their growing to adulthood in general—won't just be a celebration for your family and friends, but also a cause for the whole community to rejoice.

---

*Dana Kurzweil and her husband, Rabbi Irwin Kula, suggest that you don't wait for a child's bar or bat mitzvah to train them in the systematic giving of charity, but rather, starting at an earlier age, set aside a sum of money, put before them some of the choices, and let them discuss and decide where to give.

## T U E S D A Y

# *The Questions All Parents Should Ask Themselves*

I f praying three times a day, studying Torah, and observing all the Jewish ritual laws were sufficient to guarantee that a child would be an ethical, kind human being, it would be fitting for Jewish parents to focus all their efforts on ensuring that their children are ritually observant.

And if sending one's child to an excellent school, one that pushes students both academically and intellectually, were sufficient to ensure that he or she would grow up to be ethical and kind, then it would likewise be fitting for parents to focus exclusively on developing their children's intellectual capacities and sending them to superior academic institutions.

However, history has repeatedly taught us that a person can be a well-educated accomplished professional or ritually observant, yet be unethical.

If you want your children to grow up to be good people, then special emphasis on cultivating goodness must be part of their upbringing. Such focus has too often been lacking, among Jews and among Americans of all backgrounds, religious and secular. Not inculcating such values in children is both false to the spirit of Judaism (see, for example, Day 120), and perilous to our country's future. To take the most extreme example, the Holocaust did not come about because Germany lacked intelligent people, but rather because it lacked sufficient good ones.

Dennis Prager suggests five questions all parents should ask themselves. Answer these questions when your children are still young, and you will have the opportunity to alter your children's, and the world's, future:

♦ Would I rather have a kind child with average intelligence and grades, or a brilliant child who wasn't kind?

- How much time do I devote to developing my child's ethics, relative to fostering other achievements?
- Do I reward my child's acts of kindness as much as I do good grades or athletic achievements? Do I react less severely to character deficiencies than to scholastic or other shortcomings?
- Do I monitor my child's behavior toward other children, and show strong disapproval when she mistreats another child? For example, if my child invites a friend to the house, and is then invited to the home of a friend she would rather be with, would I allow her to cancel the first appointment?
- Do I repeatedly insist that my child thank people?*

As Dennis Prager concludes: "It is difficult to raise a good student, but it is much more difficult to raise a good person. It is a relentless job. In the long run, however, the parents of good children who are moderately successful are far happier than the parents of successful children who are moderately good."

In most cases, it is not our values that are wrong, but our priorities. When we assess what sort of people we want our children to become, the traits we often emphasize, being highly educated, musically and athletically accomplished, professionally successful and happy, are worthwhile—as long as being a good person is at the top of the list.

DAY

## 102 WEDNESDAY

# "Just as Theft of Money Is Theft, So Is Theft of Time" **

People who run late tend to see this as a minor fault, explaining, "Yes, I am often late. It's not a good thing."

---

*Prager, *Think a Second Time*, 37.
** *Mesillat Yesharim (Path of the Upright)*, chapter 11

Yet when you ask the victims of other people's tardiness their feelings about such habits, you will learn that the offense is rarely viewed as trivial: "He thinks he's so much more important than me that it's irrelevant if he's late. Clearly, my time isn't important to him."

Is such a response excessive? As one who tries to be punctual, and who is very annoyed when kept waiting, I confess to having had angry thoughts about the recurrently tardy.* I once came across an anonymous quote that summarizes the ethical issue involved: "A man who has taken your time recognizes no debt, yet it is the only debt he can never repay."

Jewish teachings regard wasting another person's time as a kind of stealing. Rabbi Abraham Twerski tells a characteristic story about Rabbi Abraham Karelitz (1878–1953), the great talmudic scholar known in Jewish life by the title of his book, *Chazon Ish (The Vision of a Man)*. He "once assembled a *minyan* [quorum of ten] in his home for *Mincha* [the afternoon prayer service], and one of the people told him that he was due at an appointment shortly. The Chazon Ish sent him on his way, stating that keeping the other person waiting was theft of time, and one cannot pray on stolen time."

If the Chazon Ish understood Jewish ethics as forbidding one from fulfilling the commandment of prayer on "stolen time," how much more would it condemn your keeping another waiting just because you chose to sleep late, took a telephone call even when you knew you were already running late, or overscheduled your day without taking into consideration the person who would be waiting for you. Similarly, Jewish ethics, to cite one common example, would mandate that doctors who are running late with their appointments ask their secretaries to call patients who have not yet arrived and warn them of the delay.

You might think of yourself as essentially a good-natured person who "sometimes" runs a little late. But from the perspective of Jewish ethics, routinely keeping other people waiting turns you into a thief.

---

*In kinder moments, I realize that there frequently are deep-rooted psychological reasons why some people run late; in other words, their behavior often is more self-destructive than aggressive.

THURSDAY

# What It Means to Sanctify God's Name

It sometimes happens that a waiter or store clerk makes an error in my favor while computing a bill or giving me change. Whenever I catch such a mistake, I point it out. What I find a little sad is the great gratitude expressed by the people to whom I indicate the error. Experience has taught them that many people who indignantly demand repayment for any error that disadvantages them are happy to pocket mistakes made in their favor.

Indeed, such behavior is so common that people who act honestly are credited with being unusually good. This provides an easy opportunity for a person to show others how his religious teachings elevate him not only when the person stands before God in prayer, but also when he or she interacts with others in the marketplace.

An unusual talmudic story tells of a rabbi who was so anxious to show a queen the goodness of Judaism that he risked his life to do so. Fortunately, most of us can bring credit to our religion without jeopardizing our lives:

> Rabbi Samuel...went to Rome. The Empress lost a bracelet and he happened to find it. A proclamation was issued throughout the land that if anyone returned it within thirty days, he would receive such-and-such a reward, but if after thirty days, he would lose his head.
>
> He did not return it within the thirty days but thereafter.
> She said to him, "Were you not in the province?"
> He replied, "Yes, I was here."
> She said, "But did you not hear the proclamation?"
> "I heard it," said he.
> "What did it say?" she asked.

He replied, "If anyone returns it within thirty days, he will receive such-and-such a reward, but if he returns it after thirty days, he will lose his head."

She said, "In that case, why did you not return it within the thirty days?"

He said, "Because I did not want anyone to say that I returned it out of fear of you, whereas, in fact, I returned it out of fear of the Almighty." She said to him, "Blessed is the God of the Jews." *

In a case more applicable to our daily lives, the Talmud tells of Rabbi Shimon ben Shetach, whose disciples purchased a donkey for him from a non-Jew. After taking possession of the animal, they discovered a very valuable pearl entangled in its neck, and gleefully told their teacher, "From now on, you will not need to weary yourself [working]."

"Why not?" the rabbi asked them.

"We bought you a donkey from an Ishmaelite, which has a pearl entangled in its neck."

Rabbi Shimon asked them, "Did its former owner know about the pearl?"

"Of course not," they replied.

So he said to them, "Go and return it."

The students argued with him that since the error was made by a gentile [and since gentiles at that time did not return money when a Jew made a business error], he should keep the jewel.

"What do you think?" replied Rabbi Shimon. "That Shimon ben Shetach is a barbarian? Shimon ben Shetach would rather hear 'Blessed be the God of the Jews' than gain any profit in this entire world." **

The next time you're tempted to keep something that you shouldn't, remember the view of Rabbi Shimon ben Shetach: a Jew who takes advantage of a business error made by a gentile is acting not like a Jew, but like a barbarian.

---

*In the story of Rabbi Samuel, I have followed almost verbatim the translation of Louis Jacobs, *Jewish Law*, 50.
**Palestinian Talmud, *Bava Mezia* 2:5.

F R I D A Y

# The Special Obligation of Religious Jews to Sanctify God's Name

Yitta Halberstam Mandelbaum once ran into Rabbi Shlomo Carlebach, the great Chasidic composer and singer, in Liberty, New York. She accompanied him as he went into a coffee shop, where he ordered a soda to go. Informed that the price of the can was fifty cents, he handed the clerk two dollars and told her to keep the change.

Convinced that Reb Shlomo did not know the mechanics of tipping, Yitta said to him, "When you order to go, you don't give a tip, and certainly you don't give a $1.50 tip on a fifty-cent soda."

Reb Shlomo smiled and said to her, "Holy sister, Yitta, I know, I know. But I'm trying to make up for *unzer tierla yiddalach* (our sweet Jews) who don't give tips, and consequently make a *chillul Hashem*" (defame God's name).

When non-Jews with whom you interact know that you are Jewish, you are no longer merely an individual. Fair or unfair, like it or not, you become an ambassador of the Jewish people to the non-Jewish world. If you act cheaply, boorishly, or otherwise badly, you run the risk that not only will people dislike you, but that they will also draw unpleasant conclusions about all Jews. Because of your bad behavior, another Jew might suffer someday.

If such reasoning strikes you as paranoid or far-fetched, consider whether you have ever been treated badly by a member of another religious, racial, or ethnic group and subsequently made some disparaging generalization about the whole group. If you have, and I know few people who have not, then realize that your bad behavior can help generate animosity not only against yourself but against all Jews.

On the other hand, when you act generously or nobly, as Shlomo

Carlebach did, you bring honor to yourself, the Jewish people, and God. That is what it means to be *mekadesh Hashem,* to sanctify God's name.

May you have a Shabbat Shalom!

SHABBAT

During the course of this Shabbat, try to review the material from the preceding six days, and use some of the texts studied as the basis for discussion during the Shabbat meals:

Day  99. Pray for Someone Else Today
Day 100. Raising Your Child to Be a Mensch
Day 101. The Questions All Parents Should Ask Themselves
Day 102. "Just as Theft of Money Is Theft, So Is Theft of Time"
Day 103. What It Means to Sanctify God's Name
Day 104. The Special Obligation of Religious Jews to Sanctify God's Name

Shabbat Shalom!

SUNDAY

# When Is the Best Time to Repent?

According to one talmudic statement, there is apparently no need to rush one's repentance: "Rabbi Eliezer said, 'Repent one day before your death.'"

Then again, Rabbi Eliezer's students quickly realized that this guideline is singularly unhelpful:

"But does a person know on what day he [or she] is going to die?"

"All the more reason, therefore, to repent today, lest one die tomorrow. In this manner, one's whole life will be spent in repentance."

—Babylonian Talmud, *Shabbat* 153a

The advantage of repenting daily is that doing so can safeguard a person against becoming involved in more serious sins. Most people who end up doing horrific things did not always act abominably. Usually their careers "in crime" started with small acts of evil, after which their bad behavior escalated. The Talmud teaches that the first and second time a person does something forbidden his conscience is usually troubled; by the time he or she performs the act a third time, it has turned into a habit, and the person will have almost convinced himself or herself that the action is permitted. But if you review your behavior often, you are more apt to curtail evil acts before they become a habit.

At some point this evening, although it may feel strange, take a pen and paper and try to review your day. See if you can think of anything you did that was wrong, or that you might do differently:

♦ Review your interactions with people, particularly those that might have ended on a bad note. Did you contribute to the problem? Were you unfair in anything you said or did? Were you rude to anyone, such as by pushing ahead on a line, receiving a service and not saying "thank you," or remaining in a bus seat even when you saw an old person standing?

♦ Did you engage in any financial interaction that perhaps was immoral? For example, did you try to persuade someone to become involved in a deal without fully disclosing all its downsides?

♦ Did you speak unfairly *about* or *to* another person? For example, did you spread a rumor, or critique someone at work in a tactless, demoralizing manner?

♦ At home, were you impatient with your children or spouse? Did you listen attentively when they wished to discuss something with you? If you expressed criticism to a family member, did you do so fairly and lovingly?

Also mark down acts you did that were honest or kind. Take pride in them; this will motivate you to want to keep doing such deeds in the future.

It is told of Rabbi Levi Yitzchak of Berditchev (circa 1740–1810) that he would sit down nightly with paper and pen and review his actions for that day. When he finished, he would review the list and say to himself, "I did some things today that were wrong, that I shouldn't have done. But I won't do them tomorrow."

Even if your list contains some deeds of which you're not proud, don't let them demoralize you. Rather, regard your list as a challenge through which you can elevate yourself. As was noted earlier, the Chasidic Rebbe Nachman of Bratslav taught: "If you are not going to be better tomorrow than you were today, then what need have you for tomorrow?"

I wish you a good today, and an even better tomorrow.

MONDAY

# Acknowledge Your Sin and Accept Responsibility

I know a man who seldom acknowledges his errors. Whenever something bad happens to him, he invariably claims that it is either due to bad luck or is someone else's fault. I once told him that of all the people I knew, he was the one for whom I felt least optimistic about the future. Since he was never to blame for any of the bad things that happened to him, there was nothing he could do to improve his increasingly unhappy life. He could only hope that he would stop having bad luck, and that other people would stop treating him unfairly or getting him into trouble.

In the Jewish tradition, the first step in repentance is *hakarat hachet*, recognizing the sin one has committed. For most of us, that is hard, and always has been. The Bible tells us that when Adam and Eve sinned in the Garden of Eden, God confronted Adam, asking him why he had eaten of the forbidden fruit of the Tree of Knowledge. Instead of acknowledging responsibility for the sin, Adam blamed Eve (and by implication God), "The woman You put at my side—she gave me of the tree and I ate." When God turned to Eve, she in turn blamed the snake: "The serpent duped me, and I ate" (Genesis 3:12–13).

Some years later, God demanded an accounting from Cain as to the whereabouts of his brother Abel, whom Cain had just murdered. Instead of confessing the great evil he had done, Cain taunted God with a mocking question: "Am I my brother's keeper?" (Genesis 4:9). Thousands of years later, Samuel denounced King Saul for disobeying a divine edict. His response? He lied and tried to defend his behavior (I Samuel 15).

A few years after that, the prophet Nathan attacked David for committing serious sins. But David's response was different from Adam's, Eve's, Cain's, and Saul's; he admitted his guilt, confessing, "I stand guilty before the Lord" (II Samuel 12:13). God, presumably delighted that finally a human being had owned up to his evil, instructed Nathan to tell David that his punishment would now be less severe.

Someone who can't acknowledge responsibility and guilt cannot and will not change. And just as a disease cannot be treated until it first is diagnosed, a sin or an evil cannot be corrected until it is acknowledged and admitted. So, if you wish to repent of bad acts you have committed, the first—and for many of us, the most painful—thing you must do is acknowledge, without rationalization and justification, the wrong you have done.

Here is an exercise: Sit down alone and see if you can think of one or two things you have done in your life, or are now doing, that you know are unfair and wrong. Even if you are not yet ready to undo the wrongs you have committed (if, indeed, it is possible to undo them fully), at least recognize your guilt, as did David. Just becoming aware of bad deeds will start to affect how you behave.

DAY

108  TUESDAY

## *Ask for Forgiveness Even When You're Not Fully in the Wrong*

A woman I know had been in an unhappy marriage that culminated in divorce. Even afterward, she and her husband, who shared joint custody of a child, continued to have a miserable relationship. Their phone conversations were punctuated with shouts, accusations, and endlessly rehashed grievances.

One year, on Yom Kippur, it suddenly occurred to her that she had been unfair, at least in part, to her ex-husband. Sitting in synagogue that day, she told me, it had become clear to her what she must do: She had to seek out her ex-husband and acknowledge and apologize for the unfair and cruel things she had done to him during their marriage. For ten years she had invested such emotional energy in recalling every cruelty he had committed that it had never occurred to her to acknowledge any personal responsibility for the marriage's misery.

Two days later she met her "ex" for lunch. When she told him the reason for the meeting, and expressed her apology for specific wrong things she had said and done, he sat in his place, stunned and profoundly moved. For the first time in many years they spoke to each other honestly and fairly, neither one pointing a finger of blame. This happened several years ago, and their relationship is now calmer than it has ever been. The woman told me she feels that an enormous burden of anger and guilt has been lifted from her.

According to the codes of Jewish law, the first step in repentance is "recognition of one's sin" (see yesterday's entry). But once such recognition is made, the goal is to move on to the next two steps in repentance: asking forgiveness from the person you have hurt (even when you think that he or she shares in the blame for what happened), and undoing as much of the damage as you can.

DAY

109    WEDNESDAY

## Tipping Even Those Whose Faces You Don't See

Tipping is a social convention that has as much to do with cowardice as with good service. Thus, although I tip generously those who have been unusually helpful or pleasant, I rarely withhold a tip from one who has been a bit rude or painfully slow in providing service.

On the other hand, there is one individual whom most people ignore, even when the service is exemplary: the housekeeper who cleans one's hotel room. We don't ignore a taxi driver, the bellman who takes our bags, or a waiter, because we see those people's faces. However, although the housekeeper does us a service, we rarely see her face or interact with her, and so most of us don't leave a tip. Even if you do not believe a tip is required, shouldn't you leave a note expressing thanks to her for the service she has provided you?

Part of cultivating a virtuous character is learning to express appreciation to those whom we don't see. After all, prayer is about expressing gratitude to the One whom we *never* see, but who has bestowed on us the greatest gift, life. Tipping a housekeeper is about expressing gratitude to one with whom we don't, or rarely, come into personal contact but who has bestowed on us a lesser but much appreciated gift: a clean room.

DAY

## 110 | THURSDAY

# What If You Could Read Your Obituary Today?

The world's most famous set of awards are the Nobel Prizes. Presented in literature, peace, economics, medicine, and the sciences, they were created a century ago by Alfred Nobel (1833–1896), a man whose fortune was amassed through the production of explosives; among other things, he invented dynamite.

What motivated this Swedish munitions manufacturer to dedicate his fortune to honoring and rewarding those who benefited humanity? According to an account I heard from Rabbi Harold Kushner, the creation of the Nobel Prizes came about through a chance event. When Nobel's brother died, a newspaper ran a long obituary of Alfred Nobel, believing that it was he who had passed away. Thus, Nobel had an opportunity granted few people: to read his obituary while alive. What he read horrified him: the newspaper described him as a man who had made it possible for more people to be killed more quickly than anyone else who had ever lived.

At that moment, Nobel realized two things: that this was how he was going to be remembered, and that this was *not* how he wanted to be remembered. Shortly thereafter, he established the awards. Today, because of his doing so, everyone is familiar with the Nobel Prize, while relatively few people even recall how Nobel made his fortune.

Thinking about how one's obituary is going to read (whether or not it is published in a newspaper or is just written in the hearts and minds of those who know you) can, and often should, motivate one to rethink how he is spending his life. One rabbi I know prepares for Yom Kippur each year by writing two versions of his obituary. In the first, he sets down how he thinks it would be written, and in the second, how he would *want* it to be written. His goal, of course, is to narrow the gap between who he is and who he would like to be.

So if, God forbid, you were to die today, what would your obituary say about you? Would it read the way you want it to read? And if not, what can you do now to change it?

FRIDAY

# The Infinite Ways of Doing Good

Danny Siegel, founder of the Ziv Tzedakah Fund, is a genius (a term I use very deliberately) at uncovering charitable efforts that meet specialized needs. In so doing, Siegel reminds us that there are limitless human needs, and thus countless opportunities to help others.

A recent issue of his fund's newsletter highlights a number of "Mitzvah heroes" who have started some of the charities that the Ziv Tzedakah Fund helps support:

♦ Under the auspices of her synagogue, Merrill Alpert of Encino, California, runs drives to acquire infant car seats, which are donated to agencies that pass them on to families who cannot afford to buy them.

- Donni Engelhart of Chicago collects new and used wigs for individuals with cancer.
- John Beltzer of Songs of Love in New York supervises a network of professional songwriters, lyricists, and technicians who compose individualized, personal songs for children with life-threatening diseases. To date, they have written 564 songs.
- Some years ago, Herman Berman of Los Angeles was distressed to learn that many bagel stores throw away unsold bagels that are only a few hours old, and started soliciting them, donating the food for distribution to poor people. To date, Berman, whom Siegel hails as "the King of the Bagel People," has given away over 322,000 bagels.
- Nancy Berman-Potash of Florida, concerned that local shelters for battered women are often too full to accept new residents, advises people on how to expand the network of hotels providing free rooms for battered women. As Siegel writes: "She will give you all the necessary details to allow many women (and many children) to move forward with their lives. You may *literally* be saving lives."
- Kathy Freund of Portland, Maine, has created the Independent Transportation Network, comprising three hundred volunteer drivers who transport elderly people.
- Craig Kielburger of Toronto has devoted years of efforts to championing the rights of child laborers in Asia. He has launched many projects, among them one by students of Broad Meadow School in Quincy, Massachusetts, who have raised $150,000 to establish a school for the Asian children.
- Under the supervision of Victoria Ginsberg, the fifth-grade class at the Ramaz Yeshiva of New York City has collected and donated more than 250,000 pounds of food over a period of six years.

If you wish further information about these and other such *gemilut chesed* (acts of kindness) projects, and how to establish them in your community, call or write Danny Siegel at the Ziv Tzedakah Fund, Inc., 263 Congressional Lane, No. 708, Rockville, MD 20852, (973) 763-9396. As Anne Frank reminds us in her diary: "How wonderful it is that nobody need wait a single moment before starting to improve the world."

May you have a Shabbat Shalom!

S H A B B A T

During the course of this Shabbat, try to review the material from the preceding six days, and use some of the texts studied as the basis for discussion during the Shabbat meals:

Day 106. When Is the Best Time to Repent?
Day 107. Acknowledge Your Sin and Accept Responsibility
Day 108. Ask for Forgiveness Even When You're Not Fully in the Wrong
Day 109. Tipping Even Those Whose Faces You Don't See
Day 110. What If You Could Read Your Obituary Today?
Day 111. The Infinite Ways of Doing Good

Shabbat Shalom!

# WEEK 17

D A Y

113

S U N D A Y

# "You Shall Not Place a Stumbling Block"

*You shall not place a stumbling block before the blind. You shall fear your God: I am the Lord.*
—Leviticus 19:14

Upon first reading, this would seem about the simplest of the Torah's 613 commandments to observe. However, Jewish law so expanded the meaning of this verse that it eventually turned into one of the most ethically demanding laws in the Torah:

> What is the meaning of "You shall not place a stumbling block before the blind"? Before one who is "blind" in respect to a certain matter. If he seeks advice from you, do not give him advice which is not fit for him. Do not tell him, "Leave early in the morning," so that robbers might mug him; "Leave in the afternoon," so that he might be overcome by heat. [Rashi, the most important Jewish commentator on the Torah, cites yet another example: Do not advise someone to sell a field and buy a donkey, when you yourself are intending to buy a field and sell a donkey.] And lest you say, "I am giving him good advice," the matter is known to [your] heart [and to God, Who knows all hearts]; as it is written, "You shall fear your God; I am the Lord."
>
> —*Sifra*, Leviticus

A person who gives another bad advice can always defend himself with the claim that he thought he was being genuinely helpful. That is why, the Rabbis claim, this Torah law is followed by the words, "You shall fear your God." True, you might be able to fool your neighbor, but God will know whether your advice really was well intentioned, or whether it was malicious and self-serving.

Thus the primary but not exclusive meaning assigned this law in post-biblical Jewish sources is to avoid providing another with misleading or self-serving advice.

In addition, any time someone comes to you for advice and you have an interest in the matter at hand, you are obligated either to refrain from offering advice or to inform the person of your personal interest (in a case, for example, where a friend solicits your advice on whether he should leave a job, and you are interested in applying for the position). Jewish law forbids pretending to be helpful while framing your advice so as to help you pursue your "hidden agenda."

Even when you are certain that your motivation is pure, Jewish law still obliges you to inform the other party of your interest in the matter. Why? Because we can so easily delude ourselves into thinking that we are doing the right thing for another person when in fact we are simply rationalizing what is in our own self-interest. For example, say you are an insurance salesman who represents different companies, some of which pay you higher commissions than do others. How can you advise a customer fairly as to which is the best policy for her to purchase, when it is in your self-interest that she buy the policy that will yield you the largest commission?

Meir Tamari, the former chief economist for Bank of Israel, and perhaps the leading contemporary scholar on Jewish business ethics, reports on how an insurance agent who wished to act in accordance with Jewish ethical teachings resolved this dilemma. Fearful that the policies he was encouraging his clients to buy "were more a reflection of his own potential earnings than the needs or benefits of the specific client," the man programmed his computer with all the data regarding the client, and let the computer choose the best policy. An elegant solution to a seemingly insoluble problem!*

Yet another way in which people transgress this command is by taking advantage of another's "blindness" (that is, their inability to see clearly) in a specific matter. Thus, while Jewish law would permit one to own a liquor store or a bar, it would forbid selling liquor to a person one knows to be an alcoholic (whether one can do so as a practical matter is a separate question). Because alcoholics generally lack the internal strength to drink in moderation, one is forbidden to manipulate or encourage their addiction; that would constitute a violation of this dictum.

In short, if you have doubts about whether you are acting ethically in any situation, ask yourself the following: "If the situation were reversed, and the person with whom I am dealing acted toward me in the manner I am now acting toward him, would I feel that I had been wronged?"

*Regarding the implications of the verse "You shall not place a stumbling block..." for how one treats the literally blind and deaf, see Day 58.*

---

*Tamari, The Challenge of Wealth, 43. Larry Gellman, a stockbroker and student of Jewish business ethics, has an additional take on this commandment: "This law forbids us to take advantage of another's blindness, but not of his carelessness or laziness. Since a blind person is *incapable* of seeing, he is very different, in the context of business transactions, from one who has the ability to see but makes no effort to watch where he is going. In the securities markets, this means that we are prohibited from taking advantage of insider information that comes from a privileged source that is simply not available to normal people, but we are not prohibited from benefiting from hard work that leads us to insights that others might not have."

M O N D A Y

# The Nameless Person Behind the Counter

American law today is rights-oriented; we hear much about the notion of consumers' rights. Jewish law, which is obligation-oriented, postulates that consumers have no less an obligation than do merchants to act fairly: "Just as there is wrongdoing in buying and selling, so there is wrongdoing in words: One may not say to him [a storekeeper], 'How much is this item?' if one has no intention of buying it…" (Mishna, *Bava Mezia* 4:10).

This ruling is not intended to discourage a person from comparison-shopping. If you are considering buying an item, you have every right to compare prices in different stores. What you are prohibited from doing is raising the hopes of the salesperson, to "steal" his or her time just to satisfy your curiosity or assure yourself that you have "got a good deal" on an item you already bought, or to acquire necessary information so as to buy the item at a cheaper price from a mail-order house.

I have taught this Mishna to many people, and some store owners, particularly those who owned large stores, have commented that they had no problem with people walking in, window-shopping, and even making idle price inquiries (large stores display their goods so as to encourage people to make impulsive purchases). However, the full force of this law becomes apparent when you apply it to a smaller store, where the salesperson may be the store's owner and where each sale is very important.

I first learned this law when studying in yeshiva more than twenty-five years ago, and subsequently taught it to my friend Dennis Prager, who has since made it his mission to make it known to as many people as possible. As Dennis explains, observance of the Storekeeper Law has manifold moral implications:

A number of years ago, a friend who leased many cars for his business told me that he could arrange for his car-leasing company to lease me a car at cost. When I responded that I didn't know what model of auto I wanted, he told me to go around and test various car models, and then tell him which I wanted.

His idea was a practical one, but it is precisely the type of practice forbidden by the Storekeeper Law. I could not test-drive a car at a dealer from whom I knew that I would not buy or lease the car. By test-driving a car at a dealer, I am implying that there is a possibility that I will buy the car from that dealer. Otherwise, why on earth would the dealer give up precious time for me?

To cite another way in which this law is violated: Some women go to a store to try on dresses, knowing that they have no intention of buying any dresses at that store. Or, even worse, some women purchase a dress, knowing that they will return it for a refund after wearing it to a specific function. Many men, planning to buy photographic equipment, will visit a retail camera store, take up the store's time deciding which equipment they want, then order that equipment from a less expensive mail-order house. And they knew that they would order by mail the entire time.

The most obvious reason the Mishna forbade such activity...is that a seller's hopes have been raised in vain. But the reason goes deeper: Those who violate this law are deliberately misleading people about one of the most important concerns in their life—their income.

We should not delude ourselves into thinking otherwise. Whenever we try on a dress, or ask the price of a camera, we are implying the possibility of buying the item, and this is precisely what the salesperson infers.

If you doubt this is so, the next time you go to a store, tell the salesperson, "Miss, I want you to know at the outset that though I will be trying on some dresses here, I won't buy any of them *here.* I'm only here to see what's available and to get your advice."

Obviously, if we said this, the salesperson would cease working with us. Stores do not exist in order to show items for people to buy elsewhere. [Editor's note: It is also all right to say, "I'm not buying today, just looking." That way, a salesperson will not feel the need to spend time with you.]

There is yet another level to this law. It makes us keenly aware that we have obligations even toward people we generally regard as beyond our obligation. Ever since I learned of this law, I have never regarded people who work in stores the same way as I did before. Whenever I enter a store, I am forced to recall my obligation to those working there.*

The adoption of this simple law will transform how you view salespeople; they become not just individuals there to answer your questions and satisfy your needs, but autonomous human beings with hopes and feelings.** You will, as Dennis Prager notes, be forced "to establish something of an I-You relationship with the person behind the counter, rather than retaining the usual I-It relationship that we have with people whom we meet only in a service capacity."

That is the genius of this one simple law from the Mishna; it reminds you that the nameless person behind the counter is, like you, a human being "in God's image."

---

*Prager, *Think a Second Time*, 14–16.
**In an instance where you want information from someone from whom you will not be buying, you should surf the Internet or call the manufacturer; that way, no one's hopes will be artificially raised. Alternatively, a friend offered another solution to the dilemma of test-driving a car from a place where you won't be buying: to generously compensate the salesman from whom you don't buy the car. As he told me: "After such a test drive helped me select a car, I was able to lease the car for considerably less elsewhere. So as not to violate this talmudic law, I returned and gave the salesman a hundred dollars for the service and time he had provided."

## T U E S D A Y

# Acts of Kindness (1): Looking Backward

The Jewish morning prayer service contains a talmudic passage that you should recite, whether or not you pray every morning:

> These are the precepts for which a person is rewarded in this world and whose principal reward is preserved for him/her in the World-to-Come. They are:
>
> honoring one's father and mother;
> performing deeds of kindness;
> early attendance at the House of Study morning and evening;
> providing hospitality to guests;
> visiting the sick;
> participating in making a wedding;
> accompanying the dead [to the grave];
> concentrating on the meaning of prayers;
> bringing peace between fellow men;
> and the study of Torah is equal to them all.*

Many people rush through their daily prayers, but you should slow down when you get to this one, and do the following: As you read each of the ten prescribed activities, think of a time (preferably, but not necessarily, in the recent past) when you carried out that particular commandment. For example, try to recall an instance when you appropriately fulfilled the injunction "Honor your father and mother," or recall a specific act of kindness you have performed for another. What emotions do you feel? Use this feeling to ensure that you will engage in the activity again by the end of the week.

---

*In the daily prayerbook, and based on Babylonian Talmud, *Shabbat* 127a.

Some of the regulations listed in this prayer are more ritualistic in nature, such as "concentrating on the meaning of prayers." Keep in mind that if you review the prayer in this manner, noting when and how you have observed these precepts in the past, you will also be fulfilling the injunction to "concentrate on the meaning of prayers."

Anyone who wishes to lead an ethical life must engage in regular introspection. For example, in the process of doing the exercise just described, you might discover that you rarely if ever observe some of these precepts. Therefore, reciting this prayer can serve as a daily goad to performing the sort of introspection that leads not just to good thoughts but also to good deeds.

DAY

116 WEDNESDAY

## Acts of Kindness (2): Looking Ahead

Turn again to the remarkable prayer we discussed yesterday.

These are the precepts for which a person is rewarded in this world and whose principal reward is preserved for him/her in the World-to-Come. They are:

honoring one's father and mother;
performing deeds of kindness;
early attendance at the House of Study morning and evening;
providing hospitality to guests;
visiting the sick;
participating in making a wedding;
accompanying the dead [to the grave];
concentrating on the meaning of prayers;

bringing peace between fellow men;
and the study of Torah is equal to them all.

As you recite each of the ten commandments that are rewarded both in this world and the next, pause and consider how you can fulfill one of these precepts today:

♦ *Honoring one's father and mother.* What can you do today to show respect and love for your father and/or mother? What can you say or do for them that will make them feel cherished or honored by you? At the very least, make sure you call or visit them today. If your parents are no longer alive, what can you do to honor their memory? Perhaps give charity in your parents' memory, transmit some wisdom you learned from them, or do something for a sibling that you know they would have wanted you to do (see, for example, Day 124). All these activities are of course equally suitable if your parents are alive.

♦ *Performing deeds of kindness.* Think of the people you know, starting with your family and closest friends, then extend outward. What acts of kindness are one or more of these people in need of? What can you do to help? For some people, what might be needed is nothing more than some kind words. An older person perhaps needs an unrushed telephone call from you, while others may require the opportunity to talk to you about some dilemma they are facing.

(By strange coincidence, if indeed there are coincidences, just as I was writing the preceding paragraph, my phone rang. The caller was a dear friend whose wife has recently been diagnosed with cancer. He wanted to discuss with me the various and sometimes contradictory advice they had received from the doctors they have consulted. It was also clear that what he needed was the opportunity to discuss this at length, without feeling rushed. To listen with a sympathetic and empathetic ear can also be act of *gemilut chesed.*)

For others, what might be required is something more concrete. For example, do you have a friend who has lost a job and is now looking for work? Consider whether there are people with whom you can speak who might be in a position to offer your friend employment? (See Day 183.)

If you are truly ambitious, make a list of people you know, and think what acts of kindness you can perform for them. Obviously, you don't have to set out to do all these acts today—although you can try to do at least one—but planning the good you can do has one wonderful effect: you are more apt to do it.

*Tomorrow we will review several more of these precepts.*

DAY

117

THURSDAY

# *Acts of Kindness (3): Looking Ahead*

The Hebrew word to pray, *l'hitpallel,* literally means "to judge or examine oneself." This meaning surprises many people, since prayer normally is thought of as petitionary, coming before God and telling Him what we want. In fact, the prayer book contains very few individual petitionary prayers. Even when a person beseeches God, it is usually for something that will be good for the Jewish people and the world (of course, at any point during the service or during the day, one can compose a personal, petitionary prayer to God).

The definition of *l'hitpallel* clearly conveys what the primary goal of the prayer service is: to motivate us to service. That is why the Rabbis included in the morning service the talmudic extract we have been studying for the preceding two days.

These are the precepts for which a person is rewarded in this world and whose principal reward is preserved for him/her in the World-to-Come. They are:

honoring one's father and mother;

performing deeds of kindness;

early attendance at the House of Study morning and evening;

providing hospitality to guests;

visiting the sick;

participating in making a wedding;

accompanying the dead [to the grave];

concentrating on the meaning of prayers;

bringing peace between fellow men;

and the study of Torah is equal to them all.

As you read this prayer, again ask yourself what you can do today, or in the coming days, to carry out one or more of these precepts:

◆ *Providing hospitality to guests.* Have you recently opened your home to guests? (See, for example, Day 159.) The Jewish tradition is particularly desirous that people do so for a Shabbat or holiday meal.

◆ *Visiting the sick.* Do you know of someone who is sick whom you have not visited, or have not visited for a long time? Stop delaying and go now. If the person lives at a distance, call him or her up. Also, it is particularly meritorious to visit a sick person who has no family or friends; such is sometimes the case when a person has to go to another city to be treated. (For suggestions from the Jewish tradition on how to act when visiting the sick, see Day 32.)

◆ *Bringing peace between fellow men.* Do you have friends or relatives who are feuding? Before you answer no, or skip over this paragraph, think: Do you know people who are not talking to each other? If so, are you in a position to help them reconcile? If both feel warmly toward you, and trust that you are not prejudiced in favor of the other, can you do something to bring peace, or at least a lessening of tensions, between them? Will you do it today?

Similarly, consider attending the house of study (the synagogue) more frequently, and being more conscientious about going to funerals and helping bring unmarried people together.

Finally, the text reminds us that the study of Torah is equal in significance to all the other commanded activities. The Talmud records the following debate: "Rabbi Tarfon and the other rabbis were once staying …in Lydda when the question was raised before them: 'Is study greater, or practice?' Rabbi Tarfon said, 'Practice is greater.' Rabbi Akiva said, 'Study is greater.' Then they all answered and said, 'Study is greater, for it leads to deeds' (*Kiddushin* 40b).

Study a Jewish text today; perhaps read a section of the weekly Torah portion. As a medieval Jewish proverb teaches, "In prayer we speak to God, but in study God speaks to us." *

As much as any prayer I know, this prayer, which we have studied for the past three days, has the power to transform and elevate our lives.

DAY

## 118  FRIDAY

# *The Least Time to Spare, the Most Time to Give*

The power of reading a story about saintly behavior is that a certain number of readers will someday find themselves in the situation described in the tale and, because of it, will act differently than they would have otherwise. With this in mind, I transmit a story from Yitta Halberstam Mandelbaum's *Holy Brother*, a remarkable collection of tales about Rabbi Shlomo Carlebach, a troubadour who spread Jewish music and love wherever he went.

One person whom Yitta interviewed told her that some years earlier, when she was waiting to board a fully booked morning flight from Toronto to New York, an airline official announced, "There are two people who have medical emergencies and desperately need to get back to New York in a hurry. We're asking for two volunteers to give up their

* Cited in Sherwin and Cohen, *How to Be a Jew*, 47.

seats for the sake of these people. The next flight to New York is in three hours. We know it's a great sacrifice, and we're sorry to put you in this position. Is there anybody here who is willing to extend themselves to help these people?"

"One hand immediately shot up in the crowd. 'I'm ready,' shouted a hearty voice....It was Shlomo Carlebach." How impressive, given that among the things for which Rabbi Carlebach was known was his extraordinary busyness. He was constantly traveling from concert to concert, and meeting with people and counseling them far into the night.

As the woman who was present that morning told Yitta, "Rest assured, of all of us gathered there that morning, it was Shlomo who probably had the most compelling need to get back fast. He had the least time to spare. But miraculously, he also had the most time to give." *

May you have a Shabbat Shalom!

S H A B B A T

During the course of this Shabbat, try to review the material from the preceding six days, and use some of the texts studied as the basis for discussion during the Shabbat meals:

Day 113. "You Shall Not Place a Stumbling Block"
Day 114. The Nameless Person Behind the Counter
Day 115. Acts of Kindness (1): Looking Backward
Day 116. Acts of Kindness (2): Looking Ahead
Day 117. Acts of Kindness (3): Looking Ahead
Day 118. The Least Time to Spare, the Most Time to Give

Shabbat Shalom!

* Mandelbaum, *Holy Brother,* 160–61.

# WEEK 18

# God's Four Questions

What matters most to God?

Different religions offer different answers. For example, most Christians believe that what matters to God is a person's faith in Jesus. Fundamentalists teach that if you have this belief, you will be granted eternal salvation; if not, God will punish you with eternal damnation.

What is Judaism's belief about what concerns God most?

A fascinating answer is offered in a talmudic passage (*Shabbat* 31a) in which the Rabbis speculate on the first questions a person will be asked when he or she dies and comes before the heavenly court.

Before you read further, stop for a moment and mark down what questions you think the Rabbis believed would be asked, and what questions *you* think should be addressed to people about their lives.

You may well have thought that the first question would be about faith ("Did you believe in God?") or ritual ("Did you observe the Jewish holidays and *kashrut* scrupulously?"). It is not. Rather, it is "Did you conduct your business affairs honestly?"

As the Rabbis understood God's will, a decent life—even a God-fearing life—is defined first and foremost by being honest with others, particularly in monetary matters. If you cannot answer this question affirmatively, God is not going to be impressed with statements of faith and ritual observance.

Second: "Did you set aside time to study Torah?"

A desire to be good does not necessarily guarantee goodness. Think of people you know and dislike. Do they think of themselves as bad people? Probably not, even though they might have done some very bad things. However, because most people judge themselves by their intentions and not by their deeds, these people think of themselves as good.

Judaism has specific guidelines in the Torah, the Talmud, and Jewish law on how to be a good person. If you don't study these books, when a moral dilemma arises, you won't know what Judaism believes is the right thing to do.

Third: "Did you try to create a family?"

Obviously not all people get married, and not all couples can have children (childless couples can, one hopes, adopt). Yet this emphasis on establishing a family has characterized Judaism since its inception. The Torah records in detail Abraham and Sarah's efforts to have a child, and the Patriarch's exertions to find a suitable wife for his son Isaac. The patriarchs and matriarchs were concerned with establishing a family because they wished to guarantee that there would be people to pass on the ideals of belief in God and in His commands of justice (see, for example, Genesis 18:19) after they died. Similarly, establishing a family helps ensure that Judaism's teachings and challenges, such as the commitment to giving charity and working "to mend the world," will be transmitted for another generation. And for the vast majority of people, marrying and raising children makes them better people. People who do not have children can also help transmit ideals to the next generation—for example to their nieces, their nephews, and their friends' children.

Fourth: "Did you hope for the world's redemption?"

The first three questions are "micro," and addressed toward the individual: Were you honest? Did you study Torah? Did you try to establish a family? If Judaism were concerned only with the individual, affirmative responses to these questions would be sufficient. But Judaism is also concerned with *tikkun olam,* repairing the world under the rule of God. This forces a serious Jew to think in bigger terms than just his or her own life and that of his or her family. We have obligations to make this world a more moral one. That we can't necessarily bring about perfection in our lifetime does not free us from doing what is possible. As Rabbi Tarfon taught, "It is not your obligation to complete the task [of perfecting the world], but neither are you free to desist [from doing all you can]" (*Ethics of the Fathers* 2:21).

# Do You Scream When You Should?

One of the strangest discussions in Jewish religious literature concerns a child born with two heads. A talmudic commentary (*Menachot* 37a) raises the question of whether such a child is entitled to one or two shares of its father's inheritance, and notes that a similar case was raised before Solomon, the wisest of kings. He had ruled, "Let them pour boiling water on the head of one child and see if the other one screams. If he does, then it means that the children are not regarded as twins, but as one. However, if the second child does not feel the suffering of the first, then they are to be regarded as separate individuals."

For the sake of the child destined to have boiling water poured on his head, one hopes that this debate was hypothetical. But the late Rabbi Joseph Soloveitchik, of blessed memory, argued that for us it is not hypothetical at all. In his essay *Kol Dodi Dofek* ("My Beloved's Voice Calls to Me"), he writes, "If boiling water is poured on the head of a Moroccan Jew, the prim and proper Jew in Paris or London must scream. And, by feeling the pain, he is loyal to the nation." *

A friend told me that throughout his twenties and thirties he was very active in the protest movement for Russian Jewry, but that since the Soviet Union fell apart and the Jews were free to leave, he hadn't found himself actively involved in any social justice cause. Recently, when someone had challenged him, "When was the last time you went on a protest march?" my friend responded, "I can't remember." The other

---

*My wife, Dvorah, worked for many years as a translator, editor, and assistant for the Nobel Prize–winning Yiddish writer Isaac Bashevis Singer. She was once with Mr. Singer at a lecture in Alabama, when a woman told him, "I was reading your story 'One Night in Brazil,' about a couple who fall out of a hammock and are brutally bitten up by mosquitoes. The description was so vivid, I started scratching my own arms." Mr. Singer answered, "Wouldn't it be a better world if we all scratched our arms when other people were itching?"

person answered, "I don't understand. Are there no injustices going on now in the world? Is there nothing left to scream about?"

As Jack Doueck, author of *The Hesed Boomerang* (see Day 363), wisely reminds us, "When boiling water is poured on the head of a human being anywhere in the world, others must scream."

# *Paying a Laborer's Wages Promptly*

*You shall not abuse a needy and destitute laborer, whether a fellow countryman [a Jew] or a stranger [a non-Jew].... You must pay him his wages on the same day, before the sun sets, for he is needy and urgently depends on it; or else he will cry to the Lord against you and you will incur guilt.*
          —Deuteronomy 24:14–15

*"For he is needy and urgently depends on it"—Why did this worker climb the ladder [to build a house], suspend himself from a tree [to pick fruit], and risk death? Was it not for his wages?*
          —Babylonian Talmud, *Bava Mezia* 112a

Day laborers (for example, domestic workers or handymen) must be paid by the end of the day in which they do their work. The Torah assumes that such people need their wages immediately ("for he is needy and urgently depends on it"), so that any delay in compensating them is regarded as a particularly serious sin ("he will cry to the Lord against you and you will incur guilt").

If someone works for you on a permanent basis, Jewish law allows you to develop a mutually agreeable system for payment; still, you are required to render payment no later than nightfall on the day when the money is due. In the case of a contractor, payment should be made upon the job's completion.

Clearly this law was intended to protect society's weakest, most economically vulnerable members, those most apt to be exploited because there is little they can do about it. A woman in her seventies told my mother of her impoverished Brooklyn childhood, during which her mother would sew and mend garments, and the daughter, my mother's friend, would deliver them to local homes. The woman told my mother that although many customers were affluent (at least in comparison with the dressmaker's family), "You would be shocked how often they would tell me that they didn't have the money ready, even when it was a small sum, and then tell me to come back a day or two later to collect it."

Under Jewish law, if these people truly did not have the money available (though if they knew the dresses were due to be delivered, they were obligated to be ready with the payment), then it was *their* responsibility to go to the dressmaker's house and bring the money, rather than waste the young girl's time by forcing her to make a return trip to collect money that was rightfully hers.

Most people regard debts they owe to banks and institutions that can repossess items in their possession as their most pressing obligations. But according to the Torah, the most pressing debts you have are to those who work for you.

WEDNESDAY

# What a Worker Owes His Employer

*A man must not plough with his ox at night and hire it out by day, nor must he himself work at his own affairs at night, and hire himself out by day. And he must not undertake fasts or other ascetic deprivations, because the ensuing weakness will diminish the amount of work he can perform for his employer.*

> *Rabbi Yochanan went to a place and found the school-teacher was fatigued. He asked the cause. They said to him, "Because he fasts." He said to the man, "You are forbidden to act in this manner."* *

—Palestinian Talmud, *Demai* 7:3

A worker expecting to be paid a regular salary must be capable of performing a normal workload. From Judaism's perspective, an employee who takes on other jobs or who engages in other activities, such as partying, that keep him up late, and comes to work groggy from lack of sleep engages in a form of thievery from his boss. (Obviously, when one informs one's employer of the extra workload, and receives the employer's agreement, there is no issue of dishonesty.) The same applies to a person who comes to work with a hangover.

Similarly, one is obligated to give a full day's work during work hours. Perhaps this sounds like a truism, but many employees violate this norm, engaging in long personal phone conversations or "bull sessions" while at work, and/or playing games on their computers. Maimonides addressed the issue of the employee's responsibility in his code of Jewish law:

> Just as the employer is enjoined not to deprive the poor worker of his hire or withhold it from him when it is due [see yesterday's entry] so is the worker enjoined not to deprive the employer of the benefit of his work by frittering away his time, a little here and a little there, thus wasting the whole day deceitfully. Indeed, the worker must be very punctilious in the matter of time....

—Moses Maimonides, *Mishneh Torah,*
"Laws of Hiring," 13:7

My father, Shlomo Telushkin, of blessed memory, worked for many years as an accountant for Ezras Torah, a charitable Jewish organization.

---

*While this teaching would apply to a teacher who engaged in exhausting ascetic behavior, if the teacher's exhaustion was due to his taking on extra work to make up for an inadequate salary, the fault then would be with his employer, not with him.

Its longtime director Rabbi Joseph Henkin was one of the great rabbinic scholars of the last generation. Throughout the day, telephone calls came in for Rabbi Henkin soliciting his advice on questions of Jewish law. My father told me that Rabbi Henkin would mark down in a little notebook the amount of time he spent on each such call, making sure to make up the time; that way, Ezras Torah would not be paying him for time spent on non-work-related matters.

Such behavior represents a standard of uprightness beyond most of us, but one that the Talmud expects of people who wish to be *fully* honest. It describes the behavior of Abba Hilkiah, a saint whose prayers the Rabbis solicited during a drought. Once, when prayers for rain were needed, two rabbis went to seek his assistance. They found him hoeing in the field, and "greeted him, but he took no notice of them." Later the scholars accompanied him as he walked home. There he and his wife prayed for rain, which immediately fell.

The Rabbis thanked Abba Hilkiah and asked, "When we greeted you, why did you not welcome us?" Abba Hilkiah answered, "I was a laborer hired by the day, and I said to myself [that since I am being paid by the day], let me not interrupt [my work even for a moment]" (Babylonian Talmud, *Ta'anit* 23b).

When it comes to time, the Jewish view of honesty was perhaps best expressed by Rabbi Moshe Chayyim Luzzatto, author of the eighteenth-century *Mesillat Yesharim* (*The Path of the Just*), a classic of Jewish moral teachings: "Just as theft of money is theft, so is theft of time" (chapter 11; for a further discussion of this maxim, see Day 102).

The stealing of time is, of course, but one way in which an employee can defraud his employer. It is equally wrong to pad one's expense account or call in sick and be paid for the sick day when one is healthy.

# *What We Owe Our Siblings*

Michael Gold, a prominent rabbi and writer, describes a bitter fight he once had with a younger brother. For a full year the two did not speak. But during this period Rabbi Gold learned that his brother, who had lost his job, was far behind on his mortgage payments, and was in danger of losing his house. Gold and his wife immediately sent him a check for a thousand dollars. Because the two were still not speaking, he received no acknowledgment from his brother. Later, though, they did reestablish contact, and his brother repaid the money. Still later, they reconciled and became very close.

"Why did I send him the money?" Gold asks. "I suppose it goes back to my childhood and the strong emphasis my parents put on being close to my brothers. I remember my father showing me a picture from Boy's Town in Nebraska of an older sibling carrying a younger, with the caption, 'He ain't heavy, he's my brother.' My father told us that 'that's how I want you boys to be.' Perhaps by caring for my brother, I was fulfilling the commandment to honor my parents." *

Gold's insight is profound. Except for an extreme circumstance (such as if your sibling is a vicious criminal or a highly abusive person), it is an act of the grossest disrespect to your parents, whether they are living or dead, to disassociate from your siblings. As a parent of young children, I know how important it is to me that they help each other, and ideally love each other, throughout their lives. And this is a universal parental desire. Rabbi Jack Riemer, who has spent decades collecting ethical wills bequeathed by Jewish parents to their children, writes that one of his favorites was that written by Rose Weiss Baygel, a European-born woman who migrated as a child to Cleveland: "My dear children: I am writing this in the bank. This is what I want from you children: Evelyn, Bernice, and Allen to be to one another—good sisters and

* Gold, *God, Love, Sex and Family*, 54–56.

brother....Be good to each other. Help one another if, God forbid, in need. This is my wish." (See Day 197 for a further discussion of this and other ethical wills.)

But what should you do if your sibling has different interests from yours, or a less refined temperament, or just bores you? Michael Gold offers good advice: "We do not need to be our brother's best friend; we do need to be our brother's keeper." In other words, treat your siblings the way you want your children to treat one another.

An exercise: Over this coming month, make sure that you speak to each of your siblings at least once a week.

DAY

### 125    FRIDAY

# Anger: Three Thoughts Before You Explode

If you have a bad temper, write the three statements below on a card and keep it with you at all times. When you are ready to erupt, and about to say the kind of hurtful things that will wound and humiliate another, take out the card and consider the statements on it. They were written some eight hundred years ago by Rabbi Menachem Meiri, one of medieval Jewry's great sages. In his book *Sefer Hamidot*, Meiri writes that these were the statements a king instructed his servant to show him whenever he lost his temper:

- ◆ You are a creature, not the Creator.
- ◆ You are flesh and blood and will perish.
- ◆ God will show you mercy only if you show mercy.

Take particular care to stay calm on the Shabbat. When Jewish thinkers describe the Shabbat, they often speak of it as an island of peace in a troubled world, and focus on it as a time for families and friends to come together. Therefore, this Shabbat, and during the some-times hectic moments of preparation before the Sabbath, don't lose your temper, even when you feel provoked. Don't be guilty of making the traditional Sabbath greeting, *Shabbat Shalom* ("May you have a peaceful Sabbath"), a lie in your house and for your family.

And with that thought, may you have a Shabbat Shalom!

DAY

## 126     S H A B B A T

During the course of this Shabbat, try to review the material from the preceding six days, and use some of the texts studied as the basis for discussion during the Shabbat meals:

Day 120. God's Four Questions
Day 121. Do You Scream When You Should?
Day 122. Paying a Laborer's Wages Promptly
Day 123. What a Worker Owes His Employer
Day 124. What We Owe Our Siblings
Day 125. Anger: Three Thoughts Before You Explode

Shabbat Shalom!

# WEEK 19

S U N D A Y

## What Does It Mean to Honor and Revere Your Parents?

*Honor your father and mother.*
—Exodus 20:12

*Let each of you revere his mother and father.*
—Leviticus 19:3

What does it mean to honor your parents? To revere them?

According to the Talmud, honor is expressed through the performance of positive acts, and reverence through the avoidance of negative ones. Thus, "honor means that a child must give [his parent] food and drink, clothe and cover him, and lead him in and out [when a parent is old and needs a helping hand]."

In short, children are required to do for elderly parents precisely the acts that parents did for them when they were young and vulnerable: feed, clothe, and protect them. But while Jewish law obligates parents to spend their own money to provide for their children's needs, it does not require children to use their own financial resources to cover their parents' expenses (for example, children are permitted to dip into their parents' savings).

"Revere" means "that a child must neither stand nor sit in his [father's] place, nor contradict his words, nor tip the scale against him" (siding with a father's or mother's opponents in a dispute; see *Kiddushin* 31b).

When I was growing up, my father had a set place at the dinner table. As long as he was alive, neither my sister nor I ever sat there. I don't even know if my father would have minded (I never recall him raising the issue), but I would have felt presumptuous had I sat in his seat.

As for "nor contradict his words," the Talmud probably meant this quite literally; a child should never dispute with a parent, except when the parent has instructed him or her to violate a Jewish law (see tomorrow's entry). Today, most parents would be alarmed if their child passively acquiesced to everything they said and commanded, without ever expressing disagreement. Nonetheless, the principle underlying the talmudic law is still applicable. Thus, I understand this law as mandating that even when you disagree with a parent, you must do so in a respectful and fair manner (and, whenever possible, in private).

For many children, this is difficult. I have heard children say awful things to their parents, including "I hate you!" and "I don't give a damn what you want, I'll do what I want!" From Judaism's perspective, such statements constitute "parent abuse," and are strictly forbidden.

Regarding "nor tip the scale against him," Jewish commentaries explain that you should not side with your parents' opponents. My mother, who grew up in New York City's Lower East Side, told me of an incident from her childhood. Workers at a store owned by a neighbor went out on strike, and the owner's son joined the strikers' picket line. While Jewish law would not obligate the son to agree with his father's policies, it would insist he not publicly humiliate his father by so closely identifying with his opponents.*

While Jewish law rules that parents are entitled to honor and respect, it also permits them to forgo making these demands of their children. For example, my parents made it clear that it was fine with them for my sister and me to express disagreement with things that they said. However, even though parents are permitted to forgo their honor, they are never permitted to allow their children to hit or curse them.

The commandment to "honor your father and mother" is one of the few for which the Torah promises a reward, "so that your days may long

---

*Obviously, all such laws have exceptions. If one's parent is evil, one may oppose him or her. Thus, Exodus records that when Pharaoh decreed the drowning of male Hebrew infants, his own daughter saved Moses. Much later, King Saul made numerous efforts to murder David, but two of Saul's children, Michal and Jonathan, thwarted him and saved David.

endure..." (Exodus 20:12). There is indeed a pragmatic aspect to fulfilling this commandment: our children will see how we look after our parents and know how to look after us.

MONDAY

# What You Don't Owe Your Parents

Parents who demand total obedience from their children have no right to do so: According to Jewish ethics, God is the only one entitled to absolute obedience.

Most notably, children are not required to honor their parents' wishes when the parents instruct them to do something that Judaism regards as immoral or forbidden by Jewish law (such as desecrating the Sabbath). According to Rabbi Shlomo Ganzfried (*Kitzur Shulchan Aruch* 143:1), "If a child is told by his father not to speak to or forgive someone with whom the child wishes to reconcile, he or she should disregard the father's command." Such a command would be justified only if the person whom the father wished the child to shun was a particularly evil person and/or a dangerous influence.

Today, with the widespread breakdown in the nuclear family, this ruling is violated in ways that Rabbi Ganzfried might not have anticipated. For example, a friend of mine was involved in an acrimonious divorce. A short time later he noticed that his oldest daughter was very uncomfortable in his presence, and kept trying to cancel their weekly meetings. When he questioned her, the girl revealed that her mother, with whom she lived, had told her, "You have a choice. You can love your father or you can love me, but you can't love us both."

Jewish law regards offering the daughter such a choice as immoral, and obliges her not to heed her mother's words. No parent (except in the most extreme of instances) has the right to try to alienate his or her child from the other parent.

Similarly, children are not required to obey a parental demand to be dishonest. The Talmud, citing the case of a child who finds a lost object and who is ordered by his father to keep it instead of returning it to its owner, rules that the son should ignore his father's order (Babylonian Talmud, *Bava Mezia* 32a). Obviously a young child will feel uncomfortable disobeying a parent's order. But an older child should resist allowing a parent to force him or her to engage in a form of theft.

Likewise, it is wrong for a parent to instruct a child to lie about his or her age for the sake of a financial advantage, such as, "Tell the man selling the movie tickets that you're only eleven so you can get in cheaper." In such a case, the child should tell the parents that he or she feels it is wrong to tell such a lie.

Parents sometimes issue commands that, while not directly contravening Jewish law, may still cause their children heartbreak. For example, many parents try to break up a child's relationship with the person the child loves. But as long as he or she wishes to marry a person whom Jewish tradition permits the child to wed (such as a fellow Jew), the child is not obligated to obey his or her parent's wishes.* That's been true of Jewish law from time immemorial. Two thousand years ago the Talmud ruled, "A father is forbidden to marry off his daughter while she is a minor. He must wait until she is grown up and says, 'I want [to marry] so-and-so" (*Kiddushin* 41a).

As a child, you owe your parents many things: gratitude, attention (expressed through visits and phone calls), honor, and even a sense of reverence. What you don't owe your parents, however, is control of your conscience.

---

*Parents certainly have the right to express their reasoned opinions as to why they believe the relationship is inappropriate. They just have no right to insist that the child accept their view.

# *Escort Your Guests*

In Jewish tradition, hospitality has as much to do with good-byes as hellos (indeed, in Hebrew, the same word, *shalom*, is used both for "hello" and "good-bye"). And while American etiquette dictates escorting guests to the door, Jewish law teaches that one should accompany one's guests into the street. When I was eleven years old, I traveled with my family on my first trip to Israel. My father took me to meet the venerable sage and saint Rabbi Aryeh Levine (see, for example, Days 62 and 181). When our visit finished, the elderly rabbi escorted us out of his house and walked with us for a block. Just to have met and spent some time with so great a man made my father and me feel very special; having him personally escort us added to our sense of privilege.

When people leave our house in a car or taxi, my wife insists on waiting till the guests drive away, and we all stand and wave. Some years ago, friends in Dayton, Ohio, brought me to the airport after a lecture, then waited with me inside the terminal. They told me that they never left the airport until after the plane departed. When I asked why, I learned that many years earlier the man had brought his elderly parents to the airport for a flight to Florida, and then left. Moments later, while the plane was still on the ground, his mother had a fatal heart attack, and his father, overcome with emotion, temporarily forgot his English and reverted to his native Yiddish. Needless to say, the tragedy of the mother's death was intensified by the confusion that followed. Ever since, this family waits until their guest's plane has departed.

Such behavior might seem extreme, but Jewish tradition regards merely escorting your guests to the door as insufficient. Take a few dozen steps more, go out with them into the street, and let them experience the honor and affection you feel for them.

# *Two Pieces of Paper*

One lesson the Rabbis deduced from God's having originally populated the world with but one person, Adam, is that each individual should feel that "for my sake was the world created" (Mishna, *Sanhedrin* 4:5). Obviously the Rabbis wished to encourage each person to feel special, though it is also true that one who spends too much time meditating on the fact that "for my sake was the world created" can become selfish and obnoxious.

To guard against people learning the wrong lesson from this rabbinic teaching, the early-nineteenth-century Chasidic master Rabbi Simcha Bunam suggested that every person carry in his or her pockets two pieces of paper. On one should be written, "For my sake was the world created," while the other should contain the words Abraham recited when he entreated God to spare the cities of Sodom and Gomorrah: "I am but dust and ashes" (Genesis 18:27).

Each paper should be consulted at the appropriate time. When you are feeling arrogant, impressed by how much more you have accomplished than others, by how much smarter, generous, insightful, witty, and popular you are, consult the sheet, "I am but dust and ashes." After all, it was Abraham who said that, and while you may indeed be more accomplished than your colleagues, are you greater than Abraham?

Then again, during moments of despair (and moments of arrogance and despair may even occur on the same day) remind yourself, "For my sake was the world created." There is always some special mission for you, something in this world that you, and only you, can accomplish.

Two pieces of paper: Write down the words, and put them in your pockets, now.

# Read and Listen to Points of View with Which You Disagree

*For three years there was a dispute [actually many disputes] between the School of Shammai and the School of Hillel, the former asserting, "The law (halacha) is according to our view," and the latter asserting, "The law is according to our view." Then a voice issued from heaven announcing, "The teachings of both are the words of the living God, but the law is in agreement with the School of Hillel."*

*But [it was asked] since both are the words of the living God, for what reason was the School of Hillel entitled to have the law determined according to their rulings?*

*Because they were kindly and humble, and because they studied their own rulings and those of the School of Shammai, and even mentioned the teachings of the School of Shammai before their own.*

—Babylonian Talmud, *Eruvin* 13b

Rabbis Hillel and Shammai, who lived just before the Common Era, were the leading sages of their age. Hillel remains to this day one of the preeminent figures of Jewish history.

The schools they founded were involved in hundreds of disputes concerning how Jewish law should be applied. While the Jewish tradition has always sanctioned debate, there was a risk that numerous divergent rulings on Jewish law could lead to a schism. And so, this talmudic story tells us, a heavenly voice emerged to declare that the law should follow the view of Hillel and his disciples.

Significantly, the heavenly voice ruled in favor of Hillel and his disciples, even in areas of ritual dispute, for moral reasons: he and his followers were "kindly and humble."

The wording of the passage suggests that Shammai's followers had grown somewhat arrogant. Certain that they possessed the truth, they no longer bothered to listen to, or discuss the arguments of, their opponents. Their overbearing self-confidence led them to become morally less impressive (the language of the Talmud suggests by implication that they were not "kindly and humble"), and probably led them to become intellectually less insightful (after all, how insightful can you be if you are studying only one side of the issue?).

Because the School of Hillel studied their opponent's arguments, when they issued a ruling they were fully cognizant of all the arguments to be offered against their own position. Thus, their humility not only led to their being pleasanter people, but also likely caused them to have greater intellectual depth.

We can all learn a lesson from the behavior of Hillel and his followers: Don't read only books and publications that agree with and reinforce your points of view. If you do so, and many people do, you will never learn what those who disagree with you believe (at best, you will hear a caricature of their position, presented by people who, like you, disagree with it). It would be a good thing in Jewish life if Jews in the different denominations, or in different political camps, started reading newspapers and magazines of the groups with which they disagree on a regular basis.

If you seldom hear, read, or listen to views that oppose your own, and if almost everyone you talk to sees the world just as you do, your thinking will grow flabby and intolerant. That is often the case with ideologues on the right and left, both in religion and in politics.

As this text teaches us, humble people are not only more pleasant human beings, but in the final analysis they may well be the only ones who will have something eternally important to teach.

# It's Not Only What You Do for Your Parents That Counts—It's Your Attitude

A son who feeds his elderly father expensive chickens would seem to be a model child, while one who sends his old father out into the fields to perform backbreaking physical toil would seem to be despicable.

The Talmud reminds us that appearances can be deceiving:

A man may feed his father fattened chickens and inherit hell, and another may put his father to work treading a mill and inherit the Garden of Eden.

How is it possible for a man to feed his father fattened chickens and inherit hell?

There was a man who used to feed his father fattened chickens. Once, his father said to him, "My son, where did you get these?" He answered, "Old man, old man, shut up and eat, just as dogs shut up when they eat." Such a man feeds his father on fattened chickens but inherits hell.

How is it possible for a man to put his father to work in a mill and still inherit the Garden of Eden?

There was a man who worked in a mill. The king ordered that millers be brought to work for him. Said the man to his father, "Father, you stay here and work in the mill in my place [and I will go to work for the king]. For if insults come to the workers, I prefer that they fall on me and not on you. Should floggings come, let them beat me and not you." Such a man puts his father to work in a mill and yet inherits the Garden of Eden.

—Palestinian Talmud, *Kiddushin* 1:7

Although cruel kings no longer conscript Jews into forced labor details, this talmudic teaching remains relevant. There are children who provide for their parents' financial needs but treat them disrespectfully, or make them feel like burdens.

Respect or disrespect for one's parents is displayed in several ways, most obviously in how one speaks to them. A man who feeds his father but addresses him contemptuously is regarded by the Jewish tradition as having acted despicably, just as it would regard one who gives a beggar a large contribution but humiliates the person with cruel words. Traditional Jewish culture also sets great store by how one speaks *about* one's parents. Thus, in the blessings that are recited after eating (*Birkat Hamazon*) at one's parents' home, one speaks of one's father as *avi mori* (my father, my teacher) and mother as *eemi morati* (my mother, my teacher).

Respect for parents is also reflected through ongoing attention to their needs. If your parents live near you, visit them often and have them over to your home. Speak to them on the telephone *several* times a week (particularly if one of your parents is widowed and lives alone), even if your calls are brief. Accompany them, when possible, to a doctor's appointment. If they're hospitalized, be sure you visit often. And, on an ongoing basis, solicit their opinions and advice, and involve them in your lives and in those of your children.

It is wonderful to be financially generous to your aged parents, but make sure that you are also generous with respect. Not everyone has money to offer parents (and indeed many parents do not need such help), but almost all of us are in a position to help fulfill their emotional needs (see Day 164). And this, too, is part of the mitzvah of "Honor your father and mother."

May you have a Shabbat Shalom!

DAY

## 133     S H A B B A T

During the course of this Shabbat, try to review the material from the preceding six days, and use some of the texts studied as the basis for discussion during the Shabbat meals:

Day 127. What Does It Mean to Honor and Revere Your Parents?

Day 128. What You Don't Owe Your Parents

Day 129. Escort Your Guests

Day 130. Two Pieces of Paper

Day 131. Read and Listen to Points of View with Which You
Disagree

Day 132. It's Not Only What You Do for Your Parents That
Counts—It's Your Attitude

Shabbat Shalom!

# WEEK 20

DAY

134    SUNDAY

# *"Educate a Child According to His Way"*

Children do not emerge from their mothers' wombs as blank slates, their lives determined solely by heredity and environment. As every parent quickly learns, children come into the world with distinctive personalities and temperaments.

A friend of mine once confessed that yelling did not work with either of his sons. The older was overly sensitive, and sharp parental disapproval was so devastating to him as to be cruel and counterproductive. The younger had a skin so thick that he simply shrugged off his parents' high-pitched voices and angry disapproval, responding only to more reasoned discourse. In both cases, the parents had to find the technique best suited to influence each child.

"Educate a child according to his way," the Book of Proverbs (22:6) teaches. In other words, while all your children are entitled to be treated with equal love, they should not be treated the same, because each is unique. It is your obligation as a parent to ascertain your child's emotional way, and to treat him or her in a manner that recognizes and values that way.

Similarly, as a parent, you are obligated to be conscious of your child's special intellectual and artistic abilities or interests. A luggage manufacturer might want every piece produced in his factory to come out precisely alike, but children are not luggage. Yet I've met parents who have very definite views about precisely what sort of person their child should be, and who do not take into account the child's personality and interests. Such an attitude denies a child's very individuality, for it is not a child's obligation to fulfill his or her parents' unfilled dreams and unlived lives. For example, although you might not have much interest in science or literature, if your child shows an affinity for those areas, you are obligated to help her cultivate it.

In theory this may seem obvious, but in practice many parents want their children to emulate them in all ways, including personality, and intellectual and professional interests.

To educate a child according to his way is to recognize that your child is separate from you, and from his brothers and sisters as well. Therefore, treat your child as the individual he or she is, and with the same recognition of a distinctive identity that you wish others to extend to you.

An exercise: To incorporate this principle into your life effectively, once a week (starting tonight, or perhaps on Friday evening when you bless your children; see Day 13), take a moment to praise each of your children by highlighting a unique talent or attribute he or she possesses. This will compel you as a parent to discover what is particular and distinctive about each of your children.

M O N D A Y

## Don't Threaten Your Children with Physical Punishment

A story from the Rabbis: A child had broken a bottle and the boy's father threatened to box his ears. Fearful of his father's wrath, the child went outside and killed himself by jumping into a deep pit. As a result of this and similar incidents, the Rabbis taught: "A person should not threaten a child even with [as small a thing as] boxing his ears. Rather, he should punish him immediately, or say nothing" (the minor tractate of *Semachot* 2:5–6).*

These wise words of the Rabbis are frequently ignored, with terrible consequences, as witness a 1998 *New York Times* story datelined Morrilton, Arkansas (October 24):

> An eight-year-old boy fatally shot himself at home this week while his mother was outside getting a switch to whip him because of a bad report card, the police in this town thirty-five miles northwest of Little Rock said today. On Wednesday afternoon, the boy, Christopher Parks, apparently climbed onto a dresser to get a gun that was hanging from a nail on the wall, straightened a doily he had wrinkled, then shot himself in the head, Detective Rusty Quinn said. Christopher, who was in the third grade, died on Thursday.

*The New York Times* headlined the article, "Bad Report Card Caused Boy's Suicide, Police Say."

The headline, of course, was absurd. It was not the bad report card that caused the suicide, any more than it was the breaking of the bottle

---

*In yet another instance, the Rabbis advise that "if you must strike a child, hit him only with a shoelace" (Babylonian Talmud, *Bava Bathra* 21a), which, when you analyze it, means that you should make sure that you never physically hurt a child.

that caused the child in the Rabbis' story to kill himself. Rather, the parents' response to the report card (and presumably to other incidents that preceded it) and to the breaking of the bottle impelled the suicides (coupled, in the Arkansas instance, with the easy availability of a loaded gun). And while it is true that children threatened with beatings do not normally kill themselves, some children are more fearful, or emotionally unstable, than others; parents must be aware of the emotional havoc they wreak when they issue dire threats against their children. In William Butler Yeats's autobiography, the poet cites the wise words of William Middleton: "We should not make light of the troubles of children. They are worse than ours, because we can see the end of our trouble and they can never see any end."

Many parents make cruel threats. My wife told me that she was recently with our children at a restaurant when she overheard a mother saying to her young son, "You're not polite. If you don't change, I'm going to have to trade you with another family for a nicer child." Evidently, such a woman does not think that she needs to be a nicer mother.

Be compassionate to your children. Don't make cruel threats.

DAY

## 136      T U E S D A Y

# Enter a Mourner's Home with Silence

The Bible tells us of several terrible disasters that befell Job. Within a span of hours his wealth was lost and his ten children were killed when a building collapsed upon them; soon after, he became afflicted with very painful boils.

As Job sat on the ground mourning his children, his three closest friends came to visit him. Immediately upon seeing Job, they tore their garments, wept, and sat down on the ground with him. For seven days and nights they didn't speak, "for they saw that his grief was very great" (Job 2:12–13; 3:1).

Only when Job spoke did his friends finally speak as well.* Basing itself on the behavior of Job's friends, the Talmud rules: "Comforters are not permitted to say anything until the mourner has first commenced to speak" (*Mo'ed Kattan* 28b).

What is the logic behind this ruling?

One's goal in paying a *shiva*** call to a mourner is to comfort him or her. Yet one does not always know what sort of comfort the mourner most needs. Perhaps you will start speaking about the dead at just the moment he or she desperately needs to speak about something else. Or perhaps you will try and divert the mourner by speaking about a lighter subject (I've often heard people in *shiva* houses talk of sports events) at just the moment when he or she needs to speak about the deceased. And, perhaps the mourner just doesn't want to speak at all.

For most of us, silence is uncomfortable. Rabbi Jack Riemer notes, "We are afraid of silence. I get into the car, I turn on my radio. I get into the elevator, they play music for me. Why? Because we're afraid to be alone for two seconds with ourselves. It's okay to be quiet. It's okay to just sit and listen. It's okay to not fill the air with small talk and cheap talk and sports talk. Just leave enough silence in which something can be felt."

Riemer, a close disciple of the late Rabbi Abraham Joshua Heschel, recalls how Heschel, among the most eloquent and poetic of Jewish philosophers, maintained total silence when visiting a friend who was mourning:

> I remember that when Rabbi Wolfe Kelman, of blessed memory, lost his sister, Dr. Heschel, of blessed memory, said, "We have to go." We went to the airport, we flew to Boston, got into a cab and went to the house. Heschel walked in, he hugged them, he sat silently for an hour. He didn't mumble a single cliché, "How old was she?" What difference does it make? "Time will heal." Time

---

*Ironically, once Job's friends started speaking, they said terrible things to him, in essence telling him that his and his children's sufferings were punishments from God for their sins. Previously moral models of silence, Job's friends turned into immoral models of speech (see Day 360).

**Shiva* refers to the seven days of mourning that commence after burial. During this time (except for Shabbat and certain Jewish holidays), mourners are not supposed to leave their home or engage in normal workday activities.

won't heal. "I know how you feel." You don't know how I feel. None of the clichés. He just sat there in silence for an hour. And then he got up, hugged them, and we left. I learned that you don't have to be glib. You just have to care.*

Jewish tradition ordains one phrase that all those who make a *shiva* call say upon departing: "May God comfort you among all those who mourn for Zion and Jerusalem."

This simple statement reminds the mourners that they are not alone in their suffering; they are part of a community. Also, by mentioning the sorrowful fate of Zion (the destruction of the Temple in 70 C.E., and the eventual exiling of the Jews from their homeland), the guest reminds the mourner that suffering is a part of the human condition. But it is also not the last word. In our century, Zion has been restored. And the mourner, too, will know happiness again.

DAY

137    WEDNESDAY

# "Don't Take My Grief from Me!"

As discussed yesterday, Jewish ethics dictate that one who visits a house of mourning say nothing until the mourner initiates the conversation. But what then?

Years of rabbinical experience have taught me that one must learn first what *not* to say. Often, visitors' well-meaning but unthoughtful and tactless comments inflict great anguish upon mourners. Author Doug Manning tells of a young woman he knew whose child had died. She sat at home in total despair, her body racked by uncontrollable sobbing.

Her family and friends, uncomfortable with the intensity of her

* In Wolfson, *A Time to Mourn, a Time to Comfort,* 202.

pain, tried to console her with conventional clichés. "There, there, now—get hold of yourself." "You can't carry on like this." "Come on, now—stop crying."

The young woman looked up at them with fiery eyes. "Don't take my grief from me. I deserve it! I am going to have it!"

In a nuanced and sensitive treatment of the ethical responsibilities of those who visit mourners, Jewish educator Dr. Ron Wolfson offers a list of clichés many of us have uttered to those who have suffered the death of a loved one. And while some of these comments may be appropriate to tell someone many months after a loved one's death, they are *all* unsuitable during those early anguished weeks:

"You have to get on with your life."
"I know exactly what you're going through."
"She lived a long life."
"You're lucky you had her for so long."
"Be thankful you have another child."
"You're young; there's plenty of time to have another child."
"Don't cry."
"Don't take it so hard."
"Get a grip on yourself."
"Calm down."
"Be strong for the children."

The most compassionate thing one can do is simply to accept and validate whatever the mourner is feeling: "It's okay to cry." "You must be hurting so much." "It's hard for me to imagine what you feel."

As Wolfson concludes:

Experts in condolence agree that one of the most important gifts you can give to someone in grief is the full, complete, and non-judgmental acceptance of the person's feelings, thoughts, attitudes, and behaviors, no matter how explosive, no matter how "embarrassing," no matter how much you want desperately to calm the person down, to reassure them that things will be better....*

*Wolfson, *A Time to Mourn, a Time to Comfort*, 202–24; Wolfson cites the story told by Doug Manning in *Don't Take My Grief Away*.

As the anguished young woman, pained by her comforters' clichés, reminds us, your job when visiting a mourner is not to take the person's grief away, but to give comfort through your presence. That is all you can do, but if you do it well, *that* is a mighty thing.

DAY

## 138 THURSDAY

# "You Shall Not Carry God's Name in Vain": An Unforgivable Sin

The third of the Ten Commandments, generally translated as "You shall not take God's name in vain," is usually understood as prohibiting, among other things, using God's name in a curse, or as mandating that one write "God" as "G–d."

It long puzzled me, however, that this is the only one of the commandments whose violation God warns He will never forgive ("for the Lord will not absolve one" who violates this commandment [Exodus 20:7]). After all, taking God's name in vain seems a less serious offense than murdering, stealing, or committing idolatry.

Once, while I was studying this commandment with Dennis Prager, he noted that the literal meaning of the Hebrew is "You shall not *carry* God's name in vain." In other words, what the commandment prohibits is doing something evil or false in the name of God. This, for example, is, from Judaism's perspective, one of the sins fundamentalist Islamic terrorists commit when they call out *Allah Akbar* (God is great) while carrying out acts of murder. The same was the case when Yigal Amir, a Jew, assassinated Prime Minister Yitzhak Rabin in the name of God and Judaism.

Rendering this verse as "You shall not carry God's name in vain," makes it clear why God won't forgive the violation of this commandment. It is the only one of the Ten Commandments the violation of which turns God into a victim. A person who commits murder, steals, or swears a false oath discredits himself or herself, but a person who does a murderous or odious act in God's name alienates people from God as well. Thus, God suffers from the acts of those who do evil in His name.

Therefore, religious Jews must constantly remember that people witnessing their behavior are forming impressions not only of them but of God and the entire Jewish people. The same applies to one whose name is recognizably Jewish, or one who wears a Star of David, or one who takes off work for Jewish holidays. If people know you to be a Jew, you represent the Jewish people, and if people know you to be religious, you represent the Jewish God as well. That is an awesome responsibility, but it also represents an extraordinary opportunity to be *mekadesh shem shamayim,* to sanctify God's name.*

As the Talmud teaches:

> "And you shall love the Lord your God" (Deuteronomy 6:5): This means that you should cause God to be loved through your acts. Thus, if a person studies Bible and Mishna…and is honest in his business dealings, and speaks gently to people, what do people say about him? "Happy is the father who taught him Torah. Happy is the teacher who taught him Torah. Woe unto those who haven't learned Torah. This man studied Torah; see how noble his ways are, how good his actions…." But when a person studies Bible and Mishna…but is dishonest in business, and does not speak gently with people, what do people say of him? "Woe unto him who studies Torah….This man studied Torah; look how corrupt are his deeds, how ugly his ways." *Yoma* 86a

*See also Days 103 and 104.*

---

*Rabbi David Woznica notes: "If you take this commandment seriously, it can regularly and significantly change the way you act. On an airplane, if you order a kosher meal, thereby alerting the flight attendants and those seated nearby that you are Jewish, you can do great good for God and the Jewish people by acting particularly nicely. Similarly, if you act rudely or otherwise inappropriately you can cause great harm."

FRIDAY

# When It's Good to Be a Fool

Some eighteen hundred years ago, a man left a will containing a clause that confounded the rabbinic courts: "My son shall not receive his inheritance until he becomes foolish." Two prominent rabbinical judges sought out the great scholar Rabbi Joshua ben Korcha to solicit his view as to this unusual provision's meaning. As they approached his house, they found him crawling on his hands and knees in the field, a cord protruding from his mouth. The rabbi was being led like a horse by his small son.

The men said nothing, and withdrew to Rabbi Joshua's house to wait for him. When he arrived, they showed him the will. Laughing, Rabbi Joshua commented, "As you live, this business you are concerned about, acting like a fool, applied to me just a few minutes ago." He explained that it was clear that the will's author didn't want his son to inherit until he married and had a family, for "when a man has children it is not unusual for him to act like a fool when it comes to them" (*Midrash Psalms* 93:12).

In a memoir reminiscent of this rabbinic tale, Professor Susannah Heschel, daughter of the great religious scholar and moral leader Rabbi Abraham Joshua Heschel, recalls:

Even after twenty-five years...when I think of [my father] my first memories are either of his humor and playfulness, or of his gentle, quiet conversations with me. I remember his delight in my childhood games, playing school or house or zoo with me, down on the floor with dolls and toys....At my childhood birthday parties, he loved to make up games for the children to play (sometimes to my annoyance, since he usurped the center of attention!), and our most frequent after-dinner family activity was reenacting my day at school: I was the teacher, my mother and father had to play the mischievous pupils.*

These whimsical stories remind us that life is rarely always serious. True, Jewish tradition imposes some very sober obligations on parents (to teach their children Torah, a profession, and how to be ethical people) and on children (to honor their parents and be in awe of them; see Day 127). But as these tales about Rabbi Joshua ben Korcha and Rabbi Abraham Joshua Heschel remind us, your children are not supposed only to honor you, they are also supposed to enjoy you.

This Shabbat, make sure you set aside a specific time to do something playful, humorous, and purely enjoyable with your children.**

May you have a Shabbat Shalom!

D A Y

### 140    SHABBAT

During the course of this Shabbat, try to review the material from the preceding six days, and use some of the texts studied as the basis for discussion during the Shabbat meals:

Day 134. "Educate a Child According to His Way"
Day 135. Don't Threaten Your Children with Physical Punishment
Day 136. Enter a Mourner's Home with Silence
Day 137. "Don't Take My Grief from Me!"
Day 138. "You Shall Not Carry God's Name in Vain": An Unforgivable Sin
Day 139. When It's Good to Be a Fool

Shabbat Shalom!

---

* *Jewish Week*, January 1998, 14.
** Rabbi Irwin Kula notes that Rabbi Joshua's advocacy of "playing the fool" with your children achieves two goals: It humanizes parents, thereby balancing the aura of respect in which Judaism encourages children to hold parents, and it enables parents to show their love and emotions more easily.

# Helping Non-Jews

Although American Jews constitute just over two percent of the country's population, the United Jewish Communities (formerly, the United Jewish Appeal) is one of America's largest charities, a remarkable fact, given that many other causes appeal to a constituency some forty times larger than the UJC's.

This legacy of Jewish giving to Jewish causes is so well known that many people are unaware that Jewish law mandates that Jews give charity and support to non-Jews as well. The Talmud teaches that "the purpose of the entire Torah is to establish peace" (*Gittin* 59b). In the interest of spreading peace and good feelings between all humankind, it dictates:

> We must provide help for the non-Jewish poor as well as for the Jewish poor; we must visit non-Jews when they are sick as well as our fellow Jews when they are sick; and we must attend to the burial of their dead as well as the burial of our own dead; for these are the ways of peace (*mipnei darkei shalom*)...
>
> —Babylonian Talmud, *Gittin* 61a

Because all human beings are created in God's image, all, except those who are truly evil, are worthy of help. If committed Jews generally give a disproportionately high percentage of their charitable disbursements to Jews, that should be because Jews generally can rely only on other Jews to support their causes, and not, God forbid, because Jews are indifferent to gentile suffering. Indeed, one often finds that the Jews most attuned to the sufferings of other Jews are those most attuned to non-Jewish suffering as well. In Yitta Halberstam Mandelbaum's *Holy*

*Brother,* the author relates a story told to her by a member of Rabbi Shlomo Carlebach's Manhattan-based congregation:

He was about six feet two, white as a sheet, and had stringy blond hair cascading down to his shoulders. His rumpled, torn and dirty clothes emitted a dank and sour odor. Yet only moments before, seemingly oblivious to the offensive smell, Shlomo Carlebach had led the young man proudly to my side, his arm draped warmly around his shoulder, exclaiming cheerfully, "Sister Anne will gladly help you!"* Surreptitiously, Shlomo whispered into my ear, "Please give him as much food as he wants to eat."

I sprang to my feet, ran into the kitchen and heaped generous amounts of food onto a plate. In a matter of minutes, the young man had devoured the meal, so I went back into the kitchen for seconds. This too was consumed rapidly, so I went back again for more. Finally, when he appeared satisfied, I looked at his blond hair and blue eyes and blurted out rather impolitely, "Are you Jewish?"

"No, ma'am," he replied courteously. "I'm a Christian from Texas."

"So, how'd you end up at our *shul* dinner?" I asked.

His eyes lifted heavenward. "I was sitting on a bench in Central Park late this afternoon, when your Rabbi walked by. I had never met or seen him before, but he took one look at me, turned around and walked right up to me. With the kindest eyes and sweetest smile, he asked ever so gently; 'Brother, do you need a meal?' I started to cry and gratefully told him yes, I desperately did. He gave me the name and address of your synagogue, and told me to come right over. He said there was good food and plenty of it. That's how I came to be here tonight. I really don't know what I would have done if your Rabbi hadn't come by," the blond Texan said slowly. "I'll tell you honestly, this is the first meal I've eaten in three days. When he walked right up to me and asked, 'Brother, do you need a meal?' I said to myself, 'This man here is surely an angel from God.'"

* At the Carlebach *shul* (synagogue), members are known as Brother and Sister.

What a wonderful story to remember the next time you find yourself inundated with too much junk mail and are tempted to throw out every letter, including appeals from charities with which you are unfamiliar. Better to remember that you, too, like Shlomo Carlebach, have the opportunity to be an "angel of God" in another person's life.

DAY

142

MONDAY

## Schedule Kindness into Your Day

In traditional Jewish culture, the study of Torah, Talmud, and other Jewish texts is regarded as the most sacred act in which a human being can engage (see, for example, Day 117), one to which committed students try to devote as many hours a day as possible. In secular society, ambitious people are driven to work long hours, often to the exclusion of other activities. The sort of thinking that leads one to devote oneself *exclusively* to studying religious texts or to advancing oneself professionally can unbalance and distort a person. As Rabbi Israel Meir Kagan, known in Jewish life as the Chaffetz Chayyim, wrote, "You occasionally see a Jew learning as much Torah as he can. He values his time and does not waste any for fear he will not study as much as he should. But if he does not set aside part of the day to do deeds of kindness—he is a fool." *

Schedule kindness into your day, whether it means visiting one who is sick, making a call on behalf of someone who is searching for work, or conferring with a person who needs advice. If you don't schedule in kindness (such as, "Between two and two-thirty today, I'm devoting myself to helping others"), you are likely to forget to do it.

---

*Chaffetz Chayyim, *Michtivei ha-Chaffetz Chayyim he-Chadash,* vol. 2, II, page 85; cited in Shapiro, *Minyan,* 127–28.

Take out your calendar and examine your schedule for tomorrow. If you have nothing penciled in that will help another, why don't you do so now? And if your first tendency is to think, "Tomorrow looks too crowded; maybe I'll do it next week, or when I get over this busy period," then remember the words of Rabbi Nachman of Bratslav: "If you're not going to be better tomorrow than you were today, then what need have you for tomorrow?"

DAY

## 143     TUESDAY

# *Don't Be a Pious Fool*

Some years ago, at a party, I entered into a conversation with a Swiss woman. She soon started declaiming her view that there was no moral difference between the United States and the Soviet Union. At the time, the USSR was not only a totalitarian dictatorship but also an antisemitic regime that oppressed its Jewish citizens, provided support to foreign governments that sponsored international terrorism, and engaged in an unusually brutal war against the Afghan people. During our discussion, it also emerged that this woman was a religiously observant Jew.

One of the first thoughts that went through my head was that I had come across a personality type the Mishna describes as "a pious fool" (*Sotah* 3:4). Jewish writings offer several examples of such people; for example, one who refuses to stop his prayers while someone is drowning, or one "who sees a woman drowning in the river and says, 'It is not proper for me to look at her [immodestly attired] as I save her.'"

Rabbi Benjamin Blech has written, "To allow a human being to drown because you are busy telling God how much you care about Him and His world is the ultimate hypocrisy." * Jewish tradition would similarly regard as a "pious fool" one who engaged in pointless self-

---

* Blech, *Understanding Judaism,* 54.

destructive acts, such as a person whose life is endangered by fasting, but who nonetheless eats no food on Yom Kippur.

Similarly, this woman's willingness to bless God before eating bread while showing a stony heart to the victims of Soviet cruelties thrust her into the category of the *chasid shoteh,* a pious fool.

God wants us to respond to suffering by stopping, not ignoring, it. He wants us to fight evil, not deny it. And yet some religious people, Christians as well as Jews, ignore this obvious truth.

In 1982, when the Soviet Union was still, in President Reagan's famous and accurate words, "an evil empire," and there were religious Christians languishing in Soviet prison camps for practicing their faith, the Reverend Billy Graham visited Russian churches, where he told the parishioners that God "gives you the power to be a better worker, a more loyal citizen, because in Romans 13 we are told to obey the authorities." According to Graham, the government in power, even if evil, is entitled to its citizens' loyalty and hard work, while God is entitled to their faith and prayers.*

Any time you assume that what matters more to God is how you act toward Him than how you, or your government, treats human beings, you are acting like a "pious fool."** The matter could be serious (as in observing rituals while ignoring the evils perpetrated by a totalitarian regime) or relatively minor. Rabbi Israel Salanter once cautioned, "It is not uncommon for an energetic individual to rise in the middle of the night [to offer the *Selichot* prayers, recited at dawn in the weeks before the New Year] and make such noise in rising from the bed that he wakes the entire household....He is blissfully unaware that his loss outweighs his gain." (In other words, it would have been preferable had he been less "pious" and stayed in bed, thus not depriving other people of their sleep.***

---

*On the Reverend Graham's 1982 trip to the Soviet Union, see George Will, *The Morning After,* 368–69.

**I do wish to note that I have great respect for other activities of Reverend Graham, but specifically because of his great prominence, the gaffe he committed in the Soviet Union was magnified greatly. How must Christian opponents of communism in the Soviet Union have felt when America's most famous Christian instructed them that God wanted them to obey their evil authorities?

***Rabbi Israel Salanter's cautionary words are cited in Dov Katz, *T'nuat Ha-Musar (The Musar Movement),* vol. 1, 355.

God demands from us piety *and* goodness. Jewish ethics teaches that when your piety exceeds your goodness, God is not impressed. The world could do with more piety—but not with more pious fools.

## WEDNESDAY

# Don't Serve Liquor with an Overly Generous Hand

A common stereotype of Jews is that we are sober. An old Yiddish song is gracelessly titled "Shikker Is a Goy" ("[Only] a Gentile Is a Drunk").

Aside from this song's hostile stereotyping of gentiles, we now know that there are many Jews who drink excessively. An important way to help discourage such abuse is to make liquor less freely available. At many household celebrations, liquor flows freely, particularly at weddings and bar and bat mitzvah receptions. Aside from enticing those who have a predilection to become drunk to do so, such easy availability encourages many moderate drinkers to drink to excess.

A Torah law ordains "you shall not bring bloodguilt upon your house" (Deuteronomy 22:8). In its original context, the law mandates building a parapet for one's roof, so that a guest will not go up there— something that was commonly done in the ancient world—slip off, and die. More than fifteen hundred years ago, the Talmud established that the biblical rationale for erecting the parapet should be broadened to include prohibitions against housing a vicious dog or owning a rickety ladder, either of which can lead to injury or death (*Ketubot* 41b).

Perhaps the time has come to broaden this law again, to include not serving liquor with an overly free hand to guests at your house or party. It would seem to me that this verse also imposes upon parents the obligation to ensure that liquor is not consumed at parties involving their teenaged children. We know that almost half of the deaths due to automobile accidents in the United States (some twenty thousand fatalities a year) result from people driving after having drunk excessively.

Make sure that the legacy of a wedding, party, or any social occasion you host is deep pleasure and well-being among your guests, not "bloodguilt upon your house."

THURSDAY

## True Hospitality: Did You Ask Your Wife?

A famous talmudic passage teaches that "a woman is more apt to begrudge guests than a man" (*Bava Mezia* 87a). For understandable reasons, this passage, with its implication that women have stingier dispositions, is commonly regarded as misogynistic. Rabbi Berel Wein, who inspired me with the title and the idea for this entry, disagrees: "This is not a discriminatory remark, nor is it even a critical comment. It is an objective statement regarding the one who really bears the burden of hosting guests in the home." *

Throughout history, and in most homes today, the cleaning, cooking, and caring for guests falls mainly on the woman. It is unsurprising, therefore, that "a woman is more apt to begrudge [the] guests" whom her hospitable husband suddenly brings home. Wein does not regard a man who brings home surprise guests as a generous figure; rather, he is, in the words of a Yiddish expression, "a *tzaddik* (a righteous person) on someone else's shoulders." The first person to whom you owe consideration is your spouse.

For three thousand years, Abraham has been the model for Jewish hospitality. The Torah records how he invited travelers who apparently were Bedouins (he didn't know that they were angels; see Genesis, chap-

---

*Wein, *Second Thoughts*, 25–26.

ter 18, and Day 159) into his tent. Wein notes that what marks Abraham's hospitality as particularly impressive is that he shares *equally* with his wife, Sarah, in providing for the guests' needs. While Sarah is baking bread for them, he "runs to the cattle" to have the meat prepared, and arranges to bring his guests water and provide them with a place to rest. As Wein concludes: "Abraham is a full partner with Sarah not only in the joys and merit of hospitality, but in its preparation and menial work as well." That is why true hospitality requires a fair division of labor.

Before you invite a guest home, make sure that doing so is all right with your wife. Then, once the guest is there, make sure that the burdens, as well as the pleasures, of this wonderful mitzvah are shared by you both.

DAY

## 146    FRIDAY

# Don't Embarrass Your Guest, Don't Embarrass Your Children

Rabbi Akiva Eiger (1761–1837) was entertaining visitors at his Shabbat table when a guest accidentally knocked against the dining-room table and caused a cup filled with red wine to spill on the white linen tablecloth. Even before the mortified guest could react, Rabbi Eiger nudged the table with his leg and knocked over the wineglass in front of him. "Oh, there's something wrong with the table," he reassured the guest. "I had better get it fixed after Shabbat."

"Let your colleague's dignity be as dear to you as your own," a teaching from *Ethics of the Fathers* (2:13), obviously was internalized by this great rabbinic sage. Indeed, such sensitive considerations should be exhibited to our children as well. Rabbi Neil Kurshan recalls instances when his children have spilled drinks at the table. Unlike Rabbi Eiger, whose only concern was to spare his guest embarrassment, his instinct has been to turn on them and make accusations: "What is the matter with you? How can you be so clumsy? I have to wear these pants tonight. Don't you know that you can't get grape juice stains out of a tablecloth?"

Of course, such explosions don't help; the child feels badly as it is. How much better, Rabbi Kurshan notes, if when such things happened we would say, "'Don't worry. It was an accident. Let's clean it up together.' But on some nights, when life has been hectic or otherwise pressured, it's much easier to be angry than to be concerned about the feelings of a little child."*

A well-known Jewish vision of the afterlife describes it as a *yom she-koo-lo shabbat,* a day of everlasting Sabbath, a day in which, among other things, no guests or children are made to feel ashamed because of a minor accident they caused.

May you have a Shabbat Shalom!

DAY

## 147    SHABBAT

During the course of this Shabbat, try to review the material from the preceding six days, and use some of the texts studied as the basis for discussion during the Shabbat meals:

Day 141.  Helping Non-Jews
Day 142.  Schedule Kindness into Your Day
Day 143.  Don't Be a Pious Fool
Day 144.  Don't Serve Liquor with an Overly Generous Hand
Day 145.  True Hospitality: Did You Ask Your Wife?
Day 146.  Don't Embarrass Your Guest, Don't Embarrass
Your Children

Shabbat Shalom!

*Kurshan, *Raising Your Child to Be a Mensch,* 12.

SUNDAY

# *When You Suspect Spousal Abuse*

Physical abuse of wives by husbands (and, to a much smaller degree, the reverse) occurs in the Jewish community, as in all others. There is little precise data on this phenomenon because many people involved in such relationships are too ashamed or frightened to speak about it.

The biblical law "Do not stand by while your neighbor's blood is shed" (Leviticus 19:16) at the very least obligates one who suspects such abuse to try to counsel its victims. The following case, titled "Lea's Story: A Successful Intervention," and written by Shirley Lebovics, L.C.S.W., a psychotherapist and marriage counselor in Beverly Hills, California, was published in *Shalom Bayit: A Jewish Response to Child Abuse and Domestic Violence.* It describes how a rabbi helped a married twenty-three-year-old woman with two children, whom he had known since childhood, when he began to suspect that there was something seriously amiss in her marriage. The rabbi asked her to stop by his office, and when she mentioned some difficulties in her marriage, he encouraged her to elaborate:

> Lea was initially reticent. Throughout the conversation, she appeared to blame herself for the marital problems. The rabbi carefully interspersed questions to help him determine whether Lea had been a victim of abuse. For example, he asked:
>
> ◆ So, when the two of you have a bad fight, what usually happens?

- When Jacob is really angry, does he lose his temper? What does he do?
- Do you ever feel frightened of him?
- Is it hard for you to tell him what's on your mind or what you'd like?

At times, the rabbi made comments that helped Lea recognize her situation:

- It sounds like you are scared of upsetting him. What is it you think he might do?
- It sounds like when he blows up it feels like he's out of control, and you don't know what to expect.
- It sounds like you feel intimidated and can't speak to him openly.

Eventually, the rabbi learned that when Jacob got angry, he threw objects, slammed doors and yelled loudly....

The rabbi asked Lea if she had told her parents, in-laws, or friends about any of what he was hearing. [She hadn't.]

Knowing that control was a strong element in abusive relationships, the rabbi asked, "How does Jacob react if you want to go out with friends?" She stated that he insisted on knowing where she was, and disapproved of many friends with whom she liked spending time. He also never gave her any spending money to use as she wished.

Finally, confronting his strong suspicions, the rabbi asked Lea, "Has he ever slapped you, hit you, or threatened to hurt you physically?" He was told that on three occasions Lea had been slapped or pushed forcefully against a wall.

None of this information was easy for Lea to relay. At the end of the conversation, the rabbi remarked, "Lea, you may not realize this, but what you've experienced with Jacob is referred to as emotional and physical abuse. You are afraid of the man you are living with. And you have every reason to be, since his outbursts and his intimidating behaviors are very frightening things to be around. I'm extremely concerned about all of this. Conflicts and arguments may be normal in a marriage, but the way they are resolved cannot be through control and abuse."

Lea appeared shocked. She had never heard the term "abuse" in reference to marriages, let alone applied it to herself. She responded by saying tearfully, "I know I should be a better wife.... I can't help it, sometimes I just upset him and I don't mean to....I know I need to learn more how to stop getting him mad like that...."

Aware of the victim's tendency to assume responsibility for her partner's abusive behavior, the rabbi responded, "Lea, what I'm hearing you say is that you feel you provoke Jacob to be violent. Lea, whatever you may be doing, nothing justifies, excuses, or allows a man to be emotionally or physically abusive. Jacob obviously has difficulty controlling his anger. Furthermore, he has notions of his role as a husband that allow him to feel entitled to control you." *

The rabbi referred the woman to a therapist who specialized in family violence. At first she balked at going, fearing that such a meeting would enrage her husband. Eventually she saw the therapist seven times. At the time this article was written, both Lea and Jacob were in individual therapy. His treatment also included a group program aimed at teaching men how to control anger.

Although this entry has focused on the intervention of a rabbi, the questions he posed can be raised by any friend as well: "Do not stand by while your neighbor's blood is shed" (Leviticus 19:16) applies, of course, to all people.

In the final section of Lebovics' article (which will be discussed in tomorrow's entry), she analyzes six things the rabbi did that enabled him to intervene effectively, and that spared Lea from further abuse and possibly saved her life.

---

* *Resource Guide for Rabbis: On Domestic Violence,* "Lea's Story: A Successful Intervention," 61–65.

## An Abused Spouse: How You Can Help

Yesterday we discussed the case of a rabbi who suspected that a woman he knew was being abused by her husband, and how he helped her to acknowledge her situation. Shirley Lebovics, the social worker who wrote this case, has pinpointed six techniques the rabbi employed that helped the woman to speak and think clearly. These techniques can be of use to all of us who might find ourselves dealing with someone in an abusive relationship:

1. The rabbi trusted his instincts and followed through on his initial concerns without alarming Lea or ever telling her what to do. He never suggested she return home or stay there. He saw his role as raising her awareness and helping her realize she needed professional help.

2. The rabbi encouraged her to talk by

   ♦ Refraining from expressing shock, surprise, or disappointment.
   ♦ Using a tone of voice and language that was empathic and understanding (such as "That must be really hard for you," or "I imagine this story is very upsetting to you").
   ♦ Giving her his full attention and making her a priority, thus letting her know his concerns were sincere and that her distress deserved attention.
   ♦ Asking open-ended questions that would help her disclose as much as possible (such as, "Tell me more about that," or "What was that like for you?")

3. The rabbi did not attempt to hear Jacob's side of the story and decide who was at fault or telling the truth. Very often it can

become confusing when the husband explains how he is provoked. The listener may find himself feeling like an arbitrator or judge of who is the true victim in the relationship. When there are elements of fear and control in a relationship, it is unnecessary for the rabbi to try to determine who provokes whom. It is the abusive relationship that must be addressed.

4. The rabbi never minimized Lea's statements, and made sure to validate her feelings of fear. In this circumstance, Jacob was not in the city. Had he in fact been in town, it would still have been crucial to interview Lea alone. Women often cannot voice what is happening at home in the presence of their spouse and should not be expected to do so. Even when interviewed alone, women may tend to minimize their experiences because of their own self-blame and embarrassment.

5. The rabbi let Lea know he was not judging her or trying to determine who was at fault. Women sometimes feel that men (particularly rabbis) are their husbands' allies and will not understand their situation. They also often feel rabbis may disapprove of any initiation on the woman's part to separate.

6. Once aware that abuse was occurring in this marriage, the rabbi made an appropriate referral to a family violence counselor for Lea, rather than encouraging her to return home and continue seeing a marriage counselor with her husband. In cases of domestic violence, marriage counseling is inappropriate. It is important to keep in mind that abuse never "goes away" by itself. It may be tempting for a rabbi to hope that lecturing a batterer, or suggesting how his wife might avoid provoking her husband, will sufficiently address the problem. Keep in mind that these are ineffective interventions and that the safety of the victim is at stake.

Shirley Lebovics' guidelines for rabbis obviously apply to all of us who suspect that someone we know is being abused. And the biblical command "Do not stand by while your brother's [i.e., neighbor's] blood is shed" (Leviticus 19:16) obligates us to become involved.

TUESDAY

# Maimonides' Advice: How to Change Negative Behavior

The twelfth-century philosopher and rabbinic scholar Moses Maimonides (*Rambam*) believed that human beings should avoid extremes and pursue a *shvil hazahav,* a golden mean, in all their actions. For example, one should not dress in the most expensive garments every day, but neither should one dress in rags. One should give between ten and twenty percent of one's net income to charity, but one should not give more than twenty percent, either, thereby squandering one's resources (see Day 236). One should not subsist on a minimal diet, but neither should one accustom oneself to dining on the best foods and wines. One should not respond in anger to every insult and act of disrespect, but neither should one become like a corpse, totally indifferent to what people say *to* and *about* one (*Mishneh Torah,* "Laws of Character Development" 1:4).

But what if you already suffer from one of these negative characteristics? What if you are very stingy, or a gourmand, or too quick to become enraged? In such instances, Maimonides argues, merely making an effort to shift to the "golden mean" will be insufficient, since your natural tendency will be to revert to the negative characteristic. A commentary to Maimonides offers the following illustration: "If a bamboo cane is bent in one direction and you wish to straighten it, simply holding the cane straight is of no use, for it will spring back. You have to bend it in the opposite direction, and then it will straighten."

In practical terms, this means that the best hope for curing a bad trait is *temporarily* to go to the opposite extreme. If you are stingy, then, for the next two months, respond with some contribution to every charitable appeal directed to you, and write out checks for at least twice as much as you normally give to established charities in your community.

If your tendency is to walk by and ignore beggars on the street, then, during these coming months, give to them, and let your generous contributions be accompanied by gracious words such as "God bless you."

If you have become accustomed to eating at fancy restaurants and drinking very fine wines, then, over the coming two months, go to inexpensive restaurants, and drink much cheaper wines. At home, eat less expensive cuts of meat than you are used to eating.

If you have a quick temper, then do everything in your power to control it. In Maimonides' words: "We tell the wrathful man to train himself to feel no reaction even if he is…cursed" (*Mishneh Torah*, "Laws of Character Development" 2:2). One possible suggestion is to fine yourself when you lose your temper, and make the fine, which you then donate to charity, a sufficiently high sum to deter you from losing your temper (for a further discussion of how this method works, see Day 156). If even after you work on your temper, you see that you still cannot control it, then you are morally obligated to seek professional help; one who cannot control the expression of his rage inflicts massive emotional pain on those around him.

At the end of two months (Maimonides himself does not designate a specific length of time in which to engage in such behavior, other than to say that one should follow the new course of behavior "for a long time"), test the waters: see if you can become charitable without reverting to stinginess, eat good food without again becoming a gourmand, and express anger in moderation and proportionate to the provocation.

A temporary period of extremism can be the ticket to breaking bad personality and character traits, but the goal of such behavior is not to practice extreme behavior for the rest of your life; rather it is to lead one back to the "golden mean." *

Before you close the book, think for a moment: What negative traits do you have that might profit from a two-month excursion to the opposite extreme? If you cannot think of any, ask your spouse or a close friend if they have any suggestions for an area of your life that needs improvement. And remember, do not respond with anger and oversensitivity when they come up with one.

---

* See Jacobs, *Jewish Personal and Social Ethics,* 15–17.

# The Unending Obligation to Be Kind

Eighteen months before he died, my father suffered a stroke that left him partially paralyzed and often disoriented. Yet, though he suffered almost continuous pain, my father's sweetness of character remained unchanged. Until the end of his life, whoever came into his presence was greeted warmly, and whoever brought him something was always thanked.

In behaving as he did, my father, who was a deeply religious man, was acting as the Jewish tradition expects, for the obligation to be kind extends for all of one's life.* Thus, a few days before he died, Rabbi Simcha Zissel Ziv asked that all his clothes be washed. Some time earlier he had made it known that he was bequeathing his clothing to the poor, and he wished to make sure that they received clean garments.**

Dov Katz, author of a five-volume study of Rabbi Israel Salanter and the Musar movement he founded, tells a remarkable story about this great rabbi's final night:

> During the last year of Rabbi Israel Salanter's life, he was ill, and the Jewish community hired a guardian to accompany him. The guardian was a good-natured but simple man. Late one night, when Rabbi Salanter felt that his death was imminent, he spent the final moments of his life explaining to the guardian that he shouldn't fear, or be nervous about, being alone in a room with a corpse.***

---

*Obviously I don't wish to denigrate those whose bitterness is occasioned by extreme physical pain or who become highly irritable because of mental illness.

**The story is told in Himelstein, *Words of Wisdom, Words of Wit*, 104.

***The account of Rabbi Salanter's final night is contained in Katz, *T'nuat Ha-Musar* (*The Musar Movement*), vol. 1, 376.

These stories remind me of an observation made in *Man's Search for Meaning*, Viktor Frankl's account of his experiences in a Nazi concentration camp. In the hell of Auschwitz, Frankl was struck with the realization that human beings always retain some measure of free will: "We who lived in concentration camps can remember the men who walked through the huts comforting others, giving away their last piece of bread. They may have been few in number, but they offer sufficient proof that everything can be taken away from a man but one thing: the last of the human freedoms—to choose one's attitude in any given set of circumstances, to choose one's own way."

There are those who die in bitterness or with a curse on their lips, and there are people whose fineness of character and concern for others remains with them to the end.

DAY

## 152     THURSDAY

# "What's Hateful Unto You..."

Religious scholars often resist offering concise definitions of their faith's essence. Such reluctance is understandable. To one who has spent twenty, thirty, or more years studying a discipline or way of life, it seems unlikely that its essential truth can be reduced to a few sentences. Thus, some two thousand years ago, when a non-Jew approached Rabbi Shammai and asked him to define Judaism's essence while he stood on one foot, the irate rabbi picked up a builder's rod and chased the man away.

Undeterred, the non-Jew went next to Shammai's colleague, Rabbi Hillel.

Hillel not only treated the man gently, but also regarded the question as a fair one. He answered, "What's hateful unto you, don't do unto your neighbor. The rest is commentary. Now, go and study" (Babylonian Talmud, *Shabbat* 31a).

With this concise definition, Hillel established the Golden Rule as Judaism's essential teaching. With his insistence that the man "go and study," he underscored that knowing how to apply the Golden Rule to behavior can require years, perhaps a lifetime, of study.

The same page of Talmud records the story of two other would-be converts who approached Shammai and were chased away: One wished to accept the laws of the Torah, but not of the Oral Law (the teachings and laws of the Rabbis as offered in the Talmud).* Another wished to become a Jew on condition that he be appointed high priest. Both then came to Hillel. He converted them, then showed the first man, through logic, why Judaism is inexplicable without an Oral Law, and the second, through study, why the Torah would not permit a convert (or any Jew not born into a priestly family) to become a high priest.**

So which approach is correct, Shammai's refusal to "reduce" Judaism to an ethical essence, or Hillel's openness to doing so?

Let the Talmud have the final word: "Some time later, the three converts met in one place. They said: "Shammai's impatience sought to drive us from the world, but Hillel's gentleness brought us under the wings of the *Shechina* (divine presence)."

DAY

153    FRIDAY

# "Not Everything That Is Thought Should Be Said"

A man I know was speaking at a family celebration about his father, who had died many years earlier under tragic circum-

---

*This is comparable to a would-be citizen of the United States announcing that he accepts the validity of the American Constitution, but not of any of the Supreme Court decisions elaborating on it.

**Hillel's willingness, in all these instances, to encourage those interested and attracted to Judaism to convert, suggests an attitude of great openness to those wishing to become Jews.

stances. After he finished his poignant remarks, a friend said to him, "Your life is so good now. Appreciate it, and stop dwelling on the sad events of your past." This response both hurt and offended the man. While appreciative of the many things in his life that were now going well, he still suffered the pain of the early loss of his father.

Often, people who offer unsolicited criticism lack internal censoring devices. When a thought comes into their head, they express it, although the thought might well be painful, and not necessarily useful, to the recipient.

If you have the tendency to share unsolicited critical comments with people, try to be guided by Rabbi Israel Salanter's words: "Not everything that is thought should be said." Aware of how often people spread inappropriate information and unfair opinions, he added, "And not everything that is said should be repeated. And not everything that is repeated should be remembered."

Rabbi Salanter's advice applies with particular force to those who pride themselves on their supposedly keen sense of humor. Such people often get themselves into trouble, or cause pain to others, by making tasteless, if sometimes funny, jokes at inappropriate times. An old Yiddish witticism teaches, "Who is a hero? One who can suppress a wisecrack."

May you have a Shabbat Shalom!

DAY

## 154   SHABBAT

During the course of this Shabbat, try to review the material from the preceding six days, and use some of the texts studied as the basis for discussion during the Shabbat meals:

Day 148. When You Suspect Spousal Abuse
Day 149. An Abused Spouse: How You Can Help
Day 150. Maimonides' Advice: How to Change Negative Behavior
Day 151. The Unending Obligation to Be Kind

Day 152. "What's Hateful Unto You…"

Day 153. "Not Everything That Is Thought Should Be Said"

Shabbat Shalom!

# WEEK 23

DAY

155     S UNDAY

## *A Day of Kind Deeds*

On an airplane flight I took, a young woman was struggling with three small children. One was crying, another was running up and down the aisles, while the third was speaking very loudly. Needless to say, the mother found herself on the receiving end of angry looks and muttered comments. But then a middle-aged woman came over and offered to help. For the rest of the flight, this woman walked up and down the aisles quieting the crying baby, and enabling the beleaguered mother to calm and placate her other two children.

I was impressed by the woman's behavior and embarrassed that I had not gone over to help. And as I watched her carrying the baby, it occurred to me that all of us should periodically (once a week, once a month, or at least once a year) make performing deeds of kindness our number-one priority for twenty-four hours. Thus, if you are on a plane and you see someone struggling with a dilemma like the beleaguered mother, don't complain, or look away, but step over and help.

In New York City, where I live, there are constant opportunities to do kind acts. For one thing, the city is filled with old, frail people, some of whom return home from supermarkets with packages too heavy for them to carry. Offer to help. Similarly, at street corners, one frequently sees weak, elderly people standing nervously, afraid that while they are crossing the street a green light will turn to red. Be a Boy Scout and help them get across.

If you are more ambitious, there is much you can do. I know a woman who is well into her seventies and who lives in a residential building for older people on small incomes. Several times a week she bathes women residents older and weaker than herself, those in their late eighties and nineties.

Kindness is carried out through words as well as acts. Spend time with those who need someone with whom to commiserate or who might need your advice. Let them fully express their dilemma and don't "rush them."

And be especially kind to those who are closest to you, your family. Make a special effort not to snap at your children, and to play with them whatever game they want to play with you.

For twenty-four hours live the way you know in your heart God wants you to live all the time.

DAY

### 156    MONDAY

## An Expensive Technique for Overcoming Anger

I know a very wealthy man who became a religious Jew. He had a quick temper and cursed a lot, which seemed inconsistent with his otherwise pious behavior. A rabbi who had helped influence the man to become religious explained to me, "He's trying to cut down on his cursing. So we've made a deal. Every time he curses, he fines himself $180 and then donates the money to a Jewish cause. So far, he's donated tens of thousands of dollars."

This incident happened more than fifteen years ago, and I've fallen out of touch with the man. I don't know if the $180 fines helped him curb his cursing, but I suspect they did.

If they didn't, perhaps $180 was an insufficient disincentive to stop him from engaging in what had become a deeply ingrained habit.

But the technique is an old and sound one.

A medieval moralistic Jewish text known as *Reishit Chochmah* (*The Beginning of Wisdom*) suggests a similar teaching to those who can't seem to control their anger: "Decide on a sum of money that you will give away if you allow yourself to lose your temper. Be sure that the amount you designate is sufficient to force you to think twice before you lose your temper."

If you are making an effort to control your temper, do this: Over the next week or month, every time you express anger that is disproportionate to the provocation, make a donation to charity. As *Reishit Chochmah* notes, the sum has to be enough to inhibit you, and should be over and above the amount of charity you would otherwise give; in other words, it must act as a fine.*

If this technique doesn't work, here's another suggestion: Give the money to a cause you otherwise would not support.** If you are an Orthodox Jew, give it to a Reform or Conservative institution; if you are Reform or Conservative, donate your money to an Orthodox one. You might not be happy to send money to a cause of which you disapprove (this alone could cause you to exert greater control over your temper), but at least your anger will then do something for the cause of Jewish unity.

If you find this technique too expensive for your liking, do nothing at all to curb your temper. In the course of a few years, this approach will not cost you any money—but it might cost you your friends, your spouse, and your relationship with your children.

It is worth thinking about *Reishit Chochmah*'s suggestion. It might cost you a lot of money, but in the long run it's cheap.

---

*The suggestion of *Reishit Chochmah* is cited in the ArtScroll edition of Nachmanides, *A Letter for the Ages* (*Iggeret HaRamban*), 30–31.
**Psychologist Solomon Schimmel suggests such a technique in his book, *The Seven Deadly Sins*, 105.

# When You're Angry at Your Spouse: Putting Things into Perspective

Alfred Lunt and Lynn Fontanne, one of the most famous theatrical acting couples in history, were married for over fifty years. An interviewer once asked Ms. Fontanne if she had ever considered divorcing, and she responded, "Divorce, never; murder, often."

This jocular response reflects a painful truth. Married couples, even those deeply in love, often irritate each other, and frequently find themselves expressing anger that is excessive and unfair. Minor issues that should provoke annoyance at most sometimes impel intense outbursts, during which cruel comments are made, and painful incidents from the past are recalled.

On other occasions, when one partner is in pain, the other responds unfairly. We find one such incident in the Bible. Jacob loved his wife Rachel deeply. However, when she complained to him bitterly of her childlessness, "Give me children or I shall die" (Genesis 30:1), he did not hold her in his arms, or tell her how much he loved her, whether she had children or not. Instead, he responded with words that could only intensify her pain: "Can I take the place of God who has denied you fruit of the womb?" (Genesis 30:2).

Some time later, Rachel gave birth to Joseph; still later, she died while giving birth to Benjamin. I wonder how often Jacob thought back to the cruel words he had said to Rachel in a moment of anger, and how much he regretted them when it was too late to take them back.

Anger often emanates from one of the least admirable human qualities, pettiness. There are times when anything our spouse does gets on our nerves. While in petty moods (and for some people, these can last for days or months), we may well exaggerate our spouse's bad qualities, while minimizing or taking for granted his or her good ones.

I am writing these words a week after a Swissair plane crashed in the Atlantic Ocean, killing over two hundred people. It was subsequently revealed that the plane's passengers had learned some six minutes before the plane went down that it was going to crash. My wife said to me that she was wondering what the couples on the airplane must have said and done during those final terrible moments. Of one thing she was certain: "Nobody said, 'I really can't stand the way you always left your clothes on the floor,' or 'I hated the way you were so careless about your spending.'"

That plane must have been filled with people making statements of eternal love, of couples expressing to one another the hope that they would be reunited in heaven or on earth, and with requests of forgiveness for betrayals and cruel words that had been said. Those last moments, for all their terror (God willing, may no one ever again have to bear such terror), must also have been moments of great beauty.

Shouldn't we think about that the next time we're about to "blow up" at our spouse for not taking out the garbage?

WEDNESDAY

## Treating Your Employees with Respect

Every once in a while, someone tells me a story that makes me ashamed of being human—not stories of Nazi horrors, but of the little indecencies and humiliations human beings inflict on one another. Thus, a nanny was telling me recently about a friend who worked for a wealthy family on New York's Upper East Side, whose duties included preparing the children's dinner. However, the nanny was not permitted to eat the food she prepared for the children; her employers set aside cheaper food for her.

The Talmud understands Deuteronomy 23:25 ("When you come into your neighbor's vineyard, you may eat grapes until you are satisfied...")

as mandating that a worker engaged in harvesting an employer's crop has the right to eat as much as he wants while he is working* (employees, however, do not have the right to take food home with them).

Compassionate and morally obvious as this law sounds, it is frequently violated even by people who probably claim to believe that the Bible's teachings are true. Rabbi Joseph Hertz, in his well-known Torah commentary, tells of a wealthy Italian landowner who, when he harvested his grapes, "fastened iron muzzles to his miserable, fever-stricken workmen, so that it might not occur to these poor peasants, working for starvation wages under the glowing sun of southern Italy, to satiate their burning thirst and their gnawing hunger with a few of the millions of grapes of the owner."**

If you trust a person enough to care for those who are most precious to you, your children, care for them enough to let them eat the food you offer your children and yourself.

DAY

159    THURSDAY

## Abraham, the Model of Hospitality

Although the Bible doesn't tell us very many details about Abraham's life, Genesis 18 makes it clear that he was an exemplary host whose behavior still has much to teach us about how to act toward guests.

---

*Another Torah verse (Deuteronomy 25:4) gives the same right even to animals: "You shall not muzzle the ox when he treads the corn."

**Hertz, *The Pentateuch and Haftorahs*, 854. Even when Jewish law, basing itself on the Torah, allowed for a form of indentured servitude (such servitude was imposed for a maximum of six years upon Israelites who had stolen and could not repay the value of the theft, or upon those who sold themselves to pay off their debts), the Talmud legislated that such workers be treated more than fairly. Thus, basing itself on the biblical verse that "your brother shall live well with you," the Talmud ruled that if a master slept on a bed with pillows, his slave had to be given an equally comfortable bed, and if the master had but one pillow, he had to give it to the slave (*Tosafot* on *Kiddushin* 20a). A master was also required to feed his servants before himself (Maimonides, *Mishneh Torah*, "Laws of Servants," 9:8).

It was a hot day in ancient Canaan, and Abraham was sitting at the entrance to his tent. Since the previous chapter reported that the elderly Abraham had just been circumcised (17:24), he might well have been recuperating. Yet, as soon as he sees three men walking in his direction, Abraham stands up and runs to them. When he reaches them, he bows respectfully and pleads with them to be his guests.

Abraham offers the men water to wash with, a loaf of bread to eat, and a shady spot to rest. When the guests accept his invitation, Abraham hurries to the tent to ask his wife Sarah to prepare some cakes; then he goes to the youth tending his cattle, and arranges with him to slaughter and prepare a calf. As soon as he can, Abraham brings the food to his guests, and attends to their needs while they eat.

The first thing we learn from Abraham is graciousness (he makes it clear to the strangers that he will feel *honored* if they accept his invitation): "My lords, if I find favor in your eyes, please don't pass your servant by."

Abraham is also intent on supplying the travelers immediately with all that they need. Indeed, the action that recurs most often in this biblical account is rushing. Abraham *rushes* to greet the men, *rushes* over to Sarah and his servant and asks them to work *quickly* to prepare the food. He is also the most attentive of hosts, standing by his guests as they eat, so that he can quickly provide for all their needs.

Finally, Abraham delivers more than he promises. "I will fetch a loaf of bread that you may sustain yourselves," is what he initially tells his guests, but he soon provides them with cream and milk, followed by a sumptuous feast of meat from a tender calf and cakes. Jewish tradition learns from Abraham's behavior: "The righteous say little and do much" (Babylonian Talmud, *Bava Mezia* 87a).

For thousands of years, Abraham has been the role model for Jews who wish to practice the mitzvah of hospitality (*hachnasat orchim*).* He actively seeks out guests, rushes to meet their needs, and gives even more than he has promised. Who wouldn't want to be entertained by such a host?

* See also Day 145.

## There Is No Such Thing as a Free Lunch

A nineteenth-century story tells of two Eastern European rabbis who were traveling together and ate a meal at an inn owned by a pious widow. While eating, one rabbi engaged in a long, detailed conversation with the rather talkative woman; the other sat quietly and, when not eating, turned his attention to a holy text he was studying.

When they rose to leave, the widow refused to let the rabbis pay for the meal. Outside, the more convivial of the two turned to his friend, commenting, "It seems to me that you are guilty of stealing a meal from that woman."

His friend looked up in astonishment. "She herself told us that we didn't have to pay."

"She didn't want us to pay money," the first rabbi answered. "But the payment she wanted was that we listen and talk to her. This you didn't do."

Guests, not just hosts, have ethical obligations. For example, Jewish tradition teaches that during the *Birkat Hamazon* (the blessings after the meal), guests are to invoke a special blessing for the family that has hosted them.* And as the above story reminds us, they have obligations to be considerate and polite, and to bring pleasure to the person who is hosting them. Guests should therefore express gratitude for what they are served, make efforts to be sociable (and not sit at the table quiet and withdrawn), and, as every parent knows, a guest brings great joy to his or her hosts by finding things about the family's children to compliment.

Jewish law inserts one additional, surprising obligation on a guest. If he has been treated with truly generous hospitality, the guest should *not*

---

* "May the merciful One bless the master of this house, the mistress of this house, both them and their family, and all that they have."

go about praising his hosts to many people; lavish praise might cause others to descend on the host family and exploit their generosity.

But most of all, engage your hosts. If they need to speak, lend them your ear.

May you have a Shabbat Shalom!

SHABBAT

During the course of this Shabbat, try to review the material from the preceding six days, and use some of the texts studied as the basis for discussion during the Shabbat meals:

Day 155. A Day of Kind Deeds
Day 156. An Expensive Technique for Overcoming Anger
Day 157. When You're Angry at Your Spouse: Putting Things into Perspective
Day 158. Treating Your Employees with Respect
Day 159. Abraham, the Model of Hospitality
Day 160. There Is No Such Thing as a Free Lunch

Shabbat Shalom!

# WEEK 24

162     SUNDAY

## How Fear of God Can Make You a Better Person (1)

Most of us associate "fear of God" with hellfire-and-brimstone religious traditions. For example, some people believe that if they disobey any one of God's commandments, or have incorrect theological beliefs, the Lord will impose horrifying and possibly eternal punishments upon them.

Although I find such teachings abhorrent, the Torah does several times specifically enjoin, "And you shall fear God" (see, for example, Leviticus 19:14). However, a study of the verses in which this term is used suggests that two benefits can accrue from fear of God, neither of which has to do with eternal damnation, or with living in a state of permanent terror.

First, such fear can be liberating. Most of us are intimidated by some other people; in nondemocratic societies, almost everyone fears government officials. Exodus' opening chapter tells of Pharaoh's order to the two midwives working with the Israelites to murder all newborn male babies at birth. However, the women disobey Pharaoh's command and save the children. What motivates their disobedience? "The midwives, fearing God, did not do as the king of Egypt had told them" (Exodus 1:17); in other words, they feared God more than they did Pharaoh. The other Egyptians only feared Pharaoh, which is why they, unlike the midwives, followed his subsequent order to hunt down and drown the Israelite infants.

This story is the first instance in any recorded literature of an act of civil disobedience, and as such it establishes a pattern that has been observed ever since. Throughout history, a disproportionate percentage of dissenters in authoritarian and totalitarian societies have been religious. Like others, these people fear their country's leaders and their ability to punish, torture, and kill them. But they fear God and His moral law even more, which is what liberates them to resist evil.

In a democratic society such as we have in the United States, where people have no reason to fear that their leaders will imprison or kill them,* citizens have an even greater responsibility not to permit themselves to be deterred from doing what is right by fear.

We should all bear in mind the midwives' story during times when we see an authority figure acting unfairly; like the midwives, we should try to thwart him or her. For example, if our boss is unfair to a fellow employee and, even worse, wants us to join with him in his unfair behavior, we're forbidden to do so. Perhaps we fear our boss, but we're instructed to fear God even more.

Yes, fear of God can be very liberating.

A second way in which fear of God can make you a better person is discussed in tomorrow's entry.

MONDAY

## *How Fear of God Can Make You a Better Person (2)*

Few of us are saints; many if not most of us are aptly characterized in an early biblical assessment of human nature: "The tendency of man's heart is toward evil from his youth" (Genesis 8:21). This verse helps explain why many people act immorally or unfairly when

---

*I once asked Elie Wiesel if he had been fearful before he criticized then President Reagan at a White House ceremony over the president's forthcoming 1985 visit to a Nazi cemetery in Bitburg. Wiesel answered that he hadn't been afraid: "What could the president do to me?" he said. However, Wiesel did note that, having grown up in a European town where the police were often bullies and antisemites, he still had a fear of policemen.

they are confident that they won't get caught, or when dealing with people weaker than themselves.

The Torah, understanding the strong human proclivity for evil, legislates, "You shall not curse the deaf or place a stumbling block in front of a blind person; you shall fear your God" (Leviticus 19:14). Why does the Torah append the words "you shall fear your God"? Obviously, even a brazen person would be cautious before tripping another, if only out of fear that the tripped person would exact revenge, or would send a stronger relative or friend to do so. But one who trips a blind person seems to have nothing to fear, because the victim will not know who hurt him.*

It is specifically when we are dealing with those weaker than ourselves that the Torah reminds us to fear God:

- ◆ "You shall honor the old and you shall fear God" (Leviticus 19:32).
- ◆ "Take no interest [from one who has become impoverished], but you shall fear God" (Leviticus 25:36).
- ◆ "You shall not rule over [your servant] ruthlessly, but you shall fear God" (Leviticus 25:43).

The last commandment serves to remind us that throughout history many people have mistreated their servants, certain that there was little if anything their underlings could do about it. Specifically because masters have no reason to fear servants, the Bible reminds them to fear God.

Fear of God means having a sense, an understanding that you are accountable to more than yourself, that you must not experience yourself as all-powerful. That is why "fear of God" in the Torah is mentioned in the context of unequal power relations. Therefore, whenever you are dealing with a person in a weaker position than yourself—an employee in the workplace, a nanny, a handyman, a cleaning woman—and are tempted to take advantage of your stronger position, remember, "And you shall fear God."

*The Rabbis broadened this law to prohibit giving another advice intended to benefit oneself (see Day 113), understanding this verse as prohibiting taking advantage of one who is "blind" in the matter at hand. In such cases it would be impossible for a court of law to prove that the person giving the advice knew it was wrong. Thus, the verse reminds us to fear God, who knows whether our intentions were honorable or dishonorable.

TUESDAY

# Express Gratitude to Your Parents

A friend of mine long harbored resentments toward his parents. "They never tried to understand who I really was," he told me, "and, worst of all, they ignored me. They just didn't spend time with me."

Years later, when he married and had a child, his attitude softened: "The fact that I survived my infancy with all my limbs and fingers intact is testament to how carefully my parents must have watched over me."

My friend's own parenting experiences made him realize how often even his parents must have risen from a deep sleep in the middle of the night to calm and feed him. As I once heard a woman explain: "Only when I became a mother did I realize how much my own mother loved me."

Such parental efforts merit gratitude. As the classic thirteenth-century *Sefer Hachinnuch,* a Hebrew volume that lists and explains the Torah's 613 commandments, explains (Commandment 33): "The root of this commandment [to honor your father and mother] is that one should recognize and do acts of kindness to those who have done good to him." The author writes that a child who does not act kindly toward his parents is an ingrate, "and this is an evil and despised trait."

A century ago, Oscar Wilde wrote, "Children begin by loving their parents; after a time they judge them; rarely, if ever, do they forgive them." In contrast to Wilde's cynicism, the Jewish tradition reminds us that even if we go through a period of alienation from our parents, we are still bound to honor them (see Day 242), and to show gratitude as well.

How should this gratitude be expressed? The most obvious way is verbally, through statements of love, affection, gratefulness, and appreciation. But the Talmud, speaking in a different context, also teaches the concept of "measure for measure"; thus, gratitude should be expressed in the same manner in which the deeds evoking the gratitude were performed. For example, if, during a bleak financial period in your life, a friend loaned you money, "measure for measure" dictates that when that friend needs money, you extend a loan to him. Similarly, your parents spent much time caring for you when you were young, and time is the most precious of all commodities. So, too, must you spend time with them and on their needs as they grow older and require assistance.

It does not have to be the same amount of time that your parents spent on you. Nonetheless, it is important to visit your parents often, if possible, to let them share in the joy of seeing and playing with your children, their grandchildren, and to speak to them on the phone frequently (particularly when one parent becomes widowed). Over the course of several years, I learned that two of the rabbis who most influenced my own development spoke to their widowed mothers every day. Both of these men are among the busiest people I know, yet they made sure to find the time for their mothers.

A suggestion: In addition to other conversations you have with them over the coming month, call your parents every Friday before Shabbat.

DAY

165    WEDNESDAY

## *When Your Mate and Your Parents Are in Conflict*

Jewish law places extraordinary emphasis on filial devotion; indeed, "Honor your father and mother" is perhaps the best known of the Ten Commandments. But if your spouse and parents do not get along (I am referring here to a clash of personalities, not a case of actual mistreatment), Jewish ethics insists that your primary loyalty must be to your spouse. It roots this obligation in the first biblical verse that speaks of marriage: "Therefore shall a man leave his father and mother and cling to his wife, so that they become one flesh" (Genesis 2:24).

Marriage means that one leaves one's parents' home to set up a new one. And your spouse is entitled to know that your first (but not exclusive) loyalty is to the home he or she has created with you.

Thus, if a dispute erupts between your spouse and your parents, even if you disagree with your spouse, you should avoid arguing in your parents' presence. Better that you speak privately with your husband or wife, and explain the reasons for your feelings; otherwise he or she might conclude that you care more for your parents than for him or her.

Similarly, it is probably imprudent to share with your parents dissatisfactions that you have with your spouse. Speak to your husband or wife about areas in which you feel unhappy, talk with a therapist and/or a close friend, but be very cautious before you go to your parents and express these feelings. For one thing, they probably are not the best people to advise you; while helpful advice generally is offered by those who can assess you objectively, few parents can be objective when their own children's interests are involved. For another, those personality traits of yours that might be contributing to your tensions with your spouse might well be traits that one or the other of your parents has; yet another reason that it will be hard for a parent to assess the situation objectively.

A series of rabbinic responsa have established that you should not allow a parent to move into your house against your spouse's wishes. These rulings were written during periods when Jewish law was often biased toward males, and the person opposing the move was the daughter-in-law.

The message for parents? Be careful before you intervene in your child's marriage, or offer critical insights about your son- or daughter-in law. As an old Jewish proverb teaches, "Every mother-in-law should remember that she was once a daughter-in-law."

# "From a Child Is Beautiful, Anything"

Allen Sherman, the comic songwriter best known for "Hello Muddah, Hello Faddah" was once in the middle of an intense conversation with his wife when his young son entered to show off a drawing he had just finished. The childish scrawls were quickly dismissed by Sherman, who was annoyed at having his conversation interrupted. The boy, hurt by his father's rejection of the picture, threw it down on the floor, rushed up to his room, and slammed the door.

The slamming door reminded the now abashed Sherman of a door that he had slammed twenty-five years earlier. One morning he had heard his Yiddish-speaking grandmother announce that she needed a "football" for a large party she would be hosting that evening. Although the young Sherman wondered why his grandmother needed a football, he was determined to procure one for her. He went around his neighborhood and finally found one boy, a bully who punched him in the nose before agreeing to give over his football in exchange for Sherman's best toys.

Sherman took the football home, polished it till it shone, and left it for his grandmother. His mother saw the football first, and became upset with him for leaving his toys around. When he explained that it was for his grandmother's party, his mother burst into laughter: "A *football* for the party? Don't you understand your own grandma? Not a football, *fruit bowl*. Grandma needs a fruit bowl for the party."

The embarrassed boy ran up to his room, slammed the door, and refused to come down to the party. But a little later his mother came up to fetch him. When she brought him downstairs, he saw his grandmother proudly walking around the room with a large bowl filled with a variety of beautiful fruits and, in the middle, the polished football he had brought home. When a guest asked his grandmother to explain what a football was doing in the middle of her fruit bowl, she told him about the gift from her grandson and added, "From a child is beautiful, anything." *

Over the years, several friends have told me of gifts they brought their parents that were greeted with halfhearted enthusiasm and sometimes with none at all. That they related these events as adults indicates how much these childhood memories still rankled.

Children deserve better; they deserve to have adults who understand, as did Allen Sherman's grandmother, that "from a child is beautiful, anything."

DAY

## 167 FRIDAY

# "This Is the Most Delicious Muffin I Have Ever Tasted"

*Ben Zoma once saw a crowd on the steps of the Temple Mount. He said...*"Blessed is He who has created all these people to serve me." For he used to say, *"What labors did Adam have to carry out before he obtained bread to eat? He plowed, he sowed, he reaped, he bound the sheaves, threshed the grain, winnowed the chaff, selected the ears, ground them, sifted the flour, kneaded the dough, and baked. And only then did he eat. Whereas I get up and find all these things done for me. And how many labors did Adam have to carry out before he obtained a garment to wear? He had to shear the sheep, wash the wool, comb it, spin, weave it, and only then did he have a garment to wear. Whereas I get up and find all these things done for me. All kinds of craftsmen come to the door of my house, and when I rise in the morning, I find all these things ready for me.*

—Babylonian Talmud, *Berachot* 58a

---

* Allen Sherman, "A Gift of Laughter," in Jay David, ed., *Growing Up Jewish,* 63–66.

Clearly, Rabbi Ben Zoma specialized in the mitzvah of expressing gratitude (*hakarat hatov*). Thus, viewing an enormous crowd of people, the sort of sight that provokes some to misanthropic observations ("a herd of sheep," "a mindless mob"), inspired gratitude in Ben Zoma. Not just gratitude, but *creative* thanksgiving. He did not say, "Look at these people, each one of them created in God's image." Though such a statement would be true, it would not necessarily inspire in him a personal reaction to each person in the crowd. Instead, Ben Zoma conjured up how many of the people in the faceless group helped him in his daily life, preparing his food and garments, and thereby enabling him to devote himself to his passion, a life of Torah.

Mendel Sternhull, a man who spent much time with Rabbi Shlomo Carlebach, used to speak of his ability to compliment and express gratitude...even for a muffin.

On one occasion Sternhull sat with Reb Shlomo in a dingy restaurant, presided over by a sour-looking proprietress and waitress. The woman was unusually homely, and unpleasant as well. Sternhull was happy when she put down their breakfast order and returned to the counter. But after taking one bite of the muffin she had brought him, Reb Shlomo summoned her back. "My most beautiful friend," he said to her gently, "are you by any chance the person who baked this muffin?"

"Yeah, I am, what about it?"

"I just want you to know that this is the most delicious muffin I have ever tasted in my life."

The woman gave a hint of a smile, thanked him, and started to walk away.

"And I also want you to know," Reb Shlomo continued, "that I have eaten muffins all over the world, but none came close to this one."

Again, the woman thanked him, but Reb Shlomo still was not finished. "And *mamesh* (truly), I have to thank you because I was so hungry, and you did me the greatest favor in the world by so expertly baking this muffin, which is surely a taste of the World-to-Come."

By now the woman was smiling broadly: "Well, gee, thanks a lot. It's very nice of you to say so. Most people never comment when the food is good; you only hear from them when they have a complaint."

Reb Shlomo went on to ask the woman about the special ingredients she used in preparing the muffin, and listened attentively. He was specific with his compliments as well, commenting on the muffin's airy texture, its buttery and fragrant quality. Sternhull recalls that he was watching Reb Shlomo's paean to a muffin with a mixture of amazement and amusement, until he gazed at the woman: "I was taken aback. The homely woman was no more. A few minutes with Shlomo had done the trick. She was transformed. She had become beautiful."

"From Shlomo I learned many things," Sternhull later recalled, "but foremost among them was *hakarat hatov* (acknowledging the good another has done for you) and how to give compliments. And maybe one day, if I really work hard at my growth…I'll also be able to acquire Shlomo's blessed ability—to sing hymns to muffins and make people beautiful." *

This Shabbat and this week pick one thing each day to examine à la Reb Shlomo; it could be a dish your spouse cooked, your child's artwork, a piece of work by an employee. Learn from the master, Shlomo Carlebach, how to offer praise.

And may you have a Shabbat Shalom!


DAY

## 168    SHABBAT

During the course of this Shabbat, try to review the material from the preceding six days, and use some of the texts studied as the basis for discussion during the Shabbat meals:

Day 162.  How Fear of God Can Make You a Better Person (1)
Day 163.  How Fear of God Can Make You a Better Person (2)
Day 164.  Express Gratitude to Your Parents

* Halberstam, *Holy Brother*, 138–39.

Day 165. When Your Mate and Your Parents Are in Conflict

Day 166. "From a Child Is Beautiful, Anything"

Day 167. "This Is the Most Delicious Muffin I Have Ever Tasted"

Shabbat Shalom!

# WEEK 25

DAY

## 169   SUNDAY

## *When You Hear That Someone Is Taking a Long Trip, Make Sure That They Take Along Some Extra Money*

The Talmud teaches that God protects those who are on a journey to do good: "Emissaries on their way to do a mitzvah will never come to harm" (*Pesachim* 8b). Based on this teaching, the custom developed among religious Jews that when someone departed for a long, particularly a dangerous, trip, relatives and friends would give him or her money to distribute as charity at the traveler's destination.

This charitable donation elevated the trip from merely a business journey or a pleasure jaunt into an opportunity to carry out the important mitzvah of charity. Jews refer to such funds as *shaliach mitzvah gelt*, or "money for an emissary to do good."

My father took this custom seriously. Whenever I departed for Israel or any other overseas trip, he gave me eighteen dollars to distribute to beggars, or for any other worthwhile cause I encountered. Upon arriving in Israel, my most frequent destination, one of my first stops would be at the Western Wall; there I would find beggars or other poor people to whom I would distribute the money.

It is considered particularly meritorious to give money to people embarking on a dangerous trip. Thus, in the late 1960s, when the saintly Reb Aryeh Levine sent a contribution to Magen David Adom (the Israeli equivalent of the Red Cross) to purchase food to be distributed to the starving citizens of the besieged African region of Biafra, the head of Magen David Adom told the representative he was dispatching there: "Here is Reb Aryeh's contribution....You know what the Sages say, that emissaries on their way to do a mitzvah will never come to harm."

The next time you hear of someone going on an overseas trip, give him or her money to dispense as charity. In addition to the good this money will do for the recipient, this gift will also change the nature of the trip for the traveler. Whether her trip is for business or pleasure, she will find, upon arriving at her destination, that she has to think for several minutes about whom she should donate her charitable funds to; then she will spend the extra minute or two disbursing them.

Can you think of a more beautiful way to help another person start a business or pleasure trip?

DAY

170    MONDAY

## *Steady Giving*

A charitable person does not wait to be asked to give; he knows that there are those in need whether or not a formal request has been addressed to him. That is why Jewish law and tradition encourage one to give repeatedly: "It is good to give charity before praying" (*Shulchan Aruch, Orach Chayyim* 92:10).

To fulfill this suggestion, many synagogues have a *pushke* (charity box) passed around during the weekday service (Jewish law prohibits handling money on the Sabbath and most holidays); participants are expected to contribute, even if it is just a small amount.

A talmudic teaching suggests a special type of donation prior to fast days such as Yom Kippur: "The merit of fasting is the charity [dispensed]" *(Berachot 6b)*.

Many people find the Yom Kippur fast very difficult. Over the years I have heard some people claim that they feel so hungry during the course of the day that they find it difficult to focus on praying. If the pangs of hunger can be so painful, then let something good emerge from them: Let them remind us that there are people who feel such hunger hundreds of days a year. The sixteenth-century Maharsha (Rabbi Solomon Elazar Eideles) notes that this talmudic passage served as the basis for an old Jewish custom; prior to a fast, people would dispense as charity the amount of money they would be saving on food that day.

Unfortunately, this custom is less widely known among modern Jews, and should be revived. Before Yom Kippur or Tisha Be'Av* this year, figure out how much your family spends weekly on food and divide the sum by seven, and send that amount to a charity that feeds the hungry. Indeed, in the *Haftorah* (prophetic reading) read on Yom Kippur, Isaiah cites God as declaring, "This is the fast I desire...to share your bread with the hungry" (Isaiah 58:6–7; obviously, the food is meant to be shared either before or after the fast).

On Yom Kippur, God has commanded us not to eat. But we can learn from the hunger we feel on this very special day to do what we can to help others to eat. For this is a divine command as well.**

---

*The fast day that commemorates the destruction of both the First and Second Temples; it falls on the ninth of the month of Av (usually between mid-July and early August). While Jewish tradition legislates several half-day fasts (from morning till night), Tisha Be'Av and Yom Kippur are the only two full fast days; they last from sundown to the next day's nightfall.

**Many synagogues participate in "Project Isaiah," in which food is collected before the Kol Nidre service on Yom Kippur eve and donated to the poor. An organization founded by Leonard Fein, Mazon, urges Jews to donate three percent of the cost of a bar mitzvah or bat mitzvah, wedding, or other celebration to feed the hungry.

T U E S D A Y

# *Prevention of Cruelty to Animals: What the Torah Says*

Which of the Ten Commandments deals in part with animals?

If you do not come up with the answer, don't feel bad, most people don't. The Fourth Commandment, which legislates the Sabbath, ordains that on that day "you shall not do any work—you, your son and daughter, your male and female slave, *and your cattle...*" (Exodus 20:9).

This is one of several Torah laws that legislate the humane treatment of animals. Deuteronomy 25:4 rules, "You shall not muzzle an ox while it is threshing," for it is cruel to do so to an animal that is working in the presence of food. And just as another Torah law permits one who is working in a field to eat while he is working (but forbids the employee from carrying away any food; see Deuteronomy 23:25–26 and the Babylonian Talmud, *Bava Mezia* 87b), so does the Torah grant animals the same right.

Deuteronomy 22:10 forbids harnessing two animals of unequal strength (e.g., an ox and a donkey) in a field, for one will suffer frustration, the other strain.

The legal term for the Jewish laws that protect animals from suffering is *tza'ar ba'alei chayyim*, the prevention of cruelty to animals.

Because Jewish law regards human beings as superior to animals (unlike animals, people are created in God's image), it permits people to eat them. Still, the laws of kosher slaughter (*shechitah*) mandate killing them as quickly as possible. If there is any nick in the slaughterer's knife or delay in the act of killing, the animal is rendered unkosher, its meat forbidden. Thus, those who slaughter animals have an economic as well as a religious incentive to kill animals as painlessly as possible.

Perhaps the cruelest act that a parent can endure is to see his or her children being killed. The Babylonian king Nebuchadnezzar, the biblical archetype of a sadist, was so enraged at King Zedekiah for leading a revolt against him that after he captured the king, he murdered Zedekiah's two sons in his presence, then blinded him, so that the death of his sons would be the last thing Zedekiah would ever see (II Kings 25:7). In more recent times, the Nazis often delighted in murdering Jewish children in the presence of their parents.

A Torah law prohibits treating animals in the way that people like Nebuchadnezzar and the Nazis treated human beings: Thus, Deuteronomy 22:6 rules that if a person comes across a nest of birds, he cannot take the mother bird with the young, but must send the mother away to spare her feelings. Concerning the rationale for this law, Maimonides writes, "for the pain of the animals under such circumstances is very great" (*Guide to the Perplexed* 3:48).

Though these laws were intended to protect animals from cruelty, they were equally intended to discourage human beings from acting cruelly. Biblical and rabbinic law understood that a person who acts cruelly to animals will act similarly toward human beings. That is yet another reason why it is so important for parents who see a child tormenting a cat, or tearing apart an insect, to stop the child firmly, and to impress upon him or her the Jewish laws mandating the kind treatment of animals.

Kindness to animals is so important that it is regarded as a hallmark of a good person. "A righteous person knows the soul [alternatively "the needs"] of his animal" (Proverbs 12:10).

A thought: If you have a pet, give it an extra treat once a week; make the Shabbat special for your pet, too.

D A Y

172

W E D N E S D A Y

## Can Veal Be Kosher?

Numerous Jewish laws (see yesterday's entry) regulate the kind treatment of animals. For example, one must feed an animal before one feeds oneself, and one must permit an animal to eat of the food in the field in which it is working. And when it comes time to slaughter an animal that one intends to eat, one must do so in as rapid and painless a manner as possible.

However, the raising of veal throughout most of the world does not, in my view, conform to the biblical and rabbinic laws protecting animals from unnecessary suffering. Until recently the conditions have been truly horrific:

> After being allowed to nurse for only one or two days, the veal calf is removed from its mother, with no consideration of its need for motherly nourishment, affection, and physical contact. The calf is locked in a small slotted stall without enough space to move around, stretch, or even lie down. To obtain the pale tender veal desired by consumers, the calf is purposely kept anemic by giving it a special high-calorie, iron-free diet. The calf craves iron so much that it would lick the iron fittings on its stall and its own urine if permitted to do so; it is prevented from turning by having its head tethered to the stall....The calf leaves its pen only when taken for slaughter." *

Having checked with rabbinic authorities involved in supervising *kashrut*, I have been assured that this treatment no longer occurs. The calves are now confined to stalls in which they can sit and stand, and are not tethered to the stall. However, there is not sufficient room for them to walk around. Also, I was assured that calves are no longer taken from their mothers within a day or two of birth, but only after two to three weeks. The rabbinic authorities with whom I spoke did not believe that such treatment constituted *tza'ar ba'alei chayyim*, the cruel treatment of animals, since the calves had never been accustomed to roaming around, and so did not suffer from such confinement.

I was not convinced. To me it seems that even if such calves were subsequently slaughtered according to the laws of *kashrut*, their meat should still be forbidden. To say that it is permissible to confine an animal in this manner for weeks (such a calf is normally slaughtered at

---

* Schwartz, *Judaism and Vegetarianism*, 28.

eighteen to twenty weeks), as long as one follows certain ritual guidelines when slaughtering it, strikes me as wrong. The Bible and Talmud wished to protect animals from unnecessary suffering. To eat veal, unless you have checked and made sure that it was raised in free-range conditions, is to be an accessory to cruelty to animals—to show animals a hard heart so that you can have soft meat. If enough people, starting with you and me, stop eating veal unless we check to make sure it was raised in humane conditions, the cruel treatment of young calves will stop. Either no more veal will be sold, or all calves will be raised in free-range conditions. The answer is in our hands.

DAY

173     THURSDAY

## Should a Jew Wear Fur?

The question almost sounds humorous. The affinity of Jews for fur is well known; as I learned when researching a book on Jewish humor, it is even the subject of jokes: "What does one mink say to another?" "See you in *shul* next Shabbos."

In recent years, animal-rights activists have strongly objected to the wearing of furs. In a sensitive, nuanced treatment, Rabbi Nachum Amsel, author of *The Jewish Encyclopedia of Moral and Ethical Issues*, suggests a number of parameters that would render some furs "kosher" for wear, and others forbidden:

If wearing furs provides for a legitimate human need, then man can use the fur. Therefore, if animal fur will indeed keep a person warmer than other materials, [this is] a legitimate need [and] animal fur would be permissible. However, if warmth can be equally provided from another material that would prevent killing of animals, then a Jew might be required to wear a coat of that other material. Similarly, if the only reason a person wears the fur coat is to "show off" one's wealth or to engage in a mere fashion statement, that would be considered a frivolous and not a legitimate need. It should be pointed out that even when furs are permitted, they may not be acquired from animals that were trapped and put through torturous pain, when the same animals might have been bred on a farm and killed painlessly. Using trapped animals in this case would entail a violation of *tza'ar ba'alei chayyim*, unnecessarily causing pain to animals.*

Indeed, if you do not check into how the animal was killed, you may well be an accessory to great cruelty. It is not uncommon for such animals to be trapped in spring-loaded steel leg-hold traps, and to suffer an average of fifteen hours of pain before they are clubbed to death by a trapper. Rabbi Bradley Artson, who believes that people should simply not wear fur, notes that "these traps are often so painful to the animal that it often chews off its own leg in terror, limping off to die of infection, loss of blood or starvation." For every animal trappers intend to catch, they trap two or more others, including dogs, cats, and deer; trappers call these undesired victims "trash animals." As regards animals raised on farms, Artson notes that conditions on many farms are so horrific that in one year alone, 450,000 animals died of heat stress. Methods for killing animals include suffocation, poisoning, and the insertion of an electrode into the animal's anus. Furthermore, the wearing of fur causes large-scale killing of animals; one forty-inch coat requires the death of sixty minks, forty-two foxes, or forty raccoons.

While indeed some animals might be killed in the painless manner advocated by Rabbi Amsel, thereby rendering furs quite possibly "kosher" for wear, Rabbi Artson reaches a different conclusion: "Fur looks elegant only on its original owners; on human beings, it is a sign of callous barbarity."**

*Amsel, *The Jewish Encyclopedia of Moral and Ethical Issues*, 11.
**Artson, *It's a Mitzvah!*, 204–5.

# When Giving Enough Is Not Enough

The great nineteenth-century scholar Rabbi Joseph Dov Soloveichik was once sitting with his students when a man approached him with a strange question: "Is it permitted for me to drink milk instead of wine at the Passover Seder?"

"Are you forbidden to drink wine for health reasons?" the rabbi asked.

"No, it's just that wine is too expensive. I can't afford it."

Instead of answering the man's question, the rabbi gave him twenty-five rubles. "Now you can have wine at your Seder," he said.

After the man left, a student asked the rabbi. "But why did you have to give him twenty-five rubles? Five would be more than enough to purchase the required amount of wine."

Rabbi Soloveichik answered, "If he intended to use milk at the Seder, that means he also doesn't have money for meat [Jewish law forbids having milk and meat at the same meal], and he probably also doesn't have money for the other items served at the Seder. I wanted to give him enough so that he could have a complete Seder."

Now, a twentieth-century version of this story: A couple I know were speaking to an elderly male friend who was suffering from horrendous back pain. The woman asked the man if there was any medication that could relieve the pain.

"There is, but it costs sixty dollars, and I can't afford it."

That evening the woman gave the man a thousand-dollar check, and suggested that he immediately go and buy the medicine.

As she explained the large gift to her husband, "If he is in such pain and still is not buying that medication, it must mean that he lacks money for many other things as well."

There are many people who ask for too much for themselves, but there are also people who ask for too little. Learn to recognize such people, as did Rabbi Soloveichik and this woman. They understood that sometimes you have to give more than enough if you truly want to give enough.

May you have a Shabbat Shalom!

## SHABBAT

During the course of this Shabbat, try to review the material from the preceding six days, and use some of the texts studied as the basis for discussion during the Shabbat meals:

Day 169. When You Hear That Someone Is Taking a Long Trip, Make Sure That They Take Along Some Extra Money
Day 170. Steady Giving
Day 171. Prevention of Cruelty to Animals: What the Torah Says
Day 172. Can Veal Be Kosher?
Day 173. Should a Jew Wear Fur?
Day 174. When Giving Enough Is Not Enough

Shabbat Shalom!

SUNDAY

# What Does the Sick Person Need?

Rabbi Aaron Levine tells of a woman who visited a sick woman in the hospital and brought her a new raincoat. She told the patient, "The weather is bad. Soon you'll need the raincoat." *

Here was a woman who carried out the commandment of *bikur cholim* with a sense of imagination. Her gift and words inspired the sick woman, encouraging her to think of herself as a person who would be well soon, and so would be returning to a normal life.

Rabbi Hanoch Teller tells of how the late Jerusalem sage Rabbi Shlomo Zalman Auerbach (known throughout the Jewish world as Reb Shlomo Zalman), once visited a rabbinic scholar who was weak and near death. When the sick scholar saw Reb Shlomo Zalman, he apologized for an article he had written years earlier criticizing something the rabbi had published. The rabbi assured the man that he had no reason to apologize; the critique had been neither personal nor unfair. Therefore, Reb Shlomo Zalman continued, "there is no need for you to ask forgiveness. However, you are absolutely wrong in your opinion and in the reason that you differ." Reb Shlomo Zalman's criticism energized the sick man and the two rabbis engaged in a vibrant extended argument over the issue.**

Reb Shlomo Zalman knew that what he could best offer this sick man was not pity, which was what so many of his other visitors had been offering him, but a final chance to be summoned once more into the "rigorous debate of…issues that had been the very essence of his

*Levine, *How to Perform the Great Mitzvah*, 39.
**Teller, *And from Jerusalem*, 318–20.

life. All the resuscitative devices in the hospital could not provide the give-and-take of learning—the very oxygen of life—of which he was currently denied."

In 1986, my father, Shlomo Telushkin, of blessed memory, had a stroke from which he never recovered. Until the day he was afflicted, my father worked full-time as an accountant. One of the clients whom he served, and who was particularly special to him, was the Lubavitcher Chasidic movement. My father also served as the personal accountant for Rabbi Menachem Mendel Schneersohn, the Lubavitcher Rebbe. One day while my father was still in the hospital, I received a call from one of the Rebbe's top aides, who had an accounting question he wished me to pose to my father. I expressed my puzzlement at the request; it was only a few days since my father had regained consciousness, and he was still somewhat confused. The man explained that at a meeting of the Lubavitch leadership earlier that day, an accounting question had come up, and the Rebbe had said, "Ask Shlomo." When he was reminded how sick my father was, he repeated, "Ask Shlomo." Of course, knowing that the question came from the Rebbe, I went to my father's room and posed it to him. My father offered an immediate response; it turned out that the question had not been difficult. What I realized at that moment was the Rebbe's brilliance and compassion. He knew how sick my father was, but also understood how important it was for my father, lying in a hospital bed, confused and half-paralyzed, to still feel productive.

When you visit a sick person, think of what he or she most needs. Then, if it is in your power, give it to him or her, whether it be a raincoat, an argument, or just a question.

# Should a Doctor or a Close Family Member Tell the Truth to a Person Who Is Dying?

Telling "the truth, the whole truth and nothing but the truth" can have a devastating impact upon a sick person. Thus, the Jewish tradition is very tolerant of lies told to people with serious and possibly terminal diseases. The Bible tells us that when Ben Hadad, an ancient king of Aram, became ill, he sent a messenger to inquire of the Israelite prophet Elisha if he would recover. Elisha told the messenger that the king would die, but that the messenger should tell him, "You shall surely recover" (II Kings 8:7–10).

Rabbi J. David Bleich, a contemporary legal scholar, notes that the medieval philosopher Gersonides (1288–1344), in commenting on this passage, suggests that absolute candor can hasten a patient's death. Thus, lack of truthfulness in such situations is not only permissible or commendable, but even mandatory.

Bleich notes that Jewish law sanctions withholding from a patient all information that could demoralize him or her. Thus, the Talmud teaches that a patient should not be informed of the death of a close relative lest it hasten his or her demise (*Mo'ed Kattan* 26b).

According to Rabbi Bleich, the mere "possibility of adverse reaction is sufficient reason for eschewing a policy of full disclosure." He goes on to note how fear itself can bring about death. For example, deaths are regularly reported of people who have ingested sublethal quantities of poison, or who have inflicted minor, nonlethal wounds on themselves: "In these cases, the sole cause of death is simply the victims' belief in their impending doom."

But if someone is suffering from a disease that is usually fatal, is it right to withhold this information? Don't people need forewarning so as to settle their affairs and to repent?

Basing himself on the *Shulchan Aruch*, Rabbi Bleich writes that a patient should be instructed to take care of his affairs and make appropriate arrangements, but the patient also must be told that such advice should not be construed as an indication that death is near. Furthermore, although Jewish law encourages people to recite the *vidui* (confession) before dying (see Day 289), a person must be counseled that "many have confessed and have not died, while many who have not confessed have died" (*Shulchan Aruch, Yoreh Deah* 335:7 and 338:1).*

The *Chokhmat he-Adam*, Abraham Danzig's early-nineteenth-century code of Jewish law, reports that "the officers of the *Hevra Kadisha* [the organization that deals with the dead and the dying] in Berlin and a number of other communities would visit all sick persons on the third day of their illness. By assuring the one thus visited that *all* sick people were treated equally, regardless of their condition's severity, they were then able to discuss matters pertaining to final preparations and death as a matter of community policy." **

Rabbi Bleich believes that the policy of the nineteenth-century Berlin community should serve as a model for present-day physicians who counsel seriously ill patients. They should make it clear that they offer identical advice about taking care of one's affairs to all patients, and not only when they fear the worst. "In this way, the patient will neither be lulled with a false sense of security, nor will he perceive a cause for undue alarm."

While I believe that the guidelines suggested by Rabbi Bleich are applicable to *most* cases, *most* of the time, there clearly are exceptions. The Bible itself notes one: When King Hezekiah fell desperately ill (circa 701 B.C.E.), the prophet Isaiah came to him with a most dispiriting message: "Thus, said the Lord: Set your affairs in order, for you are going to die; you will not get well" (II Kings, 20:1).***

Perhaps God wished Isaiah to speak so bluntly because when one

---

*Bleich, *Judaism and Healing,* 27–33.
**Herring, *Jewish Ethics and Halakhah for Our Time,* 62.
***Interestingly, this prophecy didn't come true. When Isaiah left Hezekiah's room, the king prayed fervently to God, and the prophet soon returned to tell him that God was moved by his prayers and would extend his life by fifteen years.

speaks to a nation's leader, one must sometimes speak hard truths, so that he will provide for his succession, something he would not do if he thought that he would soon recover.

But there are other exceptions as well. Psychiatrist Samuel Klagsbrun treated a man who had been admonished by his wife's physician to lie to her about the severity of her condition, a strategy that had horrible consequences. The couple had been married for fifty years. She had cancer that had already spread, and she was dying. "The couple had literally spent their entire lives together, both in work and private life. Together they ran a little scientific publishing house. Being old German-born Jews, they didn't know how to connive or pull punches. They were very straight shooters."

The man told Dr. Klagsbrun that they had never lied to one another about anything. However, the oncologist treating the woman told the husband that he would stop treating her unless the husband agreed to go along with his stratagem of never telling a patient the full gravity of his or her illness. The husband, grateful that so distinguished a doctor was treating his wife, agreed.

When the woman saw her husband speaking to the doctor, she would ask him what was discussed. The husband would hem and haw, and say that they had spoken about medical insurance or the doctor's bill. And he would then tell his wife, "You know you're doing fine, it's wonderful."

"The woman, seeing her husband's face, and knowing his face very well, knew fully that something else was being said. She knew her condition, she understood her own internal system. Not knowing a pact had been made, she felt something was being withheld from her for the first time in their marriage....The woman lapsed into a delirious phase at this point. Whatever the reason or the source of the delirium, she became incoherent and confused. After a while she became paranoid and began accusing her husband of all sorts of things. She accused him of being a traitor to her, of betraying her. Of course there was an element of truth in it. Then her paranoia escalated into all sorts of other fantasies."

Afraid that the doctor would drop his wife as a patient if he told her the truth, the husband said nothing. Eventually "the woman died in a paranoid state, filled with vilification against her husband, with rage and hatred. She died screaming at her husband. The husband after her death could not go back to the publishing house they had both created. It was too filled with her. And so he sold it for a pittance. The husband, in a massive depression, was referred to me for treatment. The treatment consisted of my helping him vent his rage against the unfair edict of the doctor which forced him to be with his wife in her dying in a way that contradicted completely the way he had been with her in living. It was a lie, a monstrous lie. Her death was a lie, a lie forced upon this man by the doctor's awful condition." *

Jewish ethics sanction lying or withholding information from a patient when doing so will help the patient, and when telling the truth will harm him or her. This approach is to be followed most of the time. But, as Dr. Klagsbrun reminds us, guidelines are only guidelines. Sometimes an ugly truth is far better than a pretty lie. (For an example of when a pretty lie is preferable to an ugly truth, see Day 72.)

T U E S D A Y

# Is Your Work Sacred?

Rabbi Jeffrey Salkin once found himself in conversation with a taxi driver who was taking him to the airport, and whose family had been members of the congregation where he now was rabbi. "So what do you say to a Jew like me who hasn't been in a synagogue since his bar mitzvah ceremony?" the driver asked as they sat in heavy traffic.

"We could talk about your work," Rabbi Salkin answered.

"What does my work have to do with religion?"

---

*The reminiscence of Samuel Klagsbrun is found in Riemer, *Jewish Insights on Death and Mourning*, 57–58. My friend Dr. Stephen Marmer, a psychiatrist, has told me that one of his medical school professors advised students that when a patient has died and the doctor is calling the relatives, they should be told that the patient has taken a turn for the worse, lest they become so upset that they get into an accident on the way to the hospital. When they arrive, the doctor should tell them that their relative was informed they were on their way, but that he or she died before they could get there.

"Well, we choose how we look at the world and at life. You're a taxi driver. But you are also a piece of the tissue that connects all humanity. You're taking me to the airport. I'll go to a different city and give a couple of lectures that might touch or help or change someone. I couldn't have gotten there without you. You help make that connection happen. …I heard on your two-way radio that after you drop me off, you're going to pick up a woman from the hospital and take her home. That means you'll be the first nonmedical person she encounters after being in a hospital. You will be a small part of her healing process, an agent in her reentry into the world of health. You may then pick up someone from the train station who has come home from seeing a dying parent. You may take someone to the house of the one that he or she will ask to join in marriage. You're a connector, a bridge-builder. You're one of the unseen people who make the world work as well as it does. That is holy work. You may not think of it this way, but yours is a sacred mission." *

There are few jobs so intrinsically secular that they can't be understood as in some ways spiritual and thus transformed into holy work. Consider the most secular of businesses, clothing, an industry long associated with Jews. Salkin notes that this field of work can also be associated with spiritual nobility and some of Judaism's very basic commandments. For example, religious Jews daily offer the following blessing to God: "Blessed are You, Lord our God, King of the universe, Who clothes the naked." By helping God to carry out this mission, those who provide clothing are doing spiritual work. Consider how much better people who are well clothed feel about themselves. Similarly, Salkin argues that people who work in the bridal end of the garment business are helping in the fulfillment of the mitzvah of *hachnasat kallah*, helping the bride and groom to marry. (As an additional spiritual act, a person who works in this field might consider donating some out-of-fashion wedding apparel to a bride with limited means.) A clerk in a clothing store who compassionately helps overweight people or people with physical disabilities find appropriate, attractive clothing is bringing spirituality and ethical sensitivity into his or her work.

If you are a teacher, a doctor, a lawyer, an accountant, a peace officer, or a receptionist, you are provided with many opportunities to do

* Salkin, *Being God's Partner*, 65–68, 171.

God's work even as you are doing your own. Rabbi Shlomo Zalman Auerbach once ran into Rabbi Aryeh Levine, the great Jerusalem saint, in the days before Yom Kippur. Rabbi Levine, to whom people routinely came to solicit a blessing, was heading for the home of Dr. Miriam Munin, a well-known local physician. "Since she treats people so well and with such kindness," Reb Aryeh explained, "I am going to her house to ask her for a blessing." *

As Reb Aryeh Levine understood, whatever work you do can help you to achieve spiritual greatness.

An exercise: Prior to going to work in the morning, spend a moment uncovering the deeper meaning of your work. Where in your work is there the opportunity to upgrade the world, or to enhance the quality of someone's life? Locate that opportunity, and spend a moment meditating about it.

W E D N E S D A Y

## Is Abortion Murder? Should a Woman's Right to an Abortion Be Absolute?

To most conservatives and liberals, the answers to the above questions seem obvious. People on the right, particularly the religious right, generally believe that life starts at conception and that abortion is murder. Liberals generally maintain that life starts at birth, and that since a woman should have the right to do what she wants with her body, she should be allowed to abort her fetus, at least during the first six months of pregnancy.

Strangely, many people who embrace these positions do not neces-

* Raz, A Tzaddik in Our Time, 356–57.

sarily live their lives according to them. For example, even among those who hold that life begins at conception, one rarely finds miscarriages being mourned with the same intensity that the death of a human being is mourned. And while all religious traditions have funeral ceremonies for infants who have died, I know of no religious ceremonies for expired fetuses. On the other hand, many who claim to believe that a woman should have the right to do what she wants with her body oppose legalizing prostitution.

Judaism's answer to the above questions? No and no.

Regarding the equation of abortion with murder, the Jewish view is that a fetus is "a part of the mother" (literally, "the mother's thigh"), and has no independent identity. Thus, if a gentile woman who has a child wishes to convert to Judaism, both she and her offspring must undergo conversion. However, if she, even in the ninth month of her pregnancy, converts to Judaism, the fetus also acquires a Jewish identity.

According to the Torah, the fetus's life cannot be equated with that of a human being. Thus, it rules that a man who murders a pregnant woman is subject to the death penalty, but if the attacker causes the pregnant woman's fetus to be lost, but no other injury ensues, he is only subject to a monetary fine (Exodus 21:22–23). The presumption behind this ruling is that while a murderer should be executed (see, for example, Exodus 21:12–14), one who causes the abortion of a fetus is not a murderer, because a fetus is not a human life.

The Mishna (circa 200 C.E.) rules that an abortion is permitted when the mother's life is at stake: "If a woman is in hard labor [and her life is in danger], they cut up the fetus within her womb...because her life takes precedence over that of the fetus" (Mishna, *Ohalot* 7:6).

Does this therefore mean that endangerment of the mother's life is the sole grounds in Jewish law for permitting abortion? Those who interpret this Mishnaic ruling stringently rule yes. However, more liberal Jewish scholars point to yet another Mishnaic ruling to prove that Judaism permits abortion even when it is only the mother's *mental well-being* that is at stake.

In a ruling that was probably theoretical, the Talmud declared that if a woman was sentenced to death, and subsequently found to be pregnant, the fetus should be aborted and the execution proceed as scheduled (Mishna, *Arachin* 1:4). Jewish law regarded delaying an execution as a form of "torture" for the prisoner, and hence forbidden.*

What, then, can one conclude is Judaism's attitude toward abortion?

It is not murder, but because the fetus is a potential life, it should not be performed except for a very serious reason. Thus, Jewish ethics would condemn abortion practiced as a kind of after-the-fact birth control, or because the child is of the "wrong" sex.** There would be grounds, however, for permitting abortion because of serious endangerment to the mother's physical or emotional well-being (such as might occur if the pregnancy resulted from rape, or if a woman learned that she was to give birth to a child with Tay-Sachs or some other severe disease or deformity).***

In all questionable cases, one should consult with a qualified rabbi.

*I suggest that the ruling was probably theoretical because the Talmud notes that executions of any kind were rare, and occurred about once every seven years. Even if this statement is an exaggeration, it still suggests that executions were uncommon.

**If the would-be parents have strong feelings about not raising the child in such cases, they should consider going through with the pregnancy and putting the child up for adoption.

***Some Orthodox scholars—perhaps the majority—disagree with the above. Dr. Fred Rosner, an Orthodox medical scholar, contends that most Orthodox rabbis would not permit abortion in cases of incest or rape, and would question whether the birth of a deformed child would prey so much on the mother's mind "as to constitute impairment of her health."

Regarding the right of a raped woman to abort a fetus, I have long been impressed by the ruling of the nineteenth-century rabbi Yehuda Perilman that "[A woman] differs from 'mother earth' in that she need not nurture seed implanted within her *against her will;* indeed, she may 'uproot' seed illegally sown."

It seems to me that those rabbis who would deny a raped woman the right to abort a fetus are demonstrating less compassion for a woman who has been violated than the talmudic rabbis did toward a woman who had committed a capital offense.

# Should a Woman Have the Right to Do What She Wants with Her Body?

The response given to this question usually reflects the speaker's political orientation. Conservatives, particularly those of the religious right, answer no, a woman should not have an absolute right to do what she wants with her body, particularly if what she wants to do is abort her fetus. Liberals, also understanding this question as referring to a woman's right to abortion, argue that women should have the right to do whatever they want with their bodies.

Judaism argues that one's body (male or female) belongs to God, and that God's will, as revealed in Jewish ethical teachings, should determine what one can and cannot do with it. Thus, for example, Jewish law forbids suicide, regarding it as a form of murder. It also prohibits Jews from arranging to have their dead bodies cremated, regarding this act as disrespectful to the body. The Torah also forbids tattoos: "You shall not…incise any marks on yourselves" (Leviticus 19:28).

Jewish law also forbids taking such life-threatening and mind-destroying drugs as heroin and cocaine, because it is wrong to imperil one's health and mental well-being needlessly. It would also prohibit a pregnant woman from smoking, since the ingestion of nicotine might well inflict permanent damage on the fetus she is carrying (see Day 36).

From Judaism's perspective, whether or not an abortion should be permitted should be based on the reasons for terminating the pregnancy (see yesterday's entry) and not any absolute right of a woman—or, for that matter, a man—to do what she wants with her body.

FRIDAY

# Rabbi Aryeh Levine and the Mitzvah to Visit the Sick

Rabbi Aryeh Levine (1885–1969) was one of the great figures of modern Jewish life, a saint with few parallels in Jewish history. Shortly after he died, his friend Simcha Raz interviewed hundreds of people who knew him, and set down their recollections in *A Tzaddik in Our Time.* Many of the book's stories reflect Reb Aryeh's lifelong commitment to visiting sick people. I have selected three that suggest the many ways in which one can carry out the mitzvah of *bikur cholim* (visiting the sick).

*He would make sure to visit those who most needed his help:*

In the very neighborhood where he lived, there was a woman bedridden by a long, severe illness. This was Rivka Weiss…who was known for her charitable work and her Jewish learning. Now, during her difficult illness, it was Reb Aryeh's custom to visit her at least once a week.

Reb Aryeh knew how devout the woman was. On Yom Kippur, the most solemn day of the year, she would certainly want to fast. So right in the middle of this solemn holy day, wrapped in his white robe and *tallit,* Reb Aryeh left his place in the synagogue and set out for the home of the sick lonely widow who had to remain alone. When he entered he made straight for the kitchen and prepared a cup of tea. Then he searched and found some biscuits in the pantry, put them on a plate, and entered the woman's room. He ordered her to take the tea and biscuits and start eating at once. And under his compelling gaze she could not refuse.

After she had obeyed and eaten and drunk, her eyes lit up. And at his command she promised that she would eat more on this holy day, just as on any other day.*

*He would visit not only the physically ill but the mentally impaired:*

[Reb Aryeh's son recalls]: Once, as we were walking, a man came over to my father and asked, "How is your relative getting along in the mental hospital?" My father answered, "The Lord be praised" (*Baruch Hashem*), and we continued on our way. "Father," I asked, "what relative do we have that is in the mental hospital?" Then he told me that once he had visited the hospital to ask or recommend that someone be taken in for treatment; and since he was already there, he went visiting through the wards. One man there caught his attention: the poor soul was full of welts and wounds, and, needless to say, my father became interested in him at once.

Well, the other patients explained, "After all, we are ill, you know; and there are moments when we get wild and out of control. Then the orderlies restrain us by force, and at times they even hit us. Now, we all have relatives and families. So the orderlies are always a bit afraid that a visitor will come and find that they have injured his relative, and of course he will complain and raise a hue and cry. That poor invalid over there is the only one here with no family, no relatives at all. So...whenever the orderlies lose their temper, he bears the brunt of it.

Without a word, my father went over to the orderlies and told them that the patient was his relative. From that time on he remained my father's "relative"; and so he went to visit him every *rosh chodesh* (the first day of each new month), and brought him little presents.

So it remained commonly accepted knowledge at the hospital, and eventually outside it, that this was a relative of Reb Aryeh.**

*He would visit and help the parents of sick children:*

There is an instructor at the Etz Hayyim school [in Jerusalem, where Reb Aryeh taught for many years] whose memory goes back to a time when a child of his was seriously ill, and his wife and he

---

*Raz, *A Tzaddik in Our Time*, 136–37.
**Ibid., 129–30.

had to stay by his bedside at night—until the effects began telling on their nerves and health. One night Reb Aryeh turned up at their home [with his wife]. "Go to sleep now, both of you," said the good rabbi. "The two of us will stay with your child. You see," he explained with his own brand of genial, charming apology, "we have to talk something over very important, and we cannot do so at home, where the children may eavesdrop."*

In addition, when Reb Aryeh would visit someone at a hospital, he would make sure to ask the nurses about patients who were not receiving visitors, and then spend time with them.

There is an art to knowing how to behave when visiting the sick. Who better to teach us how to carry out this commandment than Reb Aryeh Levine, this mitzvah's consummate artist.

May you have a Shabbat Shalom!

DAY

## 182    SHABBAT

During the course of this Shabbat, try to review the material from the preceding six days, and use some of the texts studied as the basis for discussion during the Shabbat meals:

Day 176. What Does the Sick Person Need?
Day 177. Should a Doctor or a Close Family Member Tell the Truth to a Person Who Is Dying?
Day 178. Is Your Work Sacred?
Day 179. Is Abortion Murder? Should a Woman's Right to Abortion Be Absolute?
Day 180. Should a Woman Have the Right to Do What She Wants with Her Body?
Day 181. Rabbi Aryeh Levine and the Mitzvah to Visit the Sick

Shabbat Shalom!

* Ibid., 132.

DAY

**183**

SUNDAY

## *Help Someone to Find a Spouse, Help Someone to Find Work*

I have a dear friend who has introduced more than a hundred couples who subsequently married. I once asked him how he was able to keep so many people in mind, and thereby "fix up" individuals with others who were appropriate for them. He opened up his wallet and took out a small stack of folded sheets. Listed on them were the names, ages, and other relevant information about unmarried people whom he knew, and who were interested in meeting someone romantically. That way, whenever he heard about a person who was looking to meet someone, in addition to taking down the information, he could quickly scan the names already on his list and see if he knew somebody who was appropriate.

What a wonderful, practical system! Without such an approach, much as we might want to do a favor for another, we will usually forget who it is we wish to assist.

Such a system is of course insufficient by itself. You must also have the desire and persistence to help another person. Thus a rabbinic friend of mine learned that a member of his congregation, a man who worked for a company that was downsizing, had just lost his job. After expressing sympathy to the man, my friend asked him questions about his previous job, and the vocational skills he had; he then requested that the man send him a sheet with other pertinent data.

As soon as he received the information, my friend called up another member of his congregation, who owned a large factory, described the plight of the first man, and asked the factory owner if he had any job openings available. The man asked my friend if he could vouch for the unemployed man's character, which my friend could, and the factory owner promptly hired him.

My friend told me that this was one of his happiest days in the rabbinate. He felt blessed that he had been given the opportunity to fulfill what Jewish tradition regards as the highest degree of charity. As Maimonides teaches:

> The highest degree [of charity], exceeded by none, is that of the person who assists a poor Jew by providing him with a gift or a loan, or by entering into a partnership with him, *or helping him find work* [my emphasis]; in a word, by putting him in a position where he can dispense with other people's aid.
>
> —Moses Maimonides, *Mishneh Torah,*
> "Laws Concerning Gifts to the Poor," 10:7

Obviously, you don't have to be a rabbi to do this kind of favor for someone. When you hear that a friend is looking for work, or for a mate, write down the person's name and pertinent data, and keep the information in your wallet or purse. If you have the desire and persistence to help others, you will find that you will be granted many more opportunities than you would ever have imagined.

DAY

## 184 MONDAY

# *Do Good . . . Now*

*If a commandment comes your way, don't delay [fulfilling it].*
—*Mechilta Bo,* Parasha 9

Many of us have impulses to do good for another, but if we don't act on them quickly, we often don't do so at all. We hear that a person whom we know is sick and wants visitors and we have the impulse to go see him or her, but if we don't act immediately on that feeling, either by making the visit or scheduling a definite time when we will, we usually don't go at all.

Sometimes we have acted unfairly toward another and feel the impulse to apologize and undo the damage. But the impulse passes, and we never contact the person. Or we hear of a family in dire need of money; our heart is moved, and we know that we want to help them. But if we do not write the check right away, we often never do so.

Today, and this week, when you have an impulse to do good, do not just remain in your seat, thinking, "Look how moved I am. I must be a good person."

Instead, act on the impulse. As the Rabbis taught, "If a commandment comes your way, don't delay."

Do it. Now.

TUESDAY

# *Teach Your Child Torah*

*The father is obliged to...teach [his son] Torah.*
—Babylonian Talmud, *Kiddushin* 29a

Jewish law roots the obligation of parents to teach their children Torah to the words recited in the *Sh'ma* prayer: "Take to heart these instructions with which I charge you...and you shall teach them to your children" (Deuteronomy 6:6–7).

Throughout history, Jews have understood this verse as obligating Jewish parents to provide their children with a basic Jewish education. In theory, a parent can fulfill the obligation himself by actually teaching his children Hebrew, the Torah, the prayer book, and Judaism's other holy works. But while parents should certainly involve themselves in their children's Jewish education, most discharge this obligation by sending their children to Jewish schools.

There are two types of Jewish schools in the United States: the less intensive afternoon or Sunday Hebrew schools (also known as "supplemental schools") and the Jewish day schools and yeshivot. Parents who are concerned that their children acquire the ability to read and understand Jewish texts will generally send them to day schools, and yeshivot, whose curricula allot, in addition to the full range of secular studies, two to three hours a day or more to Jewish studies. While this may sound demanding, it is necessary if one wishes to study an entire culture (basic Jewish literacy requires knowledge of Hebrew, the Bible, the prayer book [siddur], the Talmud, and Jewish ethical teachings, history, literature, and life-cycle events), and to feel literate and integrated in two civilizations. Today, all of Judaism's major denominations have day schools. In most larger cities a parent can generally find one that more or less corresponds to his or her Jewish worldview.

Afternoon schools, which have a much more limited time span in which to teach children Judaism, generally find it difficult to do more than teach children a very basic Hebrew vocabulary, prepare them for a bar or bat mitzvah, and expose them to the joys of the Jewish holidays. An additional problem is that most parents who send their children to afternoon schools discontinue their children's Jewish education after bar or bat mitzvah (at age thirteen for boys, twelve for girls).* A story told by Rabbi Bradley Artson demonstrates how self-defeating and short-sighted such an approach is:

A member of my synagogue confided to me that his daughter, then eleven, would surely become a bat mitzvah. The father insisted that his daughter learn the basics of a religious background, but after that she would choose whether or not to continue in Hebrew school. I listened and then asked whether he would also allow her to choose to discontinue her science classes after she turns thirteen. Would his daughter, I wondered, be allowed to choose never to take another writing course in school? Incredulously, the father said no, his daughter must continue with both science and writing, because no thirteen-year-old is in a position to make such an

---

*Terminating a child's Jewish education at thirteen also conveys the message that Judaism is only for children.

important choice as that....In establishing this preference [for science, writing, and secular knowledge over Judaism]...we convey to our children that ultimate questions—What is my place in the universe? What is the purpose of life? and How are we to treat other human beings?—need concern us only until puberty.*

Do not let your child's Jewish education end many years earlier than his or her secular one.

DAY

### 186     WEDNESDAY

# Teach Your Child the Value of Human Life

Some years ago, Dennis Prager was traveling on a plane. The woman seated next to him received a vegetarian meal, he a kosher one. When they started talking about their culinary preferences, the woman told him she thought it wrong to kill animals, arguing, "Who are we to say that our lives are more valuable than that of an animal?"

Prager, sure that the last statement was hyperbolic, told her, "I certainly understand your opposition to killing animals, but you can't really mean what you said about people not being more valuable than animals. After all, if an animal and a person were both drowning, which would you save first?"

After a long pause, the woman answered, "I don't know."

Shortly thereafter, Prager started asking high school students throughout America, "If your dog and a person you didn't know were drowning, whom would you try to save first?"

During the fifteen years he posed this question before thousands of

---

* Artson, *It's a Mitzvah!*, 4. Of course, such a standard imposes upon parents the responsibility not only to send their child to a Jewish school, but to make sure it is a school that raises, confronts, and helps shape ethical behavior.

students in secular schools, no more than a third ever voted to save the person. As Prager came to understand, "With the breakdown of religion, the belief that human beings are created in the image of God is no longer taught. From where, then, does the belief in human sanctity derive? What nonreligious reason could be offered for regarding people as more valuable than animals?"

Some nonreligious people have tried to offer such answers, but their arguments are not convincing. For example, they contend that human beings are more valuable than animals because they are more intelligent. But should that be the basis of the greater value of human life? If a dog were drowning next to a severely retarded child, should the child's life then not take precedence? Further, if we root human superiority in human intelligence, does that imply that if two people are drowning, we should always save the one who is more intelligent?

Others argue that a human being should be saved first out of natural empathy for a fellow person. They reason as follows: If I were drowning next to a dog, I would want to be saved first; thus, if I see another person drowning next to a dog, I should save him or her first. However, this example proves nothing. If I were drowning next to another human being, I would wish to be saved first; that doesn't prove that my life is more valuable, but only that all of us, humans and animals, wish to survive.

Judaism teaches that human beings are more valuable than animals because they alone are created "in God's image" (Genesis 1:27). This does not mean that God, like human beings, has a body, but rather that people share with God, but not with animals, an awareness of good and evil.* This awareness, and the ability to choose to lead a moral and holy life, endows human life with an inherent sanctity that is greater than animal life.

That is also why it was only in religious schools that Prager routinely found students voting to save a human being over an animal. Students there, including those who owned pets, understood that the biblical teaching that human beings are created "in God's image" means that a

---

*The words "good" and "bad," when applied to animals, are usually synonymous with "obedient" and "disobedient." A dog trained by anti-Nazi fighters to attack Nazi soldiers was no more making a moral choice to do good than a German shepherd trained by Nazi officers to attack concentration camp inmates was making a moral choice to do evil.

person, even though a stranger, has more inherent value than an animal (as regards Judaism's attitude toward animals, see Days 95 and 171).*

Present Prager's question to your children. If they tell you that they would save their pet, talk to them about the notion of people's creation "in God's image," and Judaism's belief that while animals have great value, that of humans is sacred and infinite.

DAY

## 187      T H U R S D A Y

# A Pragmatic Reason for Forgiving Others

What if someone hurts you and begs forgiveness, but you just don't want to give it? Perhaps you think their plea is not fully sincere, you are still hurting too much, or maybe you just want to inflict a little suffering on the person who hurt you.

But there is a pragmatic reason for readily granting forgiveness; it is one of those acts for which Jewish tradition promises a generous and unique reward from God: "Raba said...Whose sin is forgiven? The sin of him who forgives sins [committed against him- or herself]" (Babylonian Talmud, *Megillah* 28a).

In other words, if you are merciful to those who offend you, then God will be merciful to you when you offend Him. I understand this talmudic teaching as a kind of divine common sense. If you are unforgiving to those who have offended you, then you forfeit the right to ask God to treat you with the mercy that you are unwilling to extend to others. Conversely, if you are compassionate, that entitles you to a greater

---

*Some people have challenged Prager's question with their own: "What if a dog were drowning and Hitler were drowning, whom would you save?" In the case of an exceptionally evil person, one should save the dog, not because dogs are more valuable than human beings, but because people like Hitler don't deserve to be alive. Thus, even if Hitler were drowning alone, it would still be wrong to save him.

portion of God's compassion. (For a discussion of whether certain sins are so serious as to be beyond forgiveness, see Days 193 and 269.)

Ben Sira (also known as Ecclesiasticus), one of the books of the biblical Apocrypha, expresses the same thought: "Forgive your neighbor the wrong he has done [you], and then your sins will be pardoned when you pray. Does anyone harbor anger against another, and expect healing from the Lord? If one has no mercy toward another like himself, can he then seek pardon for his own sins?" (Ben Sira 28:2–4).

Therefore, the next time someone asks you for forgiveness, be merciful. Can you think of any easier way to obtain forgiveness for your own sins?

DAY

## 188    FRIDAY

# *Charity Is Not Enough*

Some people use their keen intelligence to deceive others, some employ it to find loopholes and technicalities that will gain them personal benefits, and some use it to find innovative ways to spare fellow human beings from shame.

Such is the subject of an unusual story in the talmudic tractate *Shabbat*. The third-century Babylonian sage Samuel was sitting with his friend Ablat, a gentile astrologer, when a group of workers walked by. Ablat pointed to one man and said, "That man is going but will not return; a snake will bite him and he will die." Samuel, who seems to have accepted Ablat's belief in astrology, but who believed that prayer and good deeds could reverse one's fate, answered, "If he is an Israelite, he will go and return." Some time later the men returned, including the one whose death Ablat had predicted. Ablat ran over and took off the man's knapsack; inside, he found a snake cut in half.

Samuel went over to the man and asked him, "What did you do [to escape your fate]?"

The man answered, "Every day, I and all the other workers pool our food, and eat it. But today, I saw that there was one man who had no bread, and he was ashamed. So I told all the other men, 'Today, I will collect the food.' When I came to that man, I pretended to take bread from him, so that he should not be ashamed."

Samuel said to him, "You have done a good deed" [that is, it was the merit of this good deed that caused God to spare you from the deadly snake; *Shabbat* 156b].

Feeding the hungry is a great good, but for this unnamed worker it was not enough simply to make sure that the man without food be permitted to share in the communal meal; he wished to spare him from shame as well as hunger.

To spare the poor from shame as well as hunger is the Talmud's ideal. And those who practice it are entitled to a special portion of God's miracles.

May you have a Shabbat Shalom!


DAY

## 189    SHABBAT

During the course of this Shabbat, try to review the material from the preceding six days, and use some of the texts studied as the basis for discussion during the Shabbat meals:

Day 183. Help Someone to Find a Spouse, Help Someone to Find Work
Day 184. Do Good…Now
Day 185. Teach Your Child Torah
Day 186. Teach Your Child the Value of Human Life
Day 187. A Pragmatic Reason for Forgiving Others
Day 188. Charity Is Not Enough

Shabbat Shalom!

# WEEK 28

## Find Work for the Developmentally Disabled

The New York–based National Jewish Council for the Disabled regularly takes out advertisements in Jewish journals, challenging readers: "Do you want to do something really meaningful for a person who is developmentally disabled?" The ad goes on to quote from Maimonides' code of Jewish law, the *Mishneh Torah:* "The highest degree of aid to a Jew in want is...providing work for him so that he may become self-supporting" ("Laws Concerning Gifts to the Poor," 10:7; see, for example, Day 183). As the ad suggests, consider whether there is a position in your place of employment that would suit a developmentally disabled person.

Twenty, thirty, or fifty years ago, I am certain that no ads like this appeared in Jewish or general journals. When you hear people wax nostalgic about the "good old days," they are not thinking about the status of physically or mentally handicapped people. In the past, these people were routinely discriminated against and ignored. In the case of retarded children, parents would sometimes try to keep the child's existence a secret, even taking him or her out for walks at night, when they were less apt to run into others. In the even more distant past, societies such as that of Sparta in ancient Greece sanctioned the killing of newborn, imperfectly formed children through exposure to the elements.

Today, however, the world is becoming far more welcoming to the developmentally disabled, and there are American companies that purposely set out to hire people with disabilities to fill jobs that are within their capacity. My beloved nephew Meir, who has Down's syndrome, works in a cafeteria at Boston University.

Are you in a position to offer work to someone who has a physical or mental disability? There are other *mitzvot* that are as great as this one—but I can think of few that are greater.

MONDAY

## An Employer Must Know How His Employees Live

There are some employers who host annual parties at their homes for their employees. Such a generous gesture conveys the sense that one regards one's employees with respect and affection.

However, a tale told in the Talmud implies that equal if not greater good might be accomplished by employers periodically visiting their employees' homes, particularly those of lower-salaried workers.

On one occasion, the second-century Rabban (Rabbi) Gamliel, the wealthy, scholarly, and somewhat autocratic leader of his age, publicly humiliated Rabbi Joshua. Outraged by Gamliel's behavior, the other Rabbis deposed him and appointed another in his place.

Regretting his behavior and wishing to regain his former position, Gamliel went to Rabbi Joshua's home to apologize. Upon entering the house, he saw that its walls were black. He said to Rabbi Joshua: "From the walls of your house, it would seem that you earn your living as a charcoal burner" (alternatively, a blacksmith; in either case, a difficult and low-paying job).

Rabbi Joshua responded: "Woe to the generation whose leader you are, and woe to the ship whose captain you are! For you know nothing of the troubles of the scholars, how they make their living, and how they sustain themselves" (*Berachot* 28a).*

---

*Hurt as he was by Gamliel's condescending arrogance, Rabbi Joshua forgave him only on his third plea, when Gamliel beseeched forgiveness in the name of his [Gamliel's] distinguished father; on the need to forgive by the third appeal, see Day 269.

I thought of this dramatic encounter some years ago, when Congress was debating a bill to raise the minimum wage. There were those who argued against the raise, though they were well aware that a person who worked forty or even fifty hours a week was earning a salary barely sufficient to support one person, and certainly not enough to support a spouse, let alone children.* I wonder how many of the congressmen who opposed raising the minimum wage for adults had ever visited the home of, or befriended, a person who had to subsist on such a salary.

Rabbi Joshua's belief that the world would be a more compassionate and better place if the Rabban Gamliels of the modern world (the leaders and employers) visited the homes of the working poor remains valid today.

TUESDAY

# Confession and Your Neighbor's Soul

As has been noted (Days 107 and 108), Jewish law insists that when we have sinned against another, we must confess our wrongdoing to the person, undo as much of the damage committed as possible, and beg for forgiveness. Sometimes, however, Jewish ethics argues that it is better *not* to detail why you are requesting forgiveness. For example, if you have said very ugly things about someone, it may be unwise to relate exactly what you uttered, since the listener will suffer

---

*Some people supported the raise, but wanted an exception made for teenage employees, arguing that a higher minimum wage would make employers more reluctant to hire teenage employees. In fairness, I would note that some of the opponents of raising the minimum wage felt that doing so would provide a relatively small number of workers with a better income while ensuring that a larger number would be unemployed. I disagree, but it would be unfair to characterize as unethical those who opposed raising the minimum wage because they thought that doing so would lead to more unemployment and suffering.

great anguish from hearing you articulate the cruel things you said (though you would still be obligated to go and tell everyone to whom you made your unfair comments that what you said was wrong and unfair).

Sometimes, when you have sinned very deeply against another, your obligation might require you to remain silent and suffer pangs of guilt, for to speak up might only compound your original sin. In Somerset Maugham's diary, he relates the following:

> He was a successful lawyer, and it was a shock to his family and his friends when he committed suicide. He was a breezy, energetic, exuberant man, and the last person you would have expected to do away with himself. He enjoyed life. His origins were humble, but for his services in the war he had been granted a baronetcy. He adored his only son, who would succeed to his title, follow him into the business, go into Parliament and make a name for himself. No one could guess why he had killed himself. He had arranged it so that it should look like an accident, and so it would have been considered except for a small oversight on his part. It was true that his wife was causing him a certain amount of anxiety....She was not mad enough to be put in an asylum, but certainly not sane. She suffered from severe melancholia. They didn't tell her that her husband had committed suicide, but only that he had been killed in a motor accident. She took it better than was expected. It was her doctor who broke the news to her. "Thank God I told him when I did," she said. "If I hadn't, I should never have had another moment's peace in my life." The doctor wanted to know what she meant. After a while, she told him: she had confessed to her husband that the son he doted on, the son on whom all his hopes were set, was not his.

It seems to me that telling this truth at the time this woman chose to do so was a far more evil act than her original act of adultery. Such malevolent truth-telling must be avoided. For while confession may be good for one's own soul, our responsibility should extend to the other person's soul as well. And there are times when confessing one's sins to another can be terrible for that person's soul.

# How Can One Repent Who Has Committed the Ultimate and Unforgivable Sin?

In 1922, three extreme right-wing, antisemitic assassins murdered Walter Rathenau, Germany's foreign minister and a Jew. When the police tracked down the killers, two committed suicide, while the third, Ernst Werner Techow, was captured. A short time later, Rathenau's mother sent a letter to Techow's mother:

> In grief unspeakable, I give you my hand—you of all women the most pitiable. Say to your son that, in the name and spirit of him he has murdered, I forgive, even as God may forgive, if before an earthly judge your son makes a full and frank confession of his guilt...and before a heavenly judge repents. Had he known my son, the noblest man earth bore, he would have rather turned the weapon on himself. May these words give peace to your soul.

It is striking that Mrs. Rathenau did not offer her son's murderer unconditional forgiveness. Instead she made two demands: that the murderer make a full and frank confession of his guilt, thereby accepting whatever punishment the court imposed upon him, and that he offer true repentance before God.

Mrs. Rathenau's letter had a belated but profound effect on Techow. Released from prison for good behavior after serving only five years, he soon found himself living in a Germany ruled by the Nazis, the very people who most supported his murder of Rathenau. However, Techow came to truly repent his antisemitism and his horrible act. In 1940, after France surrendered to Germany, he went to Marseilles and helped more than seven hundred Jews escape to Spain with Moroccan permits. Some had money and paid him; others were penniless, so Techow arranged their escapes free of charge. As he remarked to a nephew of Rathenau's, whom he happened to meet: "Just as Frau Rathenau conquered herself when she wrote that letter of pardon, I have tried to master myself. I only wished I would get an opportunity to right the wrong I've done." *

In ancient Jewish life, when a murderer was led out to be executed, a court official instructed him to say, "May my death be an expiation for all my sins" (Mishna, *Sanhedrin* 6:2). So, although Judaism teaches that there is no full forgiveness for murder in this world, if a person who commits murder devotes his life to repentance and acts of goodness, there might be in the next.

DAY

194    THURSDAY

## When a Jew Acts Dishonestly Toward a Non-Jew

Some years ago, I was delivering a lecture on Jewish ethics when a questioner posed this challenge: "One of the things that turned me off to Judaism was when a rabbi at my yeshiva taught that Jewish law rules that if a non-Jew makes an error in favor of a Jew in a business dealing, the Jew is not required to return the extra money. Is that true?"

I responded with a question: "Did your rabbi also teach you that a Jew is permitted to eat pork on Yom Kippur?"

"Of course not," he responded.

---

*Techow's story was first told in "My Favorite Assassin," by George Herald, an article that appeared in *Harper's*, April 1943. A very powerful dramatization of this incident, which appeared on the radio program *Eternal Light,* is printed in Rabbi Jack Riemer, ed., *The World of the High Holy Days,* 179–80.

"That, of course, is generally true. But in a Nazi concentration camp, if it was necessary for a person to eat pork on Yom Kippur to stay alive, Jewish law would instruct him to do so. Yet for a rabbi to say that a Jew may eat pork on Yom Kippur, without explaining the context, is to tell a falsehood. Similarly, to teach that Judaism rules that a Jew is permitted to be dishonest in a business dealing with a non-Jew, as your teacher did, is also to tell a falsehood. True, the Talmud did say that a Jew was not required to correct a mistake made by a gentile in a business dealing. But this ruling was issued in a society in which non-Jewish governments and laws discriminated against Jews, and non-Jews were not required to correct business errors made by Jews. In such societies it would seem that the Rabbis made a *pragmatic* ruling that Jews weren't required to practice a higher business morality toward non-Jews than non-Jews were required to practice toward them. However, it is one thing to say that a rabbi with the stature of a Hillel or Akiva ruled that where non-Jews are permitted to be dishonest with Jews, Jews are permitted a *measure* of dishonesty with non-Jews.* But it is an altogether different matter to imagine that a Rabbi Hillel or Akiva would have said, as your teacher apparently believed, 'Even in a society in which Jews have equal rights, a society in which non-Jews are obligated to be fully honest in their dealings with Jews, even in such a society, Jews don't have to correct business errors made by non-Jews.' Such reasoning turns a Rabbi Hillel or Akiva from being pragmatists into condoning theft."

Dishonesty is dishonesty, and, regrettably, there have always been some dishonest Jews. However, for a Jew to attribute his dishonesty to Judaism is to turn God into his accomplice in crime. Such an act is known in Jewish law as a *chillul Hashem,* a profaning of God's name; it is one of a very few sins that the tradition deems unforgivable.

---

*I emphasize a "measure" of dishonesty, because cheating or stealing from non-Jews is, and always was, forbidden (e.g., "Stealing from a non-Jew is worse than stealing from a Jew because of the profanation of God's name," Tosefta, *Bava Kamma* 10:15).

# One Boss in a Million

In December 1995, Boston businessman Aaron Feuerstein had just returned home from his seventieth birthday party when a phone call informed him that his Malden Mills textile factory in Lawrence, Massachusetts, had burned down. Twenty-six employees had been injured, some seriously.

Three thousand people worked at Malden Mills. When the employees saw the devastation wrought by the fire, they assumed, as one worker put it, "The fire's out of control. Our jobs are gone."

The fire was indeed out of control, but Feuerstein was not. An Orthodox Jew who studies both the Talmud and Shakespeare daily, Feuerstein recalled how his father liked to quote the Mishnaic aphorism "In a place where there is no man, be a man" (*Ethics of the Fathers* 2:5). In the immediate aftermath of the fire, he met with a thousand employees and told them, "When all the textile mills in Lawrence ran out to get cheaper labor down south, we stuck. We're going to stay—and rebuild."

Two days later, wages were due. "Pay everyone in full," Feuerstein ordered. "And on time." Along with the payroll checks, Feuerstein included a $275 bonus for Christmas, and a note: "Do not despair. God bless each of you."

The following day, Feuerstein convened a meeting of all his employees and announced, "For the next thirty days, it might be longer, all employees will be paid full salaries." Over the following weeks, Feuerstein dipped into his own resources to make these payments. As an employee at the meeting called out, "When you work for Aaron, you're somebody."

Later that day, Feuerstein, himself a leading philanthropic supporter of Orthodox and other Jewish causes, went on his annual pre-Christmas route around Lawrence, disbursing $80,000 to such organizations as the Salvation Army, Neighbors in Need, and the Bread and Roses Soup Kitchen.

Did either American or Jewish law require Feuerstein to act as he did? No; that is why his generous actions received national acclaim, and were the subject of numerous articles in magazines and newspapers.*

But in addition to feeling compassion for his employees and wanting to rebuild his business, Feuerstein was also obeying the dictates of an exalted Jewish value, sanctifying God's name (*Kiddush Hashem*). In a noted talmudic passage that helps define the meaning of this term, it is related how Rabbi Samuel acted toward a Roman empress with such nobility of character that she declared, "[If this is the type of people Jews are, then] Blessed is the God of the Jews" (see Day 103).

Aaron Feuerstein's behavior reminds us that piety is tested not just in the synagogue or around a Sabbath table, but also in the marketplace. Those who do anything for money show that money is their most important value. Those who risk their fortune, as Aaron Feuerstein did, to act with compassion, show that God and His ethical demands is their highest value. That is what it means to sanctify God's name.

May you have a Shabbat Shalom!

## 196      S H A B B A T

During the course of this Shabbat, try to review the material from the preceding six days, and use some of the texts studied as the basis for discussion during the Shabbat meals:

Day 190. Find Work for the Developmentally Disabled
Day 191. An Employer Must Know How His Employees Live
Day 192. Confession and Your Neighbor's Soul
Day 193. How Can One Repent Who Has Committed
the Ultimate and Unforgivable Sin?
Day 194. When a Jew Acts Dishonestly Toward a Non-Jew
Day 195. One Boss in a Million

Shabbat Shalom!

*Peter Michelmore. "One Boss in a Million," *Reader's Digest*, October 1996, 94–99.

SUNDAY

# *Have You Written an Ethical Will?*

The will, the final document most parents bequeath their children, contains no advice or life lessons, or anything to say about love or a parent's hopes about the kind of lives his or her children will live. Rather, it has one focus: the disposition of the dead person's assets.

Necessary as such a will is, Jewish tradition is also familiar with a second type, an ethical will, also known as a *tza'va'a*. Rabbi Jack Riemer has devoted twenty years to influencing contemporary parents to take up the tradition of leaving their children an ethical will, a letter in which they record a very valuable legacy: a statement of what life has taught them, and what they hope it will teach their children.

As Riemer assures parents, you don't have to be a scholar or a professional writer to prepare an ethical will. One of Riemer's favorites was written by Rose Weiss Baygel, a woman born in Riga, Lithuania, who immigrated as a child to Cleveland. Mrs. Baygel had little formal education; she spent her teen years working in a sweatshop, and later marched on picket lines during the struggle to establish the International Ladies' Garment Workers Union. With her husband, Sam Baygel, also an immigrant, she raised and educated three children.

Late in life and while in a bank—perhaps conscious there of the material assets she would be leaving her children—Mrs. Baygel realized that she still had one important message to express to her children. So she took a plain piece of paper and wrote to them as follows:

My dear children:
I am writing this in the bank. This is what I want from you children: Evelyn, Bernice and Allen to be to one another—good sisters

and brother. Daddy and I love the three of you very much, and we did our best raising you and gave you the best education we could afford. Be good to each other. Help one another if "God forbid" in need. This is my wish.

Love all of you,
Your mother

In this, her final letter to her children, Rose Baygel expressed only one concern, that her children remain close. Undoubtedly she had seen and heard of cases in which siblings had fought court battles over an estate, or had drifted apart after their parents had died, and she did not want this to happen to her children. It is unlikely, Riemer suggests, that "children who get a last request like this one—'to love one another and to help each other'—will end up fighting each other in court, or drifting apart."

The process of preparing such a will can also teach you much about yourself. One man told Riemer, "I tried to write a letter to my family and found out that I couldn't, because we aren't really a family. We have so little to do with each other. So I had to write three separate letters, one to my wife and one to each of my children. That is a pretty sad thing to realize about yourself and your family, but I guess it is better to learn it now while you can still do something about it than it is to learn later when it is too late."

To help parents get started on what can otherwise turn into a daunting task, Rabbi Riemer and Rabbi Nathaniel Stampfer, the co-authors of *So That Your Values Live On—Ethical Wills and How to Prepare Them,* suggest the following six steps:

1. Start by writing about the important events, passions, and insights of your life. For example:

   ♦ The formative events in my life…
   ♦ The people who influenced me most…
   ♦ The people in our family and the causes for which I would like you to feel a sense of responsibility…
   ♦ The mistakes that I most regret having made in my life and that I hope you will not repeat…

◆ The important lessons that I have learned in my life…
◆ I would like to ask your forgiveness for…and I forgive you for…
◆ I want you to know how much I love you and how grateful I am to you for…

2. How to organize the ethical will:

◆ Opening: I write this to you, my _____ in order to _____.
◆ The family:
My parents, siblings, antecedents were/are…
Events that helped shape our family…
◆ Personal history:
People who strongly influenced my life…
Events which helped shape my life…
◆ Religious observances, insights:
The ritual(s) of most meaning to me…
Specific teachings from Jewish sources that most move me…
◆ Ethical ideals and practices:
Ideals that found expression in my life…
I would like to suggest to you the following…
◆ Closing:
My ardent wishes for you…
May the Almighty…

3. Personalize and strengthen the links with shared family memories, personal anecdotes, and favorite sayings.
4. Write the will on acid-free paper.
5. Decide whether you want to present the will while you are still alive, as a legacy after you die—or share it with your family while you're alive, then leave it as part of your estate.
6. Attach the ethical will as a codicil to your will concerning property. Also, if you realize that there remains unfinished business between you and your children, now is the time to make an effort to resolve the issues and make peace.*

*Riemer and Stampfer, *So That Your Values Live On: Ethical Wills and How to Prepare Them.*

Some final considerations: Never allow your ethical will to degenerate into an attempt to control your family from the grave, and make sure to omit sentiments that can leave a child with a permanent sense of hurt. The goal of an ethical will is to impart a sense of what matters to you and what you hope will matter to your children, not to leave the people you most love feeling guilty.

The Torah concludes with a mitzvah related to writing: the last of the 613 commandments legislates that every Jew should write a Torah scroll (this mitzvah is normally fulfilled by contributing money to help pay for the writing of a Torah scroll). How fitting, then, that one of the final major acts of one's life is to leave behind a little "Torah" ("Torah" means teaching) written especially for your family. What a precious legacy for those who love you, and for the grandchildren and great-grandchildren who might otherwise never know you.

MONDAY

# Three Traits That Reveal Your Character

A Hebrew pun that is cited in the Talmud suggests that a person's character is revealed through three characteristics: "his cup, his purse, and his anger" (Babylonian Talmud, *Eruvin* 65b).

Through his cup (*be-koso*): Does the person drink in moderation, or is he or she a drunk? And how does he or she act when under the influence of alcohol?

While Jewish law sanctions drinking (on Shabbat, the *kiddush* prayer is twice recited over wine, and at the Passover Seder, four cups of wine are consumed), the Bible abhors drunkenness. For example, Lot, after becoming stupefyingly drunk, sleeps with and impregnates his two daughters (Genesis 19:33–38). Leviticus severely warns priests against performing their priestly functions after imbibing liquor (Leviticus 10:8–11).

Through his pocket (*be-keeso*): Is the person generous or stingy? According to the Rabbis, a stingy person who does not give charity is like one who worships idols. Indeed, as Jewish sources note, in a certain sense he or she is such a person, for worshipping gold instead of God.

Through his anger (*be-ka'aso*): Is the person easily provoked to anger? More important, when angry, does he or she say unfair things to the one who has provoked the anger? Does he or she calm down easily and make peace with that person?

The three revealers of character—*koso, keeso, ka'aso:*

Do you drink in moderation or get drunk?

Are you generous or stingy?

Do you get angry when it is appropriate and express your anger fairly, or do you go into a rage and do and say unfair things?

*Koso, keeso, ka'aso.*

DAY

199  TUESDAY

# "Until the Day of One's Death"

*Hadrian [the second-century C.E. Roman emperor] was walking along the road near Tiberias when he happened upon an old man planting trees. Hadrian asked him, "How old are you?" And the man replied, "One hundred years old." Hadrian then remarked, "Fool, do you think you shall live to eat fruit from these trees?" And the old man replied, "If I am worthy, I shall eat; if not, as my ancestors planted for me, so I am planting for my children and grandchildren."*

—*Ecclesiastes Rabbah 2:20*

There is not much to be found in traditional Jewish sources about retirement. Throughout history, most people did not live to an age old enough to retire; even among those who did, many continued to work. Most people were poor, and families needed whatever income could be brought in.

Also, Judaism's model figures were not the sort who encouraged people to think in terms of retirement. The Bible tells us that Moses led the Israelites throughout his old age, and that "Moses was a hundred and twenty years old when he died: His eyes were undimmed and his vigor unabated" (Deuteronomy 34:7). Jewish tradition claimed that some of its greatest sages, most notably Rabbis Hillel, Yochanan ben Zakkai, and Akiva, led the Jewish people even after they were a hundred years old.

What do such role models teach us today, when people are generally expected to retire at sixty-five or seventy? What does the Jewish tradition want from the elderly?

Whether or not they have retired from their jobs, Judaism does not expect its adherents to retire from life. Old people are as bound by the commandments as are the young. In many synagogues, elderly retired people make up a large percentage of those attending daily services. Rabbi Dayle Friedman argues that obligating the old to fulfill the commandments bestows dignity on those who have been freed from many other responsibilities: "To tell older adults that they are as bound to the *mitzvot* as any other Jew is to tell them that something is expected of them, that their actions [still] matter." *

In words set down eight hundred years ago, Maimonides offers a guideline still applicable to people of all ages: "Every Jew is obligated to study Torah, whether he is poor or rich, in sound health or ailing, in the vigor of youth, or very old and feeble....Until what period in life ought one to study Torah? Until the day of one's death" (*Mishneh Torah*, "Laws of Torah Study," 1:8, 10).

Although the Jewish community has always laid great stress on the Jewish education of its young, Maimonides reminds us that old people

---

*Friedman, "The Crown of Glory," 215–16.

need to fill their lives with learning. The Book of Job suggests that the learning of the old might be of particular value: "With age comes wisdom, and length of days brings understanding" (Job 12:12).

Job's notion that "with age comes wisdom" contrasts markedly with the worship of youth and beauty in contemporary society. Indeed, the biblical and Jewish approach is inherently more optimistic. In contemporary society, which places such emphasis on one's physical appearance, our value can only decrease with time, whereas the Jewish emphasis on wisdom and experience suggests that our value can continue to increase throughout life.

DAY

200

WEDNESDAY

## *When the Old Become Frail*

*When we were young, we were treated as men [told to act like adults]; now that we have grown old, we are looked upon as babies.*

—Babylonian Talmud, *Bava Kamma* 92b

In a society whose heroes are generally actors, rock stars, and sports figures, it is not surprising that there is often a low regard for those who are physically and sometimes mentally deteriorating. Yet it is those very people whom a poetic passage in the Talmud singles out for a special measure of compassion: "Show respect to an old man who has forgotten his learning through no fault of his own, for we have learned that the fragments of the old tablets [the Ten Commandments] were kept alongside the new tablets in the Ark of the Covenant" (Babylonian Talmud, *Berachot* 8b).

The Talmud, in its mention of "the fragments of the old tablets," is alluding to one of the most famous incidents in the Torah. When Moses, coming down from Mount Sinai carrying the Ten Commandments, witnessed the Israelites worshipping the Golden Calf (Exodus 32), he threw down the tablets in fury and shattered them. Later the broken shards were gathered and put into the Ark alongside the new Ten Commandments God made for Israel. And, the Talmud enjoins us, just as the shattered remains of the holy tablets were regarded as holy and treated with respect, so too must we regard as holy and treat with respect those elderly people who have become intellectually broken and emotionally shattered.

Throughout the coming week, keep this teaching in mind as you see such people—"broken fragments of the old tablets"—in the street, on the subway, or in the synagogue.

DAY

201 THURSDAY

## Beyond the Letter of the Law

A window washer once came to a friend's apartment in Manhattan and, while preparing to clean a window, clumsily broke a valuable vase.

Did my friend have the right to insist on repayment for its value? Yes, but he didn't. Did he have the right to deduct payment from the money he owed the man to pay for the vase? Yes, but he didn't. In deciding to forgo his claim, he told me that he found himself guided by a remarkably similar case described in the Talmud:

> Some employees negligently broke a bottle of wine belonging to Rabbah son of Bar Hanan, and he seized their cloaks [when they failed to pay for the damage]. They went and complained to Rav.
> "Return their cloaks to them," he ordered.
> "Is that the law?" asked Rabbah.
> "Yes," he answered, "for it is written, 'So follow the way of the good'" (Proverbs 2:20).

He returned the cloaks to the porters. Then they complained [to Rav]: "We are poor men, we have worked all day and are hungry, and we have nothing."

"Go and pay them," Rav ordered Rabbah.

"Is that the law?" he asked.

"Yes," he replied, [for the end of the verse reads], 'and keep to the paths of the just.'" (Proverbs 2:20)*

Because the employees had been careless, Rabbah was within his rights in insisting on full payment for the damage they had caused. But because they had not acted maliciously, Rav opposed following the letter of the law, feeling that doing so would lead to a greater injustice. He therefore held Rabbah to a moral, not a legal, standard, what Jewish law calls *lifnim meshurat hadin,* going beyond the letter of the law.

In daily behavior, Judaism hopes that its adherents, particularly those who are affluent, will act *lifnim meshurat hadin* and forgive a claim against a person of lesser means.

But why, if the Rabbis believe that forgoing one's claim in such a case is the moral way to act, do they designate such behavior as "beyond the letter of the law," and not simply declare it to be binding?

Apparently, Jewish law was reluctant to declare as obligatory a standard that demands that a person give up a claim that is rightfully his. But the tradition also reminds all those who would insist upon the letter of the law (particularly when they are dealing with someone in more difficult financial circumstances than themselves) that if you want God to judge you with mercy, and not according to the letter of the law, He will first examine the standard you practiced in your dealings with others. As Rabbah taught: "Whose sin is forgiven? The sin of him who forgives sins [committed against himself or herself"; *Megillah* 28a; see Day 187]. Similarly, who is deserving of God's mercy? One who is merciful to those who have erred and who are less fortunate than oneself.

---

*Babylonian Talmud, *Bava Mezia* 83a.

FRIDAY

# Consult with Your Spouse, Consult with Your Friends

Several years ago, I went to see an older rabbinic colleague, who was upset by a letter he had received that morning.

Written by a scholar whose book had been critically reviewed in a journal on whose board my friend sat, the letter attacked many people. Concerning my friend, the author wrote, "Because you didn't stop this review from being printed, I regard you as dead." Later in the letter, he made a pun that poked fun at a rabbi whose daughter had died, and he wrote of a deceased Jewish scholar whom he disliked, "May his bones rot in hell."

I read the letter with shock, then noticed that the writer had crossed out a word, and substituted another in its place. This meant, of course, that he had not just sent the letter off in a moment of unrestrained rage, but had actually reread and edited it first.

I told my friend that there was one thing of which I was certain: this man had a poor marriage and was probably friendless.

"Why do you say that?"

"Because if a man has a good relationship with his wife, and has friends, he would show them a letter like this before sending it, and they wouldn't let him do it."

The Torah tells men that their wives should be helpmates (Genesis 2:18), while the talmudic sage Rabbi Pappa offers some unexpected advice to men married to women of small stature: "If your wife is short, bend down and whisper to her [and get her opinion]" (*Bava Mezia* 59a).

Rabbi Pappa was presumably being whimsical in restricting this advice to men married to short women; it applies, of course, to all men and women. The seventeenth-century British poet John Milton noted that the first thing in the universe God declared not good was loneliness: "It is not good for man to be alone" (Genesis 2:18). One reason for this is that people need the counsel of others; it certainly is not good to be forced to make all major life decisions alone, particularly when, like the writer of the above letter, you are distraught and/or angry.

As important as it is to share good times with one's spouse and friends, it is crucial to profit from their support and wisdom when you are facing a dilemma.

May you have a Shabbat Shalom!

DAY

## 203      S H A B B A T

During the course of this Shabbat, try to review the material from the preceding six days, and use some of the texts studied as the basis for discussion during the Shabbat meals:

Day 197. Have You Written an Ethical Will?
Day 198. Three Traits That Reveal Your Character
Day 199. "Until the Day of One's Death"
Day 200. When the Old Become Frail
Day 201. Beyond the Letter of the Law
Day 202. Consult with Your Spouse, Consult with Your Friends

Shabbat Shalom!

SUNDAY

# *"The Dust of Forbidden Speech"*

Jewish laws forbidding *lashon hara* (literally "evil speech") prohibit speaking of another in a manner that lowers his or her status (see Day 43). Jewish ethics also prohibit lowering another's reputation even when you do so nonverbally. Thus, it is wrong to make a face or roll one's eyes when a person's name is mentioned. It is also wrong to make a sarcastic comment, "Yeah, he's a real genius, isn't he?" When I was growing up, a child would often say something positive about another, then clear his throat in such a manner as to convey that he meant precisely the opposite. However, since Jewish law defines *lashon hara* as anything that lowers another person's reputation, it is irrelevant whether you convey your contempt silently or with a sarcastic tone.

Jewish legal writings designate such actions as *avak lashon hara* ("the dust of *lashon hara*"), and considers them immoral. "The dust of *lashon hara*" includes any technique by which a person attempts to damage another's name without expressly saying anything critical. For example, let's say you have received a letter that contains spelling and grammatical errors. It is morally wrong to show it to another if your goal is to lower the reader's respect for the letter writer. It is similarly wrong to show a person an unflattering photograph of another and for the two of you to laugh about the picture.

The "dust of *lashon hara*" also encompasses verbal innuendo. For example, it is wrong to imply that you know something bad about another, even if you don't reveal what it is, as in, "Don't mention Robert's name around me. I don't want to say what I know about him." And just as it is wrong to say to a person who has improved herself

"Remember how you used to act" (see Day 360), it is equally wrong to transmit a negative impression of the person's past to others, as in, "None of us who knew Barbara in her twenties could ever have guessed that she would turn out as nice as she now has."

When it comes to *lashon hara,* if your goal is to lower another person's status, then it can be done equally effectively through words, a sarcastic laugh, or sharing a letter that holds its writer up to ridicule. Each of those methods is effective, cruel, and wrong.

*Regarding another instance of "the dust of forbidden speech," see Day 317.*

*Regarding another instance of "the dust of forbidden speech," see Day 317.*

DAY

205     M O N D A Y

# A Twenty-Four-Hour Experiment

Can you go for twenty-four hours without saying anything unkind *about* or *to* anyone? When I challenge audiences to try this, invariably some people laugh nervously. They are sure they cannot go a whole day without at the very least making an unkind reference about someone.

"Then you have a serious problem," I tell them. "Because if I were to ask you to go for twenty-four hours without drinking any alcohol, and you said that you couldn't, that would mean you were an alcoholic. And if you couldn't go for twenty-four hours without smoking a cigarette, that would mean that you were addicted to nicotine. And if you can't go for twenty-four hours without speaking unkindly about or to another, that means you've lost control over your mouth, and regaining such control will require vigilance."

If you are willing to carry out this experiment, check your watch. Resolve that until this time tomorrow, you will not say anything negative about another person (except in the very rare instance where it is necessary to transmit such information; such as if you found out that a friend of yours was about to date a man who had beaten his ex-wife). Throughout the day, in your dealings with others, you will constantly monitor how you speak, and keep your anger and judgmental tendencies under control. If you need to criticize, you will restrict your criticism to the incident that provoked your ire, and not engage in a generalized attack on the person who angered you. If you get into an argument, you'll argue fairly, not allowing your disagreement to degenerate into name-calling or other forms of verbal abuse. Throughout this day, you won't disseminate negative rumors, and will refrain from defaming groups as well as individuals.

In other words, for a full twenty-four hours, you will follow the Golden Rule, and speak *about* and *to* others with the same kindness and fairness that you wish them to exercise when speaking about and to you.

A rabbi once told me a favorite expression of his grandmother: "It is not within everyone's power to be beautiful, but all of us can make sure that the words that come out of our mouths are."

When you are ready to begin this experiment, look at your watch and mark down the time.

I wish you twenty-four hours of pure, healing speech.

DAY

206       TUESDAY

## Don't Bear a Grudge

Among the hardest Torah laws to observe is one that occurs in the same verse as "Love your neighbor as yourself." Before enunciating that Golden Rule, the Torah ordains, "Don't...bear a grudge against a member of your people..." (Leviticus 19:18).

The Rabbis of the Talmud explain in very concrete terms what it means to observe this law: "What is bearing a grudge? If A says to B, 'Lend me your ax,' and B says, 'No,' and the next day, B says to A, 'Lend me your garments,' and A replies, 'Here they are. I am not like you, who would not lend me what I asked for,' that is bearing a grudge" (Babylonian Talmud, *Yoma* 23a).

Obviously the one who has hurt us clearly benefits if we observe this regulation. He has refused to lend us something, but now he'll receive what he wants, without even having to suffer the indignity of a reprimand.

However, Rabbi Abraham Twerski, a psychiatrist, reminds us that by forgoing or suppressing our grudge, we profit far more than the one who offended us. Rabbi Twerski, whose career has been devoted largely to treating alcoholism and other addictions, notes that the inability of an injured party to suppress resentments and grudges is among the most significant factors responsible for relapse among recovering addicts.

In a powerful statement of the price people pay for bearing grudges, a recovering alcoholic has written, "Carrying resentments is like letting someone whom you don't like live inside your head rent-free."

This statement is so important that I think it is worth repeating: "Carrying resentments is like letting someone whom you don't like live inside your head rent-free."

As a rabbi who has had occasion to counsel congregants, I have come across people who spend hours a day thinking about the person or the people whom they most dislike. I don't know if their angry and often vengeful thoughts cause any tangible damage to the people whom they despise, but such thinking certainly ruins their days, and sometimes their lives.

I know that on those days when I am consumed by anger, I rarely get any worthwhile writing or studying done, or have any meaningful interactions with others. How could I? My mind is constantly diverted from what I am writing, reading, or talking about by thoughts of the person against whom I have a grievance.

As Dr. Twerski so wisely asks, "Why would anyone allow that?" *

*Twerski and Schwartz, *Positive Parenting,* 171.

# Picking Up Stumbling Blocks

A yeshiva student saw a piece of paper lying on the floor. Thinking it might have fallen from a religious text containing God's name, he lifted it up. When he examined it, he saw an ordinary sheet of paper, and threw it back down.

A rabbi, observing the young man, called him over and asked him to explain his behavior. The student explained that when he saw that the paper contained no religious writings, he just let go of it.

The rabbi told him, "First of all, you should have thrown the paper in the garbage. Neatness is also a value. But more important, don't you realize that now another student or rabbi will walk by, see the paper, be concerned that it might contain God's name, and bend down just as you did to pick it up?"

Of course, pieces of paper on the ground are not the only items one should pick up. A famous biblical law teaches, "Don't put a stumbling block in front of a blind man" (Leviticus 19:14; see Days 58 and 113): The logic behind this law similarly suggests that one should also pick up anything lying in the street that may cause another to stumble. For example, if you see a rock or anything that could cause a person to trip, pick it up and put it in the garbage, or lay it by the side of the road. Also, watch out for smokers who casually drop lit cigarettes and don't stamp them out; a child could pick one up and get burned. Make it a habit to stamp out lit cigarettes.

While the Torah specifically prohibits us from putting down stumbling blocks, ethics also mandates that we raise the stumbling blocks that people or nature have laid down.

THURSDAY

# The Limits of Self-Sacrifice

*Two men are traveling together [in the desert], and one has a*
*pitcher of water. If both drink the water, both will die, but if*
*only one drinks, he can reach civilization and survive. [What*
*should the man with the water do?] Ben Petura taught, "It is*
*better that both should drink and die, rather than one of them*
*look on while his companion dies." But Rabbi Akiva came and*
*taught, [the verse in the Torah] 'that your brother may live*
*with you' (Leviticus 25:36) means [only if he can also live*
*must you share the water, but in cases of conflict] your life*
*takes precedence over his."*

—Babylonian Talmud, *Bava Mezia* 62a

In the above situation, where A and B are in the desert
and A has all the water, there are three possible courses of action:

♦ A acts as a martyr and gives the water to B.
♦ A shares the water with B and both die.
♦ A drinks the water himself.

Regarding the first possibility, Judaism would never demand that A
act as a martyr. While in certain circumstances such behavior might be
commendable (such as a person with a terminal illness giving up water
for one who is healthy), Jewish law would never make such behavior
obligatory. For if A were obligated to give his water to B, then B, in turn,
would be obligated to give the water back to A. They would, in fact,
keep passing the container back and forth until such time as rescuers
would discover two bodies in the desert, the jug of water between them.

Regarding Ben Petura's position, that A should split the water, and
Rabbi Akiva's, that A should drink the water, the Talmud never issues a

definitive ruling. Nonetheless, because of Rabbi Akiva's preeminence in Jewish law, most rabbinic authorities assume that Jewish law rules according to him. Thus, in accordance with his position, Jews in Nazi concentration camps were not required to share their insufficient food rations with other Jews who were dying of starvation.

God willing, few of us will ever encounter a situation in which we will have to choose between dying with our friend, or saving our own life while he or she dies. Nonetheless, I find that this talmudic text still has daily applications. For example, everyone would concede that if A had more than enough water to survive, he would be obliged to share it with B. But isn't that true of the life situation in which almost all of us find ourselves? Don't we have more than enough "water" and food and possessions, in a world where many people don't have enough to survive? That, of course, is one reason why Jewish law mandates that we are obligated to give charity to those in need. Like Rabbi Akiva, it does not demand that we give away the one jug of water we need to survive, but it legislates that we give to charity at least ten percent of our net earnings, so that we can survive and others can as well (see Day 50).

DAY

209  FRIDAY

## "Go and Gather the Feathers"

Children chant, "Sticks and stones can break my bones, but names can never hurt me." Adults know better, that throughout history, people have used names and words to incite others to pick up sticks and stones and knives and guns to hurt other people.

Words can also hurt individuals in another way, by damaging their reputation in a manner that never can be undone. A nineteenth-century Jewish folktale tells of a man who went about town slandering the rabbi. One day, realizing that many of the things he had said were unfair, he went to the rabbi's house and begged for forgiveness. The rabbi told the man that he would forgive him on one condition: that he go home, take a feather pillow from his house, cut it up, and scatter the feathers to the wind. After he had done so, he should then return to the rabbi's house.

Though puzzled by the rabbi's strange request, the man was happy to be let off with so easy a penance. He quickly cut up the pillow, scattered the feathers, and returned to the rabbi.

"Am I now forgiven?" he asked.

"Just one more thing," the rabbi said. "Go now and gather up all the feathers."

"But that's impossible. The wind has already scattered them."

"Precisely," the rabbi answered. "And though you truly wish to correct the evil you have done, it is as impossible to repair the damage done by your words as it is to recover the feathers."

This Shabbat and this week, before you speak negatively, and perhaps unfairly, of others, make sure you are not spreading feathers to the wind, feathers that you will never be able to retrieve.

May you have a Shabbat Shalom!

DAY

## 210    SHABBAT

During the course of this Shabbat, try to review the material from the preceding six days, and use some of the texts studied as the basis for discussion during the Shabbat meals:

Day 204. "The Dust of Forbidden Speech"
Day 205. A Twenty-Four-Hour Experiment
Day 206. Don't Bear a Grudge
Day 207. Picking Up Stumbling Blocks
Day 208. The Limits of Self-Sacrifice
Day 209. "Go and Gather the Feathers"

Shabbat Shalom!

211        SUNDAY

## *Make Sure You Have a Friend Who Can Criticize You*

A friend was at a charitable organization's annual dinner and found himself sitting next to a very wealthy woman. When the wealthy woman began speaking, she expressed many bitter criticisms of others in attendance. Her nasty comments ruined my friend's evening; he soon came to understand that because of this woman's great wealth, people listened to her views without contradiction (my friend himself was afraid to say anything because his wife engaged in business dealings with the woman's husband). No one, it seemed, had ever told her to curb her tongue.

Every one of us, *without exception,* needs people whom we can trust to speak fairly and critically to us when we act wrongly. Chapter 11 of the Second Book of Samuel tells of a shocking sin committed by King David. From his palace roof in Jerusalem, he saw a beautiful woman in a nearby home, and had his servants bring her to him. After sleeping with and impregnating the woman, David arranged to have her husband, an officer in his army, killed in battle, and then married her.

There were people in David's court who knew about his sin, most obviously the servants who brought the woman to the palace, and those to whom they likely confided this information. But no one said anything to the king. Finally the prophet Nathan confronted and reproved David (see II Samuel, chapter 12, for Nathan's words, a model of how to rebuke another). If not for him, David would have remained an unrepentant sinner. Because of Nathan, he repented.

Do you have at least one friend (it could be your spouse) who speaks honestly to you, and who can criticize you? If you don't, then you don't have any real friends.

MONDAY

## Bar Mitzvahs and Bat Mitzvahs, and the Need for a New Kind of Hero

A talmudic passage informs us that some eighteen hundred years ago, "funerals in Israel became so costly that the expense was more difficult for some relatives to bear than the death itself. Some relatives even abandoned the corpse and ran away." Others, we can imagine, spent large sums of money and impoverished themselves.

This unfortunate situation finally ceased when Rabbi Gamliel, the preeminent leader of his generation and a wealthy man, "left orders that his body be carried to the grave in a simple linen garment."* Said Rabbi Pappa, "'And now it is the general practice to carry out the dead even in rough cloth worth only a *zuz'*" (*Ketubot* 8b).

Gamliel's example proved so powerful that ever since, *religious* Jewish funerals have almost always followed his model. Even among wealthy religious Jews, funerals and caskets remain simple and relatively inexpensive.

The Jewish community today needs a Rabbi Gamliel to change the nature of bar mitzvah and bat mitzvah receptions. It is now common for wealthy Jews to spend in excess of $60,000 on such celebrations, and for many other Jews to spend $30,000 or more.

Out of the desire not to appear cheap or unloving to their children, many less prosperous Jews feel forced to spend far more on such parties

---

*The costly garments in which dead people were interred had been one of the largest funeral expenses. Since coffins weren't then used in Jewish funerals, all passersby could see the simple garment in which Rabbi Gamliel was interred.

than they can or want to. Furthermore, lavish parties often end up diminishing, sometimes even eliminating, the religious significance of the bar mitzvah.* For many of the celebrants, what counts is the "bar," not the mitzvah.

The time has come for some wealthy moral heroes to throw a simple bar or bat mitzvah celebration, one in which the party is very pleasant and celebratory, but not lavish. If the first people to host such an event fear that their acquaintances will regard them as "cheap," or that rumors will spread that they are suffering financial difficulties, let them stand up at the party and announce that the $70,000 (or whatever sum) they are saving will be donated to charities of the bar or bat mitzvah's choice.

If in several of our largest Jewish communities, prominent affluent Jews threw a simple bar or bat mitzvah, the good they would do for many of their less affluent fellow Jews would be almost incalculable.**

*Mazal tov!*

DAY

## 213    TUESDAY

# Start Your Day with Gratitude

*I did not make the air I breathe
Nor the sun that warms me....*

---

*An article in *New York* magazine (March 9, 1998) described a bar mitzvah reception where $20,000 was spent on a display of fireworks, another where Las Vegas headliner Natalie Cole charged $150,000 to sing at a party on the aircraft carrier *Intrepid*, and a third in which a computer was rented to morph a boy's image with his girlfriend's to show what their offspring might look like. The article also detailed a bat mitzvah for which the parents commissioned a sixty-foot-long mural depicting the Beatles, the bat mitzvah girl's favorite group. The guests who were seated at the table called "Yellow Submarine" were greeted by a centerpiece consisting of a tank filled with live fish.

**The Gerrer rebbe has set down very specific guidelines for his many thousands of Chasidic followers concerning what should be served and spent on a celebratory meal. In recent years as well, the UAHC, the organization of Reform synagogues, has issued a guideline to its members, noting that "Many of our bar and bat mitzvah social events have exploded into excessive celebrations. We must resist this relentless commercialization of our sacred events."

*I did not endow the muscles*
*Of hand and brain*
*With the strength*
*To plough and plant and harvest....*
*I know*
*I am not*
*A self-made man.*
—Rabbi Ben Zion Bokser

I know many individuals, particularly children and teenagers, who do two things every day that they hate: going to sleep at night and getting up in the morning. Some of my friends claim they are not fully human and sociable until they drink their morning cup of coffee.

The Jewish tradition ordains a different way of getting your day off to a pleasant beginning: Let your first words be an expression of gratitude and joy. Upon arising, the first words a Jew is supposed to utter are a prayer:

*Modeh ani le-fa-necha, melech chai ve-kayyam, she-he-che-zarta be nishmati be-chem-la, rabba eh-mu-na-techa.* (I am grateful before You, living and eternal King, for returning my soul to me with compassion. You are faithful beyond measure.)

If you don't already do so, start each day this week with the *Modeh Ani,* thanking God for the most precious gift of all—life. If you already say this prayer upon arising, then for the next week make a special effort to focus on the words as you recite them; make sure your recitation is not mechanical. Before you say the *Modeh Ani,* think of at least one reason you are truly happy to be alive, and the sense of awe and gratitude will follow automatically.

WEDNESDAY

# If You Have a Tendency to Complain About Others

$A$re you one of those people who make it known when you feel you have been treated unfairly? Do you write letters of complaint when an employee is rude, an airline runs late, or a job is performed inefficiently?

You have every right to do so, but are you sure you always act fairly? A just person makes sure to make his or her satisfaction, not just disapproval, known. Dennis Prager suggests that if you are one of those who often write letters of complaint, resolve that for every one of those you write, you will also write one thank-you note. There is something petty and selfish in only making your displeasure known.

In his "Laws of Character Development," Maimonides makes the point that the only way to correct a character flaw is by temporarily going to the other extreme (see Day 150). For example, if you consistently arrive late for appointments, make certain that for the foreseeable future you arrive not on time, but early. Similarly, if you have a tendency to complain about others, set yourself a fixed period during which you search for ways to praise people. Perhaps you could profit from a suggestion of Rabbi Rami Shapiro, who has habituated himself to write thank-you notes to helpful people. He keeps a stack of stamped note cards handy: "I write to store managers, to authors of books that have moved me, even to friends now and again. In a similar vein, I praise helpful employees to their managers."

Rabbi Shapiro cites advice he heard from David Reynolds, founder of Constructive Living: "Say 'thank you' at least ten times each day."* Reynolds's advice is reminiscent of the Jewish tradition that encourages an "attitude of gratitude" to God for all the good things in one's life by

---

*Shapiro, *Minyan: Ten Principles for Living a Life of Integrity,* 137.

ordaining a minimum of one hundred blessings (*berachot*) to be recited each day.

For the rest of the day, monitor your behavior, don't change it, and ascertain in the course of one day how many times you said thank you. If the number falls short of ten, or you see that there are times when you should have said "thank you," but didn't, seek out opportunities the following day to say "thank you" at least ten times. And if you find opportunities to say it twenty times, who knows, you might help hasten the coming of the Messiah.

DAY

215     THURSDAY

## *Respect Your Family's Privacy*

Believing that their children don't, or shouldn't, have secrets, many parents enter their children's rooms without knocking. Jewish tradition opposes such behavior; the Talmud specifically enjoins, "Do not enter your house suddenly" (that is, without knocking or announcing yourself. *Pesachim* 112a).

Another text extends this prohibition to intruding on your friends. The proof text for this prohibition derives from Genesis. Early in chapter 3, Adam and Eve sin against God's command by eating fruit from the forbidden Tree of Knowledge. When God confronts them, He calls out first, "Where are you?" (Genesis 3:9). From this, the Rabbis deduce that, "a man should never enter his fellow's house suddenly, and we all can learn *derech eretz* (good manners) from the Almighty, Who stood at the entrance of the Garden of Eden and called to Adam...(*Derech Eretz Rabbah* 5:2).

Obviously, God the All-Knowing knew where Adam and Eve were, but He didn't wish to come upon them suddenly. God's behavior should serve as an eternal model of etiquette for us all. Don't startle people.

The next time you find yourself about to push open the door to your child's room, restrain yourself—then knock.

F R I D A Y

# "What Does a Good Guest Say?"

*Ben Zoma used to say: What does a good guest say? "How much trouble has my host gone to for me. How much meat he set before me. How much wine he brought me. How many cakes he served me. And all this trouble he has gone to for my sake!"*

*But what does a bad guest say? "What kind of effort did the host make for me? I have eaten only one slice of bread. I have eaten only one piece of meat, and I have drunk only one cup of wine! Whatever trouble the host went to was done only for the sake of his wife and children."*

—Babylonian Talmud, *Berachot* 58a

Unfortunately, many of us delude ourselves into believing that we are good at expressing gratitude when we are not. Thus, we think that thanking our hosts at the end of an evening is sufficient. But if you have ever left a social event after telling your hosts what a wonderful time you had, and then spent the ride home engaging in a critical character analysis of the very people who have just hosted you, you have practiced ingratitude, not gratitude.

I know that when my wife and I entertain, we spend hours preparing the house and planning the event so that our guests can spend as pleasant an evening as possible. The thought that some of them might afterwards dissect us critically pains me. And I don't think I am being paranoid in suspecting that many of them do so; I realize how often I have acted that way myself.

After you leave the home of people who have tried to provide you with a pleasant evening, the fairest thing is not to say anything disparaging about them. If you find that you can't abide by this rule, at least don't do so during the ride home. Hold off for twenty-four hours. Then, when you finally make your comments, they will probably be toned down. Also, before you voice criticism, think of the efforts these people made to provide you with an enjoyable evening. Is it fair to respond to their behavior with critical observations?

It is unjust to partake of others' hospitality, to thank them and then, like a spy, utilize information you acquired by being in their house to criticize them and diminish their status. If you are certain that the observations you make about others are rarely negative or spiteful, then ask yourself if you would be willing to speak in the same way if you knew your hosts could hear your conversation. If you would not be, then are you sure it is right to make these comments to others?

Of course, it is not enough just to try to refrain from saying critical things. As Ben Zoma suggests, you must cultivate gratitude: "How much trouble has my host gone to for me," is a good starting point for one who wishes to become a good guest at the table of life.

May you have a Shabbat Shalom!

DAY

## 217     SHABBAT

During the course of this Shabbat, try to review the material from the preceding six days, and use some of the texts studied as the basis for discussion during the Shabbat meals:

Day 211.  Make Sure You Have a Friend Who Can Criticize You
Day 212.  Bar Mitzvahs and Bat Mitzvahs, and the Need for a
            New Kind of Hero
Day 213.  Start Your Day with Gratitude
Day 214.  If You Have a Tendency to Complain About Others

Day 215.  Respect Your Family's Privacy
Day 216.  "What Does a Good Guest Say?"

Shabbat Shalom!

# Week 32

## Sunday

## *Questions to Ask Yourself Before You Criticize Another*

People who are very free in expressing their negative views of others are often unaware of how much pain and agony they are causing. I know a woman who dreads her mother-in-law's extended visits, because the older woman expresses whatever it is about her daughter-in-law's manner of running the house of which she disapproves. I know another woman who prides herself on being frank and telling people, even those she knows only slightly, what it is about them that needs improvement.

Your spouse, relatives, or friends might well have traits that annoy you, but not everything that bothers you about another person need be mentioned. Even when you witness things of which you disapprove, it is best to reserve your criticism for important matters of immediate concern. Otherwise, hold your tongue. A woman I know was about to leave on a trip with her husband when a neighbor criticized her for going away and leaving her children with a nanny. The words were not helpful; they had the effect of putting a damper on the woman's trip.*

---

*The critical neighbor might well have felt that her comments were important. However, telling someone about to depart on a trip why you think it is wrong for her to do so is not going to stop the person from taking the journey. If you feel the matter is important, better either to have the discussion well in advance of the trip, when alternatives can be considered, or to wait till the woman returns and discuss it then, when things are less harried and the person is less apt to be defensive.

The Talmud records an unusual story about Rabbi Shimon bar Yochai. An ardent second-century C.E. opponent of Roman rule over Israel, Rabbi Shimon learned that the government had issued a death sentence against him, and fled with his son to a cave. A miracle occurred, and a carob tree and a well were created to provide them with sustenance.

For twelve years the two men remained in hiding, spending their days in Torah study. Finally, word reached them that the death sentence had been annulled. When they went out from the cave, they saw people plowing and sowing. Having accustomed himself to spending all his time studying Torah, Rabbi Shimon was outraged: "These people forsake eternal life to engage in temporal life." He cast so withering a glance upon all he saw that, in the words of the Talmud, everything, including crops, was "immediately incinerated." At that point a heavenly voice called out, "Have you emerged to destroy my world? Return to your cave!" Only after a year had passed, and presumably the two men were ready to judge those who lived differently from them more moderately and fairly, were they deemed fit to live among normal people (*Shabbat* 33b).

The next time you find yourself ready to start telling someone just what it is about him or her of which you disapprove, first ask yourself these questions:

- ♦ Are my words necessary?
- ♦ Am I being fair in my critique, or might my criticism be exaggerated?
- ♦ Will my words hurt the other person's feelings, and if so, is there a way to say them that will minimize the hurt?
- ♦ Are my words likely to bring about a change in the other person's behavior?
- ♦ How would I feel if someone criticized me in the same way I'm criticizing another?
- ♦ How do I feel about offering this criticism? Am I looking forward to doing so? Since a person who has acted inappropriately is most likely to change his or her behavior when the criticism is delivered lovingly, if you find yourself looking forward to admon-

ishing another, don't do it. Your motives are probably insincere, and your criticism will be ineffective.

Don't speak up until you have answered these questions adequately.

M O N D A Y

# Knowing When to Step Aside

*In justice shall you judge your fellow human being.*
—Leviticus 19:15

This Torah injunction to judge one's fellow fairly was directed to judges. Thus, the Talmud's Rabbi Pappa cautions a judge not to adjudicate the case of someone he either loves or hates, for "in the case of a loved one, one does not see his faults; in the case of a hated one, one does not see his merits" (*Ketubot* 105b).

Michael Katz and Gershon Schwartz, authors of *Swimming in the Sea of the Talmud*, broaden the applicability of this talmudic injunction to cover contemporary situations, including instances unrelated to courts and judges. In so doing, the authors show how even the best intentioned people can act unwisely and unfairly when their own emotions are engaged:

A father who has been coaching Little League for several years gets his own son on his team. Several friends suggest that it is not the best of situations to be your child's coach, but the father thinks he can handle it. In a critical game, with the championship on the line, the coach picks his son to be starting pitcher, despite the boy's mediocre record. The child has a bad outing; the opposition hits practically everything he throws. Despite the unhappiness of the other team members, and over the complaints of many parents in the stands, the coach refuses to take his son out and put in a new pitcher. Later he blames the defeat on the bad calls of the umpire and the poor fielding of the players. What the coach-father refused to acknowledge is that it is so very difficult to see the shortcomings of those we love. A coach has to treat all his players equally; a father has to show special attention to his own child. Sometimes these two roles are mutually exclusive.

A supervisor at work is asked to put together an evaluation of one of the firm's employees who is being considered for a promotion. Just last year, however, the two women fought bitterly over the way a job was being handled. Harsh words were exchanged, and feelings were hurt. The employee questioned the supervisor's competence and submitted a complaint to the boss. The supervisor has never forgotten, or forgiven. Now, *she* will have the last word, making sure that the employee pays for what she did to her. Despite the fact that everyone else values the employee and raves about her work, the supervisor cannot find anything positive to say about her.

Perhaps there are those who can objectively assess the work or abilities of a person they either love or hate, but such people are rare. Katz and Schwartz point out that that is why the earlier cited Rabbi Pappa "suggests we acknowledge this and step aside, allowing someone more objective and less involved to judge the situation and make the difficult decisions." *

The Torah commands us to judge fairly and with justice. When our feelings are too charged for us to be objective, we are obligated to step aside.

*Katz and Schwartz, *Swimming in the Sea of the Talmud*, 195–96.

T U E S D A Y

# *When You've Judged Another Unfairly*

The First Book of Samuel begins with the story of Hannah, a married woman who is deeply distressed over her inability to conceive. She enters the Israelite temple at Shiloh, where she weeps and quietly beseeches God to give her a child.

Eli, the high priest, seeing Hannah's lips moving, but hearing no sound, assumes she is drunk. He walks over and reproves her, "How long will you make a drunken spectacle of yourself? Sober up!" (1:14).

Hannah is wounded by Eli's harsh words: "Oh, no, my lord, I am a very unhappy woman." She explains to him that she has been pouring out her heart to God because of her anguish and distress.

How embarrassed Eli must have been when he realized how unfairly he had spoken to Hannah. Instead of obeying the Torah injunction, "In justice shall you judge your fellow" (Leviticus 19:15), he had leaped to an unjust conclusion.

As soon as Eli realizes his error, he blesses Hannah that she go in peace and that God grant her all that she has requested. A year later, the future prophet Samuel, whom the Bible compares to Moses and Aaron (Psalms 99:6), is born to her.

Many of us behave like Eli; when we see someone do something we do not understand, we condemn the person without knowing all the facts. One sin to which Jews confess on Yom Kippur is "for the sin we have committed before You by hasty judgment [of others]." The cruel conclusions to which such hasty judgments can lead have been highlighted in "On the Street," a poem by Roger Bush:

She was pretty and she smiled at the men approaching.
I could see her in profile. A sweet thing and cheeky, too.
Embarrassed males turned away.

Quickened their pace; looked guilty, some blushed.
But undaunted, she met with an expectant smile the next,
Only again to be refused.
Soliciting, I thought; a prostitute; in broad daylight;
Until she turned,
And I saw she was selling buttons for charity.

He staggered down the steps and fell, Lord,
A crumpled mass on the footpath.
His bottle broke and liquid spilled across the walk.
He's drunk, I thought. Disgust. Disdain. Until…
Two girls rushed from a nearby car and cried,
"It's Daddy. Please help. He's ill."

He caught my gaze. This greedy-eyed young man,
He too had seen the open handbag on the aged arm,
With the few dollars exposed to view,
He stalked the prey, and the old woman just window-shopped.
He'll grab and run, I thought, but no,
Quietly, he tapped her shoulder, pointed to the bag,
Exchanged smiles.
They went their way.
O Lord, forgive me, forgive me.
Why do I always think the worst of your children?

If you have judged another unfairly, particularly if you have shared your low estimation of the person with others, you are obligated to go to all the people to whom you have spoken ill of the person, and confess to them how wrong you were.*

Second, like Eli, you should do a favor or some act of kindness for the person whom you misjudged.

Finally, start trying to judge people less critically and more compassionately.

---

*Does ethics dictate that you should also tell the person whom you slandered what you said about him or her to others? Usually not. If the person learns what you said, this may cause him or her terrible pain (see Day 192).

# "Therefore Was Man Created Singly"*

In ancient Israel, when a witness stepped forward to offer testimony in a capital case, the judges gave him an extended and very somber warning. First they informed him that his testimony could not be based on conjecture or hearsay, and that he would be subjected to an extremely detailed cross-examination. They also reminded him that civil cases differ from capital ones: in a civil case, if a witness lies or errs and later wishes to repent, "he may gain atonement through monetary restitution, but in a capital case the blood of the innocent, executed through false testimony, and that of his descendants who might have been born to him will haunt the witness to the end of time."**

But this admonition was still deemed insufficient. The court then subjected the witness to yet one more biblical lesson:

Therefore was man [in Hebrew, *Adam,* the name both of the first person and also the word for "person"] created singly, to teach us that whoever takes a single life it is as though he destroyed a whole world, and whoever saves a single life it is as though he saved a whole world.

It is also meant to foster peace between people, because no one can boast to his neighbor: "My ancestor was greater than yours." ...

It also serves to dramatize the greatness of the Holy One, blessed be He, for a person strikes many coins from one mold and they all resemble each other, but the King of Kings, the Holy One,

---

*Mishna, *Sanhedrin* 4:5.

**The Rabbis then offered the witness a lesson in the Bible, reminding him that when Cain murdered Abel, God denounced him with an oddly worded denunciation: "Your brother's *bloods* cry out to Me from the earth" (Genesis 4:10). Since there is no plural for "blood" in Hebrew, the Rabbis understood "bloods" as implying Abel's blood and that of all his unborn descendants.

forms all mankind from the mold of the first man, and each is unique. Therefore, each person is obligated to say, "For my sake was the world created."

—Mishna, *Sanhedrin* 4:5

As this passage makes clear, Jewish ethics insists upon the great value of the individual. The Rabbis based this on God's creation of one man, Adam. Had Adam died, the world would have died with him. From this, the Rabbis deduced that each human being, created in the image of God and of Adam, is as valuable as a world.

Troublingly, in many Mishnaic texts, one finds a somewhat different wording: "...whoever destroys a single *Jewish* life it is as though he destroyed a whole world, and whoever saves a single *Jewish* life it is as though he saved a whole world." But this reading makes no sense. Adam was not Jewish (the first Jew was Abraham). All we can learn from Adam's life is the sacredness of each individual, not the sacredness of each *Jewish* individual. Because all human beings descend from Adam, and because they are created in the divine image, all human life is sacred. Clearly, *this* was the Mishna's original wording.

This text is also an effective antidote to racism. All people are descended from the same man, so all people are related. There are no superior and inferior races.

Finally, the text teaches that each individual is unique. When a government or a ruler mints coins, each coin looks precisely the same. But God fashioned human beings, and each looks different (even identical twins have different fingerprints). Therefore, each person should feel a sense of pride: He or she is created in God's image, and is like no one else who was ever created.

About the most religious act a person can do is relate to those whom he or she meets as having been created in God's image and possessing infinite value. One who follows this guideline will show respect to all people, not just the wealthy and prominent. Similarly, perhaps the most irreligious act one can do is to treat another human being without respect. Doing so shows that one does not really believe that person to be in God's image. Therefore, while the mistreatment of a person is a sin against him or her, it is also a sin against God.

Finally, as the Mishna reminds us, to treat yourself badly also is a sin. If the world was created for your sake, aren't you worthy of respect and kindness?

T H U R S D A Y

## "If Someone Wishes to Kill You, Get Up Early and Kill Him First"*

While Jewish law teaches that each human life possesses infinite value (see yesterday's entry), it also ordains that a human being who murders innocent people forfeits his right to live. The only biblical law repeated in each of the Torah's five books is that ordaining capital punishment for premeditated murderers (see, for example, Genesis 9:6, "Whoever sheds the blood of man, by man shall his blood be shed").**

Regarding those who set out to murder others, the Book of Exodus teaches that if a thief tunnels into a house at night and is discovered, the householder has the right to kill him. At first reading, this ruling seems surprising, since Jewish law forbids killing someone who is committing a property offense. However, the Torah assumes that a thief breaking into a person's house at night, aware that it is probably occupied, is prepared to kill the householder; therefore, if the householder preemptively kills the thief, "there is no bloodguilt" (Exodus 22:1). The sole exception is when the householder has reason to be certain that the thief has no intention of killing him or her (see Exodus 22:2).

---

*Babylonian Talmud, *Sanhedrin* 72a.
**See also Exodus 21:12, Leviticus 24:17, Numbers 35:31, and Deuteronomy 19:11–13 and 19:19.

In the Talmud's language, "If someone wishes to kill you, get up early and kill him first."* The logic informing this talmudic teaching applies to national as well as individual threats. Prior to the Six-Day War, Israel's Arab enemies repeatedly made it clear that they intended to destroy her, a threat that prompted Israel to launch a preemptive attack on June 5, 1967. Similarly, in the early 1980s, Iraq was preparing an atom bomb for use in a war against Israel. In 1981, when Israel orchestrated a destruction of the Iraqi nuclear reactor that could produce the bomb, Jews throughout the world understood this attack as the legitimate fulfillment of this talmudic dictum.**

According to Jewish ethics, and as this talmudic teaching makes clear, both individuals and nations have the right to prepare preemptive attacks against those who plan to destroy them.

D A Y

223

F R I D A Y

## *Be Conscious of the Goodness and Sweetness in Others*

The Bible, Talmud, and Midrash are fascinating in their willingness to describe even their greatest figures' faults. Thus the Bible

---

*A friend has argued with me that this rabbinic aphorism in support of self-defense is so obvious that it does not need to be taught. But is it truly so obvious? Less than sixty years ago, Mahatma Gandhi, regarded as one of the twentieth century's great saints, argued that it would be better to let the Nazis conquer the whole world than for the Allies to fight against them (see Day 30). And two thousand years ago the New Testament attributed to Jesus the teaching, "Offer the wicked man no resistance, but if anyone strikes you on the right cheek, offer the other also" (Matthew 5:39).

**The rest of the world was far less sympathetic, and Israel was almost universally condemned for bombing Iraq's nuclear reactor. Since the Iraqi government had made clear its extreme animus and its desire to destroy Israel, the question is why was so much of the world opposed to what Israel had done?

does not hide Joseph's youthful arrogance (Genesis 37:5–11), Isaac's naïveté about his sons' characters (Genesis 27), and David's adultery (II Samuel 11–12). In the Talmud and Midrash as well, we learn of flaws in otherwise great rabbinic figures. We are not informed of them in order to lower our estimation of these rabbis, but to tell us how they overcame these failings—and, by extension, how we may overcome our own (see Day 150 for Maimonides' advice on how to overcome negative habits and behavior).

Of one prominent rabbi we learn:

Rabbi Yannai was taking a walk, and he saw a man of impressive appearance [who appeared to be a scholar]. Rabbi Yannai said to him, "Would you be my guest?"

He said, "Yes."

So Rabbi Yannai took him to his house, and gave him food and drink. He spoke to him of talmudic matters and found that the man knew nothing; then he spoke about the Mishna, the Aggadah, and the Bible, and saw that the man was ignorant of them all. Then he said to him, "Take the wine cup and recite the blessing."

The man said, "Let Yannai make the blessing in his own house."

Rabbi Yannai said, "Can you repeat what I say to you?"

He said, "Yes."

Then say, "A dog has eaten Yannai's bread."

The man jumped up, seized Yannai, and said, "You have my inheritance, which you are withholding from me."

Yannai said, "What inheritance of yours do I have?"

The man answered, "Once I passed a school and I heard the voices of the children reciting, 'The Law which Moses commanded us is the inheritance of the congregation of [all the children of] Jacob' (Deuteronomy 33:4); they did not say, 'the inheritance of the congregation [only] of Yannai."

Then Rabbi Yannai said, "What merit have you [that is, what good deeds have you done] that you should eat at my table?"

The man said, "I never heard malicious gossip and repeated it, nor did I ever see two people quarreling without making peace between them."

Said Rabbi Yannai, "You have such fine qualities [*derech eretz*] and I called you a dog." *

Sometimes we know a few details about a person and make unfair assumptions about him or her, but when we look deeper, we learn of virtues we never imagined. "Man looks at the outward appearance, but God sees into the heart," the Bible teaches (I Samuel 16:7). There are times when we have to learn to try and look with God's eyes.

May you have a Shabbat Shalom!

DAY

## 224    SHABBAT

During the course of this Shabbat, try to review the material from the preceding six days, and use some of the texts studied as the basis for discussion during the Shabbat meals:

Day 218. Questions to Ask Yourself Before You Criticize Another
Day 219. Knowing When to Step Aside
Day 220. When You've Judged Another Unfairly
Day 221. "Therefore Was Man Created Singly"
Day 222. "If Someone Wishes to Kill You, Get Up Early
            and Kill Him First"
Day 223. Be Conscious of the Goodness and Sweetness in Others

Shabbat Shalom!

* *Leviticus Rabbah* 9:3.

SUNDAY

# The Good That You Do Lives On

In many synagogues throughout the world, there is an adult who volunteers to be the "candy man." Throughout the long Saturday-morning service, he dispenses chocolates and other candies to children attending services. I once heard Rabbi Jack Riemer reminisce about what influenced him to become his congregation's candy man:

I got the custom from Mayer Grumet, who sat in front of us in the synagogue in which I grew up [in Pittsburgh]. Mayer Grumet was not a very rich man. He had a bit of a grocery. He was not a very great scholar, or even a very observant Jew. But he had one wonderful quality: he loved kids. So every Shabbat that he came to *shul,* he came with a bag of Hershey bars. And I have to confess that when I was a child, I didn't go to *shul* only to hear the rabbi's sermon or to hear the cantor. I went to *shul,* at least in part, in order to get a Hershey bar from Mayer Grumet. And now I do it. And I don't think that I ever planned it this way, but somehow the example of what he did registered inside me. And who knows? Someday one of the kids in my synagogue now may grow up to be the candy man for the kids of the next generation because of me. Who knows in what city or what country that will be, but it could happen. And if it does, then Mayer Grumet, who has been gone for over forty years, will still be affecting kids forty years from now.

In addition to the immortality that Judaism believes God bestows on human beings, good deeds also bestow life beyond death. As a friend once told Rabbi Jeffrey Salkin, "Every time I recommend a book to my child to read, and that book had been recommended to me by Mrs. Cohen, my fourth-grade teacher, that's [part of] Mrs. Cohen's immortality."

As one grows old and approaches death, is there a more pleasing consolation than knowing that the good you have done for others will go on being done, even by people you have never met and will never know?

MONDAY

# When It's Right to Be Early

Shmaryahu Levine, the early Zionist leader, claimed that throughout his whole life he had tried to be late to a Jewish meeting and never succeeded.

Jewish events have a well-deserved reputation for starting late. And so, when Rabbi Shlomo Zalman Auerbach, the great Jerusalem sage, was asked to officiate at a wedding, the driver who escorted him timed his pickup to bring the rabbi to the wedding hall about half an hour after the wedding's scheduled time.

When the rabbi asked the driver why he had come late, the young man answered, "Wedding ceremonies always start late, and I didn't want to waste the rabbi's time."

Rabbi Auerbach wasn't satisfied with this explanation. "There are so many things a bridegroom has on his mind. There are countless worries. ...One of his concerns is that the rabbi who is performing the ceremony arrive on time. I cannot bear the thought of my contributing to the *chassan's* [groom's] anxiety. I do not mind arriving half an hour early. I can sit on the side and not be a bother to anyone. Anything is better than adding to the bridegroom's worries." *

A woman I know went to her daughter's school to watch her per-

* Teller, *And from Jerusalem, His Word,* 170–72.

form in a second-grade play. She arrived at the school just a moment or two before the play was to begin. All the other second-graders seemed excited, but her daughter was crying as she ran over to her mother. "I didn't know if you were going to come," she blurted out between sobs.

The mother told me that she resolved on that day always to come early to such events.

While we should always strive to be on time, when the event is extremely important to the other person, don't try to be on time; try to be early. At worst, a few minutes of your time will be wasted, and if you encounter unexpected delays, you will still be on time. Alternatively, always carry a book or article with you; that way, even if you are early, you need not waste any time.

The commandment to "love your neighbor as yourself" means to do for another person what you would like others to do for you. When it is important to you that others be on time, you appreciate it when they arrive punctually or even a little early. Do the same for them.

DAY

## 227 TUESDAY

# "His Mercy Is Upon All His Works"

On two occasions when the Bible describes a utopian world, the creatures inhabiting it are vegetarian. Thus, in the Garden of Eden, God instructs Adam and Eve to restrict their diet to vegetables and fruits (Genesis 1:29). Later, during the time of Noah, God gives humankind permission to eat meat (Genesis 9:3). But the prophet Isaiah, envisioning a future messianic age, sees it as one in which even the animals will be herbivorous, a world in which "the wolf shall dwell with the lamb and the leopard lie down with the kid," and "the cow and the bear shall graze, and their young shall lie down together" (11:6,7).

Although permission to eat meat was apparently granted initially as a concession to human nature,* meat-eating has long since become an important part of traditional Jewish culture. In Jewish tradition, one of the characteristics of a joyous holiday meal is that both meat and wine are served (Babylonian Talmud, *Pesachim* 109a; obviously, vegetarians and recovering alcoholics should not feel bound by this tradition, since eating meat or consuming liquor would destroy the joy of the holiday for them.)

Nonetheless, Jewish law never wanted the permission to eat meat to lead to an indifference to animal suffering. Thus the slaughtering of animals was strictly regulated, and great effort was expended to limit their pain (see Days 171 and 172).

And although the Rabbis regarded human life as far more valuable than animal life (because people, unlike animals, are created "in God's image"), they also maintained that the treatment of animals is of concern not only to animals and humans; it very much matters to God. Of no less a figure than Rabbi Judah the Prince (editor of the Mishna, and the most distinguished rabbi of the early third century C.E.), the Talmud relates:

> The sufferings of Rabbi Judah came to him because of a certain incident, and left him in the same way. What was the incident that led to his suffering?
>
> A calf was once taken to be slaughtered. It [escaped, and] ran to Rabbi Judah, where it hid its head under his cloak, and cried.
>
> Rabbi Judah, however [pushed it away, and] said, "Go. It was for this that you were created."
>
> It was then said [in heaven], "Since he has no pity, let us bring suffering upon him." [For the next thirteen years, Rabbi Judah suffered from various painful ailments.]
>
> And how did his sufferings end?
>
> One day his maid was sweeping the house, and she came upon some young rats. She was about to sweep them out of the house, when Rabbi Judah stopped her. "Let them be. As it is written in Psalms, 'His mercy is upon all His works'" (145:9).
>
> It was then said [in heaven], "Since he is merciful, let us be merciful to him" [and he was immediately healed].**

---

*The Talmud teaches, "A man should not eat meat unless he has a special craving for it" (*Hullin* 84a).

** *Bava Mezia* 85a.

In traditional Jewish thought, a tender concern for animals has long been regarded as an important characteristic of a great leader. A famous rabbinic Midrash suggests that Moses' kindness as a shepherd was one of the factors that motivated God to choose him to lead the Jews from Egypt:

Once, while Moses was tending the flock of his father-in-law, Jethro, one young sheep ran away. Moses ran after it until the sheep reached a shady place, where he found a pool of water and began to drink. When Moses reached the sheep, he said: "I did not know you ran away because you were thirsty. Now, you must be exhausted [from running]. Moses put the sheep on his shoulders and carried him [back to the herd]. God said, "Because you tend the sheep belonging to human beings with such mercy, by your life I swear you shall be the shepherd of My sheep, Israel." *

WEDNESDAY

# Be Kind to Your Enemy's Animal

In the most famous episode of Mario Puzo's novel *The Godfather* a gangster arranges to cut off the head of a horse belonging to a man who has tried to thwart him, and deposits the bloodied head on the man's bed. The Torah, composed some three thousand years earlier, rules that even if you hate someone, you are forbidden to take it out on his family members, or even on his animal: "When you see the donkey of your enemy lying under its burden and would refrain from raising it, you must nevertheless raise it with him" (Exodus 23:5).

The Torah does not legislate that if you see your enemy himself

* *Exodus Rabbah* 2:2.

struggling with a heavy load, you are obliged to help him (though obviously Jewish ethics would encourage you to do so). But it rules that you cannot let an animal suffer because of a personal dispute between you and its owner. Although the heavily laden animal is the obvious beneficiary of this Torah law, a third-century C.E. rabbinic midrash highlights how obedience to this regulation can also transform your relationship with your antagonist:

> Rabbi Alexandri said: Two donkey drivers who hated each other were walking on a road when the donkey of one lay down under its burden. His companion saw it, and at first he passed on. But then he reflected: Is it not written in the Torah, "If you see your enemy's donkey lying down under its burden…"? So he returned, lent a hand, and helped his enemy in loading and unloading. He began talking to his enemy: "Release a bit here, pull up over there, unload over here." Thus peace came about between them, so that the driver of the overloaded donkey said, "Did I not suppose that he hated me? But look how compassionate he has been." By and by, the two entered an inn, ate and drank together, and became fast friends. [What caused them to make peace and to become fast friends? Because one of them kept what is written in the Torah.]
> —*Tanhuma, Mishpatim #1**

Many people find it hard to be fair to someone they dislike, let alone to the hated person's animal. The Torah teaches us how to be fair to both.

*With minor variations. I have followed the translation of William Braude in Bialik and Ravnitzky, eds., *Book of Legends*, 459.

THURSDAY

# "Seek Peace and Pursue It"

$M$any Jews, aware of the talmudic teaching that there are 613 commandments in the Torah, believe that the goal of a committed Jew's life is to observe all 613. But that is not the case. For example, one commandment prescribes that a man who divorces his wife write her a "bill of divorcement" (Deuteronomy 24:1–3).* Are you obligated to carry this out? Only if you get divorced, but obviously it is far preferable to remain happily married and never have the need to practice this particular commandment.

There are other biblical laws like this one, that need to be observed only when the opportunity presents itself. For example, Exodus 23:5 legislates (see yesterday's entry), "If you see the donkey of your enemy lying under its burden, and would refrain from raising it, you must nevertheless raise it with him." The operative word here is "if." *If* you see your enemy's donkey struggling under its burden, you are obliged to help your enemy and his animal, but you're not required to go around looking for struggling donkeys needing help.

Concerning peace, however, the Psalmist teaches, "Seek peace and pursue it" (Psalms 34:15). The Rabbis understand this to mean, "Seek peace where you are, and pursue it elsewhere" (*Leviticus Rabbah* 9:9).

While "Seek peace where you are," imposes upon us an obligation to reconcile with those with whom *we have* had a fight, what does "pursue it elsewhere" mean?

Ask yourself: Within your family or among your friends, are there those who have had a falling out, and what can you do to reconcile the feuding parties? Apparently, according to the Psalmist's teachings, one should not wait for the feuding parties to come to you; they likely never will. Instead, "pursue" the opportunity. Speak with them and try to influence them to make up.

---

*According to the Torah, only a man can issue a *get*, a divorce. However, Jewish law was later amended to prohibit a man from issuing a *get* against his wife's wishes (see Day 253).

F R I D A Y

# On Loving Yourself

The biblical verse that explicitly ordains "Love your neighbor as yourself" contains the implicit commandment to "love yourself."

To love oneself not only has implications for how we regard and treat ourselves, but also for how we treat others. For example, I wonder if there has been an abusive parent throughout history who loved himself or herself. People who despise themselves are far more likely to act brutally to their children and others than people with a better self-image.

A two-hundred-year-old Chasidic story reflects how caring about oneself can affect how one treats others. Rabbi Dov Baer of Mezeritch (1704–1772), successor to Israel Baal Shem Tov, the founder of Chasidism, went with several disciples to solicit a charitable donation from a wealthy man. At the man's house, Dov Baer learned that the rich man lived in penurious circumstances. He ate old dry bread, and seldom had meat and fruit at his meals. Instead of focusing on the donation he had intended to solicit, Dov Baer argued with the man on the need for him to live better, to have fresh bread at his table, and to augment his vegetable dinners with meat, fruit, and desserts.

Upon leaving, Dov Baer's disciples expressed amazement at his behavior. "What do you care what that man chooses to eat? What business is it of ours?"

"You don't understand," Dov Baer answered. "If that man eats fresh bread, then at the very least he'll give poor people stale bread. But if he himself lives on stale bread, he'll assume that the poor can get by on stones."

In short, the Torah's command reminds us not only to love our neighbor, but to love and treat ourselves well, too.

May you have a Shabbat Shalom!

S H A B B A T

During the course of this Shabbat, try to review the material from the preceding six days, and use some of the texts studied as the basis for discussion during the Shabbat meals:

Day 225.  The Good That You Do Lives On
Day 226.  When It's Right to Be Early
Day 227.  "His Mercy Is Upon All His Works"
Day 228.  Be Kind to Your Enemy's Animal
Day 229.  "Seek Peace and Pursue It"
Day 230.  On Loving Yourself

Shabbat Shalom!

# WEEK 34

S U N D A Y

## "There Is No Messenger in a Case of Sin"

That every human being is created in God's image should make each of us feel valued; it means that we are God-like in that we know good from evil. But such knowledge has a downside, for since we know good from evil, that means that we bear responsibility for the evil we do, *even* if we are commanded to do so by a parent, boss, or military superior.

Thus, the Talmud rules that if a parent instructs a child to keep a lost object he has found rather than return it to its owner, the child should disobey (*Bava Mezia* 32a). Since biblical law commands one to return a lost object, the parent is commanding the child to violate God's law, a demand that he or she hasn't the right to make. Obviously, a very young child, even one familiar with Torah law, will feel uncomfortable flouting a parental order. A more mature young person, however, should not allow a parent to force him or her to participate in an act of thievery.

Similarly, although most Americans would regard a boss who orders an employee to do something illegal (such as billing for an exaggerated number of hours, or using lower quality materials than that for which the client is paying) as bearing the major responsibility for the crime committed, Jewish law insists that the one who actually commits the crime is the one upon whom blame primarily falls.* As the Talmud reasons, "There is no messenger in a case of sin" (*Kiddushin* 42b). Normally, one cannot blame a messenger for the content of the message he delivers; no matter how evil or infuriating it is, blame should be directed only against the one who sent the message. But if a person is sent to perform an evil act, he cannot defend his behavior by saying that he was only acting as another's messenger. Because "there is no messenger in a case of sin," the person who carries out the evil act bears responsibility for the evil he or she does. As the Talmud asks rhetorically, "When the words of the master [God] and the words of the pupil [a human being] are in conflict, whose words should be obeyed? [Obviously, the master's]" (*Kiddushin* 42b).**

The same ethical reasoning applies to crimes ordered by a military superior. At war crimes trials of Nazi murderers, the defendants often tried to evade responsibility by claming that they were "just following orders." From Judaism's perspective, such a claim is nonsense. Why should a Nazi officer's order "You shall murder" carry more weight than God's command "You shall not murder"?

In October 1956, on the eve of the Sinai campaign against Egypt, the Israeli government ordered Israeli Arabs to stay in their homes.

---

* That the one who performed the evil act is held accountable does not, of course, absolve the one who ordered the act from moral responsibility.

** Thus, if A instructs B to do wrong, and B does so, then B is regarded as acting of his own accord, for were he merely following instructions, he would obey God's command in preference to that of the person ordering him to act wrongly.

Some Arab villagers in Kfar Kassim, perhaps unaware of the curfew, went out to work. When Israeli troops encountered them, they opened fire and killed forty-nine people.

At their court-martial, the soldiers defended themselves with the claim that they were just following orders. Eight soldiers were convicted by an Israeli court that ruled that no "order" from a superior officer could justify killing innocent people.

Whenever a "superior" orders you to do something evil, or even just unfair, bear in mind that your true superior, God, is the superior of the one who issued the order.

MONDAY

## The Power of Goodness

In *Do Unto Others*, Rabbi Dr. Abraham Twerski, a psychiatrist and a Chasidic rabbi, offers the ultimate *bikur cholim* (visiting the sick) story, a powerful example of how the mitzvah of visiting the sick can transform and elevate the life of both the ill person and the visitors:

> Yossi was born with a defective heart. His parents were advised that he would need an operation when he turned seven, and that the operation was best done in America.
>
> Yossi's parents, both Israelis, knew no one in America, so when the time came, a mutual friend put them in touch with me, and I found a medical center in Pittsburgh, where I live, where the surgery could be performed. Several months later, Yossi and his parents arrived.
>
> Neither Yossi nor his parents understood a single word of English, so I put out the word in the Pittsburgh community for anyone who spoke Hebrew to contact me. Twenty-nine people volunteered, and I contacted all of them for an emergency meeting.
>
> At this meeting, I explained the predicament. Yossi would be

hospitalized for at least two weeks, and it was absolutely essential that an interpreter be available at all times. There was no way he could make himself understood to the staff. I asked people to volunteer several hours of their time to be in attendance, and we arranged a schedule that covered twenty-four hours a day for two weeks. Each person had an assigned time, and we agreed that one person would not leave until the next arrived. The plan operated like clockwork. Yossi and his parents were never left alone, and not only was there effective interpretation, but the family also received the support of interested people. The postoperative period was not without many anxious moments, and Yossi's parents swear that without the moral support of so many friends, they could never have survived it.

The entire hospital was impressed by this community cooperation and devotion, and when Yossi was discharged, the surgeon waived his bill! The family had no insurance coverage, and the hospital wrote off whatever they could and gave them the lowest rate. This was paid through donations made by friends of the small community that had sprung up around Yossi. Before Yossi left for home, a gala party was held, attended by the volunteers, contributors, surgeon, and other members of the hospital staff. Tearful good-byes were said, there was much embracing, lots of people gave of themselves and got back this: they had helped to save a little boy. Along the way, each one discovered qualities inside them that might never have been tapped if not for Yossi. On top of this, many friendships had been formed during this period, and these people who had not known each other became close friends, having worked for a common cause.

Six years later, on a visit to Israel, I made a surprise visit to Yossi, but he wasn't home: he was playing basketball! I went to the playground and could not stop my tears of joy when I saw the robust little boy who had once been so hampered by illness playing a game of hoops. On my return to Pittsburgh I contacted the participants in Yossi's operation for a reunion, and we all bonded again as we shared the news. One man originally had been reluctant to help because he was so terrified of hospitals. Now he related that he no longer hesitated to visit friends when they were ill; he had gotten over a phobia that had controlled him.

It's twenty years later. Yossi is happily married and has a child. He sends cards twice a year, which we circulate. In this way the group stays in touch, and when a member needs help or wants to share happiness, we are there. What we did for Yossi pales in comparison to what Yossi did for us. Each of us is stronger as a result of this event. That is the power of goodness.*

TUESDAY

# Teach Your Child a Profession

Judaism advocates a life of balance; for example, it condemns as unbalanced a parent who takes care to provide for a child's spiritual needs (by raising the child in a religious household and teaching him or her Torah), but does not prepare the child to live as a productive adult who can earn a living. In the Talmud's words, "The father is obliged ...to teach [his son] a trade or profession....Rabbi Judah says: Whoever does not teach his son a trade or profession teaches him to be a thief" (Babylonian Talmud, *Kiddushin* 29a).

In today's world, where women have equal work opportunities and equal needs to earn money, a parent would be obligated to ensure that daughters as well as sons are taught a trade or profession.

What is the link between not training a child for a profession and teaching him or her to become a thief? A human being who has no productive way to make money will be drawn to making it in unproductive and illegal ways.

*Twerski, *Do Unto Others*, 16–18.

Of course, the acquisition of work skills alone is no guarantee of honesty. There are honest and dishonest doctors, lawyers, accountants, teachers, and business executives. That is one reason why Jewish law puts such emphasis on the obligation of parents to teach their children Torah (Babylonian Talmud, *Kiddushin* 29a). Indeed, the Rabbis believed that the most powerful way to produce honest citizens is through the combination of a life of Torah accompanied by labor: "Rabban Gamliel ...says: The study of Torah combined with a worldly occupation is an excellent thing, for the energy needed by both keeps one away from sin. All Torah study that does not have work accompanying it must in the end come to nothing and be the cause of sin" (*Ethics of the Fathers* 2:2).

As Rabban Gamliel reminds us, neither the acquisition of professional competence alone nor of Torah competence alone guarantees moral competence. A life that combines religious/moral and professional training almost always does.

DAY

235　WEDNESDAY

## *Teach Your Child That What Matters Most to God Is Goodness*

The Hebrew word for parent, *horeh,* is related to that for teacher, *moreh.* From Judaism's perspective, the parent's most fundamental task (in addition to providing a child with love and proper physical care) is to teach one's child to be a committed Jew and a kind and moral person.

Although many parents acknowledge the supreme importance of raising their children to be good people, in practice most parents convey an entirely different set of priorities to their children. For many years,

Dennis Prager has been asking parents to ask their children of all ages, "What do you think matters most to your mother and father—that you be successful, popular, musically or athletically talented, or good?" Parents who do this often have been shocked to learn that very few children listed being a good person as their parents' highest priority.

However, being good *is* first in Judaism's scale of values. As noted earlier (see Day 120), the Talmud teaches that the first question addressed to every human being after he or she dies is not "Did you graduate in the upper ten percent of your class?" or "Did you make a lot of money?" but "Did you conduct your business affairs honestly?" And the prophet Micah (eight century B.C.E.) taught that the essence of what God wants of human beings is "to do justice, love mercy and walk humbly with God" (Micah 6:8). Thus there are great figures in the Jewish tradition who were not professionally successful (Rabbi Joshua ben Hannaniah was a poor man who earned his living making needles; Jerusalem Talmud, *Berachot* 4:1) or popular (many of Jeremiah's fellow Israelites wanted to kill him) or musically or athletically talented (if the great nineteenth-century rabbinic scholar Rabbi Israel Salanter had such talent, scholars have yet to learn about it). What unites these people is goodness.

The traditional texts (the Torah and Talmud) are the Jewish tradition's source for teaching goodness. Therefore, a commitment to Jewish ethics requires parents to ensure that their children receive an education that emphasizes Judaism's insistence on ethical behavior (for example, sending your child to a Jewish school that puts primary emphasis on observance of Judaism's ritual laws and does not place sufficient emphasis on the ethical ones would not fulfill this requirement). Make sure you check out the values taught at the school to which you send your children with the same intensity with which you examine the school's academic credentials.

A parent who provides for his or her child's material needs and who has sent the child to good schools has done much. But if a parent has not reared his or her child with a comprehensive system of ethical values, and with an understanding that what matters most to God is goodness, then the parent has not fulfilled the most important task the Jewish tradition imposes upon him or her as a *horeh:* to be a *moreh.*

THURSDAY

# Don't Give Away Too Much

Several years ago I came across a book titled *Women Who Date Too Much and Others Who Should Be So Lucky.* Perhaps this entry should have been called "People Who Donate Too Much and Others Who Should Be So Generous."

Surprisingly, Jewish law does teach that there *is* such a thing as being too generous. Thus, while it is appropriate to give ten percent or more of your income to charity, the Rabbis of the Talmud passed an ordinance that no one should give away more than twenty percent of his or her income (*Ketubot* 50a).

Their rationale? They feared that overgenerous giving would cause the donor to become impoverished and end up needing help from others. Some historians speculate that the Rabbis' ruling, which was issued during the rise of early Christianity, was directed against the Christian idealization of poverty, as epitomized by the vows made by monks and nuns.

For its part, Judaism has long deemed poverty a curse. As a *midrash* teaches: "Nothing in the world is more grievous than poverty, the most terrible of all sufferings....For one who is crushed by poverty is like one to whom all the troubles of the world cling and upon whom all the curses of Deuteronomy (28:15–68) have descended. Our Rabbis said: If all the sufferings and pain in the world were gathered [on one side of a scale] and poverty was on the other side, poverty would outweigh them all" (*Exodus Rabbah* 31:12 and 31:14).*

The battle persists between those who idealize total giving and

---

*I suspect this *midrash* is hyperbolic, given that most people would find the death of their children a more horrifying prospect than poverty. Nonetheless, many other Jewish texts attest to the horrors and degradations imposed by poverty. Ecclesiastes taught, "A poor man's wisdom is scorned, and his words are not heeded" (10:16), and the Talmud noted: "When the bread basket is empty, strife comes knocking at the door" (*Bava Mezia* 59a).

those who question its fairness or logic. Thus, after *People* magazine published an article about a man's decision to donate his life savings to Habitat for Humanity, a well-known charity that helps build and repair houses for poor people, it published the reactions of two letter writers, reactions that in certain ways mirror early Christianity and Judaism's different approaches.

The first letter extolled the man's generosity: "In a world in which there is such growing concern about Social Security and building your own nest egg, I am truly encouraged by this man's faith in the all powerful and loving God to take care of his family's needs."

The second writer was far less approving. "Has this man gone crazy? Does he really believe God wanted him to give his life savings away? How could he not think of his family's future when his capability of supporting them ended? Who is going to donate to their needs? If he wanted to give something, how about his time?" (*People,* February 9, 1998, page 4).

Admittedly, not many people are likely to be tempted by the notion of giving more than twenty percent of their income or savings to charity, let alone donating everything. But the rabbinic ruling reminds us that what Judaism particularly esteems is a life of passionate moderation. Give charity, and do so joyfully (see Day 8), but don't make a onetime gift of everything that you have. Better that you give generously, and do so for a long time. As the medieval *Orchot Tzaddikim* (*Paths of the Righteous*) reminds us, it is better to give away over a period of years a thousand gold pieces than to make a onetime donation of a thousand gold pieces.*

Give generously, and may you be able to do so for many years to come.

---

*Rabbi Irwin Kula demurs: "It is not at all clear that this is always true. Imagine a situation in which 'a thousand gold pieces' will enable a person to start a business that will employ many people for the foreseeable future versus one piece of gold that will buy one person some meals."

# Can a Religious Person Be Cruel?

Judaism's answer, one that may be surprising to many people, is no. Surprising, because throughout history there has been no shortage of people who have claimed to be religious and who have been horribly cruel. In fact we, as Jews, were often victims of such people.*

In truth, from Judaism's perspective, for a religious person to be cruel makes as much sense as a person starting an organization called Carnivores for Vegetarianism. If you eat meat, you are not a vegetarian. If you treat other people meanly and cruelly, you are not a religious person, and Judaism regards you as sinning against both humankind and God. Thus, in speaking of a person who humiliates another, the Midrash says: "If you do so, know whom you are humiliating. [As the biblical verse teaches]: 'He made him [Adam] in the likeness of God'" (*Genesis Rabbah* 24:7). In other words, because Judaism teaches that all human beings are created in God's image, any act of cruelty toward another is simultaneously an act of aggression against God.**

Some two thousand years ago the Talmud delineated kindness as the hallmark of a religious Jew: "The Jewish nation is distinguished by three characteristics: they are merciful, they are bashful [alternatively, modest] and they perform acts of loving-kindness" (*Yevamot* 79a). While I know more than a few Jews who are distinguished neither by modesty nor bashfulness, the Rabbis took this definition so seriously that they claimed that one who is cruel cannot only not claim to be religious, he cannot claim to be a Jew at all. "Whoever is not merciful to his fellow

---

*Thus, the Crusaders claimed to be the most pious of Christians, yet they marched through towns murdering Jews who refused to be baptized, while the Inquisitors of Spain tortured individuals in the name of God.

**That is why, when the Crusaders and Inquisitors murdered innocent people, they also were attacking their Creator. And even if one can rationalize a religious person assaulting another human being, how can a person who claims to be religious assault God?

men is certainly not of the descendants of our father Abraham" (Babylonian Talmud, *Beizah* 32b).

Until the words "cruel religious person" become an oxymoron, people of all faiths will have much to atone for. (For an example of what should be another oxymoron, see Day 296.)

May you have a Shabbat Shalom!

DAY

## 238     SHABBAT

During the course of this Shabbat, try to review the material from the preceding six days, and use some of the texts studied as the basis for discussion during the Shabbat meals:

Day 232. "There Is No Messenger in a Case of Sin"
Day 233. The Power of Goodness
Day 234. Teach Your Child a Profession
Day 235. Teach Your Child That What Matters Most
        to God Is Goodness
Day 236. Don't Give Away Too Much
Day 237. Can a Religious Person Be Cruel?

Shabbat Shalom!

SUNDAY

# The Antidote to Arrogance

Upon seeing a very large crowd, many of us dismiss the people within it as a mob. To counteract the natural tendency to devalue people who are part of a throng, Jewish law ordains a special blessing to be recited upon seeing a large number of people: "Blessed is He who is wise in secrets, for just as no two faces are alike, so, too, are no two minds exactly alike" (Babylonian Talmud, *Berachot* 58a). The blessing reminds us that each of these people is an individual like ourselves, with a special relationship to God, and that just as God knows our mind, so too does He know the mind of each person in the crowd.

Of course, it is not only crowds that incite in many of us feelings of arrogance. Many people feel superior upon meeting others less attractive, less intelligent, less professionally successful, less educated, and less popular than they are. The Talmud tells of one rabbi who, feeling self-satisfied after learning much Torah with his teacher, was greeted by a very ugly man, and responded, "Empty one, are all the people in your town as ugly as you?" (see Day 335).

If you have tendencies toward conceit, and few of us don't, be guided by the words of Bahya ibn Pakuda, author of the classic eleventh-century Jewish text, *Chovot Halevavot* (*Duties of the Heart*):

> A sage was once asked: "How come you are accepted as the undisputed leader of your generation?" He replied: "I have never met any person in whom I did not detect some quality in which he was superior to me....If he was less wise than I, I considered that on the Day of Judgment he will be held less accountable than I, for my transgressions were committed with full knowledge, while his were committed in error. If he was older, I would reason that the merit

which he already acquired must exceed mine. If he was younger, I calculated that his sins were fewer than mine....If the man was richer, then perhaps his wealth has enabled him to surpass me in serving God [through acts of charity]. If he was poorer, I would consider him to be contrite and of a humbler spirit than I. Thus, I honored all men and humbled myself before them" (chapter 10).

The antidote to arrogance: When you meet people, instead of examining them for faults, seek out the quality in which they are superior to you, and from which you can learn.

## Don't Pretend to Virtues You Don't Have

An old Jewish joke tells of a synagogue where, one Yom Kippur, the cantor stood up to begin the service when he suddenly was overcome with trepidation. He rushed over to the ark containing the Torah scrolls, and cried out to God: "Lord, I am not worthy to lead this holy congregation in prayer. What am I but dust and ashes?"

The rabbi, overwhelmed by the cantor's words, ran over to the ark and called out to God: "I am nothing in Your eyes. What have I ever done that is worthy?"

At that point the *shammes* (synagogue assistant) was also moved. He jumped up from his seat, ran to the ark, and called out, "God, I am a man of no value, a miserable sinner, a nothing."

The rabbi tapped the cantor on the shoulder and said, "Now look who's calling himself a nothing!"

Although we all want others to think well of us, being obsessed with what others think often prevents us from becoming the kind of person we want everyone to believe we are. This applies to all areas of life, not just ethical ones. For example, I knew a man whom I long thought of as wealthy; he lived in an enormous house set on two acres of land in one of San Francisco's most expensive neighborhoods, drove a Rolls-Royce, and owned a business that employed hundreds of people.

One of his daughters confided that shortly before his death he took her out to breakfast, and begged her forgiveness for the rather small inheritance he would be leaving her brother and her. He explained that he had spent so much money maintaining an ostentatious lifestyle so as to impress his neighbors that he had used up many millions of dollars.

Because this man was so concerned that everyone think of him as rich, he became much less rich than he otherwise would have been.

In the Jewish joke, the rabbi and cantor obviously understand that humility is an important virtue. But what matters more to them than being humble is that people perceive them as humble. Because of this concern, they lose their humility.

My grandfather Rabbi Nissen Telushkin, of blessed memory, told me of a man he knew who, as a highly respected member of the community, was entitled by Jewish tradition to occupy a prominent seat at the front of the synagogue. Instead, he chose to sit in an undistinguished seat in a back row. But my grandfather soon noticed that the man's eyes were constantly darting about to see if people were noticing how humble a seat he took for himself.

My grandfather told him, "It would be better to sit in the front of the synagogue and think you should be sitting in the back, than to sit in the back and think the whole time you should be sitting in the front."

If you find it very important that people know of a virtue you possess, be careful: you probably don't yet possess it as fully as you think. And you won't, until what matters more to you is what God thinks, not other people.

But then, who am I to preach?

I am reminded of the words of Rabbi Israel Salanter, who was preaching in a synagogue, reproving people for their failings, and urging them to improve themselves. He commented, "I too am guilty of these failings. In truth, I am preaching to myself aloud, and if what I am telling myself is of use to you, then please use it."

# "Love Your Neighbor": What Is the Neighbor's Responsibility?

I was working in my office one morning when a dear friend called. His mother had been operated on the previous afternoon; now the doctors found that they needed to perform a second procedure. When I asked my friend if he wanted me to come and sit with him in the hospital, he answered, "I would really appreciate that."

I headed straight for the hospital, and spent the rest of the day with him. As soon as I arrived, it became immediately apparent that it was very important to him that I was there, and I was very happy that I could spend this time with him.

I wondered later what would have happened had my friend not been so direct—if, when I had asked him if I should come, he had answered, "No, I'm fine. Don't bother." In such a situation, particularly given that other circumstances during the preceding three days had prevented me from working, I might well have stayed on the phone with him for another few minutes, asked him to call me and tell me how the operation went, and then hung up.

Because my friend was direct and told me what he really needed, I could respond to his need. And because I knew him to be a fair person and not manipulative, I knew that his appeal for me to be with him was real.

This put me in mind of a popular Chasidic story, one that has long both moved and bothered me. It is told of Rabbi Moshe Leib of Sassov that he startled his followers one day by telling them:

How to love men is something I learned from a peasant. He was sitting in an inn along with other peasants, drinking. For a long time he was as silent as all the rest, but when he was moved by the wine, he asked one of the men seated beside him, "Tell me, do you love me or don't you love me?" The other replied, "I love you very much." But the first peasant replied, "You say that you love me, but you do not know what I need. If you really loved me, you would know." The other had not a word to say to this, and the peasant who had put the question fell silent again. But I understood. To know the needs of men and to bear the burden of their sorrow, that is the true love of men.*

To the rebbe of Sassov, the lesson was obvious; to love others is to know what hurts them and to know what they need. I certainly know when I'm in pain how much I appreciate those who can intuit my suffering and the reasons for it.

But I also have compassion for the second peasant. His love for his friend might have been very real, even if he did not know why the other was in pain. It seems to me that it is the responsibility of the one who is in need to tell others what he or she needs.

Although many human traits split pretty evenly along gender lines, my impression is that there are many women who want their spouses or partners to know what it is that they need without their having to state it explicitly.

I understand the commandment "Love your neighbor" as implicitly obliging us to do what we can to make it possible for our neighbor to act lovingly toward us. This means that we have a responsibility to make it clear to others what it is we need. Our neighbor is not a mind-reader. He or she might not even be intuitive, but this does not make the person a bad or unloving neighbor.

So, don't just love your neighbor, make sure you give your neighbor a chance to love you.

*Buber, *Tales of the Hasidim: Later Masters,* 86.

# "Honor Your Father and Mother": The Surprising Wording of the Biblical Commandment

Why does the Torah—in the Fifth of the Ten Commandments—command us to "honor" our parents, but not to love them? Certainly not because it is hesitant to command love; after all, it legislates "Love your neighbor as yourself" (Leviticus 19:18); "And you shall love the Lord your God with all your heart, with all your soul and with all your might" (Deuteronomy 6:5); and "You shall love him [the stranger] as yourself" (Leviticus 19:34).

Why not a commandment to love one's parents?

Two possible reasons: First, it is possible that the obligation to love your parents is subsumed under the command to love your neighbor (that is, since your parents are also in a certain sense your neighbors, you are required to love them).

But the real reason, I believe, has to do with the Torah's insight into human nature. Many people, both as adolescents and adults, experience periods of alienation from their parents, and almost all go through periods of ambivalence. This is not surprising. Parents play so major a role in our lives (among other things, they are our models of what it means to be a man and a woman, a mother and a father, a husband and a wife, and an adult) that inevitably we trace some of our personal problems in relationships and in ourselves to things our parents did or didn't do.

It is to provide us with a guideline during these periods of alienation and ambivalence, during which we might not feel very loving, that the Torah enjoins us to honor our parents, and to show a measure of respect. Angry children sometimes express the kind of harsh and cruel things to their parents that they would not say, even in anger, to acquaintances and friends. I know of people who have said to their parents, "I hate you," or "I wish I had had decent parents, not you." These are precisely the sort of comments that the Torah prohibits. If you are angry with your parents, express it. But put fair limits on what you say. You are still bound, even when enraged and even when you might not be feeling love, by the requirement to show your parents honor.

*On how to express anger fairly, see Day 23.*

*On how to express anger fairly, see Day 23.*

DAY

## 243

### THURSDAY

## *If Parents Become Senile*

*Once he [Dama the son of Netinah] was seated among the great men of Rome, dressed in a silken gold garment, when his mother came and tore the garment from him, slapped him on the head, and spat in his face. But he did not shame her.*
—Babylonian Talmud, *Kiddushin* 31a\*

The Talmud mentions several stories about Dama, a non-Jew, whom the Rabbis regarded as a model practitioner of the commandment to honor one's father and mother. From the above story we learn that a child should never humiliate a parent publicly, even if he or she is disturbed and behaves abominably.

Instead, Jewish law rules that children are obliged to try to take care of a senile parent for as long as possible. Only when it is no longer possible should a child hire others to do so:

---

\*Rabbi Gershon Winkler and Lakme Batya Elior wisely suggest that it is inappropriate to teach this talmudic passage to young children, since they might understand the story as meaning that if a parent physically and/or verbally abuses them, they should remain silent. Obviously, Judaism does not advocate that children who are minors accept cruel and oppressive behavior from their parents. Because Dama, the hero of this story, was a mature man, the rabbis deemed his restraint and compassion for his mother as admirable (see Winkler with Elior, *The Place Where You Are Standing Is Holy,* 133).

If one's father or mother becomes mentally disordered, [the child] should try to indulge the vagaries of the stricken parent, until he [or she] is pitied by God [and dies]. But if he finds he cannot endure the situation because of the parent's madness, let him leave and go away, and appoint others to care for the parent properly.

—Moses Maimonides, *Mishneh Torah*,
"Laws Concerning Rebels," 6:10

In modern times this ruling would suggest that children first try and care for parents on their own, and/or with some outside help. When that is no longer possible (as in the case of a parent stricken with Alzheimer's), they should hire others to serve as primary caretakers. As for sending a parent to live in an old-age home, this should be a final step, never a first one.

Parents cared for us when we were young and very demanding, and Jewish law instructs us to try to do the same for them for as long as we can. Gur Aryeh ha-Levi, a seventeenth-century Bible commentator, believed that the commandment "Honor your father and mother" was meant specifically to address the parents' final and hardest years: "It is natural for old people to be despised by the general population when they can no longer function as they once did, but sit idle, and have no purpose. The commandment 'Honor your father and mother' was given specifically for this situation." *

DAY

244    FRIDAY

## How to Learn Empathy

When a nineteenth-century Eastern European shtetl was beset by a siege of freezing weather, the local Chasidic rebbe needed to raise funds to heat the houses of the town's poor. He set off for the home of the town's richest man, and knocked on the door.

* Gur Aryeh ha-Levi in *Melekhet Makhshevet*, cited in Klagsbrun, *Voices of Wisdom*, 198.

The man, a follower of the rebbe, answered, and invited the rebbe inside. The rebbe demurred, saying he was there but for a minute, and they could conduct the conversation on the doorstep. The rebbe then started to ask the rich man general questions about his wife and children. The man, who had come to the door dressed only in a shirt, felt his teeth beginning to chatter. "Will the rebbe please come inside?" he again asked.

The rebbe said no, then started to ask the man questions about his business.

The man was now shivering. "Will the rebbe please come inside, and tell me why he has come to my house?"

The rebbe remained outside, but told the man, "I've come to ask you for one hundred rubles. We need the money to warm the houses of the poor."

"And if I promise to give it, will the rebbe then come inside?"

"Yes."

"Then I'll give the money right now."

After the rebbe followed the shivering man into the house, the man opened his safe and gave him a hundred rubles.

He asked the rebbe, "If you knew all along what you were planning to ask me, why didn't you come in right away and ask?"

He answered. "If I had come in as soon as you opened the door, you would have escorted me to a comfortable chair in your living room, and brought out a glass of hot tea for yourself and me. We would have been seated in plush chairs, being warmed by the fireplace, and when I would have asked you for money to heat the houses of the poor, you would have offered five rubles, maybe ten. But standing outside, you experienced for a few minutes the bitterness of the cold that the poor are experiencing all the time. I wanted you to be feeling that bitter cold when I asked you for the hundred rubles."

Sympathy is a fine trait, but empathy is what really opens wide our hearts. This year on Yom Kippur, when you are sitting in synagogue and feeling hunger pangs, decide at that moment what you'll give to organizations that distribute food to the poor. And this January or February, step outside without a coat in the dead of winter; when you start to shiver, make up your mind what you will give to organizations that help the needy.

May you have a Shabbat Shalom!

S H A B B A T

During the course of this Shabbat, try to review the material from the preceding six days, and use some of the texts studied as the basis for discussion during the Shabbat meals:

Day 239. The Antidote to Arrogance
Day 240. Don't Pretend to Virtues You Don't Have
Day 241. "Love Your Neighbor": What Is the Neighbor's Responsibility?
Day 242. "Honor Your Father and Mother": The Surprising Wording of the Biblical Commandment
Day 243. If Parents Become Senile
Day 244. How to Learn Empathy

Shabbat Shalom!

# WEEK 36

S U N D A Y

## *Don't Snap at Your Spouse*

One might think that people would act most kindly to those to whom they feel closest, and restrict their rudeness, moodiness, and impatience to strangers. However, that isn't the way the world usually works. People are most often cruel to those closest to them.

I know one man who has endured many ego-destroying explosions from his wife. When she subsequently apologizes, she assures him that, according to her psychiatrist, he is the only person she trusts sufficiently to show her dark side. Indeed, many people who are extremely courteous and gracious to strangers and acquaintances have few compunctions about shouting or snapping at their spouses and children.

The Torah informs us that the Patriarch Jacob loved Rachel the most of his four wives; in fact, she is the only one whom the Bible tells us he loved. Rachel was also the only one of Jacob's wives who was infertile. In deep pain over this, and knowing her husband to be a holy man with a special connection to God, Rachel confronted Jacob and said to him: "Give me children, or I shall die!" (Genesis 30:1).

Jacob turned on his wife in fury: "Can I take the place of God, who has denied you fruit of the womb?"

What harsh words! Perhaps Jacob, frustrated by his wife's infertility,* was upset by the implication of her words that it was within his power to "give" her children. Perhaps he just found it offensive that she thought her life not worth living if she could not have children.

Whatever Jacob thought, Rachel's words, obviously prompted by pain, deserved a kinder response. As a rabbinic *midrash* comments, "Is this how one responds to a suffering person?" (*Genesis Rabbah* 71:7).

A later biblical episode similarly portrays an encounter between a childless wife and her husband, although this one concludes more gently. Elkanah, witnessing his infertile wife sinking into depression, says to her, "Hannah, why do you weep? Why don't you eat and why do you feel bad? Am I not better to you than ten sons?" (I Samuel 1:8).

While Elkanah's insistence to his infertile wife that she had no reason to feel sad ("Why do you feel bad?") might have been insensitive, his response at least conveys love and reassurance ("Am I not better to you than ten sons?") rather than scorn or fury.

Sometimes it is hard to respond to your spouse's distress with sympathy. Perhaps you feel that the other person is exaggerating his or her pain, has been complaining about it for too long, or that there is nothing you can do to alleviate the suffering and therefore would prefer to talk about something else. But whatever you feel, try to refrain from speaking angry, hurtful words. Sometimes, you won't succeed; human beings living together in close proximity are bound to annoy and antagonize

---

*Rachel later had two children.

each other occasionally. But if you often speak harshly to those who are closest to you, you must find a means to control yourself.

The Talmud notes that women generally cry more easily than men, and that husbands must be very careful not to hurt their wives (*Bava Mezia* 59a). I don't know if men have been getting more sensitive since the time of the Talmud, but I do know more than a few husbands who have been reduced to tears by their wives' cruel words.

The world is always in need of more kindness. Who deserves it more than the husband or wife who has chosen to share your life?

MONDAY

## *Are You in an Abusive Relationship?*

At one point or another, all couples argue, fight, or at least sorely try each other's patience. However, there are appropriate ways to disagree; as long as a couple's arguments take place within these ethical parameters (see Day 51), a marriage can stay healthy. Often, partners can even grow from such disagreements.

Jewish Women International (formerly B'nai Brith Women), has formulated a series of questions to help characterize a relationship in which the fighting is one-sided and unfair. God willing, you will be able to answer all the questions they pose with a "no." If you do answer "yes" to any, you may be in an abusive relationship, and should consult your rabbi, a hotline, or even a shelter (I have slightly edited some questions for the sake of clarity).

Does your partner:

- ♦ Call you names, yell at you, and swear at you?
- ♦ Put you down in front of other people?

- ◆ Tell you that you're no good?
- ◆ Act very jealously and possessively?
- ◆ Control your finances and make you ask for money?
- ◆ Try to control whom you see and what you do?
- ◆ Berate you for what you wear, what you say, and how you act?
- ◆ Blame you for his [or her] violent actions?
- ◆ Destroy your belongings or hurt your pets?
- ◆ Push, hit, kick, punch, or slap you?
- ◆ Force you to have sex?

In Judaism, *shalom bayit* (a peaceful household) is highly valued and rabbis generally will not encourage divorce if there is reason to believe that a state of peacefulness can return to a marriage. If it cannot, however, then it is wrong to stay in the relationship. The Torah itself commands, "You shall carefully preserve your lives" (Deuteronomy 4:15), which Jewish sources understand as forbidding a person from placing himself or herself in unnecessary danger. Thus, to remain in a relationship with a person who physically or emotionally torments you is forbidden. As Jewish Women International reminds those who have answered "yes" to any of the above questions: "You may be in an abusive relationship...[and] you may be jeopardizing your health and safety by staying in an unsafe situation." *

DAY

248

TUESDAY

## *Don't Be an Elitist*

The third-century C.E. rabbi Judah the Prince, editor of the six-volume Mishna, the first comprehensive collection of Jewish oral law, seems to have been a bit of an ascetic. On his deathbed he raised his hands and declared before God, "It is known to You that I have not

* *Resource Guide for Rabbis: On Domestic Violence.*

enjoyed the pleasures of this world even with my little finger" (Babylonian Talmud, *Ketubot* 104a). Virtuous as he was, Rabbi Judah suffered from a flaw: when distributing charity, he was an elitist who felt that only learned Jews should be entitled to assistance.

> Once, when there was a [famine in Israel], Rabbi Judah the Prince opened the food warehouses and announced: "Let all those who have studied Bible, Mishna, Gemara, Halacha, and Aggada come in, but those who are ignorant of Torah should not enter."
>
> Rabbi Yonatan ben Amram forced himself in [without disclosing his identity] and said to him, "My teacher, feed me!"
>
> He said to him, "My son, have you studied the Bible?"
>
> He answered, "No."
>
> "Did you study the Mishna?"
>
> He answered, "No."
>
> "If that is the case, how can I feed you?"
>
> He answered, "Feed me as you would a dog or a raven."
>
> He fed him.
>
> When [Rabbi Yonatan ben Amram] left, Rabbi Judah the Prince remained troubled, saying, "Woe is me! I have given food to one who is ignorant of Torah."
>
> His son, Rabbi Shimon, said, "Maybe that was your student, Rabbi Yonatan ben Amram, who has never wanted to gain any advantage because he has studied Torah."
>
> They checked and discovered that that was, indeed, the case. Rabbi Judah the Prince then said, "Let everyone enter." *

Though it has a comforting conclusion, this story is a disturbing one. As Danny Siegel, a Jewish writer, and himself an innovative distributor of charity, notes: "The opening lines make no sense to me."

Why did the Talmud include this story? The Rabbis who compiled the Talmud could easily have deleted it. Perhaps they related this story to remind Jews in every generation that *all* hungry people are entitled to

---

* Babylonian Talmud, *Bava Bathra* 8a. I have followed almost verbatim Danny Siegel's translation; see his *Family Reunion*, 42–43; in addition, this entry was deeply influenced by Siegel's commentary on this passage.

food. Those like Rabbi Judah, who restrict their giving to fellow religious scholars, are acting wrongly, as are those who restrict their donations to those involved in cultural activities, or to those in the world of academia.*

As the Passover Haggadah instructs us, in words that many people ignore, "Let all who are hungry, come in and eat."

## Don't Encourage Your Children to Date Wealthy People

I had a friend in college whose parents asked him the same two questions whenever he came back from a date with a new woman: "Is she pretty?" and "Is her family rich?" Others have told me that they were raised by parents with admonitions such as, "You shouldn't only marry for money, but it's just as easy to fall in love with a rich girl [or boy] as a poor one."

From Judaism's perspective, making marital choices based on money is immoral, and reflects a low character. Thus, the Talmud teaches, "Whoever marries a woman for her money will have disreputable children" (Babylonian Talmud, *Kiddushin* 70a). While many people understand this dictum as a curse, I believe it simply means that the father will have a child like himself, one who will do anything for material gain.

Marriage for money often occurs between wealthy men and attractive, much younger women. Two thousand years ago, when parents

---

*My friend Daniel Taub offers a somewhat different explanation of this tale: "There was a famine in Israel, and Rabbi Judah thought he could prioritize to whom food should be donated on the basis of scholarship. But the story seems to teach us that you shouldn't value the life of a scholar more than that of someone else, someone, indeed, who may never have had the chance to study."

arranged their children's marriages, the rabbis condemned a father who married his daughter to an old, most likely highly affluent man. As the late rabbinic scholar Rabbi Shlomo Yosef Zevin, citing the *Shulchan Aruch*, summarizes the Jewish tradition on this point: "An old man should not marry a young girl, for such mismatching leads to immorality." * Clearly, the Rabbis feared that a young woman married to a much older man would be more likely to betray the marital bond and seek out younger, more virile lovers.

Marrying for money may well lead to misery as well as immorality. As the late Rabbi Wolfe Kelman used to say, "Whoever marries for money ends up paying for it."

Whom, then, should you encourage your children to marry? People who are committed to establishing homes filled with Judaism's values, people to whom they are physically and emotionally drawn, people who have some personal and/or professional ambition, and people who are kind, very kind: the rest is commentary.

DAY

## 250 THURSDAY

# The Painful, Challenging Question Parents Must Ask Children

When King David was old, in the last months of his life, Adonijah, his oldest surviving son, went around Jerusalem boasting that he would soon be king.

How vile for a son to make it known that he is anxiously awaiting his father's death, so that he can assume power. Yet it is significant that the Bible does not regard David as blameless for Adonijah's obnoxious

---

* Rabbi Shlomo Yosef Zevin, "[The Old] by the Light of Halacha," in Lamm, ed. *The Good Society*, 129.

behavior. The text reports that throughout his son's life, his father had never scolded him when he had acted badly, nor asked him, "Why did you do that?" (I Kings 1:6).

I know a couple whose daughter cruelly mistreated her younger brother, often taunting and hitting him. The parents used to comfort the young boy, but rarely confronted, challenged, or punished the girl for her behavior. I know another set of parents who witnessed their five-year-old daughter mistreat, on a number of occasions, a slightly younger girl who was her neighbor. The younger girl would run away crying. The parents were vigilant in not letting their daughter get away with such behavior. They told her repeatedly that such behavior was unacceptable, unfair, and cruel, and challenged her about it every time it occurred.

I leave it to your imagination to guess which of these two children grew up to be self-centered and tactless, and which grew up to be fair and kind.

Some might argue that parents have limited influence, that no matter what David had done, Adonijah ultimately would have become arrogant and selfish. But the Bible, in telling us that "his father never scolded him, [asking] 'Why did you do that,'" clearly disagrees; it believes that parents, by posing the right question, over and over again if necessary, can influence their children to act more kindly, fairly, and ethically.

"Why did you do that?" A good question for children—and for ourselves as well.

DAY

251    FRIDAY

## Marriage Is Also Supposed to Be Fun

Religious people are commonly thought of as solemn, as so preoccupied with trying to fulfill their obligations that they rarely think about joy, and have little time for fun. But a look at the Torah reminds us that joy and fun are regarded by the Bible as intrinsic and important parts of the marriage relationship. Consider the language the Torah uses to discuss Isaac and Rebecca's relationship: *Yitzchak metzachek et Rivkah ishto.* One can translate this either as "Isaac was caressing [or playing with] his wife, Rebecca" or as "Isaac was making his wife, Rebecca, laugh"; from the context, the allusion appears to be sexual (Genesis 26:8).

One again finds the language of joyfulness in a distinctively unromantic passage in Deuteronomy, in which the Torah legislates one of the category of men to be exempted from military conscription (except in an instance of a war for national survival): "When a man has taken a bride, he shall not go out with the army or be assigned to it for any purpose; he shall be exempt one year for the sake of his household, to give happiness to the woman he has married" (Deuteronomy 24:5).

To give happiness to the woman one has married, to play with one's wife, to caress her, and to make one's wife laugh—all of these are not just common sense or New Age thinking, they are descriptions and prescriptions straight out of the Torah.

If you find that you and your spouse are too often overwhelmed by the burdens of raising children, finances, and a general lack of sleep and of time, you should still make sure to find time to play not just with your children but with each other. The other pressures will remain, but when a marriage is joyful and sensual, as Isaac and Rebecca's, everything somehow will still seem worthwhile.

May you have a Shabbat Shalom!

DAY

## 252 SHABBAT

During the course of this Shabbat, try to review the material from the preceding six days, and use some of the texts studied as the basis for discussion during the Shabbat meals:

Day 246. Don't Snap at Your Spouse

Day 247. Are You in an Abusive Relationship?

Day 248. Don't Be an Elitist

Day 249. Don't Encourage Your Children to Date
        Wealthy People

Day 250. The Painful, Challenging Question Parents Must Ask
        Children

Day 251. Marriage Is Also Supposed to Be Fun

Shabbat Shalom!

# WEEK 37

DAY

253     SUNDAY

## Rabbenu Gershom and the Prohibition Against Being a Snoop

One of the most famous figures in medieval Jewish history is Rabbenu Gershom, a tenth-century German Jewish scholar from Mayence, also known as *Me'or Hagolah,* "the Light of the Exile." Several far-reaching legal rulings in Jewish law are attributed to him. For example, he is credited with outlawing polygamy among Jews, something that had been permitted since biblical times.* He also ruled that a woman could not be divorced against her will, although Torah law, and the Talmud as well, had permitted this.** Since the time of Rabbenu Gershom, a couple can divorce only if both partners agree.

---

*Rabbenu Gershom's prohibition wasn't accepted by Jewish communities residing in the Muslim world, and some of their members took multiple wives well into the twentieth century.
**According to the Torah, if a man married a woman and found in her "something unseemly," he could divorce her (Deuteronomy 24:1). The Talmud records the view that the words "something unseemly" applied to anything the man didn't like about his wife (Mishna *Gittin* 9:10).

One of his less well known, but still equally applicable, rulings prohibits reading mail addressed to another. This applies even if the letter is addressed to someone with whom you're close. Thus, you're forbidden to open and read a private letter (as opposed to "junk mail," for example) addressed to your spouse or child. Unless the person to whom the letter was addressed gives you permission to read it, you are not allowed to do so.

Many people, particularly parents, violate this ruling, which often evokes understandable outrage in their children. Need one add that reading another person's even more private documents, such as a diary, is likewise forbidden?

By extension, Rabbenu Gershom's prohibition would extend to listening in on someone else's phone conversations, or listening to personal phone messages intended for someone else. As a general rule, when someone is having a private phone conversation with another, it is best to leave the room; it is difficult for a person to speak openly and unself-consciously when someone else is present.

As noted elsewhere (see Day 215), Jewish law even prohibits one from entering one's own household without first knocking, lest you invade the privacy of, and embarrass, someone inside the house. In short, Judaism takes very seriously every person's—including one's children's—right to privacy.

As noted elsewhere (see Day 215)

DAY

254

MONDAY

## *Be Generous with Power*

*When a king and a bridal party meet, the bridal party must make way for the king. Nevertheless, [the first-century C.E.] King Agrippa made way for a bride, and the sages praised him. When they asked him, "What made you do so?" he replied, "I wear a crown every day; she will wear her crown but a brief hour."*

—Post-talmudic tractate *Semachot* 11:6

A number of years ago, a Jewish journal honored a friend of mine by appointing him as one of three judges to bestow an award on a successful Jewish educator. The award carried no monetary prize, but my friend was surprised at how vigorously he was lobbied by the different candidates and their supporters.

He expressed his amazement about this to the late Rabbi Wolfe Kelman. Instead of empathizing with his astonishment, Rabbi Kelman asked him a question: "You're often asked to speak at Jewish organizations' banquets and dinners, aren't you?"

My friend nodded. For many years he has lectured extensively throughout the Jewish world.

"And so you're used to being asked to sit on the dais. But many people, including many who are doing work as important as yours and mine, never get to sit on the dais. And, just like you, they also want recognition."

Humbled by Rabbi Kelman's words, my friend returned to his function as a judge with renewed dedication.

The behavior of King Agrippa reminds us that if we are ever in a position of power, our first responsibility should be to help others, not aggrandize ourselves. Indeed, probably the most positive benefit one acquires with power is the ability to use it generously. Another friend, a prominent media figure, told me that he has pleasure calling up sick people who are fans of his radio show, and wishing them well. He knows that because of his prominence, receiving a call from him is something that these people will particularly treasure.

Rabbi Hanoch Teller tells of an instance when the late Israeli rabbi Shlomo Zalman Auerbach, a very humble man, heard of a family in America that had suffered the grievous loss of a husband and father. He was so distraught that he immediately made an overseas call to the family. When the widow picked up, he introduced himself as Shlomo Zalman Auerbach. At first his name elicited no recognition, so he said it again: "This is Shlomo Zalman Auerbach, from Jerusalem." "Oh," the woman replied with astonishment, amazed that so prominent a rabbi was calling her. Rabbi Auerbach spent twenty minutes consoling the widow, and then spoke to each of the children. To the youngest child, aware that it would help the boy's status at school, he said, "When you return to school, tell all your friends that Rabbi Shlomo Zalman called you up and spoke to you from Jerusalem." *

What all these people recognized is that perhaps the most important benefit of fame is that it enables one to help far more people than one otherwise could.

TUESDAY

# When Silence Is Golden

*Rabbi Shimon ben Elazar used to say: Do not try to appease your fellow at the height of his anger, nor speak to him words of consolation while his dead lies before him....*
—*Ethics of the Fathers* 4:23

Many people associate good manners with knowing precisely the right thing to say. But as this rabbinic teaching reminds us, there are times when good manners dictate saying nothing at all.

Such is generally the case when another has suffered an emotional blow, such as the death of a loved one. To offer comfort immediately after the death, when the mourners are still in shock, may trivialize the loss. At such a time, the greatest gift you can provide is your presence. The very fact that you are there will make the mourner feel that she is not alone in her suffering. But words of consolation, which so often imply that the mourner should not feel so bad, probably will make the bereaved feel even more isolated and alone.

Similarly, as noted in Day 136, Jewish ethics teach that when you visit a mourner, you should remain silent until the mourner initiates conversation. Your goal during a *shiva* visit is to help the person griev-

* Teller, *And from Jerusalem, His Word,* 323.

ing. If he wishes to talk about the deceased, you should follow his lead. If he needs to divert his mind and talk about something else, talk with him about whatever he wishes to discuss. And if he wishes to remain silent, sit with him and share in his silence.

Similarly, restrain your tongue when you are with a person in the heat of their anger. Many people become enraged when provoked, but after some time has passed (sometimes it can be as little as a few minutes, sometimes hours or even longer), they remain angry but are calmer. That is the time to speak with them and try to appease their anger. However, by trying to calm them at the moment of their most intense rage, you will likely stimulate even greater anger, compounded by the person's frustration that you, too, don't understand the "justness" of his or her fury.

Words should be spoken when they can do good. When they can only inflame a person's sense of desolation or anger, holding one's tongue is preferable. As Moshe ibn Ezra, the medieval Hebrew poet, reminds us: "If speech is silver, silence is gold."

DAY

256    WEDNESDAY

## *Learn Even from Those with Whom You Disagree*

Of the fifteen hundred or so rabbis cited in the Talmud, only one apparently became a heretic and left Judaism; Elisha ben Abuyah, a contemporary of the second-century Rabbi Akiva. In a midlife crisis, the reasons for which are shrouded in legend, Elisha lost his faith, and became convinced that "There is no Judge and no justice."

Understandably, the other rabbis turned on Elisha in retaliation for his rejecting them and their way of life. They stopped referring to him by his name, insisting on calling him *Acher*, "the other one." One, however, Rabbi Meir, who was Elisha's disciple and friend, refused to desert him.

He continued to see Elisha, and tried to influence him to return to Judaism. Rabbi Meir would also cite earlier teachings of Elisha that he still found valid. When others criticized Meir for not repudiating Elisha and the teachings he had learned from him, Rabbah bar Rab Shila, a contemporary of Rabbi Meir, defended him: "Rabbi Meir found a pomegranate. He ate the inside, but threw away the peel." (Babylonian Talmud, *Hagigah* 15b)*

When disagreeing with another on basic issues, many of us are tempted to repudiate the teachings of that person on all other issues. As noted elsewhere, this seems to have been one of the errors of Rabbi Shammai's disciples, who refused even to study and consider the contrary positions of the followers of Rabbi Hillel (see Day 131). By not examining what their opponents said, Shammai's students became the mental inferiors of those of Hillel (who made a point of studying opposing viewpoints), one reason why Jewish law may have rejected their teachings in favor of those of Hillel and his disciples.

In contemporary life, we must remember that liberals have things to learn from conservatives, conservatives from liberals, Orthodox Jews from Conservative and Reform Jews, and Conservative and Reform Jews from the Orthodox.

We all need to become disciples of Rabbi Meir and learn how to eat the inside of a pomegranate while discarding what we may consider its "peel."

DAY

257

THURSDAY

## Revenge and the Command to Love Your Neighbor

Many Jews are unaware that one of the Torah's 613 commandments is a ban on taking revenge, even though it occurs in

---

*There is a fine novel by Milton Steinberg on the life of Elisha ben Abuyah, *As a Driven Leaf*, which deals as well with his relationship with Rabbi Meir.

what might well be the Torah's most famous verse: "You shall not take revenge or bear a grudge against a member of your people, but you shall love your neighbor as yourself, I am God" (Leviticus 19:18).

What is the logic behind placing the injunction to "love your neighbor as yourself" alongside the prohibition against taking vengeance or bearing a grudge? All of us have sometimes acted wrongly or unfairly toward another. Thus, at any given moment, there likely are people who feel that we have wronged them, and who emotionally would like the opportunity to hurt us as we hurt them. But in instructing people to "love your neighbor as yourself," the Torah is telling us that, just as we would wish those of our neighbors whom we have wronged to love us and forgo their desire for revenge, so should we forgo the desire for revenge against those who have hurt us.

The extent to which saintly Jews have suppressed the desire to seek vengeance is perhaps best reflected in the experiences of Rabbi Abraham Isaac Kook, the chief rabbi of Palestine between 1921 and 1935. In addition to being a profound scholar and a deeply pious man, Rabbi Kook was a committed Zionist. Consequently, members of the Neturei Karta, a small group of anti-Zionist, ultra-Orthodox Jews, despised him for his political beliefs. They often spoke and wrote of him with the greatest contempt, and sometimes even cursed him.

On one occasion the daughter of a Neturei Karta leader was afflicted with a serious ailment, for which the examining physicians had but one conclusion: the young woman needed to be sent abroad to the world's leading specialist in the disease's treatment.

When the father made inquiries, he learned that the doctor was both very busy and very expensive. He was a poor man, so it was highly unlikely that the doctor would take on his daughter as a patient. However, he also learned that the doctor was a great admirer of Rabbi Kook. If the rabbi asked him to, the doctor would definitely treat the girl.

The man, who on many occasions had publicly denounced Rabbi Kook, was too embarrassed to go to him directly. Instead he sought out the rabbi's beloved friend Reb Aryeh Levine, asking him to speak up on his daughter's behalf. As soon as Reb Aryeh explained the problem, Rabbi Kook agreed to write the doctor a letter. And because he had such great reason to resent the father, he went out of his way to depict the girl and her father in favorable terms. As he told Reb Aryeh, "I will let no personal bias influence me as I write this." After he finished the letter, Rabbi Kook wrote another one, to a shipping company that almost always respected his requests, asking them to give the girl and her family a large discount.*

Throughout his life, Rabbi Kook chose not to respond in kind or with vengeance to those who hated him. As was noted earlier, he often taught: "The Talmud teaches that the Second Temple was destroyed because of causeless hatred. Perhaps the Third Temple will be rebuilt because of causeless love."

# Who Is a Hero?
# A Jewish Perspective

In almost every culture, heroism is associated with physical strength. A hero is stronger than others, one who uses his physical strength to overcome opponents, and often, but not always, to do good. The percentage of people in a society who can be heroes is limited; most lack the physical strength or courage to qualify.**

In Judaism, heroism is generally understood as referring to inner, not outer, strength. "Who is a hero?" *Ethics of the Fathers* asks. "One who overcomes temptation" (4:1).*** Thus, an impoverished man or woman who finds a valuable object belonging to another and resists the temptation to keep it, but instead returns it, is a hero. So is a person who is addicted to liquor but who doesn't get drunk. Judaism perceives

---

*Raz, *A Tzaddik in Our Time*, 115–16.

**Judaism too is familiar with this definition of a hero. Thus, the Talmud, in one limited context, defines a hero as one who "is feared by his companions on account of his strength" (*Kiddushin* 49b).

***Thus, in effect, there is no one objective measure of heroism, since each of us has our own temptations to struggle with and overcome.

overcoming temptation as not just a good thing to do, but as a heroic action.

From Judaism's perspective, a physically strong person who can't overcome his or her temptations is a weakling, and a physically weak person who doesn't give in to temptations is a hero.

What about you? What tempts you? What urges are hard for you to control? If you are tempted to be dishonest, can you resist? If you want to have a sexual relationship with someone who is forbidden to you, can you resist the urge? If you have a quick temper, can you avoid overreacting and exploding in anger?

In the outside world, heroism is a great value, but one that applies to few people and is tested infrequently. In Judaism, heroism is a possibility for everyone, and we are tested almost every day of our lives.*

May you have a Shabbat Shalom!

D A Y

## 259    S H A B B A T

During the course of this Shabbat, try to review the material from the preceding six days, and use some of the texts studied as the basis for discussion during the Shabbat meals:

Day 253.  Rabbenu Gershom and the Prohibition Against
          Being a Snoop
Day 254.  Be Generous with Power
Day 255.  When Silence Is Golden
Day 256.  Learn Even from Those with Whom You Disagree
Day 257.  Revenge and the Command to Love Your Neighbor
Day 258.  Who Is a Hero? A Jewish Perspective

Shabbat Shalom!

*An insightful discussion of heroism from a Jewish perspective is found in Nachum Amsel, *The Jewish Encyclopedia of Moral and Ethical Issues,* 249.

# WEEK 38

SUNDAY

# *Accidents Do Happen*

Dennis Prager teaches a Torah class in Los Angeles. After some three years of study, the class had reached Exodus 21, which contains, among other regulations, laws concerning damages caused by animals. Verse 35 reads, "When a man's ox injures his neighbor's ox and it dies, they shall sell the live ox and divide its price; they shall also divide the dead animal." In other words, as long as the ox hasn't previously acted in such a manner (see verse 36), its owner is obligated to pay only half of the damages.

Many class members expressed shock. "Why only half? It was his ox that inflicted the damage. Shouldn't the owner be liable for all the damage?"

"Americans today," Dennis responded, "refuse to believe in accidents. In our society, a person who suffers injury wants someone to pay, and to pay big, whether or not that person acted irresponsibly."

The Torah reasons differently. If the ox had a previous history of goring, then the owner's refusal to either slaughter the ox or to keep it penned up constitutes negligence. In such a case, the owner bears full liability (Exodus 21:36; see tomorrow's entry).

But what if the ox had been mild-mannered and unaggressive prior to this incident? What if the owner had no reason to assume that it would ever gore another animal?

Then, the Torah tells us, the owner only pays half. True, an accident has happened, and a victim (both the animal and the animal's owner) has suffered. But in a certain sense, the owner too, having had no reason to anticipate such behavior from his animal, is also a victim. To hold him responsible for all payments would seem to constitute a sort of judgment of negligence against him. So the Torah splits the payment between the ox's owner and the animal's owner.

While this might not seem a perfect solution, the alternatives offered by our overly litigious society hardly seem superior. A friend confessed to me with shame that when an employee tripped in his house (she simply lost her footing; there was no object on the floor), his first concern was that she would sue. When it became apparent that she was not badly hurt, he was as relieved at being exempted from the possibility of a lawsuit as he was at seeing the hurt woman feeling all right. The very litigious nature of our society often causes us to view others as potential plaintiffs rather than as partners or as fellow creatures in God's image.

The Torah understood that accidents happen. Sometimes a sad thing happens, and an injury occurs. But just because there's a victim doesn't mean there's a villain.

DAY

261     MONDAY
_____

## When an Accident Is No Accident

Drunk drivers who kill people frequently defend themselves with the plea that their action was an accident. From Judaism's perspective, such a defense is an absurd confusion of accident and negligence.

Biblical law distinguishes between accidents that a person couldn't have anticipated, and injuries resulting from negligence. In the case described yesterday, when an animal that had never previously displayed any violent tendencies suddenly attacks another creature, its owner is obliged to pay half the damages. But if the animal had a previous history of goring, the owner's responsibility is one hundred percent.

Why? Because once an animal gores (and the Torah's language suggests that this animal may already have done so twice), the owner knows that his animal has violent inclinations. If he chooses to keep such an animal alive, he bears moral and legal responsibility for any future injuries the animal inflicts.

Maimonides, in his legal code, the *Mishneh Torah,* rules: "Five species of animals are considered prone to cause damage from the beginning of their existence. This applies even if they have been domesticated. Therefore, if they cause damage or death by goring, biting, treading, lying down upon, or the like, the owner is liable for the entire amount of the damages. They are a wolf, a lion, a bear, a tiger, and a leopard. Similarly, a snake that bites...even if it has been domesticated." *

If you choose to raise a dangerous animal, Jewish law regards you as negligent and liable for any injuries it inflicts, even if you have taken some precautions and tried to domesticate it. Similarly, Jewish law regards you as negligent and liable if you drive after taking a number of drinks, and cause an accident.

An accident is an accident when it could not have been anticipated. When it could have been anticipated, it is no accident.

DAY

262      TUESDAY

## Don't Be a Mitzvah Hero at Someone Else's Expense

Jewish law dictates that a person wash his or her hands and recite a blessing before eating bread. On one occasion, colleagues noted that Rabbi Israel Salanter was very sparing in pouring water over his hands; in fact, he used the minimum amount permissible.

When asked why he performed this commandment in a manner that appeared almost grudging, Rabbi Salanter responded, "The water is

---

*Maimonides, *Sefer Nezikin* (*The Book of Damages*), "The Laws of Damages to Property" 1:6; translated by Rabbi Eliyahu Touger, 16.

carried to this house from a well by a servant girl. Water is heavy, and I don't wish to fulfill my mitzvah on her back."

It was part of Rabbi Salanter's greatness to notice moral issues where others saw none. On another occasion, a respected citizen invited him to be a Shabbat guest. Rabbi Salanter quizzed the man briefly as to how the Shabbat meal would be conducted, and learned that between the courses there would be extensive discussions of the Torah portion, and the singing of Shabbat *zmirot* (songs). Rabbi Salanter consented to be a guest, but only on condition that the meal be served quickly, and that the Torah discussions and singing be kept to a minimum or postponed until after the meal was concluded.

The host was stunned by the request, but acceded. The meal was served quickly and without interruption. When the dinner was finished, the host asked the rabbi, "Can you tell me what you found wrong with my normal manner of conducting the Shabbat meal, and why you insisted on this change?"

Instead of responding, Rabbi Salanter summoned the cook from the kitchen. "I want to apologize to you," he told the elderly woman. "I'm sorry that I caused you to work so hard, and forced you to bring out the courses one after another. Please forgive me."

"Forgive you?" the woman responded. "I want to thank you. Every Friday night, after having already worked here a whole day, I have to remain late, and I go home exhausted. Tonight we finished at a reasonable hour. Thank you. Now I can go home and get some rest."

As Rabbi Abraham Twerski has commented, Rabbi Salanter was a man who "understood not only what goes on in the Talmud, but also what goes on in the kitchen."

DAY

263    WEDNESDAY

## *Speak Truth to Power*

*How do we know that a disciple sitting before his master, who sees that the poor man is right [in a legal dispute which his teacher is adjudicating] and the wealthy man wrong, should not remain silent? Because [the Torah teaches]: "Keep far away from falsehood" (Exodus 23:7).*

—Babylonian Talmud, *Shevuot* 31a

Because the Jewish tradition so emphasizes the respect a student must show his or her teacher, the Rabbis feared that students would hold their tongues when they saw their teacher, while judging a case, favoring one side. Thus, the Talmud felt it necessary to warn students that when such a matter occurs, the Torah, the holiest document in Jewish life, mandates that they speak up. Quite simply, Jewish ethics teaches that you do not have the right to remain silent when another person will suffer because of your silence. Thus, in this case described in the Talmud, in which a teacher incorrectly favors a rich litigant, the student is required to speak up.* Indeed, for the student not to do so is to commit perhaps a greater offense than the teacher's, since the teacher's error is probably innocent, while the student's silence is not.

This ruling likewise implies that if you see a boss unfairly mistreating a fellow employee, you should speak up. Speak up any time when you, like the student with his teacher, have reason to believe that your words will have an impact.

Dr. Stephen Marmer, a professor of psychiatry at the UCLA School of Medicine, shared with me a cherished memory from his days in medical school:

When I was a second-year student, during one particular lecture a student rose to ask a very elementary question. The teacher glared and replied, "That is a stupid question!" The red-faced student sat down, but another student, one of the best in the class, raised his hand. Expecting a more intelligent comment or question, the teacher recognized him. The second student proceeded to say, "Professor, none of us in this class is stupid. We may be ignorant, but that is why we are here to learn. You should apologize to so-

---

*Another Torah verse makes it clear that the same would apply if the teacher was favoring a poor man over a rich one: "You shall not render an unfair decision: Do not favor the poor or show deference to the rich; judge your kinsmen fairly" (Leviticus 19:15).

and-so and to the class." At that point, all the other students applauded. To his credit, the professor did offer an apology before continuing his lecture, and even thanked the admonishing student.

As Dr. Marmer concluded, "I have never forgotten how morally courageous that was for my classmate to do."

The notion of speaking truth to those more powerful than yourself ("speaking truth to power") is a doctrine long associated with Quakers. The Bible (in its stories of Moses' confrontations with Pharaoh and the prophets' challenges to kings) and the Talmud (in its insistence that a student challenge a teacher) remind us how important and longstanding a Jewish tradition it is.

DAY

## 264     THURSDAY

# *Just How Much Are You Supposed to Fear God?*

R abbi Yochanan ben Zakkai was a master of common sense. He opposed the Jews of first-century Judea revolting against Rome, arguing that an uprising by the small Judean state against the Roman Empire was unwinnable. When people told him that God would intervene on the Jews' side, perhaps even sending the Messiah, he remained unconvinced: "If you should happen to be holding a sapling in your hand when they tell you that the Messiah has arrived, first plant the sapling, and then go out and greet the Messiah."

Years later, after the revolt failed and the Romans destroyed Jerusalem and its Great Temple (70 C.E.), Rabbi Yochanan played the key role in rebuilding Jewish life. While the last of the rebels were dying at Masada, he was establishing a new academy of Jewish learning in Yavneh, which proved a worthy successor to the Sanhedrin (the Jewish high court) in Jerusalem. Jewish tradition credits him with establishing a model of a Judaism that could survive without a Temple, without sacrifices, and even without a state.

When Rabbi Yochanan was on his deathbed, he displayed a common sense in religious matters that equaled his common sense in political ones. His disciples, aware that this was likely to be their last meeting with him, asked him for a parting blessing, and he answered, "May your fear of God be as strong as your fear of men."

"Is that all?" the students asked, astonished by such pedestrian advice.

"Would that you achieve as much as that," Rabbi Yochanan answered. "Know that when a man commits an offense, he says, 'May no man see me' [all the while indifferent to the fact that God sees everything he does]" (Babylonian Talmud, *Berachot* 28b).

The students had entered the dying rabbi's room hoping for inspirational and grandiose words. Instead, they got what they should have learned to expect from Rabbi Yochanan: commonsense wisdom. He told them a truth that is obvious but seldom noted, that most people, even those who claim to be religious, fear human beings more than they fear God. When they act unethically, they take care that no one witnesses their behavior, oblivious to the more important reality that God sees what they are doing.

Rabbi Yochanan reminds us that if we fear God as much as we fear people, if we maintain a consciousness that God is always there ("Know what is above you: an eye that sees"; *Ethics of the Fathers* 2:1), we will perform very few evil acts.

DAY

265

FRIDAY

# Don't Mouth Pious Platitudes

Once, when a young child was injured while playing in the street, the Jerusalem sage Rabbi Shlomo Shwadron put the child on his shoulders and started running to a nearby hospital. An older woman, seeing the very worried expression on the rabbi's face, called out to him, "Don't worry, Rabbi. God will take care of everything."

But as the rabbi passed her, the woman saw that the child he was carrying was her own grandson. "Chaim! Chaim!" she started shrieking hysterically, wringing her hands. "Is he going to be all right? Is he going to be all right?"

Pious, religious-sounding statements made when other people are suffering are not always expressions of deep faith. For some people perhaps they are, but for others they are platitudes. So when you're tempted to utter a platitude that costs you nothing, like telling a person in need of money "God will provide," or saying to one who has suffered a tragic loss, "Whatever God does is for the best," remember the grandmother who spoke so thoughtlessly to Rabbi Shwadron. What would you want someone to say, how would you want someone to react, if it were your child or grandchild who was injured and in danger? Certainly not in this way.

There are times when we need to learn to be silent.

May you have a Shabbat Shalom!

DAY

## 266     SHABBAT

During the course of this Shabbat, try to review the material from the preceding six days, and use some of the texts studied as the basis for discussion during the Shabbat meals:

Day 260. Accidents Do Happen
Day 261. When an Accident Is No Accident
Day 262. Don't Be a Mitzvah Hero at Someone Else's Expense
Day 263. Speak Truth to Power
Day 264. Just How Much Are You Supposed to Fear God?
Day 265. Don't Mouth Pious Platitudes

Shabbat Shalom!

# WEEK 39

SUNDAY

## *Do a Favor . . . for Your Enemy*

Because Judaism originated and developed in an agricultural society, many Torah regulations concern animals. For example, if you see an animal suffering under a heavy burden, you are commanded to help its owner release the burden, thereby minimizing the animal's discomfort (Exodus 23:5). And if you see a person loading goods on his animal, you should help him as well. But if two people simultaneously need assistance, one who is unloading an animal and the other loading, you should first help the person whose animal is being unloaded, since that creature is suffering more.

However, Jewish law offers a curious exception. The Talmud teaches, "If a friend requires unloading, and an enemy loading, your first obligation is toward your enemy, in order to subdue your evil inclination." When one rabbi raises the logical objection that in order to minimize the burdened animal's suffering, unloading should take precedence, the Talmud responds, "Even so, the motive 'in order to subdue one's evil inclination' is more compelling" (*Bava Mezia* 32b).

It is very hard to make peace with a person whom you dislike; even if you sit down together to talk, the conversation is apt to degenerate into angry recollections of past grievances and insults. A Jewish joke tells of two men who have been feuding for years. One year, just before the Kol Nidre service on Yom Kippur eve, the rabbi summons the men into his office and admonishes them, "It's absurd for you to come before God and ask for forgiveness when you can't even forgive each other." Shamed by the rabbi's words, the men shake hands and make up. Later, after the service ends, they see each other, and one says, "I want you to know that I prayed for you everything that you prayed for me."

The other man responds, "Starting up already?"

In truth, because reconciling enemies is so hard, the Talmud insists on taking advantage of any opportunity to do a favor for an enemy; the favor itself can cause your enemy to see you in a more positive light.

This is precisely the sort of ethical deed for which it is hard to prepare; the opportunity to do your enemy a favor is likely to happen on the spur of the moment. Yet knowledge of this talmudic text is apt to make you act differently when the opportunity arises. So, if you see a person whom you dislike in a difficult situation, and you are in a position to provide assistance, overcome your evil inclination, break the pattern of enmity, and help him or her out.

DAY

268 MONDAY

## Maimonides, Art Buchwald, and the Importance of Every Deed

A striking passage in Maimonides'"Laws of Repentance" suggests that we go through life always feeling as if our good and bad deeds are in perfect balance, so that the very next deed we perform will tip the balance either way. Maimonides then raises the stakes, asking us to imagine that the world is also poised in perfect balance, so that our next deed can tip the entire world to one side or the other ("Laws of Repentance," 3:4).

Rabbi Jack Riemer found a somewhat similar idea expressed in a very different idiom in a column by the humorist Art Buchwald. Follow Buchwald's advice, and not only will *you* become a better person, the world also will become a better place, and quickly. Buchwald writes:

I was in New York the other day and rode with a friend in a taxi. When we got out, my friend said to the driver, "Thank you for the ride. You did a superb job of driving."

The taxi driver was stunned for a second. Then he said: "Are you a wise guy or something?"

"No, my dear man, and I'm not putting you on. I admire the way you keep cool in heavy traffic."

"Yeah," the driver said and drove off.

"What was that all about?" I asked.

"I am trying to bring love back to New York," he said. "I believe it's the only thing that can save the city."

"How can one man save New York?"

"It's not one man. I believe I have made the taxi driver's day. Suppose he has twenty fares. He's going to be nice to those twenty fares because someone was nice to him. Those fares in turn will be kinder to their employees or shopkeepers or waiters or even their own families. Eventually, the goodwill could spread to at least one thousand people. Now that isn't bad, is it?"

"But you're depending on that taxi driver to pass on your goodwill to others."

"I'm not depending on it," my friend said. "I'm aware that the system isn't foolproof, so I might deal with ten different people today. If, out of ten, I can make three happy, then eventually I can indirectly influence the attitudes of three thousand more."

"It sounds good on paper," I admitted, "but I'm not sure it works in practice."

"Nothing is lost if it doesn't. It didn't take any of my time to tell the man he was doing a good job. He neither received a larger tip nor a smaller tip. If it fell on deaf ears, so what? Tomorrow there will be another taxi driver whom I can try to make happy."

"You're some kind of nut," I said.

"That shows how cynical you have become. I have made a study of this. The thing that seems to be lacking, besides money of course for our postal employees, is that no one tells people who work for the post office what a good job they're doing."

"But they're not doing a good job."

"They're not doing a good job because they feel no one cares if they do or not. Why shouldn't someone say a kind word to them?"

We were walking past a structure in the process of being built and passed five workmen eating their lunch. My friend stopped. "That's a magnificent job you men have done. It must be difficult and dangerous work."

The five men eyed my friend suspiciously.

"When will it be finished?"

"June," a man grunted.

"Ah, that really is impressive. You must all be very proud."

We walked away. I said to him. "I haven't seen anyone like you since 'Man of La Mancha.'"

"When those men digest my words, they will feel better for it. Somehow the city will benefit from their happiness."

"But you can't do this alone!" I protested. "You're just one man."

"The most important thing is not to get discouraged. Making people in the city become kind again is not an easy job, but if I can enlist other people in my campaign..."

"You just winked at a very plain-looking woman," I said.

"Yes, I know," he replied. "And if she's a schoolteacher, her class will be in for a fantastic day."

DAY

269 TUESDAY

## *When You Have Been Sinned Against: Your Obligation*

Jewish law requires that a person who has injured another—physically, monetarily, or through words—ask him or her for forgiveness. If the "injurer" does not do so, then, Jewish tradition teaches, even God cannot forgive him (see Day 276).

But what is your responsibility if you are the victim of the sin? How does Jewish law expect you to act when the one who harmed you begs forgiveness?

It wants you to forgive.

Putting aside the most egregious and relatively rare evils (such as requests for forgiveness made by a rapist, a kidnapper, or a mugger),* the Jewish view is that you should always forgive if the request seems sincere, and try to do so wholeheartedly.

What if you feel just too angry to do so?

Then you should work on yourself. Try to enter into the other person's mind and imagine why she might have acted as she did. Did she deceive you in a business deal? Perhaps she felt under such financial pressure that she didn't think clearly or fairly. Did he betray a secret? Maybe he told others out of a desperate need to seem important.

Some years ago my wife and I briefly employed an elderly woman as a babysitter. One day, when Dvorah suggested to our daughters that they take a few Barbie dolls on a car trip, our daughter Naomi said, "Ruth [not the woman's real name] told us to give her all our dolls, so that she could give them to poor children."

We confronted the woman, who admitted that she had sent some of the dolls to her grandchildren; others, we suspect, she sold. We were furious.

A short time later, after having arranged for the return of some of the dolls, the woman asked us to forgive her. We struggled with our

---

*I can identify no textual basis for this position, though it seems self-evident to me on logical grounds that, for example, a woman who has been raped is not obligated to forgive her tormentor. On the other hand, Professor Louis Newman, in *Past Imperatives: Studies in the History and Theory of Jewish Ethics*, argues that his reading of the Jewish tradition suggests that no crime committed against another should be beyond forgiveness. Noting that God is repeatedly described in Jewish sources as open to forgiving sins committed against Him, Newman writes: "This view of divine forgiveness logically implies that the duty of one individual to forgive another is likewise unlimited" (page 92). I am not persuaded by Newman's analogy, since God, being God, does not suffer from a sin committed against Him in the way a raped woman suffers. And Newman does note that the classical Jewish sources never explicitly address the issue of whether there are interpersonal sins so heinous as to be unforgivable. I have excluded from this discussion, as would Newman (see his book, page 244, footnote 1), requests for forgiveness made by murderers, since the only one who can grant such a person forgiveness is dead.

anger over her manipulation of our children's emotions, but then forgave her. Dvorah and I attributed what she had done to a need to appear as a generous, doting grandmother to her grandchildren.

True, once something like this happens, one does not feel particularly trusting of such a person; still, if the person seeking forgiveness seems truly contrite, it's important to let go of one's anger and to forgive.

In fact, Jewish law regards one who rejects three separate appeals from another for forgiveness as cruel (*Mishneh Torah*, "Laws of Repentance," 2:9–10).* Just because you were the victim of another's dishonesty or cruelty does not entitle you to act cruelly toward him or her, particularly when that person is trying to make amends. Revenge is sweet in fantasy, during the first throes of fury. But ultimately it is not sweet, it is just cruel.

An exercise: Is there someone who has attempted to secure your forgiveness, and whom you have rebuffed? Has the time come for you to reconsider?

DAY

270        W E D N E S D A Y

## *A Nightly Prayer Before Going to Sleep*

When I was growing up, I had a friend who was always nursing grudges. In elementary school, his anger was directed against a schoolmate he regarded as a tattletale; in college, he was furious at a fellow classmate who won a scholarship that my friend thought the student was not entitled to. Later I heard him rail against his mother for a lie she had told him many years earlier.

*This law implies that the "injurer" should be persistent in seeking forgiveness from the injured.

Although blessed with great intellectual capacities, my friend has never achieved anywhere near the success that was expected of him as a youth. Why?

I'm not a psychologist, but my theory is that too much of his intellectual energies and emotions have been directed at establishing "the case" he has against whomever is the current target of his anger. He has spent hundreds, maybe thousands, of hours dissecting, with little sympathy or empathy, the motives and actions of those who have antagonized him.

Ironically, though he is an observant Jew, my friend has never profited from a prayer the Jewish tradition suggests each person make before going to sleep. The nightly bedtime ritual of a Jew is supposed to include recitation of the *Sh'ma*, Judaism's credo statement. Prior to reciting it, one is supposed to say the following:

> Master of the universe, I hereby forgive anyone who angered or antagonized me or who sinned against me—whether against my body, my property, my honor, or against anything of mine; whether he did so accidentally, willfully, carelessly, or purposely; whether through speech, deed, thought, or notion; whether in this transmigration or another transmigration....May no man be punished because of me. May it be Your will, my God and the God of my forefathers, that I may sin no more. Whatever sins I have done before You, may You blot out in your abundant mercies, but not through suffering or bad illnesses. May the expressions of my mouth and the thoughts of my heart find favor before You, my Rock and my Redeemer.*

The prayer follows a commonsense formula of Jewish theology. First you forgive others for offenses they have committed against you; only

---

*Perhaps the most surprising feature of this prayer, which is found in the ArtScroll Prayerbook, pages 288–89, is the clause "whether in this transmigration or another transmigration," which seems to constitute a rare affirmation of a Jewish belief in reincarnation. I omitted from the middle of the prayer, following the words "another transmigration," the words "I forgive every Jew," since this limitation does not seem to me to flow from the logic of the prayer.

then do you have the right to ask God to forgive you for offenses you have committed against Him (see Day 187).*

Recite this prayer, internalize its message, and you will go to sleep calm and wake up calm. I'm thinking of making a photocopy of it, and sending it to my friend. But I had better do it anonymously; otherwise he'll get angry at me.

DAY

271 THURSDAY

# Don't Let Your Child Humiliate Another Child

Several years ago, I learned that on my daughter's school bus, some children were taunting a girl who was a new student at the school, as well as a bit overweight and unathletic. Some even made up jingles to mock her, which they sang in her presence.

When I sat down with my daughter to explain how wrong this was, I found that I was so overcome with emotion that I couldn't speak. My daughter looked at me in astonishment, amazed that what seemed to her to be a small matter—some children teasing one of their peers— had upset me so deeply.

I explained to her how seriously Judaism regards the issue of humiliating another person. "Teasing," the word children often use to describe such behavior, is chosen to hide and minimize the evil of what is being done. To humiliate and mock another child is far worse than to tease. Judaism regards such behavior as a form of murder, understanding that if such humiliation goes on for a prolonged period, it can

---

*I understand this prayer as mandating forgiveness of those who have inflicted upon you the sort of normal hurts that human beings commonly inflict on one another. It does not seem to me that this prayer entails forgiving another for extreme acts of evil and the infliction of horrific hurts (on whether such acts of evil can ever be forgiven, see Day 193, and the note in yesterday's entry).

destroy a person's self-respect, make him or her feel foolish and hated, and therefore destroy a person's life.

After we spoke, my daughter called up the girl and invited her to our house. During the phone conversation, the girl confided that though she tried to put up a strong front on the bus (telling the children who were taunting her, "I don't care what you say. It doesn't bother me"), in reality, the constant humiliation had made her feel horrible.*

If you teach your child from a young age that taunting and humiliating another human being are among the greatest evils a person can commit, you will not only help save your child's soul, you also might save another child, one unknown to you, from a life of misery and pain.

FRIDAY

# What the Fifth Commandment Demands of Parents

The Rabbis understood Jewish law as not only obligating children to honor parents, but also as obliging parents to act in a manner that enables their children to honor them. For example, the Talmud denounces a parent who hits a mature child, understanding that such an act might well provoke the child to strike back, and thereby violate a Torah law (Exodus 21:15; see *Mo'ed Kattan* 17a).

When we witness children acting disrespectfully toward parents, it might well be true that the children are at fault. But Abraham Joshua Heschel, the great rabbinic scholar and humanitarian activist, asked parents to consider another possibility: "In so many cases, it is the parent who makes it impossible for the young to obey the Fifth Command-

---

*We also alerted the school's principal about what was going on. He immediately became involved in stopping the taunting.

ment. My message to parents is: Every day ask yourselves the question, 'What is there about me that deserves the reverence of my child?'"

May you have a Shabbat Shalom!

S H A B B A T
_____

During the course of this Shabbat, try to review the material from the preceding six days, and use some of the texts studied as the basis for discussion during the Shabbat meals:

Day 267. Do a Favor...for Your Enemy
Day 268. Maimonides, Art Buchwald, and the Importance
            of Every Deed
Day 269. When You Have Been Sinned Against: Your Obligation
Day 270. A Nightly Prayer Before Going to Sleep
Day 271. Don't Let Your Child Humiliate Another Child
Day 272. What the Fifth Commandment Demands of Parents

Shabbat Shalom!

DAY

274

# Make Your Celebration a Cause for Everyone to Celebrate

Rabbi Abraham Twerski tells of the concern he experienced when he was invited to a very opulent wedding reception:

I worried over this event, not wanting to hurt either the couple or the parents, all four of whom had been in my congregation so many years [earlier, before I became a psychiatrist]. But the wedding was so, well, lavish and expensive—what other words can I use—that I thought of how wasteful it would prove to be when so many others are needy. How could I partake in such an event? How could I give my heart to it and truly wish them well?

An idea, a very obvious one actually, came to me that I knew would satisfy my dilemma. I requested that the couple give the leftover food to an operation in Milwaukee that arranges to remove such leftovers and distribute them to the needy. To my great delight, the couple had already arranged this, and indeed many of their friends in their "social set" often donated leftovers in this way.

The next idea came from Ida, a woman who attended my wife when my daughter was born. She suggested that the flowers be donated at the end of the evening to Mt. Sinai Hospital, where she worked as a nurse. Actually, it seemed like such a great idea that I wanted some of those flowers to be donated to a local psychiatric hospital where many of the patients never receive flowers.

The couple loved this idea. I danced and celebrated at the wedding, and early in the morning, thirty medical students from Marquette University came to get the flowers and distribute them.*

In recent years, a Jewish organization, Mazon (Hebrew for sustenance), has asked Jews to donate to them three percent of the cost of a celebration (such as a wedding, a bar or bat mitzvah, or a graduation party), which the organization then distributes to other organizations that feed the hungry. What a wonderful way to ensure that our celebration continues even when the party has ended! Rabbi Twerski notes that a week after the wedding he received a letter from the newly married couple relating that giving the flowers and food to those less fortunate, bringing them cheer, was a great way to start their new life, "and a good omen for a happy marriage."

*Mazal tov!*

M O N D A Y

# On Not Embarrassing the Recipient

It is not enough to give charity, Jewish tradition teaches; one is obligated to perform charitable acts in the most ethical manner possible. Unfortunately, the way to accomplish this is not always obvious. Sometimes what seems to be a charitable act is not, in fact, the most ethical course of action. Thus, the *Sefer Chasidim* (*Book of the Pious*), the thirteenth-century guidebook of pious Jewish circles in Germany, relates:

Reuben, an honest man, asked Shimon to lend him some money. Without hesitation, Shimon made the loan but said, "I really give this to you as a gift."

*Twerski, Do Unto Others: How Good Deeds Can Change Your Life, 37–39.

Reuben was so shamed and embarrassed that he would never ask Shimon for a loan again. Clearly, in this case, it would have been better not to have given Reuben a gift of that kind [paragraph 1691].

Shimon certainly did not lack a good heart. What he did lack, however, was a trait that is just as important in accomplishing good: a well-developed moral imagination, the ability to use one's mind and heart to ensure that when one performs a kindness, one does it in the manner that will achieve the most good.

A master at doing good the right way was Rabbi Aryeh Levine, one of the preeminent Jewish *tzaddikim* (saints) of the twentieth century.

For many decades, Reb Aryeh taught at the Etz Chayyim school in Jerusalem. During most of this time, many of the school's students were poor. Once, Reb Aryeh noticed a young boy coming to school in very tattered shoes. Clearly he needed a new pair, but Reb Aryeh also knew that the boy's father, a proud man, would be humiliated and offended if his son were treated as a charity case and given a pair. How does a person with moral imagination provide a boy with soles, while not paining his father's soul?

During a morning recess break, Reb Aryeh summoned the boy to his office because, he said, he needed to test him on his talmudic proficiency. He asked the boy several questions, well within the youth's grasp. "Wonderful!" Reb Aryeh said when the boy answered correctly. He gave the youngster two notes: one to be brought to a local shoemaker, with instructions to give the boy a good pair of shoes, for which Reb Aryeh would pay; the second, a note to the boy's father telling him about the "prize" his son had won.*

As important as it is to dispense *tzedaka* (charity) to those in need, it is just as important to do so without humiliating the recipient. *How* you give often matters as much as *what* you give.

---

*Raz, *A Tzaddik in Our Time,* 321.

# Is There Someone You're Ignoring Whom You Should Ask for Forgiveness?

According to Jewish law, if you have cheated another, you must first pay the person what you owe him and then beg his forgiveness. This is Judaism's route to repentance. As an oft-quoted Mishna teaches, "Yom Kippur atones for sins against God, not for those against man, unless the injured party has been appeased" (Mishna, *Yoma* 8:9).

If you are not in a position to return the money, explain your circumstances to the person you defrauded, and ask him or her to bear with you as you try to pay off as much of the debt as you can. If the person has died, you should pay the money to his or her heirs.

If you have insulted an individual or hurt him or her in some other way, acknowledge what you have done, ask if there is anything you can do to mitigate the damage or hurt you have caused, ask for forgiveness, and express the wish for reconciliation.

If the damage you inflicted on another person was severe, he or she might be unwilling to forgive. If that happens, Jewish law instructs you to make at least two more efforts to obtain forgiveness. After three requests have been made and refused, you are not required to seek forgiveness again, for Jewish law does not oblige you to spend the rest of your life begging another to forgive you.

Before you turn the page, concluding that this entry is intended for others but not for you, think hard for a moment. Is there someone whom you have hurt—a family member, friend, or business acquaintance—to whom you have never apologized? Many years ago, the novel *Love Story* popularized the line "Love means never having to say you're sorry." Jewish ethics believes the contrary. Love and goodness mean learning how not to hurt others and how to apologize when you do.

## W E D N E S D A Y

# Don't Forgive on
# Other People's Behalf

Several times a year in the United States, one hears of the murder of a young person, only later to see the victim's parents being interviewed on television, announcing that they forgive their child's killer. Almost invariably, the parents are deeply pious Christians who have been taught by their tradition that all sins can and should be forgiven.

The Jewish viewpoint on granting forgiveness, in a case where the crime was committed against another, is very different. From Judaism's perspective, although the parents in the case described above can forgive the killer for the pain he caused them, they cannot forgive the murder itself; only the victim of the crime—who in this case is in no position to do so—can forgive the crime. Some years ago, the late Rabbi Abraham Joshua Heschel was invited to speak before a group of non-Jewish business leaders. At the conclusion of his talk, one executive asked him, "Rabbi Heschel, don't you think it's about time you and the Jewish people forgave the rest of the world for the Holocaust?"

Rabbi Heschel responded with a story:

> Over fifty years ago [Hayyim Soloveitchik], the rabbi of Brisk, a scholar of extraordinary renown, revered also for his gentleness, entered a train in Warsaw to return to his hometown. The rabbi, a man of slight stature, and of no [strikingly] distinctive appearance, found a seat in a compartment. There, he was surrounded by traveling salesmen, who, as soon as the train began to move, started to play cards.
>
> As the game progressed, their excitement increased. The rabbi remained aloof and absorbed in [the book he was reading]. Such aloofness was annoying to the others. One of them finally suggested that the rabbi join in the game. He answered that he never

played cards. As time passed, the rabbi's aloofness became even more irritating, until one man said to him, "Either you join us, or leave the compartment." Shortly thereafter, he took the rabbi by the collar and pushed him out of the compartment. For several hours the rabbi had to stand, until he reached his destination, the city of Brisk.

Brisk was also the salesmen's destination. When the rabbi left the train, he was immediately surrounded by admirers welcoming him and shaking his hands. "Who is that man?" asked the salesman [who had pushed him out of the compartment].

"You don't know? It's the famous rabbi of Brisk."

The salesman's heart sank. He had not realized whom he had offended. He quickly went over to the rabbi to ask forgiveness.

The rabbi declined to forgive him: "I would like to forgive you," he said, "but I can't."

In his hotel room, the salesman could find no peace. He went to the rabbi's house and was admitted to the rabbi's study. "Rabbi," he said, "I am not a rich man. I have, however, savings of three hundred rubles. I will give them to you for charity if you will forgive me."

The rabbi's answer was brief: "No!"

The salesman's anxiety was unbearable. He went to the synagogue to seek solace. When he shared his anxiety with some people in the synagogue, they were deeply surprised. How could their rabbi, so gentle a person, be so unforgiving? Their advice was for him to speak to the rabbi's eldest son and to tell him of the surprising attitude taken by his father.

When the rabbi's son heard the story, he could not understand his father's obstinacy. Seeing the man's anxiety, he promised to discuss the matter with his father.

It is not proper, according to Jewish law, for a son to criticize his father directly. So the son entered his father's study and began a general discussion of Jewish law and turned to the laws of forgiveness. When the principle was mentioned that a person who asks for forgiveness three times should be granted forgiveness, the son mentioned the name of the man who was in great anxiety. Thereupon, the rabbi of Brisk answered:

"I cannot forgive him. He never insulted me. He did not know who I was. Had he had any idea who I was, he never would have acted as he did. He wants forgiveness? Let him find a poor anonymous Jew sitting on a train reading a book and ask him for forgiveness."

"No one can forgive crimes committed against someone else," Rabbi Heschel concluded. "It is therefore preposterous to assume that any Jew alive can grant forgiveness for the suffering of any one of the six million people who perished. According to Jewish tradition, even God Himself can only forgive sins committed against Himself, not against man." *

THURSDAY

## The Punishment of One Who Humiliates Another

I know a woman whose parents moved with her to a foreign country when she was seven years old. At her new school she was repeatedly and publicly humiliated by a teacher who mocked grammatical and vocabulary errors she made. This experience was so traumatic that, decades later, the woman still suffered paralyzing fear before speaking in front of a group.

While this young girl suffered terribly, the Talmud claims that the teacher, who never repented and begged the girl's forgiveness, would one day suffer an even more severe punishment: "One who publicly humiliates another, even though he has learned Torah and has performed other good deeds, loses his share in the World-to-Come" (*Ethics of the Fathers* 3:11).

*I first heard this story from the late Rabbi Wolfe Kelman, who heard the story from Rabbi Heschel; in the text cited herein, I have followed, in the main, the version of Rabbi Heschel's response as printed in Wiesenthal, *The Sunflower*, 164–66.

Why do the Rabbis presume that God imposes so severe a punishment for this transgression? Obviously because they perceive public humiliation as an offense that inflicts irrevocable damage. A person who is humiliated (particularly if the humiliation occurs repeatedly) frequently becomes insecure, ashamed of himself or herself, and embarrassed in the presence of others.

This strict teaching has manifold daily implications. Teachers must not humiliate students (the offense is greatly magnified if the shaming occurs in the presence of others), nor may parents humiliate their children; employers must not humiliate employees, and one involved in a dispute must not humiliate his opponent.

I once read of a man who boasted to his rabbi that he had publicly confronted a sinner, and had admonished the man so severely that the sinner's face turned red. "What's more," continued the student, who was well aware of this teaching. "I'm happy I did it, even if it costs me my share in the World-to-Come."

The rabbi wisely noted that this young man probably wouldn't be willing to lose his smallest finger for the pleasure of admonishing another. All that his statement revealed was that either he disbelieved the rabbinic teaching regarding the severity with which God views humiliating another, or that he had no appreciation of the significance of the World-to-Come.

If you have humiliated another, you must beg the person for forgiveness, and try to build her up in public to compensate for how you dragged her down. For example, if the teacher described above truly wished to repent, she should first have gone to the girl's house, acknowledged that she had done a great wrong, and asked the student for forgiveness. Then she should have stood up in front of the class, admitted that she had done a bad thing, and spoken up on behalf of the girl whom she had humiliated.

The Rabbis were clearly preoccupied with the horror of humiliating another. The Talmud records a blessing given by one sage to another. "May you never cause anyone else embarrassment and may you never be caused any embarrassment yourself" (*Mo'ed Kattan* 9b).

# *When You Can't Give Money*

For an observant Jew committed to giving charity, the Sabbath can be difficult. What do you do when you see hungry beggars soliciting contributions on the one day each week that Jewish law forbids handling money? Because of this prohibition, I generally tell the beggars that it's my Sabbath day, and that I am sorry, but that I am not carrying money.

Recently, I was walking on the Sabbath with a friend, Ari Goldman, and his daughter Emma, who carried a box filled with food items. Whenever we came across a beggar, she gave him or her something, explaining to me, "I was uncomfortable passing by a beggar and not being able to give anything. So now I never leave the house on Shabbat without taking food with me." *

Emma's suggestion impressed me, and reminded me that when a person uses her intellectual abilities to find a way to act more ethically, she can find a way to do so, even when, like Emma, that person is only ten years old.

May you have a Shabbat Shalom!

---

* *Halacha* (Jewish law) forbids carrying anything in a public domain on the Sabbath, but the area in Manhattan where we live, and hundreds of other localities throughout the United States, has established an *eruv*, a closed-in space that constitutes a domain in which carrying items on the Sabbath is permitted.

## SHABBAT

During the course of this Shabbat, try to review the material from the preceding six days, and use some of the texts studied as the basis for discussion during the Shabbat meals:

Day 274.  Make Your Celebration a Cause for Everyone to Celebrate

Day 275.  On Not Embarrassing the Recipient

Day 276.  Is There Someone You're Ignoring Whom You Should Ask for Forgiveness?

Day 277.  Don't Forgive on Other People's Behalf

Day 278.  The Punishment of One Who Humiliates Another

Day 279.  When You Can't Give Money

Shabbat Shalom!

# WEEK 41

## SUNDAY

# How to Avoid Giving In to Temptation

*Take a circuitous route, O Nazirite, but do not approach the vineyard.*

—Babylonian Talmud, *Shabbat* 13a

In the Book of Numbers, the Torah describes the law of the Nazirite, one who vows to "set himself apart for the Lord." By taking the Nazirite vow, a person obligates himself not to drink wine or eat grapes, cut his hair, or have contact with a corpse (see Numbers 6:1–21). Such a vow was usually taken for a set period of time.

In commenting upon this law, the Talmud offers the Nazirite very practical advice: "Take a circuitous route, O Nazirite, but do not approach the vineyard." In other words, since you are forbidden to eat grapes, avoid tempting yourself by going to places where grapes are present.

In a more modern context, this advice could be expanded to apply to people with different temptations. For example: "Take a circuitous route, O recovering alcoholic, but do not approach a bar." Similarly, gamblers should avoid being in casinos and racetracks, or around card games, and dieters should, among other things, avoid looking at the dessert menu in restaurants.

Because of the specific nature of the vow he has taken, it is easy for a Nazirite to know exactly what he must avoid, but for many human beings it is difficult. We have all met alcoholics who are sure they can handle one or two drinks, or gamblers who are certain they will walk away from the gaming table if they start to lose too much money. That is why self-knowledge is the first step to self-improvement. Only if a person knows his weaknesses (such as overstepping appropriate sexual boundaries, gossiping unfairly, exaggerating one's hours when charging a client) is there a hope that he will learn how to categorically avoid those things that most tempt him.

Do you know your weaknesses? And if you do, do you have strategies for guarding against them?

<br>

DAY

## 282     M O N D A Y

# *When You're Tempted to Do Something Wrong*

*Know what is above you: An eye that sees, an ear that hears, and all your deeds are recorded in a book.*
—Ethics of the Fathers 2:1

Recently, in an event that dominated American life for a full year, a president became involved in a sexual relationship while serving in the White House. The president's actions were very indiscreet, and in several ways quite disgusting. For example, he spoke by phone with a congressman concerning the dispatching of American troops to foreign danger spots, while simultaneously engaging in sexual activity with his lover. When this matter became known, the president and the woman, as well the president's wife and daughter, were tremendously embarrassed. While one might argue that the public should never have learned of such events, as I believe, in some respects the president had only himself to blame. No one forced him to do what he was doing.

Similarly, some people choose to become involved in dishonest or shady business details and are greatly embarrassed when their behavior becomes known.

All such episodes can be avoided by following the apt advice a friend of mine told me his mother gave him. If you are the sort of person who is often tempted to give in to temptation, it would be wise to write these words down and carry them with you at all times:

> Whenever you are tempted to get involved in a venture or a relationship that you think might be wrong, imagine that your involvement will be headlined in the next morning's *New York Times*. If that thought doesn't worry you, then go ahead with your plans. Otherwise, stop. Immediately.

# *When There Is No* Shalom Bayit *in Your* Bayit

Some years ago, when a Jewish friend of mine was getting divorced, the giving of the *get* (the Jewish divorce) was carried out under the auspices of an elderly European-born Orthodox rabbi. At one point he commented to my friend, "In America, too many people get divorced, in Europe too few did."

The rabbi's insight was profound. In the United States, there are divorces that appear to be avoidable, where compromise might have saved the marriage. But as the second half of the rabbi's comment indicates, this doesn't mean that *all* marriages should be saved.

Judaism regards marriage as sacred: *Kiddushin,* the Hebrew word for the wedding ceremony, derives from the Hebrew word for "holy" (*kadosh*). Nonetheless, there are times when the pain one suffers in a marriage outweighs all its benefits, and the marriage should be terminated.

*Shalom bayit,* a peaceful home, is valued highly in Judaism, and rabbis who counsel troubled couples frequently mention it (saying, for example, "I want you to go home and reestablish *shalom bayit*") in their efforts to motivate a couple to resolve their differences. But, ironically, the lack of *shalom bayit* is precisely the reason some couples *should* divorce. For if the goal of a marriage is to establish an island of peace in a difficult world, when a home is unpeaceful and likely to remain so, the marriage probably should end.

Obviously, although such a decision should not be reached lightly, neither should it be avoided at all costs. Certainly where abuse takes place, there should be a divorce, and quickly. As the Talmud puts it: "No one [woman or man] should be expected to dwell in the same den with a serpent" (*Yevamot* 112b). The Talmud also encourages a woman who is mistreated by her husband not to assume that this is her fate: "Woman was given unto life, and not unto suffering" (*Ketubot* 61a).

In addition to instances of abuse, if you truly have come to dislike or despise your spouse (or your spouse feels that way about you), and you find that you constantly seek opportunities to spend time away from him or her, then you should seriously consider divorce. An unhappily married man or woman need not assume that he or she has been sentenced to a life of quiet desperation. The Talmud tells us that Rabbi Yossi was married to a woman who would insult him in public, even in his students' presence. When a student urged him to divorce her, he indicated that he would like to, but lacked the funds to pay the divorce settlement. So the student raised the funds to enable him to buy his way out of a hellish situation (Palestinian Talmud, *Ketubot* 11:3; see Day 318).

Judaism views divorce as very sad. A poetic text declares, "If a man divorces his first wife, even the [Temple] altar sheds tears" (*Gittin* 90b). Yet, Judaism never concluded that divorce is always wrong. Why? First, when there is no reason to suffer, one shouldn't (particularly when there are no children, or the children are grown). Second, after a bad marriage, there is still the hope for a good one. As a friend of mine, a baseball fan who achieved a happiness in a second marriage that had eluded him in his first, told me: "Better to be one for two, than 0 for one."

DAY

284  WEDNESDAY

## *When Jewish Law Permits a Person to Be Publicly Shamed*

Judaism is unrelenting in its opposition to humiliating another person publicly: "Whoever shames his neighbor in public, it is as if he shed his blood" (Babylonian Talmud, *Bava Mezia* 58b). "One who humiliates another publicly, even though he has learned Torah and has performed good deeds, loses his share in the World-to-Come" (*Ethics of the Fathers* 3:11).

However, this seemingly definitive ruling has its exceptions:

> When a father who refused to support his children was brought before Rabbi Hisda, he would say, "Turn a mortar upside down in public, and have the delinquent father stand on it and declare: 'Even a raven cares for its young, but I do not care for my young.'"
>
> —Babylonian Talmud, *Ketubot* 49b

Why does Jewish ethics sanction public humiliation in this instance? Rabbi Hisda seemed to believe that a father who refuses to support children who depend on him forfeits his right to be treated as a normal human being; as the rabbi observes, the man's own behavior shows him to be morally inferior to an animal. Second, he apparently hoped that the very threat of such humiliation would stimulate the man to help his children, whose rights to eat, be clothed, and live in decent housing outweigh the negligent father's right not to be humiliated.

If you have brought children into the world, you are obligated to help support them. This seems so obvious, yet throughout the United States there are tens of thousands of men who shirk this most basic moral responsibility. My wife and I know a woman whose husband deserted her and fled the country. A well-to-do man, he has sent no money to her since he left, and made no effort to contact his sons. Yet the woman, who struggles under terrible financial burdens, periodically receives reports that he lives the life of a religiously observant Jew. If true, how absurd! After committing one of the few offenses for which Judaism permits a person to be publicly shamed, it would seem that he assumes he will buy off God's goodwill with some prayers and ritual observances.

A father's responsibilities to his young children are absolute (regarding older children who act immorally, see Day 311), and have nothing to do with whether he and the children's mother are still married.

T H U R S D A Y

# The Limits of God's Forgiveness

Is God all-powerful? Judaism says yes, He can do anything. For example, not only did God create the world, but He can even restore the dead to life (see II Kings 4:32–35). And yet there is a power that Judaism teaches that God doesn't, and refuses to, exercise. God won't forgive an injustice we have committed against another.

The belief that a piously observed Yom Kippur wins forgiveness for *all* one's sins is a myth. The Mishna teaches, "Yom Kippur atones for sins against God, not for those against man, unless the injured party has been appeased" (*Yoma* 8:9). In his "Laws of Repentance," Maimonides elaborates on this ruling:

> Repentance and Yom Kippur atone only for sins between man and God; for example, a person who ate forbidden food...and the like. However, sins between people, for example, someone who injures a colleague, curses a colleague, steals from him or the like will never be forgiven until he gives his colleague what he owes him and appeases him. It must be emphasized that even if a person restores the money that he owes the person he wronged, he must appease him and ask him to forgive him. Even if a person only upset a colleague by saying certain things, he must appease him and approach him repeatedly until he forgives him....
>
> —Maimonides, *Mishneh Torah*,
> "Laws of Repentance," 2:9*

In other words, if you have sinned against God, ask for forgiveness. If you have sinned against your child, correct the injustice and ask him

---

*I have largely followed the translation of Rabbi Eliyahu Touger, *Hilchot Teshuvah—The Laws of Repentance*, 42–44.

or her for forgiveness. If you have sinned against your spouse, resolve to change your behavior, and ask him or her for forgiveness. If you have sinned against someone in a business dealing, correct the injustice and ask that person for forgiveness.

Certainly, life would be easier if we only had to attend a synagogue service on Yom Kippur, reach deep within our souls, and ask God for forgiveness. But Yom Kippur's goal is not to make life easy; it is to transform our relationships with others and with God, to enable us to start afresh the only way one truly can, by erasing, to the extent possible, the wrong we have done.

DAY

## 286     FRIDAY

# It's Not Enough to Be Nice, Timing Also Matters

Good intentions are insufficient; one must also strive to ensure that one's good intentions bring about good results. That is why it is so important to weigh one's words *before* one speaks. Thus the second-century C.E. Rabbi Meir criticizes those whose words of consolation cause a mourner more pain than comfort:

> A person who meets a mourner after one year and consoles him, to what can he be compared? To a physician who meets a person whose leg had been broken and says to him, "Let me break your leg again, and reset it, to convince you that my treatment is good."
> —Babylonian Talmud, *Mo'ed Kattan* 21b

May you have a Shabbat Shalom!

SHABBAT

During the course of this Shabbat, try to review the material from the preceding six days, and use some of the texts studied as the basis for discussion during the Shabbat meals:

Day 281. How to Avoid Giving in to Temptation
Day 282. When You're Tempted to Do Something Wrong
Day 283. When There Is No *Shalom Bayit* in Your *Bayit*
Day 284. When Jewish Law Permits a Person to Be Publicly Shamed
Day 285. The Limits of God's Forgiveness
Day 286. It's Not Enough to Be Nice, Timing Also Matters

Shabbat Shalom!

# WEEK 42

DAY

288

SUNDAY

## *Help Non-Jews as Well as Jews*

In 1978, Rabbi Shlomo Carlebach gave a concert in Dubrovnik, Yugoslavia. When the concert was finished, Reb Shlomo took a walk and came across a young man sobbing. "Holy brother," he asked, "why are you crying your heart out like that?" The man, a non-Jew, told Reb Shlomo that he had just won a scholarship to a medical school in Paris, but didn't have the money for the plane ticket. Just that day, he had been totally unsuccessful in securing a loan.

"How much is the plane fare?" Reb Shlomo asked.

"A hundred and fifty dollars."

Reb Shlomo went through his pockets and pulled out all his cash. He counted out the money and handed it to the man, who was stunned. "You don't even know me. How do you know I'll ever pay you back?"

"It's not a loan," Reb Shlomo answered. "It's a gift."

The man was adamant that he didn't want charity, he wanted to pay the money back. Reb Shlomo wrote down his name and address, then added, "Repay me only when you truly can."

Ten years later an envelope postmarked Dubrovnik arrived at the Carlebach *shul* in Manhattan, along with a check for $150 and a note: "Because of your great kindness, I am today a successful physician in Dubrovnik, with a thriving practice. I owe everything to you and will never forget you for the rest of my life." *

Because all human beings, Jews and non-Jews alike, are created in God's image, it makes sense that Jewish law obliges Jews to dispense charity to non-Jews as well as Jews:

> We must provide help for the non-Jewish poor as well as for the Jewish poor; we must visit non-Jews when they are sick as well as our fellow Jews when they are sick; and we must attend to the burial of their dead as well as the burial of our own dead; for these are the ways of peace.
>
> —Babylonian Talmud, *Gittin* 61a

MONDAY

# The Final Words a Jew Should Speak

The ritual known as confession is so associated with Catholicism that many Jews are unaware that Judaism has a confessional

*Mandelbaum, *Holy Brother*, 75–76.

prayer, too. Unlike the Catholic confession, however, in which a person acknowledges his or her sins to a priest who has the power to grant absolution, Jewish law rules that one should recite the *vidui* (confession of sins) directly to God, and only when death is imminent. God willing, neither you nor anyone dear to you will need to recite the *vidui* in the near future. But simply being aware of this prayer's contents can influence the way you live the coming years of your life.

The *Shulchan Aruch,* the code of Jewish law, teaches:

> If one feels death approaching, he should recite the *vidui.* And he should be reassured by those around him: "Many have said the *vidui* and not died, and many have not said the *vidui* and have died." And if he is unable to recite it aloud, he should confess it in his heart. And if he is unable to recite it by himself, others may recite it with him or for him.
>
> —Yoreh Deah 338:I

What follows is the traditional text of the *vidui:*

> O my God, the God of my ancestors, accept my prayer and do not reject my supplication. Forgive me all the sins that I have committed in my lifetime. I am ashamed and abashed for all the wrong things that I have done. Please accept my pain and suffering as an atonement and forgive my sins, for against You alone have I sinned.
>
> May it be Your will, Adonai, my God and God of my ancestors, that I sin no more. With Your great mercy, cleanse me of my sins, but not through suffering and pain. Send a complete healing to me and to all those who are stricken.
>
> I acknowledge to You, Adonai, my God and the God of my ancestors, that my life is in Your hands. May it be Your will to heal me. But if You have decreed that I shall not recover from this illness, I accept the decree from Your hand. May my death atone completely for all the sins and all the transgressions that I have committed before You. Shelter me in the shadow of Your wings and grant me a portion in the World-to-Come.

Father of all orphans and guardian of widows, be with and protect my dear family, for my soul is bound up with theirs.

Into your hands do I commit my soul. You have redeemed me, Adonai, O God of truth.

*Sh'ma Yisra'el, Adonai Eloheinu, Adonai Echad* (Hear, O Israel, the Lord is our God, the Lord is One).

## TUESDAY

# *Should a Jew Donate His Organs?*

Jewish law maintains that a human body is sacred even after death; thus it generally opposes autopsies, out of the belief that cutting up a body and removing its organs constitutes *nivul hamet,* a disgrace to the dead.*

Because of Jewish law's well-known opposition to autopsies, many Jews assume that it opposes donating one's organs, since their extraction involves cutting up and somewhat mutilating the body.

For a long time I was—and still am—queasy at the thought of my body, or the body of someone I love, being cut up, and organs extracted, after death. But then I read a letter that transformed my view. It was written by a nurse in charge of transplants at a hospital to the family of a young man who had died from an injury, and whose family had donated his organs:

I would like to thank you again for your kindness and generosity in donating your son's organs to people in need of a transplant....The liver was transplanted into a twenty-seven-year-old Pittsburgh

---

* Autopsies *are* permitted in instances when death is suspicious and the police need the corpse examined so as to secure possible evidence; also in cases in which an autopsy can provide helpful knowledge for others suffering from the same illness as the deceased.

man.…He had been attending school, but the severity of his liver disease the past few months…had restricted him to staying at home. He is now doing very well. The kidney was transplanted into a twenty-six-year-old male who is married and has three small children. He is also doing very well. The heart was transplanted into a thirty-four-year-old male in Minnesota who is doing just fine.…Both corneas were transplanted. One went to an eighty-eight-year-old female and the other went to a seventy-nine-year-old female.

I know there is nothing I can say that will lessen the grief over your son's death. I hope you will find some comfort in knowing that because of your kindness and generosity, other people can have healthier and happier lives.*

After reading such a letter, can one really continue to dismiss organ transplants as a disgrace to the dead? Or are they, as educator Dr. Ron Wolfson has suggested, an act of *k'vod hamet,* an honor for the dead, since they bring healing to the living?

Wolfson goes on to ask, then answer, another question that disturbs many religious Jews: "What about the requirement [of Jewish law] that the entire body be buried? Ultimately, the transplanted tissues will receive burial when the beneficiary of the transplant dies."**

The reading from the Prophets for my bar mitzvah was II Kings, chapter 4, which tells how the prophet Elisha breathed air into the lungs of a dead boy and restored him to life. Rabbi Stanley Garfein notes that "We may not share Elisha's ability to perform miracles, but today [if we choose to donate our organs], we can share his capacity to restore and redeem life."

A famous talmudic passage teaches that "he who saves a single life, it is as if he saved an entire world" (Mishna, *Sanhedrin* 4:5). Donating your organs enables you to save "several worlds" even *after* you are dead.

Does that mean that I am no longer uneasy about donating my organs? No, I still am. The only difference is that now I know that my squeamishness is wrong.

---

*Cited in Rabbi Stanley Garfein's 1989 Yom Kippur sermon to his congregation, "Organic Immortality," printed in Riemer and Stampfer, eds., *So That Your Values Live On,* 197–202.
**Wolfson, *A Time to Mourn, a Time to Comfort,* 55.

An exercise: Check your driver's license. Do you want to sign the waiver to donate your organs?

# Listen ... Really Listen

As a young scholar, Martin Buber (1878–1965), author of *I and Thou,* the classic philosophic work on the importance of dialogue and communication, was hard at work editing a mystical text when his doorbell rang. An anxious and distraught young man asked if he could speak with Buber, who invited the man inside and answered the questions he asked. But, as he later confided, he was anxious to return to his work, and "I didn't try to answer the questions he didn't ask."

A short time later, Buber learned that the man had died, apparently a suicide. "Later...not long after, I learned from one of his friends that he had come to see me not casually, but borne by destiny, not for a chat but for a decision." The meeting's unhappy aftermath changed Buber forever. From then on, he concluded, encounters with people must take precedence over scholarship and mystical speculation.

Today, and throughout the week, when somebody seeks you out in person or over the telephone, listen. While he or she is speaking, stay focused; don't let your mind wander to other subjects, or to personal concerns.

Listen—*really* listen.

# How Not to Teach Torah

*One who is overly strict [alternatively, "an angry person"]
cannot teach.*

—Ethics of the Fathers 2:5

Why should a person's overstrictness or bad temper
disqualify him or her from educating others?

Often, students don't understand a concept the teacher has
explained. If he or she has a bad temper, students will be afraid to ask
for clarification; few people wish to be yelled at or mocked. But if the
teacher is pleasant, students feel comfortable asking questions and
seeking clarification; they will emerge from the classroom knowing the
subject matter and how to incorporate it into their lives.

An important talmudic passage underscores the harsh consequences of studying with an ill-tempered teacher: "If you find a student
who has difficulty with his studies, attribute it to his teacher's failure to
show a pleasing countenance" (*Ta'anit* 8a).

How damning a statement! A teacher whose unpleasant manner
causes a student to remain ignorant bears responsibility for the student's
ignorance.

This truth also holds for parenting. My wife has told me that I am
quite patient in explaining something for a first or second time. But by
the third time, if the person to whom I am speaking has not grasped
what I believe is quite obvious, I become impatient. That is what happened when I was teaching my six-year-old daughter, Naomi, how to
read. From time to time I would become impatient with her for not
understanding or remembering something we had reviewed several
times. After I became aware that I had done so, I said to Naomi, "Sometimes I get angry when we are studying together, and it's wrong of me
to do so. I apologize, and if I become impatient in the future, say to me,

WEEK 42

408

'Daddy, you're not supposed to get angry'" (see Day 339 for an example of how my unjustified loss of temper embarrassed me).

These words empowered Naomi (she no longer had to remain silent and passive when I showed impatience), and had an immediate and positive effect on our relationship. Letting your students or children know that you sometimes become unfairly angry, and should be reminded not to do so, shifts the responsibility for your impatience from them (that is, they are responsible for provoking you) to you. Even better is to train yourself to show impatience rarely. The Talmud holds out the great sage Hillel as a model of a teacher who never lost his temper, even when he was repeatedly asked foolish questions (Babylonian Talmud, *Shabbat* 30b–31a).

Finally, if you can't control your temper, seek professional help or try another career, one in which your temper cannot damage the egos and souls of the people with whom you work.

DAY

293

FRIDAY

## *Charity, Idolatry, and Deafness*

The Talmud is fierce in its denunciation of uncharitable people: "If a person closes his eyes to avoid giving [any] charity, it is as if he committed idolatry" (*Ketubot* 68a).

Loathsome as it is to be uncharitable, what is the logic behind comparing it to idolatry? Rabbi Adin Steinsaltz explains: "A person who knows that his money comes from God will give from his money to the poor. One who does not give to the poor, however, apparently believes that his own strength [and wisdom] are solely responsible for all he has. This is a form of idolatry insofar as he posits himself as the exclusive source of everything."

Normally, one would think that idolatry and uncharitableness are totally different, since refraining from giving charity alienates us from our fellow human beings while idolatry alienates us from God. Yet, as this aphorism indicates, withholding *tzedaka* alienates people from the Almighty as well. Rabbi Shlomo Carlebach was convinced that we put our souls at risk when we ignore the poor: "If your ears are not open to the crying of the poor, then your ears are dead, and you will not hear God calling you, either."

May you have a Shabbat Shalom!

DAY

## 294　SHABBAT

During the course of this Shabbat, try to review the material from the preceding six days, and use some of the texts studied as the basis for discussion during the Shabbat meals:

Day 288. Help Non-Jews as Well as Jews
Day 289. The Final Words a Jew Should Speak
Day 290. Should a Jew Donate His Organs?
Day 291. Listen...Really Listen
Day 292. How Not to Teach Torah
Day 293. Charity, Idolatry, and Deafness

Shabbat Shalom!

DAY

## 295     SUNDAY

# *Sanctifying the Secular*

As noted earlier (Day 144), the Torah legislates that a person putting up a new house must build a parapet on its roof. In the ancient Near East, houses were almost always flat-roofed, and people commonly walked and rested on their roofs. The Torah supplies the rationale for constructing this railing "so that you do not bring bloodguilt on your house if anyone should fall from it" (Deuteronomy 22:8).

More than a thousand years after this Torah ruling, the Talmud cited this biblical rationale to outlaw maintaining a vicious dog or a rickety ladder in one's home.

Some time ago, while studying this law with my congregation in Los Angeles, I asked members to think of contemporary activities that would either be mandated or prohibited by the biblical injunction. In the ensuing discussion, congregants came up with many suggestions:

♦ Don't keep a loaded gun in the house.
♦ Childproof your house; if you don't have small children, childproof your house before the visit of young children.
♦ Clear the walk in front of your house after a snowstorm.
♦ Install a smoke alarm system.
♦ Place guard rails on your upper-floor windows to prevent children from falling out.
♦ If your house has window bars or gratings to block thieves from entering, make sure occupants can open the rails from inside, so that a person can escape in case of emergency.

Of course, all these suggestions are nothing more than common sense. But when common sense is employed in fulfillment of a Torah law, one of the relatively few for which a rationale is given, the ensuing behavior becomes a religious activity as well. So, the next time you go down to clear your walk after a snowstorm, you can also feel that you are fulfilling a divine command. I don't know if that will make the work easier, but it should make it feel holy.

MONDAY

## Don't Be a Racist

How can a person believe that all human beings are created "in God's image," and simultaneously believe that some races are more "in God's image" than others?

Unfortunately, there are people who harbor such a belief. The history of racial hatred shows the participation of many religious people in such activities. For example, the Ku Klux Klan had churchgoing Christians among its members. And one finds Jews who seem to believe that Jews, by their very nature, have "higher souls" than non-Jews.

In truth, however, there is no room in Judaism for racism. For example, one of the important lessons the Talmud derives from Genesis's claim that God initially created the world with one person, Adam, was that this was "for the sake of peace among humankind, that one man should not say to his fellow, 'My father is greater than yours'" (Mishna, *Sanhedrin* 4:5; that is, since we all descend from the same person, no individual or race can claim to have a superior lineage).

In recent times there have been those who have argued that the biblical claim that the Jews are God's Chosen People is a form of racism. Shortly after the Nazis' rise to power, the gifted but sometimes antisemitic writer George Bernard Shaw said that the Nazis, with their doctrine of racial superiority, were merely imitating the Jewish doctrine of chosenness. Shaw's suggestion that Jewish chosenness was in some respects the basis for Nazi racism is a monstrous distortion. The doctrine of Aryan superiority was the Nazi justification for Germany exploiting other nations and murdering those they regarded as their inferiors. On the other hand, Jewish chosenness imposed on Jews special obligations. Furthermore, the fact that Judaism teaches that any person who accepts its tenets and practices—whether white, black, or yellow—becomes "chosen" proves that Judaism is not based on race. Indeed, Jewish tradition holds that the Messiah will descend from King David, who himself is a descendant of Ruth, a convert to Judaism (see Ruth 4:16–17).

One who believes in the biblical view of creation, that all people descend from Adam and Eve and are created "in God's image," cannot assume that one race is superior to another, and thus deserves privileges. The Bible teaches that all people stand equal before God: "Are you not as the children of Ethiopia to me, children of Israel?" asks the prophet Amos (9:7). "Religious racist" might not be an oxymoron, but from Judaism's perspective, it should be.

TUESDAY

# Never Practice Ingratitude

If ever there was a nation that ancient Israel was entitled to despise, it was Egypt. Over centuries, the Egyptian government and people had enslaved the Israelites, and during one brief period had attempted to murder all newborn male babies (Exodus 1:22).

Yet later, after the Egyptians had been punished with the Ten Plagues and the Israelite slaves had been freed, the Torah commanded: "You shall not abhor an Egyptian, for you were a stranger in their land" (Deuteronomy 23:8).

How can one explain this special biblical concern with not hating the Egyptians?

Rabbi Joseph Hertz, the late Chief Rabbi of the British Empire and a major twentieth-century Bible commentator, suggests that the Israelites were enjoined to remember that originally they were allowed to enter Egypt as guests during a period of severe famine in Canaan. Although the Egyptians later turned on them, this initial act of kindness should not be forgotten.*

This Torah law has ramifications in our daily lives. If you have in any way profited from another person with whom your relationship later soured, you must not allow yourself to forget the earlier good that he or she did for you. I know a woman who felt that her parents treated her coldly and favored her older sister; her general emotion toward them was fury—until she had her own child. Rising repeatedly during the night to attend to her child, she realized that her parents, too, had done many kindnesses for her.

The prohibition against ingratitude applies not just to personal kindnesses and favors, but also to intellectual influences. Thus, the Gaon of Vilna counsels, "If you find something worthwhile in a book written by another, don't ridicule parts of the book with which you disagree."

Another illustration: Let's say a person who is far removed from Judaism is influenced to become more involved by a Reform or Conservative rabbi, and subsequently becomes Orthodox. Even though this person might now disagree with Reform and Conservative Judaism and their approaches to Jewish teaching and observance, he also is morally obligated to remain grateful to those rabbis from whom he once learned. As the Talmud teaches, "Cast no mud into the well from which you have drunk" (*Bava Kamma* 92b).

DAY

298 WEDNESDAY

## *Raising Truthful Children*

*One should not promise a child something, and then not give it to him, because, as a result, the child will learn to lie.*
—Babylonian Talmud, *Sukkah* 46b

*Hertz, The Pentateuch and Haftorahs, 847.

If a parent promises a gift to a child and doesn't bring it, or agrees to take a child on a trip and then cancels, the child's initial response will be disappointment. As noted earlier, if such unfulfilled promises occur often enough, he or she will eventually conclude that that is how the real world works, that even when you assure someone you are going to do something for them, there is no need to follow through on your word.

Parents can deliver a hundred lectures to children on the evils of lying, but if their interactions with their children are often untruthful, the children will follow their parents' example instead of their words.

In one bitterly humorous talmudic anecdote, a rabbi teaches how important it is to encourage your children to be truthful:

> Rav was [constantly] tormented by his wife. If he asked her to cook lentils for him, she would cook peas. If he asked for peas, she would cook lentils.
>
> When his son Hiyya grew up, he gave her his father's messages, but reversed what his father had told him (if his father wanted lentils, he would say that he wanted peas).
>
> One day, Rav said to his son, "Your mother has improved."
>
> Said Hiyya, "[That is because] I reversed your messages."
>
> Said Rav, "That is what people say, 'Your own offspring teach you reason.' Nevertheless, do not do so anymore, for the Bible [is our highest authority, and it] says, 'They have taught their tongue to speak lies'" (Jeremiah 9:4).*

Hiyya's lies to his mother were of a harmless nature. Still, Rav was willing to forgo the convenience those lies brought him. He felt that it was more important to raise his son to be truthful, intuitively understanding that "people who tell too many white lies can become colorblind."

This quaint talmudic tale still has much to teach us, particularly that parents must not accustom children to tell lies, whether it be to

*Babylonian Talmud, *Yevamot* 63a

unwanted phone callers ("Tell them Daddy's not at home"), or to ticket sellers at movie theaters (asking a child to claim to be younger than he or she is, to take advantage of a cheaper ticket price).

If you promise your child something, carry out what you promised, for the sake of your relationship with your child, and for the sake of your child's soul.

## Empathy Is Not Natural

The Torah teaches that "man's heart is evil from its youth" (Genesis 8:21). This does not mean people are born evil; rather, human beings are born morally neutral with strong temptations toward evil. This state of affairs imposes upon parents the responsibility of raising their children to be good people, for clearly, as the Bible teaches, they can't rely on human nature to do the job. Thus, for example, parents must be vigilant in ensuring that their children don't tease other children (see Day 271). Unfortunately, children are often intolerant of those who are different, which is why parents must train their children not to mock retarded or fat children, or children who are unathletic, shy, or otherwise socially awkward.

One of the greatest cruelties occurs when children mock a peer because he or she comes from a poor family. I recently read a newspaper story about a thirteen-year-old girl named Wendy, who lived with her family in a trailer park, and attended a school largely made up of children from affluent homes. She was often subjected to a barrage of disparaging comments, ranging from the boy who insisted that she give him her bus seat ("Move it, trailer girl"), to the girl who responded to Wendy's question about where she had bought her beautiful new shirt, by laughing and saying, "Why would you want to know?" Wendy explained to the reporter that she knew that the shirt was out of her price range, but she just wanted to be part of the small talk.

On another occasion, a classmate teased Wendy about her mismatched clothes, and her humble home in the trailer park. He wouldn't stop, and finally, provoked, she kicked him in the shins. When he complained to the school authorities, they didn't punish him for his taunting words, but instead placed Wendy on suspension.*

Because the overwhelming majority of Americans claim to believe in God, the students who mocked Wendy also probably do. But what does that mean? Do they believe that God approves of what they are doing, or do they believe that God exists, but don't care what He wants?

If parents can't teach their children to empathize with another child's suffering, then all the other good things they do for them, such as sending them to academically intensive schools and spending "quality time" with them, is largely irrelevant. Furthermore, while the children depicted in this article had not learned empathy from their parents, what they had picked up (if not from their parents, then from others), was arrogance; they were certain that the poverty that had befallen this girl never would befall them. The Jewish view that parents should impart to children is very different and can help generate a sense of empathy:

> Rabbi Hiyya advised his wife, "When a poor man comes to the door, be quick to give him food so that the same may be done to your children." She exclaimed, "You are cursing our children [with the suggestion that they may become beggars]." But Rabbi Hiyya replied, "There is a wheel which revolves in this world."
> —Babylonian Talmud, *Shabbat* 151b

Children who from a young age are taught texts such as this will be far less likely to nickname a poor student "trailer girl," or to tease her about her mismatched clothing; indeed, they might well ask their parents if they could give the girl some nicer clothes.

But such texts *must* be taught, for empathy does not come naturally.

---

* *The New York Times*, 14 October 1998, 1.

## *Express Your Gratitude to the People Nearest to You . . . Now*

I know people who would never think of leaving a taxi or restaurant without thanking the driver or waitress, and leaving a generous tip. But they are sometimes far stingier with grateful words to those who do the most to enhance their lives, their spouses, family members, and friends. They suffer from what I call "emotional constipation," an inability to express love and gratitude, to thank those dear to them for specific favors and kindnesses.

The poem below was written by Rabbi Jack Riemer, who has powerfully captured the ability of kind words to heal the world, and whose words have often inspired me:

### THINGS YOU DIDN'T DO

Remember the day I borrowed your brand-new car and dented it?
I thought you'd kill me—but you didn't.

And remember the time I dragged you to the beach,
and you said it would rain, and it did?
I thought you would say, "I told you so"—but you didn't.

And remember the time I flirted with all the guys
to make you jealous—and you were?
I thought you'd leave—but you didn't.

And remember the time I spilled blueberry pie all over
your brand-new rug?
I thought you'd drop me for sure—but you didn't.

Yes, there are lots of things you didn't do,

But you put up with me, and you loved me, and you protected me;

And there were so many things I wanted to make up to you when
you returned from the war—
but you didn't.

An exercise: At some point today, think of something that someone—particularly a person with whom you're close—has done for you
and for which you haven't expressed gratitude. Commit yourself to
thanking them before or during this Shabbat.

May you have a Shabbat Shalom!

## SHABBAT

During the course of this Shabbat, try to review the
material from the preceding six days, and use some of the texts studied as
the basis for discussion during the Shabbat meals:

Day 295. Sanctifying the Secular
Day 296. Don't Be a Racist
Day 297. Never Practice Ingratitude
Day 298. Raising Truthful Children
Day 299. Empathy Is Not Natural
Day 300. Express Your Gratitude to the People Nearest to You…Now

Shabbat Shalom!

DAY

302        SUNDAY

# *Learning to Say "I Need"*

More than a century ago in Vilna, a wealthy man lost all his money. Ashamed of his poverty, he told no one of his changed circumstances, and eventually died of malnutrition.

The townspeople were horrified to learn that one of their neighbors had died, and that no one had helped. Rabbi Israel Salanter consoled the ashamed citizens: "That man did not die of starvation, but of excessive pride. Had he been willing to admit to his situation and ask others for help, he would not have died of hunger."

As Rabbi Salanter's statement makes clear, Jewish tradition obligates one who is needy to ask for assistance, just as it obligates those who have the means to provide it. The sixteenth-century code of Jewish law, the *Shulchan Aruch,* formalized this obligation to seek needed assistance in this way: "Whoever cannot survive without taking charity, such as an old, sick, or greatly suffering individual, but who stubbornly refuses to accept aid, is guilty of murdering himself...." *

The Rabbi Salanter story illustrates how excessive pride can deter people from seeking the help they need. And this applies not just to charity. I know of parents who had an adolescent son in need of psychiatric help. This occurred in the 1950s, when many people disdained such assistance. The family was too proud to acknowledge that a family member was "mentally disturbed." In addition, they feared that their neighbors might find out and think less of them. So no psychiatric help

---

*Rabbi Joseph Karo, *Shulchan Aruch, Yoreh Deah* 255:2; In a dialectical conclusion that typifies so much of Jewish legal discussion, the same passage continues: "Yet one who needs charity but postpones taking it and lives in deprivation so as to not trouble the community, shall live to provide for others." In other words, while it is commendable to suffer *some* deprivation rather than take charity, it is forbidden to endanger one's life just to avoid taking charity.

was given, and one day the young man committed suicide. Clearly, an important contributing factor to this suicide was family pride.

If you need help, particularly in a potentially life-threatening situation, seek it. It is not just your right but your obligation.

MONDAY

## *When Anonymous Giving Is Important, and When It Is Not*

When it comes to giving charity, the most important thing is not that your intentions be pure or that you give anonymously; what matters most is that the money you give does good. Thus, a true believer in the cause of the antebellum American South who anonymously endows a museum that extols the Confederacy's battle to retain slavery is doing a bad thing. In contrast, an egocentric whose gift to a cancer research center is made contingent on his name being prominently displayed in every room of the building is performing a good deed.

There are times when it's important *not* to make an anonymous gift; for example, if the announcement of your gift, particularly if it is a generous one, will prompt others to give more money than they would have otherwise.

When it comes, however, to donations made to an individual, private giving is almost always preferable; the poor person's dignity dictates that it is better that others not be aware of your gift. The Talmud teaches, "When Rabbi Yannai saw a man giving a coin to a poor man in front of everyone, he said to him, 'It would have been better for you not to have given it to him than to have given it and put him to shame'" (*Hagigah* 5a).*

---

*Obviously this reasoning would not apply in the case of one who begs in public, and who therefore is not shamed by being seen accepting charity.

If you know of someone who needs financial help, give it to him or her, but in private; tell no one else (unless it is important to tell those people who might also be inclined to offer assistance). True, the recipient will know your identity, but let that knowledge be restricted to him. You will know; he will know; God will know. Why does anyone else need to?

# When Silence Is Criminal

Under American law, you are required to testify in a court case only if you're subpoenaed. Under Jewish law, whether or not a court summons you, or even knows of your existence, you are obliged to come forward with relevant information (see Leviticus 5:1), particularly if it can help exonerate an innocent person.* "From where do we learn that if you are in a position to offer testimony on someone's behalf, you are not permitted to remain silent? From 'Do not stand by while your neighbor's blood is shed'" (*Sifra Leviticus* on Leviticus 19:16).

By implication, the same applies even in a noncourt case. For example, if someone in your community is the subject of a hurtful rumor that you know to be false, you are obliged to step forward and help clear the slandered person's name. A talmudic passage says that a person who has information that can help another but does not come forward is particularly despised by God (*Pesachim* 113b).

In short, if you have information that can save an innocent person from prison or conviction in court, or save a person's name from being ruined, you're obligated to come forward and reveal what you know. To remain silent is to "stand by while your neighbor's blood is shed."

*For an additional instance in which silence is criminal, see tomorrow's entry.*

---

*It is obviously important as well to testify to a criminal's guilt, both to support the victim (such as when a woman was raped, the defendant denies it, and your testimony can support her allegation), and to save other, future, victims of the criminal.

## *If You Learn That Someone Is Intending to Hurt Another*

Many years ago, my mother saw a young teenage boy walk into a house, and then overheard another boy nearby say to his companions, "When he comes out, we'll beat him up." A few moments later she walked over to the residence and, when the young man's mother came to the door, informed her of what she had heard. In so doing, my mother was acting in accordance with Jewish ethics, which teaches that when you learn that people are plotting to harm another, your moral, and *legal*, obligation is to inform the potential victim of the threat.

In a famous case in the late 1960s, a psychologist working at the University of California–Berkeley was treating a student, Prosenjit Poddar, who confided his intention to murder another student, Tatiana Tarasoff, for rebuffing his romantic advances. Taking the threat seriously, the psychologist informed the campus police, who in turn detained the young man for questioning, but released him when he appeared to be acting rationally. At this point the doctor's supervisor told him to say nothing further about the case to anyone; two months later, Poddar murdered Tarasoff.

From my understanding of Judaism, the doctor's obligation extended beyond informing the police; he also should have warned the intended victim. "Do not stand by while your neighbor's blood is shed" (Leviticus 19:16) means that you are forbidden to stand by when you possess information that could save another from harm; you must inform the person who is in danger. Based on this verse, too, Jewish law rules that if one is in a position to appease or deter the perpetrator, one must do so.

In the Tarasoff case, the girl's parents sued the university, the doctor, and his supervisor, and won a judgment against them. In the court's opinion, the doctor, because he was licensed by the state, had an obligation to inform the would-be victim of the threat against her life.

In most American states, however, such an obligation is not imposed upon an average individual who has learned of someone's plan to murder another. Thus, in a recent Nevada case (see Day 341), a nineteen-year-old man witnessed a close friend preparing to murder a seven-year-old girl. He walked out of the room and informed no one, including the police, of what he had seen. When the murderer was caught, and the behavior of the friend became public knowledge, the latter was not arrested, for he had violated no Nevada law. Indeed, the man was permitted to resume his college studies in California. Ironically, the school he attended was Berkeley, the very university where Tatiana Tarasoff was enrolled when she was murdered.

In the Book of Esther, the Bible tells how Mordechai overheard two men in King Ahasuerus's court plotting to assassinate him. Because he reported the conversation to his cousin Queen Esther, the king's life was saved (Esther 2:21–23). This biblical event served as an important precedent for the *Shulchan Aruch*, the authoritative code of Jewish law: "He [or she] who hears heathens or informers plotting to harm a person is obliged to inform the intended victim. If he is able to appease the perpetrator and deter him from the act, but does not do so, he has violated the law, 'Do not stand by while your neighbor's blood is shed'" (*Shulchan Aruch, Choshen Mishpat* 426:1).

DAY

306     THURSDAY

# "You Are Not as Good as You Think You Are, and the World Is Not as Bad as You Think It Is"

In Jewish tradition, there is no prophet more beloved than Elijah, who is universally known among Jews as *Eliyahu HaNavi*

(Elijah the Prophet). The preeminent hero of Jewish folklore, he is a guest at every Passover Seder, where a special cup of wine is prepared for him (as children, we all watched carefully during the time of his "visit" to try to spot any diminution in the cup's contents). And at every circumcision a chair is set aside for Elijah (*kisei shel Eliyahu*).

It therefore comes as a shock to most Jews to go back to the Bible, the original source about Elijah. Its Elijah bears no relationship to the kindly old man of Jewish folklore; he was the most confrontational of prophets. On one noteworthy occasion he led the people in killing 450 idolatrous priests of Ba'al who were trying to woo the Israelites away from monotheism. After this encounter, knowing that the idol-worshipping Queen Jezebel was planning to kill him (I Kings 19:2), Elijah fled into the desert, where he prayed to God to let him die. Convinced that he was the only committed God-worshipper left ("The Israelites have forsaken your covenant and...I alone am left"; I Kings 19:14), and that the Israelite people, as a religious entity, were coming to an end, Elijah had no desire to go on living.

God did not allow Elijah to wallow in self-pity and self-righteousness; He reminded him that there were at least seven thousand other monotheists, and He gave him new tasks and sent him on his way.

My father and teacher, Shlomo Telushkin, of blessed memory, who was by nature an optimist, explained that it was Elijah's exaggerated condemnation of all other Jews that was the kernel of the reason for his many reappearances in Jewish life. He who saw himself as the last Jew became fated to bear constant witness to the eternity of Israel, to be present when every Jewish male baby enters the covenant, and when every Jewish family celebrates the Seder (circumcision and the Seder remain the two most commonly observed Jewish rituals).

Elijah stands in a long line of despairing Jews who have erroneously prophesied the end of the Jewish people.

Likewise, whenever we are tempted to make dire assessments of the Jewish future, or dark predictions about our children's or our nation's future, we must also make sure to hold our pessimism in check. Many of us slander our times, as well as the people among whom we live. Moments of intense criticism can easily descend into moments of self-righteous and exaggerated criticism.

It is during such moments that we would be wise to guide ourselves by the words of the Chasidic rebbe Wolf of Strikov: "You are not as good as you think you are, and the world is not as bad as you think it is."

## When Pious Words Are Irreligious

A Chasidic rebbe known as the Leover instructed his followers, "If a person comes to you for assistance, and you tell him 'God will provide,' you are acting disloyally to God. For you should understand that God has sent you to aid the needy person, not to refer him back to the Almighty."

In another Chasidic story, a rebbe taught his disciples, "Everything that God has created in this world has a purpose." A follower raised his hand. "In that case, what is the purpose of *apikorsus* [heresy]?" "Heresy has a value," the rebbe answered. "When a poor person solicits your aid, imagine that there is no God to help this man, and that you alone can provide this person with assistance."

As both of these stories make clear, the irreligious response when someone solicits aid is to give or do nothing while mouthing pious words, such as "God will always help," or "Whatever God wants is for the best." As Rabbi Louis Jacobs has noted, "Pious resignation to the will of God is a virtue when practiced on one's own behalf. It ceases to be a virtue when practiced on behalf of others. There is nothing heroic in being stoical concerning the sufferings of others."

And as the second story reminds us, Jewish ethics even provides a way to be religious when you're feeling like a heretic.

May you have a Shabbat Shalom!

SHABBAT

During the course of this Shabbat, try to review the material from the preceding six days, and use some of the texts studied as the basis for discussion during the Shabbat meals:

Day 302. Learning to Say "I Need"
Day 303. When Anonymous Giving Is Important, and When It is Not
Day 304. When Silence Is Criminal
Day 305. If You Learn That Someone Is Intending to Hurt Another
Day 306. "You Are Not as Good as You Think You Are, and the World Is Not as Bad as You Think It Is"
Day 307. When Pious Words Are Irreligious

Shabbat Shalom!

# WEEK 45

DAY

309

SUNDAY

## When a Half-Truth Becomes a Whole Lie

According to Jewish ethics, it is wrong to praise what is good in the product you are selling while remaining silent about its defects. Just as you would feel cheated if someone deceived you in this manner, so you must not mislead another:

Most people are not outright thieves who simply take their neighbor's property....However, in their daily business dealings, most of
them have a taste of stealing, for example, when they permit themselves to make an unfair profit at the expense of another, claiming
that such profit has nothing to do with theft. It is both good and
honest to do everything possible to show the buyer the real value
and beauty of the article. However, for one to cover and hide a
defect is nothing less than deceit, and is forbidden.

—Moshe Chayyim Luzzatto (1707–1747), *Mesillat
Yesharim* (*The Path of the Just*), chapter 11

My mother was once called by a stockbroker whom she knew
slightly, and who urged her to buy shares in a certain company. He enu-
merated several reasons why he thought the company was poised to do
well. My mother bought the stock, which promptly fell and stayed
depressed for a long time. She later had reason to suspect that the firm
at which this broker worked had a large quantity of this stock to unload,
and instructed its brokers to encourage their clients to purchase it. Obviously the brokerage firm and this particular broker did not definitely
know the stock would fall. But had my mother been informed that they
were trying to dispose of a large quantity of stock, she would not have
purchased it. This was the "defect" and the relevant information that the
broker hid from her.

The Mishna outlaws another way in which buyers are misled:

A vendor may not combine different grades of produce in one bin
[in more familiar terms, one may not place the nicest, reddest
strawberries on top, if not all of them are of the same quality]....A
vendor whose wine has become diluted with water may not sell it
unless he makes full disclosure to the customer, and in any event
he may not sell it to another retailer, even if he makes disclosure,
for fear that the second retailer will deceive *his* customers.

—Mishna, *Bava Mezia* 4:11 (the example of the
strawberries is offered by Gordon Tucker in his
article "Jewish Business Ethics," 35)

Jewish tradition found a rationale for restraining unfair behavior in a
biblical verse, one that offers guidance for all of us in instances not cov-

ered by a specific law: "Her ways [the ways of Torah] are pleasant and all her paths peaceful" (Proverbs 3:17).

The capitalist credo "Let the buyer beware" is not Judaism's ideal. Rather, Jewish ethics would teach, "Let the seller beware."

MONDAY

# Is Your Blood Redder?

*A man came to [the fourth-century C.E. Rabbi] Rava and said to him: "The governor of my town has ordered me to kill someone and, if I refuse, he will have me killed. [What shall I do?]"*

*Rava said: "Be killed and do not kill; do you think that your blood is redder than his? Perhaps his blood is redder than yours."*

—Babylonian Talmud, *Pesachim* 25b

God willing, none of us will ever have to face so horrible a situation.* Still, the Talmud's insistence that other people's blood is as important as our own should affect our daily behavior, even in non-life threatening situations. For example, those who push ahead of others on lines are likewise guilty of thinking that their blood is redder than others and that they need not wait their turn. Therefore, before you push your own interests at the expense of others, and assert that your time is more valuable, ask yourself the question Rava posed to this man: "Do you think that your blood is redder than his?"

---

*In accordance with the talmudic teaching "If someone wishes to kill you, get up early and kill him first" (*Sanhedrin* 72a; see Day 222), Jewish law would rule that the man had the right to kill the governor since it was he, not the designated victim, who was endangering his life. However, killing the man the governor had designated would constitute murder.

TUESDAY

# Should There Be a Limit to Parental Love?

A famous story tells of a man who approached the Baal Shem Tov, the eighteenth-century founder of Chasidism, with a serious problem: "My son has drifted far away from Judaism. He leads an utterly dissolute life. What should I do?"

The sage's response was as simple as it was unexpected: "Love him more."

Such, of course, is one current of thinking regarding parent/child relations: Love for a child should be unconditional, and unrelated to his or her behavior. As the Baal Shem Tov seems to have believed, a strong dose of parental love might well motivate even an alienated and immoral child to lead a more Jewish and moral lifestyle.

In recent years, and in secular society, the alternative notion of "tough love" has gained currency. Proponents of this approach instruct parents to refrain from providing emotional and financial support to a child who is acting badly, specifically because they do love their child. For example, parents of a drug addict are told to keep the child out of their house if he indulges in this habit while living with them. Permitting such a child to remain at home, unless he is simultaneously involved in a program to break the addiction, discourages the child from improving, and might well lead to other children in the family becoming addicts.

This approach seems consistent with the advice proffered by Rabbi Judah the Chasid, author of the classic thirteenth-century text *Sefer Chasidim* (*Book of the Pious*). He writes of the need for parents to protect themselves and their other children from a child who has chosen an evil path:

> If a father has a son who is a glutton and a drunkard, he should not destroy his entire family and his other children for the benefit of

that one [by spending all his funds to indulge the addiction of the recalcitrant son]....Therefore, the father should act as if this son never existed and expel him from his house, rather than ruin himself and his family on account of one son.*

It is important to note both what Rabbi Judah the Chasid says, and what he doesn't. He does not advise cutting off all contact with a child because he violates Judaism's ritual laws (for example, there was a time when some Jewish parents observed the laws of mourning for a child who intermarried). Rather, what parents must do is avoid pouring an excess of emotion or money into one misbehaving or self-destructive child at the expense of their other children.

DAY

## 312     WEDNESDAY

# *Teach Your Child Survival Skills*

Perhaps the most surprising demand some talmudic rabbis require of a father is that he "must teach his child how to swim" (*Kiddushin* 30b). What is the connection between leading a moral, holy, and professionally accomplished life (all of which the Talmud obligates parents to help their children achieve; *Kiddushin* 29a; see Days 234 and 235), and learning how to swim?

The Talmud itself answers this question: "[Because] his life may depend on it."

At the time that the Talmud was composed, most travel over distances, and frequently even over short ones, required traversing bodies of water. Often the small boats that were used to make such trips would capsize; a person who couldn't swim would drown.

*Both the story of the Baal Shem Tov and the advice of Rabbi Judah the Chasid are cited in Isaacs, *The Jewish Book of Etiquette*, 139–40.

Thus, the obligation to teach swimming probably had nothing to do with imparting to one's children recreational skills (such as teaching a child to play basketball or golf), but rather with teaching them survival skills. In *How to Run a Traditional Jewish Household,* Blu Greenberg recalls an ugly incident in Riverdale, New York, in which several Jewish teenagers were beaten up by antisemites. The local rabbi's sensible suggestion, one entirely in keeping with this talmudic teaching, was, "The time has come to teach Jewish kids karate."

This eighteen-hundred-year-old injunction applies to activities the Rabbis could never have anticipated. Thus a parent who teaches his children the importance of obeying traffic signals and of driving carefully is not just engaging in commonsense parenting; he or she is also fulfilling an ancient Jewish law—teaching one's child how to survive in a world that can often be dangerous.

DAY

313    THURSDAY

# The Most Perfect Act of Kindness

Recently, the father of a school friend who was playing with one of my daughters was late in picking her up. Because I had an appointment scheduled, I was a bit upset with his tardiness, until he arrived and told me the reason for the delay: He had been spending the last few hours arranging the funeral of a woman who had died and who had no family. Jewish tradition regards this man's act as *chesed shel emet* (a true act of kindness). As Rashi, the eleventh-century Bible commentator, writes, "The kindness that is shown to the dead is a true kindness, for [in such a case] one does not expect to be repaid" (commentary on Genesis 47:29).

The words "for [in such a case] one does not expect to be repaid" convey that often when we do favors for others, part of us hopes that the recipient of our kindness will someday be in a position to help us.

But for obvious reasons, when we help the dead, our motives are untainted.

Jewish law has a particularly high regard for the mitzvah of helping to bury the dead. Thus, Torah law generally prohibits a priest (a *kohain*) from coming in contact with a corpse, and a high priest from ever doing so. Among observant Jews, a person who knows himself to be a *kohain* will not attend a funeral or burial except if the deceased is his wife, child, parent, or sibling. According to biblical law, a high priest is never permitted to have contact with a corpse, even for the closest of relatives (Leviticus 21:11). But reverence for the dead is so great that if a high priest, while traveling alone, comes across a dead body, he is personally responsible for taking care of its burial (Maimonides, *Mishneh Torah,* "Laws of Mourning," 3:8).

In addition to helping organize a funeral for one who has died, another way to practice *chesed shel emet* is to join a *chevra kadisha,* the Jewish organization that exists in almost all Jewish communities, which performs the rituals of purifying a dead body and preparing it for burial.*

The daily Jewish prayer book enumerates the mitzvah of caring for the dead as one of those for which one is rewarded in both this world and the next.

DAY

## 314     FRIDAY

# A Ritual Way to Make Each of Your Children Feel Special

Perhaps the best-known Shabbat ritual is the one ordaining that the holiday begin with the lighting of two candles, accompanied by a special Sabbath blessing. In many Jewish households, the

---

*The activities of a *chevra kadisha* are described in Lamm, *The Jewish Way in Death and Mourning,* see also Chipman, "Hevra Kadisha," in Strassfeld and Strassfeld, eds., *The Third Jewish Catalog,* 136–39.

custom is to light an additional candle for each child in the family. For example, every Friday evening my mother lit four candles, the two required by law, one for my sister, Shalva, and one for me. The message this extra candle sends to each child is a powerful one. As Rabbi Abraham Twerski, a psychiatrist, puts it, "How edifying it was for me to know that our home was brighter on Friday nights because I was in existence!" *

An exercise: Tonight, when you light the Shabbat candles, your children alongside you, make yourself aware of something they did in the past week that has brought light into your life. Then ask your children, your spouse, and yourself to think about something they or you did during the past seven days that brought light to the world.

May you have a Shabbat Shalom!

DAY

## 315    SHABBAT

During the course of this Shabbat, try to review the material from the preceding six days, and use some of the texts studied as the basis for discussion during the Shabbat meals:

Day 309. When a Half-Truth Becomes a Whole Lie
Day 310. Is Your Blood Redder?
Day 311. Should There Be a Limit to Parental Love?
Day 312. Teach Your Child Survival Skills
Day 313. The Most Perfect Act of Kindness
Day 314. A Ritual Way to Make Each of Your Children Feel Special

Shabbat Shalom!

---

*Twerski and Schwartz, *Positive Parenting*, 233.

SUNDAY

# A Time for Silence

Al Smith, the former governor of New York and 1928 Democratic presidential candidate, was a vigorous campaigner who was prepared for any and all insults. When a heckler called out to him, "Tell us all you know, Al, it won't take long," he responded, "I'll tell them all we both know, and it won't take any longer."

Smith's witty remark aside, the truth is that telling people all you know will, at best, turn you into a bore and, at worst, cause terrible suffering to others. Such at least was the belief of the third-century talmudic sage Rabbi Yochanan.

He based his view largely on his understanding of a law in the Torah that ordains that a child born of an adulterous or incestuous union is a *mamzer,* a bastard. Such a child is forbidden to marry all Jews except for other bastards (Deuteronomy 23:3).* Because of the law's horrific penalty, rabbis throughout the ages have exercised great ingenuity to avoid declaring a person a *mamzer.* But Rabbi Yochanan went further; he believed that Jewish law was willing to free people from the taint of bastardry—through silence. As he told his colleagues, "It is in my power [to reveal the families of impure birth in Jerusalem], but what shall I do, seeing that the greatest men of our time are mixed up therein" (Babylonian Talmud, *Kiddushin* 71a). Rabbi Yochanan apparently reasoned as follows: "Why should I announce the presence of bastards in a family, thereby destroying their marital prospects, and cause suffering to some very fine, innocent people?"

This teaching should serve as a stern reminder to those of us who

---

*The curse of *mamzerut* never ends; thus, if a Jew of normal status marries a *mamzer,* the children of their union, and their children's children, for all generations, are *mamzerim.*

casually transmit gossip and unflattering information about others, information that might lower the status of the person and/or family being discussed. Yet, either out of maliciousness or out of the desire to be perceived as knowledgeable, many people share truths that can cause great suffering to others, and damage their reputations.

Rabbi Yochanan's silence spared some righteous people shame and ostracism. He truly incorporated into his daily behavior the teaching of Ecclesiastes: "[There is] a time for silence and a time for speaking" (3:7).

MONDAY

# When Praising Someone Is the Wrong Thing to Do

*Whoever relates the virtues of his neighbor before the person's enemies, that constitutes the "dust of slander."*

—Moses Maimonides, *Mishneh Torah*, "Laws of Character Development," 7:4

If you are speaking to a group of people, among whom is one you know dislikes a certain person, don't start singing the disliked person's praises. Perhaps you believe that complimenting that person in front of his or her adversary is doing him or her a favor. The Jewish tradition does not agree.* True, it's possible that the adversary will listen in silence when your words are first uttered; his or her silence might even continue for as long as you are present. However, when you depart, the antagonist will likely start in with a litany of all that he or she dislikes about the other.

If you want to lessen a person's animosity for another, then speak

---

*If, however, the person's antagonist starts attacking him in front of a group, it is commendable for you to speak up on behalf of the person whose name is being besmirched.

one-on-one to the antagonist. But don't praise someone in a group containing the person's enemy. All you will guarantee is that the others in the group will eventually hear a delineation of all that the person's enemy dislikes about him.

## TUESDAY

# *You and Your Ex*

Asurprising talmudic tale teaches us that one of the people to whom one owes a special measure of kindness is one's ex-spouse.

Rabbi Yossi's wife used to subject him to much suffering and ridicule. Rabbi Elazar came and said, "Master, divorce her, she does not accord you the respect due you." Rabbi Yossi replied, "I cannot afford to pay her the money specified in the *ketuba*" (the marriage contract). Rabbi Elazar replied: "I will give you the money for the settlement, so divorce her." Rabbi Elazar gave him the money, and Rabbi Yossi divorced her.

She then went and married the town watchman. Some time later the watchman lost all his money and became blind, and his wife would lead him by the hand begging for charity. Once, she led him through the whole city, but no one gave them anything. He asked her, "Is there no other neighborhood in the city where we can go?"

She replied, "There is one other neighborhood, but my first husband lives there, and I am too embarrassed to go there." He beat her until she took him to Rabbi Yossi's neighborhood.

Just then, Rabbi Yossi passed by. He saw how the husband was abusing her, and he provided them with a house and food for the rest of their lives.*

*Palestinian Talmud, *Ketubot* 11:3.

Until recently, and certainly in the talmudic age, divorce was far rarer than in today's society. Thus, for the past two millennia, this story about Rabbi Yossi might well have struck most readers as more curious than meaningful or applicable. Today, however, with divorce commonplace, this story teaches us that it is usually wrong to end *all* positive feelings for a person who was once our flesh. As I once heard a divorced woman graciously say of her former husband, "Anyone whom I once loved a lot, I still love a little." True, married couples are not blood relatives, but the Torah instructs a person to regard his or her spouse as such. For example, the Bible's first words on marriage tell us, "Hence a man leaves his father and mother and cleaves to his wife, so that they become one flesh" (Genesis 2:24). Indeed, in the story cited above, the Talmud goes on to root Rabbi Yossi's kindness to his wife in another biblical verse, "and you shall not hide yourself from your own flesh" (Isaiah 58:7). A spouse might not be a blood relation, but we should look on him or her as such. Even divorce should not terminate *all* feelings for one's ex.

How sad, therefore, that divorced couples often demonize each other. While such an attitude is particularly unfortunate and irresponsible when the couple share children, this tale teaches us that it is sad even when the couple is childless. How much better to let go of the bitterness, particularly as time passes, and show a kind heart, as did Rabbi Yossi.

DAY

319

WEDNESDAY

## Solomon's Sword: How to Determine a Child's Best Interests

In Jewish tradition, King Solomon is regarded as the wisest king who ever lived. Solomon's reputation for genius came about early in his kingship, and was largely established through a case he was asked to judge. Two women had each given birth to a child. One night, while sleeping, one of the women accidentally smothered her child. She rose from her bed, and exchanged her dead child with the live child in the other woman's arms. The next day, both women appeared in front of Solomon, each claiming to be the mother of the living child.

When it became apparent that neither woman could prove the child to be hers, Solomon ordered that a sword be fetched, the child cut in two, and each woman given half. One of the women cried out in horror, "Please, my lord, give her the live child; only don't kill it." The second insisted, "It shall be neither yours nor mine, cut it in two." At this point, all became clear to Solomon. He turned to the second woman and instructed her, "Give the live child to her....She is its mother" (I Kings, 3:16–27).

I have heard and taught this story so often that I was convinced there was nothing new to be said about it, until I saw Rabbi Michael Gold's discussion of this tale. As Gold understands this ancient incident, it still has much to teach us: "The lesson of this story is that the child's self-interest [should] become the center of all decision-making."[*]

American courts have often returned or awarded children even to parents who previously abused them, and who therefore have more in common with the woman who said, "Cut it in two," than with the compassionate mother. Convinced that biological parenthood should trump all other considerations, courts have occasionally declared themselves under no obligation to take into account the child's needs.

This, however, is precisely what Solomon reminds us *must* be taken into account. It is the woman who wishes not to hurt the child to whom the child should be awarded. While the overwhelming majority of parents love their children and strive to do what is in their best interests, in those instances where they don't (such as parents who physically or emotionally abuse their children), God's desire, as personified in this story, is to do what is best for the child. Therefore, from Judaism's perspective, the person who shows that what matters most to him or her is the child's interest is the one to whom custody should be awarded.

---

[*] Gold, *God, Love, Sex and Family*, 212.

# The Special Obligation of Adoptive Parents

In a passage filled with psychological insight and acute moral sensitivity, Maimonides writes of the special obligation imposed on those who deal with widows and orphans:

> A person must be especially heedful of his behavior toward widows and orphans because their souls are deeply depressed and their spirits low. Even if they are wealthy, even if they are the widows and orphans of a king, we are warned concerning them, "You shall not ill-treat any widow or orphan."
>
> —*Mishneh Torah,* "Laws of Character Development," 6:10

As Maimonides makes clear, one must display extraordinary sensitivity when dealing with those who are most emotionally vulnerable. This applies as well in the case of parents who adopt children. All children need to know that they are special, but adopted children, who know that they were given up by their biological mothers and fathers at birth, have a special need to know how precious they are. Daniel Mosesman, who was himself adopted, writes, "I would like to say something to all adoptive parents. Please give your child all the love you can. Please hold them and hug them all the time. Please listen to them. Most of all, please let them know that their birth and their life has blessed your life." *

---

*This quote is taken from "Letter from an Adopted Child," in *Ultimate Issues:* A quarterly by Dennis Prager, 1993.

F R I D A Y

# *Don't Speak* Lashon Hara *About Yourself*

R abbi Israel Meir Kagan (1838–1933), known in the
Jewish world as the Chaffetz Chayyim, wrote several important books
on guarding one's tongue and not speaking *lashon hara,* unfairly of others (for a discussion of this topic, see Day 43). Frequently, he traveled to
Jewish communities throughout Eastern Europe to lecture on this and
other topics.

During one such trip, a man sat down opposite him on the train.
The two started to talk, and Rabbi Kagan asked the man where he was
heading. "I'm going into town to hear the Chaffetz Chayyim speak
tonight. After all, he's the greatest sage and saint in the Jewish world
today."

Embarrassed by the man's words, Rabbi Kagan demurred: "Sometimes people say such things, but it's not true. He's not such a great
sage, and he's certainly no saint."

The other man grew incensed. "How dare you disparage such a
great man!" he said, and slapped Rabbi Kagan in the face.

That evening the man attended the lecture, where he saw, to his
horror, that the man whom he had slapped was none other than the
Chaffetz Chayyim.

At the speech's conclusion, he rushed over to the rabbi. "Please,
please, forgive me. I had no idea it was you."

Rabbi Kagan smiled. "You have no reason to request forgiveness. It
was my honor you were defending. On the contrary, I learned from you
an important lesson. For decades, I've been teaching people not to
speak *lashon hara* about others. Now I've learned that it's also wrong to
speak *lashon hara* about oneself."

While it is good to be humble, the Chaffetz Chayyim's tale reminds
us that being modest does not mean denying one's virtues or disparag-

ing oneself. The Torah verse that explicitly commands us to "love your neighbor as yourself" (Leviticus 19:18), implicitly commands us to love ourselves. And just as you would not wish to hear others speaking ill of someone whom you love, so too should you not speak ill of someone you are supposed to love: yourself.

May you have a Shabbat Shalom!

D A Y

## 322     S H A B B A T

During the course of this Shabbat, try to review the material from the preceding six days, and use some of the texts studied as the basis for discussion during the Shabbat meals:

Day 316. A Time for Silence
Day 317. When Praising Someone Is the Wrong Thing to Do
Day 318. You and Your Ex
Day 319. Solomon's Sword: How to Determine a Child's Best Interests
Day 320. The Special Obligation of Adoptive Parents
Day 321. Don't Speak *Lashon Hara* About Yourself

Shabbat Shalom!

SUNDAY

# Learning to Keep Your Envy in Check

"Y ou shall not covet your neighbor's house; you shall not covet your neighbor's wife...or anything that is your neighbor's" (Exodus 20:14) is the Tenth Commandment.

At study sessions I have conducted on the Ten Commandments, people often express perplexity about this one: "What's so terrible about coveting? It's just an emotion, not a deed. Why does God forbid it?"

When it comes to ethics, people often assume that only right behavior matters. But the late Israeli Bible scholar Nechama Leibowitz noted that the Bible's concern goes far deeper than just affecting people's actions. The last six of the Ten Commandments concern relations between people. Commandments Five through Eight mandate ethical deeds (honoring one's parents and prohibiting murder, adultery, and stealing). The Ninth Commandment outlaws wrongful speech (in this case, perjury), while the Tenth, as noted, addresses and prohibits a wrongful emotion, coveting your neighbor's property or spouse. Although these commandments start by dealing with behavior, their progression makes it clear that the ultimate goal of transforming people's external behavior is to transform their inner selves.

Why? Most important, because how we feel and think will ultimately affect how we act. If you envy your neighbor's spouse or property, and don't restrain your desire, there's a good chance you will end up committing adultery, stealing, or worse. That is what happened to two of Israel's kings. David coveted Bathsheba, who was married to Uriah, an officer in his army. He slept with her and impregnated her, then, wishing to avoid a scandal, he arranged to have Uriah killed in battle (II Samuel 11). A century later, King Ahab coveted a vineyard adjoining his royal palace. When Navot, its owner, refused to sell him the land, Ahab's wife, Jezebel, hired two witnesses to testify that Navot had committed treason by cursing God and king, and had him executed. Since those convicted of treason had their estates confiscated by the king, Jezebel then presented Navot's vineyard to her husband. The prophet Elijah, who had learned of Jezebel's actions, confronted Ahab in the vineyard and shouted at him: "Have you murdered and also inherited?" (I Kings 21:19).

What had started in Ahab's case with a violation of the ban on coveting soon led to the violation of the Ninth Commandment, which forbids perjury; the Sixth, which forbids murder; and the Eighth, which forbids stealing.

The two men whom the Bible depicts as disobeying the prohibition against coveting were not poor (the kind of people whom one might expect would be most prone to coveting), but wealthy and powerful kings.

How can you safeguard yourself from a temptation that afflicts even kings? Regarding the coveting of your neighbor's possessions, it is not wrong to want more than what you have—but it is wrong to want it at your neighbor's expense. There's no evil in desiring a Jaguar, but only in wanting the one belonging to the person next door. Anyone who sincerely tries to practice the command to "love your neighbor as yourself" will feel uncomfortable coveting that which belongs to someone else.

Regarding the prohibition against coveting your neighbor's spouse, the thirteenth-century Bible commentator Abraham ibn Ezra, writing in the context of a feudal society, notes that a common man won't covet the queen; she is so far removed from him socially that it will never enter his head that he might win her away from the king. As ibn Ezra goes on to explain, God is telling us in this commandment that our neighbor's spouse is as forbidden to us as is the queen. And just as the common man will not spend hours fantasizing how he will win over the queen, so too must we not waste hours imagining how we will win over our neighbor's spouse. If we ignore this prohibition and permit ourselves to start thinking how we can seduce our neighbor's spouse, we will soon start plotting how to commit adultery. Better, rather, to internalize the Torah command: your neighbor's spouse is forbidden to you. End of issue.*

M O N D A Y

## *Don't Get Used to Other People's Suffering*

"As a very young rabbi," recalls Rabbi André Ungar, "I accompanied my senior colleague, Harold Reinhart, to a funeral...the very first I ever attended. It was a truly tragic affair, a young man killed in an accident, leaving wife, parents, and small children behind. I was overwhelmed by the family's grief, full of bewilderment, outrage, pity, the old theological questions. Driving home, Rabbi Reinhart and I sat silently in the car. After a while, I heard myself blurt out in embarrassment, 'I suppose after a time you get used to this sort of thing.' He looked over at me, frowned, and whispered, 'André, the day you get used to it, get the hell out of the rabbinate.'"**

Rabbi Stephen S. Wise was visiting China some years before the Second World War, at a time when the dominant means of transportation there was the rickshaw. The rickshaws were pulled by frail workers who coughed constantly as they dragged their burdens. During the first days of his trip, Rabbi Wise was horrified that his transportation came at the expense of such suffering. In his hotel room at night, he lay awake, listening to the penetrating, rasping coughs of the drivers outside. When he mentioned this to his hosts, they reassured him, "Don't worry. In two more weeks you will get used to it. In a month you won't even hear it."

"And so it was," Rabbi Wise recalled. Later he referred to the day he stopped hearing the coughing as the "most embarrassing day of my life." ***

*See my commentary on the Tenth Commandment in *Biblical Literacy*, 438–39.
**Blue and Magonet, *Kindred Spirits*, 46.
***Riemer, ed., *The World of the High Holy Days*, 132.

As you read the newspaper today, as you walk down the streets of your city, as you speak to friends who are having problems, remember this teaching:

Don't get used to other people's suffering.

Don't get used to other people's suffering.

Don't get used to other people's suffering.

DAY

## 325

T U E S D A Y

# *What's Wrong with Your Life? What's Right?*

Think for a minute of all the things that are troubling you: your health or that of someone you love; lack of money; insufficient professional success and recognition; problems in your marriage or with your children; a fight in which you're embroiled with a relative, friend, or colleague.

Now think of all the things that are right with your life: your love for your spouse, children, and friends; activities from which you derive pleasure; satisfactions at work; pride in your children; professional accomplishments; the good deeds you have done for others. Then consider all the good things that are right in your life that you probably rarely think about—for example, that you, and the people you love, can most likely walk, talk, hear, smell, and see.

Do the good things in your life outweigh the bad ones?* If they do, do you nonetheless find yourself focusing disproportionate attention on the problem areas, on the things that aren't working out?

Goethe tells the story of walking past a group of blind beggars in Rome, most of whom were receiving few, if any, contributions from the

---

*Judaism encourages one to focus on the good things in one's life by ordaining that a person recite a hundred blessings daily, including a blessing thanking God that one's organs are working properly (see Day 75), and thanking God for one's sight and one's clothing.

passersby. He noticed, however, one man whose plate was receiving a steady flow of donations. He stepped close to the man and saw the placard the beggar was holding: "It is springtime and I am blind." *

If it is springtime, summer, fall, or winter, and you can see, shouldn't you be grateful?

DAY

**326**

## WEDNESDAY

# Shiva, *the Final Act of Gratitude*

Some years ago I performed a funeral service for an elderly man. At one point, just before the service began, I asked his daughter where she would be observing *shiva* (the seven days of mourning) for her father. "Oh, I'm not doing anything like that," she answered. "Some friends will come over and visit tonight. But I don't believe in mourning. I believe in living life with zest." Seeing the discomfited look on my face, she added, "Besides, my father was a very positive, upbeat man. He never would have wanted me to go through an unpleasant mourning period."

Driving home, I wondered if this woman knew her father as well as she thought. Would he really have been pleased to learn that a day after his funeral, his daughter, son-in-law, and grandchildren were carrying on business as usual, working, relaxing at home, or attending a ball game or the theater? I wondered if this woman's refusal to mourn her father's death was reflective of a zestful love of life, or an unintentional expression of insufficient concern for the man who raised and supported her for so many years.

Over the years I have learned that many American Jews regard the observance of *shiva* as a burden. The thought of taking off from work and

---

* Sherwin and Cohen, *How to Be a Jew*, 16.

from one's other normal activities for seven days following the death of a parent or sibling strikes many people as excessive and unnecessary (Judaism also mandates such a period of mourning following the death of a spouse or child, but this does not seem to strike many people as excessive).

From Judaism's perspective, the refusal to mourn a parent's death for seven days is a gross form of disrespect. To carry on with one's life as if nothing significant has happened is essentially to declare the deceased's life and death to be insignificant. I suspect that few of us, including this woman's father, would want our children to regard our demise in this way.

The Torah tells us that we should treat our parents with honor and awe (see Exodus 20:12, Leviticus 19:3, and Day 127). Common sense tells us that we should also feel gratitude toward them for giving us life, for getting up in the middle of countless nights to feed and comfort us, for providing us with an education and with moral guidance. Jewish law demands, as the final act of gratitude, that we stop our lives for a week after our parents die, and do almost nothing but think about, talk about, and mourn them.

DAY

327  THURSDAY

## Repentance Is Good— Overrepentance Is Not

*Our Rabbis taught: As for the sins which one has confessed [privately to God] on one Yom Kippur, one should not confess them on another. If he repeated the offenses, then he should confess them on another Yom Kippur. But if he has not committed these sins again, yet confesses them again, then the Bible applies to him the verse, "As a dog returns to his vomit, so does a fool repeat his folly" (Proverbs 26:11).*
—Babylonian Talmud, *Yoma* 86b

The goal of repentance is to cleanse the soul; once this is achieved, one should not continue to focus on those acts that sullied it.

It seems that this teaching is directed toward helping people with obsessive personalities (the sort apt to be overwhelmed by feelings of guilt) to get on with their lives. My grandfather Rabbi Nissen Telushkin, of blessed memory, once explained the verse in Psalms, "Turn away from evil and do good" (Psalms 34:15), as meaning "Turn away from fixating on evil you may have done, and instead do good deeds." He elaborated with the following analogy: Suppose you are given a quantity of salt water that you are required to drink. What should you do? There are two possibilities. One is to remove all the salt. However, this is an arduous process; without special equipment, the average person can never remove the salt. Alternatively, one can pour so much fresh water into the salt water that eventually the salt becomes untastable.

There are certain types of sinners, my grandfather continued, who become so focused on the evil tendencies within themselves or on sins they have committed that they become depressed. However, instead of trying to root the evil out completely, something that is usually impossible to do, it is better to overwhelm the evil with the performance of much good. As Maimonides reminds us in his "Laws of Repentance" (3:1,2,5), God judges a person according to the majority of his or her actions.*

If you have sinned, do what you can to undo it, confess it, then move on with your life—and do good.

---

*"[Furthermore] this reckoning is not calculated only on the basis of the number of the merits and sins, but also takes into account their magnitude. There are some merits which outweigh many sins....In contrast, a sin may outweigh many merits. The weighing [of sins and merits] is carried out according to the wisdom of the Knowing God. He knows how to measure merits against sins" (*Mishneh Torah*, "Laws of Repentance," 1:2).

# Don't Stereotype Groups

One would think that Jewish tradition would regard *all* the words of the prophets as holy and instructive. But this is not always the case. Thus the Rabbis were highly displeased with Isaiah's statement "For I am a man of unclean lips, and I live among a people of unclean lips" (6:5). The Midrash imagines God saying to Isaiah, "Of your own self you may say, 'I am a man of unclean lips.' That I will abide. But how dare you say, 'I live among a people of unclean lips'?" (*Song of Songs Rabbah* 1:38). In a more radical passage, the Talmud speculates that Isaiah met a martyr's death at the hands of the evil King Menashe as punishment for calling the Israelites "a people of unclean lips" (*Yevamot* 49b).

Unfortunately, stereotypes, like rumors, tend to be negative (see Day 52). In condemning a whole people, Isaiah was simultaneously condemning many individuals who were innocent of the offense that had aroused his ire. Yet many of us, like Isaiah, routinely stereotype other groups. In the United States, people who hold different views on issues such as abortion, gun control, or the role of religion in public life often speak cruelly and unfairly of each other. Within the Jewish community, mean-spirited, often hateful stereotyping is done by Reform and Conservative Jews of Orthodox Jews, and by Orthodox Jews of their more theologically liberal brethren. Similar sorts of stereotyping goes on between Jews who are hawks and doves vis-à-vis Israel, and between Jews from different lands. Of course, it is equally wrong to depict non-Jewish groups and countries in stereotypical terms.

Particularly unfortunate is that such stereotyping is often done on Shabbat, as people gather together to share in relaxed and wide-ranging conversations over a Shabbat meal. How ironic that the Shabbat table, to which we invite angels (the *Shalom Aleichem* song is an invitation to angels to come join us) should be the place where some of God's creatures slander others. To us, this offense might seem minor. But to the Rabbis of the Talmud such negative stereotyping was worthy of the most serious punishment. Let's monitor ourselves this Shabbat, and try to ensure that we speak of other groups with the same delicacy and fairness we wish others to exercise when speaking of the group to which we belong.

May you have a Shabbat Shalom!

329    S H A B B A T
_____

During the course of this Shabbat, try to review the material from the preceding six days, and use some of the texts studied as the basis for discussion during the Shabbat meals:

Day 323. Learning to Keep Your Envy in Check
Day 324. Don't Get Used to Other People's Suffering
Day 325. What's Wrong with Your Life? What's Right?
Day 326. *Shiva*, the Final Act of Gratitude
Day 327. Repentance Is Good—Overrepentance Is Not
Day 328. Don't Stereotype Groups

Shabbat Shalom!

# WEEK 48

SUNDAY

## Raising Your Children to Love Both Themselves and Others

Many parents reserve their highest praise to their children for their intellectual and athletic accomplishments. Thus they compliment the child most effusively when he or she achieves intellectual distinction ("I'm particularly proud of how smart you are"), and when speaking to others, it is this aspect of their child that they praise ("Scott's so intelligent, it's just amazing").

What sort of self-image does a child develop who is not intellectually or athletically gifted, and whose parents cannot go around bragging about his or her achievements? Furthermore, is it healthy for children who are very smart or athletic to be raised to believed that these talents and abilities are truly what is most important about them?

Here is a simple suggestion, one that has the capacity to make both your children and the world happier and kinder: *Reserve your highest praise to your children for when they perform kind deeds.* That way they will learn to identify having a high self-image with being a good person. Children who grow up associating being praised and loved with the performance of ethical acts are apt to most like themselves when they are doing good. Think about that for a moment—a generation of people who most like themselves when they are doing good. What a world that would be!

*See Day 101 for a series of five questions all parents should ask themselves.*

MONDAY

# Watch Your . . . Compliments

Many Jews are aware that Judaism bans malicious gossip (see Days 43 and 44); however, far fewer know that Jewish tradition warns people to take care even when dispensing compliments. As the Talmud teaches, "A person should not [excessively] compliment another [who is not present], for though he will start by speaking positively, the conversation will soon turn to the person's negative traits" (*Bava Bathra* 164b).

What is the logic behind this? The realization that human nature generally finds more interesting what is *not* nice about a person than what *is*. Thus, even when a conversation about someone begins with compliments, and even when it is conducted by people who generally like the person being discussed, it is likely to veer off in an uncomplimentary direction. For example, if you and I are talking about someone we know in common, and I say, "I really love that guy, but there's one thing I can't stand about him," then what do you think we're most apt to spend the next ten minutes talking about? Similarly, if I ask you and a friend to talk for twenty minutes about someone you both know, it is unlikely that you will spend the whole twenty minutes saying, "Oh, you know that story which shows how nice she is? I know an even nicer story." In addition, Rabbi Saul Weiss points out that even when your intentions are pure, "pointing to a person's good actions or qualities [often directs] attention...to his bad actions and qualities."* Furthermore, compliments may evoke jealousy or envy.

Does the Jewish tradition never want us to praise another? No, it just wants to remind us how quickly discussions of another, even those that start off with compliments, can deteriorate into negative gossip. If we consciously maintain this awareness, we can guard against such a deterioration.

*Weiss, *Insights*, vol. 1, 39.

Even when you compliment someone, you still have to watch what you say.

TUESDAY

## When Legal Doesn't Equal Moral

The majority of Torah laws are very specific, whether they be injunctions to return a lost article to its owner (Deuteronomy 22:3), to circumcise a male infant on his eighth day of life (Genesis 17:12), or to prohibit perjury (Exodus 20:13).

However, sometimes a Torah law is phrased in a general manner. Such is the case with the verse "And you shall do what is right and good in the sight of the Lord" (Deuteronomy 6:18). Jewish tradition understands this as obliging one to act morally, particularly in an instance where acting strictly according to the law would lead to an injustice.

Writing in *Publishers Weekly*, the main trade journal of the book industry, Thomas McCormack notes many ways in which publishers, agents, and authors on occasion act legally but unethically. For example, authors generally receive a royalty of between 10 and 15 percent of their books' retail price. However, in many contracts, publishers insert a clause that if the book is sold to bookstores at a discount of 51 percent or higher, the author's royalty declines to 4.9 percent (10 percent of what the publisher receives). McCormack knows of instances in which publishers have offered the 51 percent discount on books that are selling well, just to decrease the author's royalty and thereby increase their own profits.

In another example, McCormack reports an instance in which an agent received a completed manuscript from an author. While the book's subject was very commercially appealing, the submitted manuscript was poorly written. The agent hired a good writer to write an excellent proposal for the book, secured a substantial advance from a publisher, and then delivered the original, poorly written manuscript.

In yet another instance, a publisher had a great idea for a book, and asked an agent to suggest one of his writers. When the agent did so, the writer produced a poor proposal and the publisher declined. Whereupon the agent announced that she felt free to sell the idea, with another writer, elsewhere.

How do people justify such behavior? According to McCormack, many people are quite ingenious at rationalizing whatever it is they want to do:

♦ "I'm just trying to keep my business alive so my employees' kids can eat."
♦ "My first responsibility is to my author, I'm only trying to do the best for him."
♦ "My agent told me it was all right."

As McCormack sadly observes: "Blessed are the amoral; everything they do is fair." *

Jewish law and common sense both recognize that the legal and the moral usually equate, but not always. The innovation of the Torah law "and you shall do what is right and good" is to remind us that in God's eyes, the immoral is *always* wrong.

DAY

333    W E D N E S D A Y

## *Using Your Evil Urge to Do Good*

*"And God saw everything that He had made, and found it very good" (Genesis 1:31). [Rabbi Nachman said in the name of Samuel: "The words 'very good'] refer to the* yetzer *hara, the evil inclination."*

* Publishers Weekly, 6 July 1998, 24.

*"But is the evil inclination a very good thing? [another rabbi challenged Rabbi Nachman]. What an astonishing thing to say!"*

*"Were it not for the evil inclination," he answered, "men would not build homes, take wives, have children, or engage in business."*

—*Genesis Rabbah 9:7*

The Bible has a decidedly sober view of human nature: "The tendency of man's heart is towards evil from his youth," is God's early assessment of human nature (Genesis 8:21). If this description strikes you as unfair, think about yourself: Are your thoughts always pure? For example, do your final thoughts before falling asleep concern what you can do the following day to relieve hunger and suffering in the world? Or are you like most people: When lying in bed and your mind is free to wander, do your thoughts often drift off in directions you wouldn't want others to know?

If so, you are in good company. Jewish tradition teaches that we all have evil inclinations; what distinguishes good people from bad is that good people resist theirs. When they can't resist these inclinations entirely, they try to channel them in good directions.

That some of one's inclinations are bad, or at least unholy, does not mean that the actions that flow from them need be bad as well. For example, a couple's main motive for mating might be lust, but that does not mean that they need be bad parents to the child that results from their act. Similarly, the fact that a medical researcher's motive for finding a cure to a disease might be to become wealthy does not make the researcher a bad person. For while the desire for wealth in and of itself is not a noble one, if one becomes wealthy by doing a great good, then one has harnessed one's evil inclination for the right purposes. If you want to be famous, try to become so for doing good. If you are wealthy, don't become famous by throwing lavish parties; rather, give lavishly so that a hospital building is built and named for you.

Almost all of us have desires for wealth and fame, and we all feel lust. If you have such ignoble impulses, don't be demoralized by them.

For Jewish ethics teaches that even when our motives are impure, the actions that result from those motives might be pure indeed.

THURSDAY

# Let Your Word, Not Your Oath, Be Your Bond

Traditional Jewish culture has long discouraged oath-taking. Oaths are generally administered in God's name, with one's hand on a Bible. Since associating God with a lie, even an unintentional one, is a particularly serious crime, many religious Jews refrain from all oaths, realizing that their testimony might contain an admixture of untruth. For example, if you are asked to summarize a conversation you had with another person, how confident are you that your recollection would be totally accurate, even if your intentions are honorable? That is why some religious Jews forgo legitimate claims if the only way to establish their case is by testifying under oath.

Because of Jewish tradition's desire to discourage oath-taking, it puts great emphasis on truth-telling, even when no oath is involved: "Rabbi Yossi ben Judah said: 'Let your "yes" be yes, let your "no" be no' (alternatively, 'Let your yes be honest, let your no be honest')" (Babylonian Talmud, *Bava Mezia* 49a).

Obeying this dictum can have clear ramifications in daily life. I know a woman whose first reaction upon being invited to an event is always to say yes. Later, when it becomes apparent that attending the affair will be inconvenient, she often begs off with a contrived excuse. This is precisely the sort of behavior that Jewish teaching criticizes as wrong. Don't rush to say yes, but once you do, you are morally obligated to follow through—even if it later becomes inconvenient to do so.

Similarly, if in a business negotiation you make a verbal commitment, abide by it, even if later on you are tempted to renege. The person to whom you said yes has the right to believe that your commitment is final (following this dictum might well incline you to be more cautious before saying yes).*

It is a sad sign for a society if people can be certain that another person's statement is truthful only when the person swears to it. A better standard would be the Talmud's: "Let your 'yes' be yes, let your 'no' be no."

DAY

335

FRIDAY

## Never Insult Another

The Talmud can sometimes be unsparing in describing the faults of its sages. Even so, few of its stories are as shocking as the one it tells of a certain Rabbi Elazar ben Shimon. One day, he was traveling on his donkey alongside a river. He was in a particularly good mood and, the Talmud adds, "feeling very proud of himself," for he had just succeeded in learning much Torah from his teacher.

Suddenly an exceedingly ugly man passed near him, and called out, "Good morning, Rabbi."

Rabbi Elazar did not return the man's greeting; instead he said to him, "Empty one, are all the people from your town as ugly as you?"

The man replied, "I don't know. But go and tell the craftsman who made me, 'How ugly is the vessel that you made.'"

The rabbi, immediately realizing that he had committed a grave sin, dismounted from his donkey. He bowed low to the ground, and said to the man, "I have spoken out of turn to you. Please forgive me."

The man responded, "I will not forgive you until you go to the

---

*According to Jewish law, one who reneges on a verbal commitment in a business deal may be formally censured by a court. The censure comes in the form of a curse: "He who exacted punishment from the generation of the Flood and from the generation of the Dispersion (see Genesis 11:1–9) will exact punishment from whoever does not abide by his word" (see Babylonian Talmud, *Bava Mezia* 49a).

craftsman who made me and tell him, 'How ugly is this vessel that you made.'"

Rabbi Elazar followed the man until the two of them reached a nearby city. When the man heard the people greet the rabbi in complimentary terms, he said, "If this person is a sage, may there not be many like him in Israel." He then explained to the crowd what Rabbi Elazar had done.

The people said to him, "Forgive him nevertheless, because he is a man of great Torah." He answered, "For your sake I forgive him, provided he does not make a habit of doing this."

I remember being shocked the first time I read this story, more than twenty-five years ago. I wondered, "How could anyone, let alone a rabbinic scholar, act so cruelly? This story must be a fiction the Rabbis made up to teach people how awful it is to make fun of another's appearance."

Now a confession, one I am embarrassed to make: Recently I was walking with two of my children, and at a red light, I saw a man standing opposite us. Although he was in no way misshapen, he was quite homely; I do remember that thought going through my head. A moment later the light changed to green, and we started to cross. As the man passed us, our eyes met, and he greeted me with a warm "Good afternoon."

I felt so ashamed and unworthy. Here was a human being standing opposite me; like me, created in God's image. And though I said nothing cruel to him, I had looked at him, and judged him wanting. How vile! To judge someone on the basis of a superficial impression, and on the basis of something over which a person has no control.

The Talmud concludes this tale by telling us the important lesson Rabbi Elazar learned from this incident: "A person should always be soft like a reed and not hard like a cedar" [as he had been to the unattractive man; Ta'anit 20a-b].

I would argue that this is a lesson we all need to learn, again and again. I have heard men say horrible things about unattractive women: "She's a dog." Or "Look in the dictionary under the word 'ugly' and you'll see her picture."

Children are particularly damaged by insults, and they are often hurt by the very people who most claim to love them: their parents. We have all heard of children told by a father or mother, "I wish you'd never been born," or "You're stupid. You're never going to amount to anything." Eleanor Roosevelt recalled how her mother would speak lovingly to her younger brothers, but as for her, "If a visitor was [at our house], she might turn and say, 'She is such a funny child, so old-fashioned, we always call her Granny.' I wanted to sink through the floor in shame."*

Judaism regards insulting or demeaning another person, particularly when done in the presence of others, as an almost unforgivable sin. Yet, when angry, many otherwise ethical people say extremely hurtful things.

So, when you are furious at another, or tempted to be witty at his or her expense (a feeling to which film, theater, and book critics often yield), remember the lesson Rabbi Elazar learned so painfully.

May you have a Shabbat Shalom!

DAY

## 336  SHABBAT

During the course of this Shabbat, try to review the material from the preceding six days, and use some of the texts studied as the basis for discussion during the Shabbat meals:

Day 330. Raising Your Children to Love Both Themselves and Others
Day 331. Watch Your…Compliments
Day 332. When Legal Doesn't Equal Moral
Day 333. Using Your Evil Urge to Do Good
Day 334. Let Your Word, Not Your Oath, Be Your Bond
Day 335. Never Insult Another

Shabbat Shalom!

* Goodwin, *No Ordinary Time,* 93.

# WEEK 49

SUNDAY

## *When Is It Permitted to Pass On Negative Information About Another?*

Lf you have an employee who performs his job inadequately, is it fair to complain to your friends and others about his faults? According to Jewish ethics, the answer is no. Those people to whom you are speaking have no need to know about your employee's deficiencies.

When, then, does Jewish law permit passing on negative information about another? When the person to whom you are speaking needs it.

For example, let's say that your incompetent employee seeks work elsewhere and you are asked by a prospective employer to assess her. In such a situation, even though your negative comments can do real damage to the person being discussed, Jewish ethics permits, and, according to some views, *obligates* you to speak truthfully, since the person to whom you are speaking has a need to know this information, and might well suffer damage if you don't transmit it. However, you are *not* permitted to pass on gossip that's irrelevant to the person's job performance (such as, "He has a poor relationship with his parents"), and you are also forbidden to make general defamatory statements ("He's just no good"). You must be specific in explaining what it was about the employee that was inadequate; traits that annoyed you might not annoy the person to whom you are speaking. For example, saying of an employee that "she rarely showed initiative" might not turn off an employer who wants a worker who follows directions precisely, and doesn't deviate.

Jewish ethics similarly permits transmitting relevant negative information to one who is planning to go into business with another. Thus, if you know for a fact that a person is inclined to show up for work at ten and leave at two, you should pass on such information, because it is relevant and useful.

*Relevant and useful.* Those are the criteria. If it is not relevant and useful, keep it to yourself. If it is, speak up.

*A third instance in which it is permitted to relate negative information is to one who is romantically involved with another person, and from whom important information is being withheld, a matter to which we will turn tomorrow.*

## Passing On Negative Information When a Couple Are Dating: The Four Guidelines of the Chaffetz Chayyim

Rabbi Israel Meir Ha-Cohen Kagan (1838–1933), known in Jewish life by the title of his most famous book, *Chaffetz Chayyim* ("one who desires life"), was the first sage to systematically gather and publish Judaism's teachings on guarding one's tongue. The large majority of his writings on this subject detail the type of information and comments about others that one is forbidden to spread. These prohibitions struck many as so extensive that a man once complained to the Chaffetz Chayyim that his writings made it almost impossible to speak at all. "On the contrary," the rabbi answered. "Just as the laws of *kashrut* don't make it impossible to eat, but instead make known that which you're permitted to eat, similarly, detailing those things you're forbidden to say enables one to speak without sinning."

In one passage, the Chaffetz Chayyim indicates the circumstances in which one is permitted to pass on negative information to a person who is romantically involved with another. Suppose, for example, that you know that one of the two parties involved in a serious relationship is withholding from the other information about a serious illness he or she has. Should you speak up?

According to the Chaffetz Chayyim, such information should be revealed, provided that four conditions are met:

1. The danger is serious and current. If the person has symptoms of a disease that won't manifest itself for *many* years, the Chaffetz Chayyim advises one to say nothing.
2. You must be very precise in the information you transmit, and avoid all exaggeration. Say only what you know, nothing more.
3. Your motives must be solely to help the person whom you are informing, and not to exact revenge against the person about whom you are speaking.
4. You should be quite certain that the information you are transmitting will affect the relationship. Thus, if you are reasonably sure that the couple are so in love that the person to whom you pass on the information will ignore it, it is better not to say anything at all.

For example, consider an instance in which you learn that a man is withholding such information. The most desirable thing to do is to approach the person and urge him, on his own, to inform the woman he is dating. Only if he refuses to do so should you speak up. The more troublesome consideration, and one I have found unanswered in Jewish sources, is determining the point in the relationship when one is required to make such information known. For example, let's say you have a friend with an illness and you go about informing every woman whom he dates of his illness. Your friend's social life, as well as your friendship, will be ruined. On the other hand, a woman who learns such information *after* she has gotten to know the more positive aspects of the man is in a far better position to judge the illness's significance for herself.

This ruling of the Chaffetz Chayyim applies to issues other than illness. A person involved romantically with another is entitled to information that might affect his or her desire to continue the relationship. I believe that a person dating someone with a violent temper, or one who has been unfaithful in an earlier marriage, has a right to know this before deciding whether or not to marry the person.

If the unhappy job of transmitting such information falls on your shoulders, remember the Chaffetz Chayyim's conditions: The information you are passing on must be significant and fairly current, you must not exaggerate, your motives must be purely to help the one to whom you transmit the information, and the information must have the capacity to affect the relationship.*

DAY

339     TUESDAY

## *Telling Your Children "I'm Sorry"*

In workshops I conduct on anger, I often ask audiences how many of them grew up in households where their parents never apologized to them, even when they did something wrong.

Thirty to forty percent of the adults routinely raise their hands. In the discussions that follow, it quickly becomes apparent that the pain of never having been apologized to is still fresh. The people describe the humiliation of being forced by their parents to say they were sorry when they had

---

*See the discussion of "Snitching and Telling Secrets," by Nachum Amsel in *The Jewish Encyclopedia of Moral and Ethical Issues*, 272–75. My understanding of this issue has been influenced by Rabbi Alfred Cohen, "Privacy: A Jewish Perspective," in *Halacha and Contemporary Society*, 213–18.

done something wrong, while knowing that no apology would ever be extended to them when they were the victims of their parents' unfair anger. What an awful message parents who never apologize send their children: "You don't have to seek forgiveness when you mistreat someone weaker than yourself." Or, "Because I raise and support you, I can treat you as I want. I don't have to say 'I'm sorry,' even when I'm wrong."

I once gave a lecture in Denver in which I asked the audience, "How many of you grew up in a household in which somebody's ill temper had a bad effect on the household?" Present in the audience that day were two of my daughters, then aged six and four. To my embarrassment and to the audience's immense amusement, my six-year-old raised her hand, and the four-year-old, seeing her sister's hand go up, did as well.

Later, when I spoke to my daughter, she explained that I often snapped at her when I was teaching her to read. I apologized for doing so ("It's wrong of me to do that. I'm really sorry. I'll try not to do that in the future, and I hope you can forgive me"). I then told her that in the future, if I became impatient, she should say to me, "Daddy, you're not supposed to get angry." Providing her with a statement to make in such a situation empowered her.

To do or say something unfair to your child is wrong, but invariably we all say unfair things to the people with whom we live. That is why learning how to apologize to your children is important. And please don't wait for Rosh Hashanah or Yom Kippur to seek forgiveness. Many people do so, and then collapse their apologies into one general statement: "I'm sorry for anything I did that hurt you." That's not good enough. You need to apologize as soon as you become aware of the hurt you have inflicted, and you need to make your apology specific ("I'm sorry that I screamed at you last night in front of your friends").

In the final analysis, the members of your household are the people who know best whether or not you are a mensch. And as my experience in these workshops has shown me, of one thing you can be sure: Thirty years from now, children who grew up in households in which their parents knew how to say "I'm sorry" will feel much better about themselves, and about you.

# Make Time for Your Children

Although devoted parents love their children more than their work, many parents find their work more interesting than their children, and so spend too much time on their work and too little with their offspring. Other parents, suffering from financial pressures, justify the small amount of time they spend with their children with the claim that they need to put in long hours just to support them. And there are parents who minimize the time spent with their children because they believe that spending time on their work is more important. For example, Rabbi Chayyim of Volozhin, the foremost disciple of Rabbi Elijah, the Gaon of Vilna, reports that the Gaon's devotion to Torah study was total: "His separation from all worldly matters was amazing to the extent that he never inquired about the welfare of his children. He never wrote letters of greeting to them and never read the letters he received from them." *

Golda Meir, the late Israeli prime minister, reflected on the children-versus-work dilemma in her autobiography, *My Life:* "Were they [my children] proud of me, then or later? I like to think so, of course, but I am not really sure that being proud of one's mother makes up for her frequent absences."

Do you spend enough time with your children? Do they feel that you spend enough time with them? If you can't be with your children as much as they would like, do they feel confident that you will make time for them when it really matters? In this instance, perception can be as important as reality. You may be sure that you will be there for them at the important moments, but ask *them* if they are confident that you

---

*This statement is found in Rabbi Chayyim's introduction to the Gaon's commentary to the *Sifra de-Tzeniuta,* 6b, and is cited in Jacobs, *Holy Living,* 51–52.

really will be. If they don't have that confidence, it is your responsibility to convince them that you will.

On this subject, I have found no words wiser than those of Rabbi Mendel Epstein: "If you are too busy to spend time with your children, then you are busier than God intended you to be."*

T H U R S D A Y

# "You Must Not Remain Indifferent"

A merican society is rights-oriented, while traditional Jewish society is obligation-oriented. Judaism insists on people actively doing good in contexts where American law would permit them to do nothing. For example, we discussed earlier (see Day 85) the law in Leviticus 19:16, "You shall not stand by while your neighbor's blood is shed." Whereas American courts have repeatedly affirmed a person's right to offer no assistance to one whose life is endangered (for instance, you have no obligation to save a toddler you see drowning in a shallow pool), the Torah obligates one to take action to save a person whose life is at risk.**

Judaism's insistence that we not stand by indifferent to others' needs applies to certain situations in which life isn't at stake. Thus, although American law would oblige one to return a lost object one has picked up (as long as it has a certain, somewhat significant value), Rabbi

---

*Cited in Brawarsky and Mark, eds., *Two Jews, Three Opinions,* 169.

**In the Nevada case mentioned in Day 305, a nineteen-year-old student from the University of California–Berkeley walked into a bathroom and witnessed his friend preparing to murder a seven-year-old girl. He did not try to stop his friend, but instead walked out and reported nothing to the police. His friend was subsequently caught and convicted of murder. But the nineteen-year-old wasn't charged by the police, since under Nevada law he had committed no crime. In addition, school officials at UC Berkeley refused demands of student groups to expel this man, also arguing that he had violated no law.

Nachum Amsel notes that the Torah is the only body of law with which he is familiar that "says that the individual *must* pick up the lost object to begin with." In the Torah's striking words, when you come across a lost item, "you must not remain indifferent" (see Deuteronomy 22:1–3).

The belief that "you must not remain indifferent" would seem to be part of the rationale behind the law that one must offer one's seat to an elderly person who is standing: "You shall rise before the aged and show deference to the old" (Leviticus 19:32). Yet how often one sees younger people on a bus or subway burying their noses in a newspaper so that they don't have to look into the face of an older person who would benefit greatly from a seat.

To cite another instance: If you have information that can help another in a court case, you are morally obligated to come forward even if you're not subpoenaed (see Leviticus 5:1 and Day 304).*

In short, if you want to be a good person, it is not enough to refrain from doing evil, you must also do good.

DAY

342     F R I D A Y

# *When You Learn Torah, Use It*

*When you rise from study, ponder carefully what you have learned; see what there is in that which you learned which you can put into practice.*

> —*Iggeret ha-Ramban* (*Letter of Nachmanides*)
> thirteenth century

Although Jewish tradition regards studying Jewish texts as a particularly valuable act, the goal of such learning is to shape behavior. Concerning one who studies but who has no intention of

---

* Amsel, *The Jewish Encyclopedia of Moral and Ethical Issues*, 238.

practicing what he learns, the Rabbis say it would be better if he didn't study at all.

Some Torah study lends itself easily to being put into practice. For example, the biblical law mandating erecting a parapet on your roof so that no one falls off suggests more than just the building of a safe structure. As Jewish law understood the Torah's admonition "so that you do not bring bloodguilt on your house if anyone should fall from it" (Deuteronomy 22:8), it obliges us to clear our house of any dangerous items. We should not keep a rickety ladder on which someone might slip, or own an aggressive dog that might bite someone (Babylonian Talmud, *Ketubot* 41b). One who studies this passage might learn, for example, to be especially careful to pick up children's toys that might cause another person to stumble (or train one's children to learn responsibility and pick up the toys themselves).

Torah portions that tell stories also often have practical implications, even if they are not accompanied by specific laws. For example, Genesis, chapters 42–45, tells the story of how Joseph forgave his brothers after they had committed an awful offense against him. Twenty-two years earlier, Joseph's brothers, who despised him for being a braggart and being their father's favorite, had sold him into Egyptian slavery. With the passage of time, and through the intervention of God, Joseph had become the highest official in the land of Egypt, second only to Pharaoh. A famine occurred in Canaan, and Joseph's brothers came to Egypt to buy food. Joseph recognized them, but they didn't recognize him. At the time of the sale he had been a smooth-faced teenager; now he was thirty-nine, dressed in clothing appropriate to his high position, and he spoke to them in Egyptian. But Joseph did not immediately divulge who he was. Rather, he put his brothers through a series of tests, designed to reveal whether their characters had grown over the preceding two decades. When he learned that they had, that they were truly contrite for what they did to him, and, most important, that they would never betray a brother again (a detail that comes out when Judah, the brother who first proposed selling Joseph into slavery, announces his willingness to become a slave in lieu of his younger brother Benjamin), Joseph revealed himself to his brothers, and told them that he forgave them for what they had done to him.

This is a worthwhile lesson for everyone to learn, particularly those (and it is not a small number) who have relatives with whom they are not speaking because of some fight that occurred years earlier. Of one thing I am certain: the slight inflicted upon them by their relative, and which they refuse to forgive, was a lot less serious than the cruelty Joseph's brothers inflicted on him.

As Nachmanides reminds us in the statement quoted at the beginning of this entry, when we study Torah, Talmud, or Jewish law we should constantly be on the alert for how we can incorporate what we have learned into our lives. The Rabbis promise an unusual reward for one who does so: "Rabbi Aha said: 'He who learns with the intention of practicing will be privileged to receive the Holy Spirit'" (*Leviticus Rabbah* 35:7).

An exercise: If you engage in some Jewish study on a daily or weekly basis, make sure you extract something from your next study session that has an impact on your daily behavior.

May you have a Shabbat Shalom!

DAY

343    SHABBAT

During the course of this Shabbat, try to review the material from the preceding six days, and use some of the texts studied as the basis for discussion during the Shabbat meals:

Day 337. When Is It Permitted to Pass On Negative Information
About Another?
Day 338. Passing On Negative Information When a Couple Are
Dating: The Four Guidelines of the Chaffetz Chayyim
Day 339. Telling Your Children "I'm Sorry"
Day 340. Make Time for Your Children
Day 341. "You Must Not Remain Indifferent"
Day 342. When You Learn Torah, Use It

Shabbat Shalom!

SUNDAY

# *One Who Calls Another Person by a Cruel Nickname*

An old Jewish proverb declares, "Everything depends on luck; even a Torah scroll in the ark." Most synagogue arks contain several Torah scrolls. The "lucky" ones are read from each week; the "unlucky" ones can go for years without being opened.

In similar fashion, some talmudic admonitions have become widely known and observed. Others are frequently ignored, which is why many Jews are shocked to learn that the Talmud regards calling another by an unkind nickname as a particularly serious offense: "All who descend to *Gehenna* [hell] will come up except three who descend and will not come up: One who sleeps with a married woman, one who shames his friend in public, and one who calls his friend by a cruel nickname" (Babylonian Talmud, *Bava Mezia* 58b).

Although the strict enforcement of this talmudic observation would lead to hell being overpopulated, the statement does underscore how seriously the Rabbis regarded calling someone by a cruel nickname. Yet those who routinely call others by hurtful nicknames frequently choose to remain oblivious to their victim's suffering. Recently a national magazine chronicled the case of an overweight teenage girl who committed suicide in response to taunting nicknames imposed on her by her peers. Two weeks later the magazine printed a letter by another victim:

As a teenager, I too was tortured by my fellow students. I was an overweight teen and was abused constantly. I could not escape it. Teachers witnessed this over and over again and did nothing. The principal told me her hands were tied. I thought of suicide but luckily I never did it....I wish all teenagers who tease others could have it happen to them so they could feel the pain and humiliation they inflict. I am signing this letter with the name they chose to torture me with for six years. How would you like to be known by an entire school as:

Big Bertha, Portland, Oregon*

At speeches I have often asked audiences, "How many of you ever endured being called by a nickname you disliked?" Invariably, one-fifth or more of the people raise their hands (others, I am sure, keep their hands down out of fear that they will be asked what the nickname was). For most of these people, the suffering was inflicted most intensely during their childhood, and by other children. That is why parents must be vigilant in stopping their children from calling other children by hostile nicknames.

Few things matter to people as much as their names. To call someone by a name that causes the person hurt is a seldom acknowledged, but very real, form of abuse.

DAY

345    MONDAY

# *When Anonymous Giving Is Not Good*

*If one gives a gift to a friend, he must inform him [and not give the gift anonymously].*
—Babylonian Talmud, *Shabbat* 10b

---

*People, 10 November 1997, 6. Another letter in the same issue reflects the anguish of a woman who had mercilessly teased another and recognized her guilt too late: "I read the story of Kelly Yeomans [the girl who had committed suicide] with tears streaming down my face, since I remember, when I was young, making fun of a girl who was bigger than me and my friends. To this day I feel horrible and realize the effect this humiliation has. That little girl will always be in my prayers...."

Judaism is commonly viewed as a legalistic religion, one that puts emphasis on deeds far more than on emotions. How moving and somewhat unusual, then, to find the Talmud expressing this emotional concern: don't give your friend an anonymous gift; rather, let the person know that you love him or her. As the Rabbis understood it, what generally matters more to the recipient than the gift is the caring behind it. That is why most people read the card accompanying a gift before opening it.

According to *Ethics of the Fathers*, God was the first one to bestow a gift, and He made sure that mankind knew that He was the giver: "Rabbi Akiva used to say: 'Beloved is man for he was created in God's image; but it is by a special love that humankind were informed that they were created in God's image; as it is written: For in the image of God did He make man'" (Genesis 1:27; *Ethics of the Fathers* 3:18).

Of course, God gave the gift of life to animals, fish, birds, flowers, and trees, as well as to people. But two things distinguish the additional gift that God gave humankind: He created them in His image, and made sure that they were aware of this. Because of this gift, each person can take pride in the fact that he or she has an aspect of divinity.

However, what would Jewish ethics dictate in an instance where the gift you are giving your friend is charity? In such a case, would it not be less humiliating to the friend if the gift were anonymous?

Many people believe so, and certainly if you have reason to assume that giving the gift anonymously will be better for your friend's emotional well-being, you should do so. But in trying to decide whether or not to reveal your identity, consider: If you had suffered a reversal of fortune and received a monetary gift, it might actually be more embarrassing not to know from whom it came. For then you would look upon everyone you knew as the possible donor, and feel ashamed at the thought that so many people knew of your plight. By making it known to your friend that you are the one helping him, he is less likely to worry that so many people know about, and are possibly talking about, his poverty.*

---

*My friend David Szonyi has doubts about my reasoning: "The poor person may well worry less that others know about his poverty than that he is emotionally 'beholden' to someone, which

In addition, being able to associate a gift with a specific individual will make the recipient feel the love the donor feels for him. The recipient also will know whom to approach if his situation becomes desperate again.

But such cases of charitable giving are the exception. Most gifts we bestow are made with the intention of bringing joy, not life's necessities, into our friends' lives. That joy is increased when we make it known to friends who it is that loves them enough to have spent the money and the time to get them a gift.

DAY

## 346

TUESDAY

# *Do You Owe Your Children an Inheritance?*

A friend once told me that he had no expectations that his affluent parents would bequeath him or his siblings an estate of more than nominal value: "What's more, it doesn't bother me. I just want my parents to spend whatever they have on themselves. I don't think parents have any moral responsibility to leave money to their adult children."

While part of me suspects that my friend's generous view of his parents' needs versus his own is related to the fact that he and his siblings have done well financially, another friend confided to me a very different reaction. When her father died, she learned that during the last years of his life, the ostentatious lifestyle he had led had greatly diminished the size of his once-large estate. The woman, who had every reason to expect that she would receive a large bequest, was upset at how little was left her and her brother.

In Judaism's view, are parents expected to leave an estate for their children?

---

is especially awkward with a friend. That's why anonymous giving of charity is preferable." Szonyi's reasoning underscores why such instances must be decided on a case-by-case basis.

Although it is difficult to isolate a definitive Jewish viewpoint on this subject, a wonderful story suggests at least one prominent scholar's view: "One day [Rabbi Choni] was walking down the road and saw an old man planting a carob tree. He asked him, 'How long will it take this tree to bear fruit?' The man answered, 'Seventy years.' He asked, 'Are you quite sure you will live another seventy years to eat its fruit?' The man answered, 'I myself found fully grown carob trees in the world; as my ancestors planted for me, so am I planting for my children'" (Babylonian Talmud, *Ta'anit* 23a).

If anything, the significance of parental bequests to children has become more pronounced during recent years. During the first few generations of Jewish life in the United States, it was taken for granted that each generation would do better financially than the preceding one; thus, the amount of money parents could leave their children generally was not significant. However, that is no longer the case. We are now living through the first generation of children who are likely in many instances to lead less affluent lives than their parents. At the same time, as many people's incomes are growing very slowly, the cost of living a committed Jewish life has grown dramatically (for middle-income parents with three children, the cost of a Jewish day school can easily consume fifteen to twenty-five percent of their earnings).

This situation has caused some committed Jewish parents to come up with more creative bequests than in the past. I know a man whose grandfather left a substantial fund with the proviso that the interest and dividends be utilized to pay the Jewish day school tuition of his grandchildren and their descendants (parents who send their children to non-Jewish schools do not receive a stipend) and the university tuition of *all* his descendants. This man's priorities were clear and, in my view, commendable: he wanted to enable his descendants to get the Jewish learning necessary to be morally educated and committed Jews, and the secular education necessary to acquire professional skills.

Clearly, two thousand years after Rabbi Choni came across the old man working in the field, planting carob trees for one's descendants remains as important as ever.

# "One Who Is Bashful Will Never Learn" *

The Jewish tradition generally regards bashfulness and a nonaggressive demeanor as good traits ** —but not when it comes to Torah study (or learning in general). As *Ethics of the Fathers* teaches, a bashful student, one too timid to ask questions, will always remain ignorant.

For a student to learn, she must be willing to ask questions and challenge her teacher. Jewish law dictates that you should do so respectfully, but that doesn't mean you shouldn't be aggressive. The Talmud tells us that Rabbi Yochanan's favorite student, and later learning partner, was Rabbi Shimon ben Lakish, known as Resh Lakish. When he died and Rabbi Yochanan fell into a depression, the other rabbis arranged for Elazar ben Pedat to study with him. Each time Rabbi Yochanan would voice his opinion, Rabbi Elazar would add, "I know another source which supports what you are saying."

One day, Rabbi Yochanan turned on him: "Do you suppose you are like Resh Lakish? Whenever I stated an opinion, Resh Lakish would raise twenty-four objections to what I said....He forced me to justify every ruling I gave, so that in the end, the subject was fully clarified. But all you do is tell me that you know another source which supports what I am saying. Don't I know myself that what I have said is right?" (Babylonian Talmud, *Bava Mezia* 84a). From Rabbi Yochanan's perspective, a student who's always agreeing, and who's too respectful to challenge and question his teacher, causes his teacher to stop growing.

More important, it is only the assertive, questioning student who can grow. The Talmud tells us that Resh Lakish grew up among gladia-

---

*Ethics of the Fathers* 2:5.
**For example, the Talmud teaches, "This people (Israel) is distinguished by three characteristics: They are merciful, bashful, and perform acts of kindness" (*Yevamot* 79a).

tors and bandits and, as a young man, was a Jewish ignoramus. But after a few years studying with, questioning, and challenging Rabbi Yochanan, he grew into one of the greatest sages of his age.

Sometimes a student remains silent out of fear that a question might offend the teacher by sounding antagonistic or heretical. If a teacher treats the inquiry in this way, then the student is probably studying with the wrong teacher.

On other occasions, shy or timid people say nothing because they are afraid to expose their ignorance in front of the other students. But if you attend a class and don't clarify a confusing matter, either you will leave perplexed and have wasted your time, or you will form an erroneous impression, and possibly pass on your ignorance or incorrect views to others. The *Shulchan Aruch* addresses this dilemma:

A student should not be embarrassed if a fellow student has understood something after the first or second time and he has not grasped it even after several attempts. If he is embarrassed because of this, it will turn out that he will come and go from the house of study without learning anything at all.
—*Shulchan Aruch, Yoreh Deah* 246:11

If your natural tendency is to hold back, you must find a way to overcome it—at least in the classroom. When you have a question, ask it. As an old Jewish proverb teaches, "Nobody ever died from a question."

# Study Judaism Fifteen Minutes a Day... Starting Now

*A foolish student will say, "Who can possibly learn the whole Torah...?" A wise student will say, "I will learn two laws today, and two tomorrow, until I have mastered the whole Torah."*

—*Song of Songs Rabbah* 5:11

If you are waiting for a convenient time to start studying Jewish texts, a time when your workload is light and your children and spouse undemanding, you are never going to learn even the basics of Judaism. In all likelihood, you are busy now, and are likely to remain so for the next several decades. That is why Rabbi Hillel cautions, "Don't say, 'when I have leisure, I will study,' lest you never have leisure" (*Ethics of the Fathers* 2:4).

A man once approached Rabbi Israel Salanter, told him that he had only fifteen minutes available a day for study, and asked: "Should I use it to study a text such as *The Path of the Upright* (an eighteenth-century book of moral exhortation), or works such as the Torah and Talmud?"

"Study the moral text," Rabbi Salanter answered.

"Why?"

"Because it will make you realize that there is something wrong with your life if you only have fifteen minutes a day to devote to study and spiritual growth."

A piercing answer. Yet, even if you can currently set aside only fifteen minutes a day for study, it is important that you start now.

My father was an accountant. When he grew very busy with his practice, my grandfather, who was fearful that my father would stop learning, suggested to him that every morning, when he finished praying, he study two laws from the Mishna (an activity that, he knew, would occupy my father for about ten to fifteen minutes). By doing so for the last thirty-five years or so of his life, my father succeeded in going through the six volumes of the Mishna several times. A friend of mine has for several months been reading two chapters a day from the prophetic books of the Bible, and has already read through most of them.

Fifteen minutes a day, whether devoted to Torah (either starting with Genesis, or following the Torah portion of the week) or later books of the Bible, studying laws from the Mishna, a small section of the Talmud, or a Jewish moral text, will yield great Jewish growth—and quickly. And Rabbi Salanter might well be right—you might soon start reordering your life in ways that will yield far more than fifteen minutes a day for study.

DAY

**349**

F R I D A Y

## *Random Acts of Kindness* *

Rabbi Israel Baal Shem Tov, the eighteenth-century founder of Chasidism, was once sitting in a large room with his followers when a poor man entered. Although there was nothing that seemed impressive about the man, the Baal Shem invited him to sit alongside him at the head of the table. Later, after the man had left, the astonished Chasidim asked the Baal Shem why he had so honored the man. Was he perhaps a hidden saint? The Baal Shem answered, "Someday, when I want a seat of honor in the World-to-Come, and they ask me what I did to deserve it, what will I answer? I will tell them that once I, too, gave a poor, perhaps undeserving, man a seat of honor."

If you examine another carefully and critically enough, as did the

---

* *Random Acts of Kindness* is the title of a book by Daphne Rose Kingma.

Baal Shem Tov's followers, you can usually find some reason why the person is undeserving. That is why Rabbi Shmelke of Nikolsberg (d. 1778) cautioned, "When a poor man asks you for aid, do not use his faults as an excuse for not helping him. For then God will look for your offenses, and He is sure to find many."

So, during the next few days, don't examine others too carefully before you decide whether or not they are worthy of help or an act of kindness. The world is filled with random acts of violence; fill it with random acts of kindness.

May you have a Shabbat Shalom!

DAY

## 350 SHABBAT

During the course of this Shabbat, try to review the material from the preceding six days, and use some of the texts studied as the basis for discussion during the Shabbat meals:

Day 344. One Who Calls Another Person by a Cruel Nickname

Day 345. When Anonymous Giving Is Not Good

Day 346. Do You Owe Your Children an Inheritance?

Day 347. "One Who Is Bashful Will Never Learn"

Day 348. Study Judaism Fifteen Minutes a Day…Starting Now

Day 349. Random Acts of Kindness

Shabbat Shalom!

**351**    S U N D A Y

# A Particularly Evil Form of Stealing

*It is worse to steal from the many than to steal from an individual, for one who steals from an individual can appease him by returning the theft; one who steals from the many, however, cannot.*

—Tosefta, *Bava Kamma* 10:14

One who defrauds another, and subsequently regrets the act, can seek out the victim, and restore to him or her that which was stolen. But one who steals from the many (for example, one who uses dishonest weights in his stores, or engages in a stock-market fraud) does not even know the identity of all his or her victims; thus, defrauding the public becomes, like murder and slander, an irrevocable wrong.

But what if such a person *does* wish to repent, is there anything he can do to mitigate his offense?

Jewish law instructs those who have cheated the many to "pay back those whom they know they have defrauded, and devote the balance to public needs" (Tosefta, *Bava Mezia* 8:26). In ancient times, helping the public might involve paying the costs of digging a well; today, such an individual might help build a park, construct a library, or otherwise benefit the community from which he stole.*

---

*This does not justify those who make themselves rich through dishonest means, and then salve their conscience with large donations to good causes.

# A Husband's Obligations to His Wife

The *ketuba*, a two-thousand-year-old document, is a wedding contract that grooms present to their brides at Jewish weddings. A legal document, it details a husband's obligations to his wife, as well as his financial responsibilities to her in case of death or divorce.

In accordance with Exodus 21:10, the groom promises the bride that "I will give you your food, clothing, and necessities, and live with you as husband and wife according to the universal custom." Thus, at the time of marriage, the man undertakes to provide his wife with such basic economic necessities as food and clothing. The last clause, "and live with you as husband and wife according to universal custom," obliges him to engage in regular sexual relations with her.

Jewish law felt the need to codify this obligation because of its belief that most woman were sexually more shy than men, and thus would be embarrassed to initiate sex. Without such a clause, the Rabbis feared, a woman married to a sexually indifferent husband could endure weeks and months of sexual neglect.

The groom also promises that "I will cherish, honor, support, and maintain you in accordance with the custom of Jewish husbands who cherish, honor, support, and maintain their wives faithfully." Therefore, a man who mocks or humiliates his wife (particularly in the presence of others), or otherwise treats her with a lack of appreciation and respect, is not only acting cruelly, but is also violating a contractual obligation he assumed at the time of marriage. Similarly, the words "and maintain you in accordance with the custom of Jewish husbands" suggest that it is a husband's legal obligation to make every effort to support his wife and family beyond the basic necessities. If he doesn't make every feasible effort to provide this support, he is violating a legal obligation he undertook.

Providing for a wife's needs and cherishing and honoring her are what a Jewish husband undertakes to do on his wedding day. To do less is, in Jewish terms, to define oneself as less than a man.

# Don't Insult Your Spouse

I know a woman whose first marriage was beset by numerous problems. She and her husband consulted a therapist, whom she told, in her husband's presence, "I'm willing to put up with our other difficulties: I only request that when he is angry at me, he not call me 'retarded.' If he just agrees to that, I'll stay married to him."

The man agreed, but didn't abide by the agreement. Whether he could not restrain his tongue, did not want to, or just did not try hard enough, when they fought, he continued to call his wife "retarded." Not surprisingly, they divorced.

The Talmud teaches that a man has to be particularly careful not to hurt his wife's feelings, "for a woman's tears are brought on more easily [than a man's]" (*Bava Mezia* 59a). As was noted earlier, perhaps men are becoming more sensitive, for I know men who are deeply wounded and sometimes reduced to tears by their wife's cruel words.

While on a lecture tour, the nineteenth-century Rabbi Israel Salanter accepted a man's invitation for Shabbat dinner. As he and his host were preparing to sit down for the meal, the man threw an angry fit at his wife for forgetting to cover the *challot*.* Wounded by her husband's words and ashamed in the presence of their distinguished guest, the woman ran off to the kitchen and remained there. Rabbi Salanter, shocked by the man's behavior, leaned over and said to him, "Excuse me, but I'm getting older and my memory is weakening. Could you

---

* Plural of *challah*; the Jewish custom is to place a cover over the *challot* until after the blessing over the wine is recited.

remind me of the reason we cover the *challot* until after we recite the *kiddush* [over the wine]?"

The man, proud to be of assistance to so prominent a sage, explained the symbolism behind the custom; the *challot* are covered so that they be spared the "embarrassment" of being exposed while all the ritual attention is being focused on the wine (normally, bread is the first item on the table to be blessed). After he finished, Rabbi Salanter rose and rebuked him: "You are so meticulous about a mere custom of not 'embarrassing' a loaf of bread. And yet you are so quick and ready to dishonor your wife and hurt her feelings. I cannot eat with you." Only when the man hurried into the kitchen and pleaded with his wife to forgive him did Rabbi Salanter consent to remain.*

People are often far crueler to their spouses than to strangers. Yet while the Torah obliges us to "love your neighbor as yourself," concerning one's wife, the Talmud teaches, "and honor her more than yourself" (*Yevamot* 62b).**

DAY

354    WEDNESDAY

## *Jews Shouldn't Be Cheap; Jewish Funerals Should Be*

Many people equate the spending of exorbitant sums of money with showing respect. That is one reason it is common for mourners to spend many thousands of dollars on ornate caskets. But logic dictates that such expenditures are irrational; corpses are buried in the ground, they don't live there. Judaism teaches that the soul survives the body; the body simply decomposes.

---

*The story about Rabbi Salanter is told by Rabbi Shlomo Carlebach and cited in Winkler and Elior, *The Place Where You Are Standing Is Holy*, 135.

**At a time when women had fewer rights both in Jewish and secular society, it is significant that rabbinic Judaism placed such emphasis on honoring one's wife. Today, in our more egalitarian age, the dictum should work equally in both directions ("and honor him more than yourself").

In ancient Israel, dead bodies were buried directly in the ground, yet people still found ways to overspend on funerals. Large amounts of money were spent on costly garments to inter the dead. Then, after the funeral, people sometimes brought food to mourners' houses in gold baskets. The Talmud tells us that the expense of funerals and mourning exerted so terrible a financial pressure on survivors that the Rabbis decided to ameliorate the situation:

> Formerly, they used to bring food to the house of mourning, rich people in baskets of silver and gold, poor people in baskets of peeled willow twigs; and the poor felt ashamed. Therefore a law was passed that everybody should bring food in baskets of willow twigs, in deference to the poor....Formerly, they used to serve drinks in a house of mourning, the rich serving in white glasses and the poor in colored glasses [which were less expensive]; and the poor felt ashamed. Therefore a law was passed that everyone should serve drinks in colored glasses, in deference to the poor....
>
> Formerly, they used to bring out the deceased for burial, the rich on a tall bed ornamented with rich covers, the poor on a plain bier; and the poor felt ashamed. Therefore a law was passed that all should be brought out on a plain bier, in deference to the poor....
>
> —Babylonian Talmud, *Mo'ed Kattan* 27a–b

> Formerly, the expense of burying the dead was harder for a family to bear than the death itself; sometimes family members left the body and fled to escape the expense. This was so until Rabban Gamliel [the leader of his generation and a wealthy man] came and adopted a simple style; [when he died] they carried him in a simple linen garment, and then all the people followed his example and carried out the dead in simple linen garments. Said Rabbi Papa: "And now it is the general practice to carry out the dead even in rough cloth worth only a *zuz*" [a small silver coin].
>
> —Babylonian Talmud, *Ketubot* 8b

Unfortunately, despite Jewish tradition's clear preference for simple, inexpensive funerals, some funeral directors try to exploit people's guilt (and what son or daughter, husband or wife, does not feel some guilt toward a parent or spouse who has just died?) to influence them to purchase an expensive casket. When Ed Koch, New York's feisty former mayor, lost his mother to cancer, he and his father told the funeral director that they were looking for a plain casket in the Orthodox tradition. Instead, the man ushered them into a room with a fancy casket: "He knew that we were looking for something simple, but he figured he'd work his hard sell on us just the same. He took us into several rooms, and in each room the caskets cost less. He didn't skip a room."

As Koch quickly realized, the funeral director was trying to shame them into buying an expensive casket. The man finally took them down to the basement, where he showed Koch and his father two simple pine boxes. But even here, one was more expensive than the other. "We were so humiliated by the ordeal that we said yes to [the more expensive one]. We could resist no further. I've never forgotten that. That man made us feel cheap, and we succumbed." *

When a beloved family member dies, one should mourn his or her loss. But that is all one should mourn. One should not mourn the cost of the funeral.

DAY

355    THURSDAY

## A Law That Needs to Be Changed

The twelfth-century Moses Maimonides is the codifier of Jewish law par excellence. He was regarded as so preeminent a rabbinical scholar and philosopher that, after his death, his fellow Egyptian Jews inscribed on his tombstone, "From Moses to Moses, there was none like Moses." In the almost eight hundred years since his death, Maimonides has continued to be regarded with awe, and with good reason; in addition to his philosophic classic, *The Guide to the Perplexed*, his legal

* Koch, *Citizen Koch*, 60–61.

writings, codified in his fourteen-volume *Mishneh Torah,* have been a major influence on all subsequent Jewish legal codes.

Thus it is very disturbing to find a teaching in Maimonides, albeit one based on a talmudic text, that can be used to cause and justify cruelty, and even death. In his "Laws of Murder and Protection of Life," Maimonides discusses the status of an unintentional killer, one who brings about the death of another through negligence. The Torah rules that in such a case the killer must flee to a specially designated "city of refuge" and remain there until the death of the high priest. If he leaves the city earlier, the immediate relatives of the victim are permitted to kill him (Numbers 35:22–28). At the time Maimonides wrote his code, the cities of refuge had not existed for two thousand years, but since he regarded the *Mishneh Torah* as the basic legislation for a future Jewish state, he codified within it the laws concerning such cities. Thus, in chapter five, paragraph five, discussing which people had to flee there and which ones did not, he writes:

> When a father unintentionally kills his son, he should be exiled (to a "city of refuge"). When does the above apply? When [the father] kills the son while not in the midst of study....If, however, he imposes punishment on his son while teaching him Torah, [secular] knowledge or a profession, and the son dies, the father is not liable [for exile or, apparently, any punishment at all].

Thus, according to Maimonides, killing a child while disciplining him should be regarded as an accident. But of course no child dies from a minor physical punishment. For physical punishment to result in death, it must be very brutal. Furthermore, in the very next paragraph, Maimonides similarly exonerates from punishment a teacher who kills a child while punishing him. Maimonides explains that parents and teachers are not punished in such an instance, "for they unintentionally killed while performing a mitzvah (commandment)."

Maimonides' writings in this regard have been among the influential sources cited to justify parents and teachers hitting children. One can only wonder how many young people who suffered in the past from learning disabilities were cruelly hit, or otherwise endured physical abuse. I think it is fair to say that teachers who hit students in the past bear considerable responsibility for the mass defection from Jewish observance a century ago.*

The great Hebrew poet Hayyim Nachman Bialik recalled bitterly how it felt to study in a Jewish school in which students were hit:

> [The teachers] knew only to hurt, each in his own way. The rebbe used to hit with a whip, with his fist, with his elbow, with his wife's rolling pin, or with anything else that would cause pain. But his assistant, whenever my answer to his questions was wrong, would advance toward me, with the fingers of his palm extended, and bend before my face and seize me by my throat. He would look to me then like a leopard or a tiger or some other such wild beast and I would be in mortal dread. I was afraid he would gouge out my eyes with his dirty fingernails and the fear would paralyze my mind so that I forgot everything I had learned the previous day.**

Such are the cruelties that can result when a great and influential scholar writes with equanimity of parents and teachers who kill a child "while performing a mitzvah." ***

---

*Many of these teachers, in turn, were also in some ways victims. Usually severely underpaid, they were expected to be able to teach, discipline, and inspire, without having had any form of teacher training.

**Cited in M. Z. Frank, "Hayyim Nachman Bialik," in Noveck, ed., *Great Jewish Personalities in Modern Times*, 175–76.

***A friend expressed great discomfort with this entry, arguing that it is unfair to blame Maimonides, who was, after all, citing rulings that are written in the Talmud. Nonetheless, I have focused my critique on Maimonides, since he chose to cite this talmudic ruling when he could also have chosen to counterbalance it by citing the Talmud's advice: "If you must strike a child, hit him only with a shoelace" (*Bava Bathra* 21a; see Day 135). Since no child ever died from being hit with a shoelace, I suspect that the rabbinic author of this maxim did not regard with equanimity fathers and teachers who killed children while disciplining them. Indeed, in his "Laws of Teaching Torah" (2:2), Maimonides does say that teachers should beat students, but not cruelly, and should use a small strap instead of a stick. My friend further argued that it is unfair to expect Maimonides to be so far ahead of his time, since he lived in an age in which brutal discipline was imposed on children and students; indeed, such brutality persisted into the twentieth century. My friend might be right; perhaps my expectations of Maimonides are unfair. I only wish to note that the lives of many individuals might have been spared physical pain and humiliation if this twelfth-century sage had chosen to cite a different, sweeter, talmudic source.

# The Holiness of Laughter

Some years ago I wrote a book, *Jewish Humor*, which attempted to explain Jewish life and the Jewish psyche through some two hundred jokes and humorous stories. I particularly enjoyed writing this book, but because its subject matter was humor, I always regarded it as one of my less important works. Then I met a psychiatrist, a devout Jew, who told me how important the book had been to him. His cousin, who had terminal cancer, had become deeply dispirited. The psychiatrist used to speak to his cousin on a daily basis, but found that their talks were becoming increasingly depressing. So he challenged the man: "I will continue to speak to you daily, but every day I want us to tell each other at least one joke."

For the ill man, searching each day for a joke helped him to realize that life was more than just pain. As for the psychiatrist, my book became the source for many of the jokes he told his cousin. The psychiatrist told me that during the final months of his cousin's life, "you were responsible for many of the laughs that we shared."

I was deeply moved. I realized that although we often feel we are doing our best work when we speak about matters of meaning and spirituality, it ain't necessarily so. Earlier (see Day 79) I related the story of Rabbi Israel Salanter, who was once seen by his students standing in the street and conversing at great length with an acquaintance. It was clear to the onlookers that the conversation was of a secular nature and somewhat humorous, since the two men were laughing. They were surprised, as it was Rabbi Salanter's practice to avoid unnecessary speech and idle chatter. When they later questioned him about his behavior, he explained: "This man was feeling very bitter, and it was a great act of kindness to cheer his sad soul and to make him forget his worries and sadness. How could I cheer his soul? By engaging in a discourse concerning fear of God and ethical self-improvement? [No!] Only by pleasant talk about general matters." *

Rabbi Nachman of Bratslav (1772–1810) was another great Jewish figure who appreciated the significance of appropriately timed humor. A man described by his biographer as a "tormented master," Reb Nachman wrote, "There are men who suffer terrible distress and are unable to tell what they feel in their hearts, and they go their way and suffer and suffer. But if they meet one with a laughing face, he can revive them with his joy. And to revive someone is no slight thing." **

May God grant you the opportunity to revive another with laughter and with joy.

And may you have a Shabbat Shalom!

DAY

## 357  SHABBAT

During the course of this Shabbat, try to review the material from the preceding six days, and use some of the texts studied as the basis for discussion during the Shabbat meals:

Day 351. A Particularly Evil Form of Stealing
Day 352. A Husband's Obligations to His Wife
Day 353. Don't Insult Your Spouse
Day 354. Jews Shouldn't Be Cheap; Jewish Funerals Should Be
Day 355. A Law That Needs to Be Changed
Day 356. The Holiness of Laughter

Shabbat Shalom!

---

* Etkes, *Rabbi Israel Salanter and the Mussar Movement*, 166.
** Arthur Green's biography of Nachman of Bratslav is entitled *Tormented Master;* the statement of Reb Nachman is found in Blue and Magonet, *Kindred Spirits,* 242.

DAY

358     SUNDAY

# Unfair Competition

"Competition brings out the best in products and the worst in people," declared David Sarnoff, the legendary founder of RCA, the great radio company and forerunner of NBC. Aware of how cutthroat some people could become, Jewish ethical teachings tried to condition them to rein in their more extreme competitive tendencies: "If a poor man is examining a cake [with the intention of buying it] and another [knowing that the poor man is about to make the purchase] comes and [buys it]...he is called a wicked man" (Babylonian Talmud, *Kiddushin* 59a).

The emphasis on the would-be cake purchaser being poor clearly is meant to underscore that he or she does not have the option of purchasing another cake if this one becomes unavailable. But Jewish tradition understands this principle as applying to more than just indigent people; thus it condemns as immoral stepping in when another has all but concluded a business deal (the contract has not yet been signed), and thus "stealing away" the business: "If a person is negotiating to buy or hire either movable or immovable property and another preempts him and buys [or hires it], the latter is an evil person. This applies also in the case of a worker seeking employment" (*Shulchan Aruch: Choshen Mishpat* 237:1).

In other words, if someone you know is pursuing a job lead, and seems to have a good chance of getting it, it is unfair for you to apply for the same job. But what if you believe that you are more qualified for the job? Indeed, is such a standard so idealistic as to be naïve and unrealistic? I don't know the answer to these questions, but it seems to me that if you heard about the job opening from the applicant, it would be unfair to try to preempt him or her by applying for the same position.

Regarding efforts to preempt a deal that another has already concluded, a friend of mine asked me if Jewish law would have sanctioned her behavior in a dispute in which she had been involved. She had reached a verbal agreement to sell to a certain publisher the paperback rights to a hardcover book her company had published, when another publisher approached her and offered more money for these rights. Her boss argued that since no contract had been signed, she had no obligation to honor the earlier agreement, and should accept the higher bid. She, in turn, argued that it was immoral to give one's word and then retract it.

I told her that her reasoning was in perfect conformity with the above ruling in the *Shulchan Aruch.* Once you have given your word, Jewish law regards anyone who pressures you to take it back as acting ruthlessly. And while Jewish ethics approves of competition, it opposes *ruthless* competition.

DAY

359

MONDAY

## Would Jewish Ethics Permit a Jew to Own a Gun Store?

Yes, but…

While I have found no explicit rabbinic response that directly addresses this question, it seems to me that the right of a person to sell weapons to the general public is contingent on his *carefully* checking into the purchasers' backgrounds. Without such checks, the owner shares in the moral responsibility for harm that ensues from selling weapons to people who shouldn't have them (similar to the moral guilt of one who serves too much liquor to a person who will soon be driving a car).

The Jewish legal ruling that comes closest to addressing this issue is found in Maimonides' *Mishneh Torah.* He rules that it is forbidden to sell heathens weapons of aggression,* although it is permitted to sell them defensive weapons (*Mishneh Torah,* "Laws Concerning Murder," 12:12; however, no matter what argument the would-be purchasers make, it would be wrong to sell arms to those who have a history of aggression).** This ruling would seem to outlaw the sale of assault weapons, as well as bullets that can penetrate bulletproof vests worn by police. It would also seem to mandate support for a waiting period before one could sell a person a weapon. During this time, the salesperson would have a moral (even if there were no legal) obligation to check into the background of the one wishing to acquire the weapon.

One piece of rabbinic advice that applies to so many other life situations also applies here: "Who is wise? One who foresees the future consequences of his acts" (Babylonian Talmud, *Tamid* 32a: see Day 30).

TUESDAY

# Wronging with Words

The more you know about a person, the more you can hurt him or her with words. While even a stranger is capable of inflicting emotional pain upon you, in order to be able to wound someone deeply, you usually need to know something about him or her.

Jewish law regards utilizing information you have about another to inflict hurt as an enormous evil. The Mishna cites several examples of how people do so: "If a person was a repentant sinner, one must not say to him, 'Remember how you used to behave.' If a person was a descen-

---

*Technically, Maimonides outlaws the sale of "weapons of war," but it is clear that he is referring to any weapons of aggression, "a knife...or any other object that could cause danger to people at large." Because Judaism is not committed to any doctrine of pacifism, Maimonides notes that "it is permitted to sell weapons to soldiers of the country [in modern terms, to the army]" since such weapons are used to defend the country's citizenry.

**David Szonyi argues that "applying Maimonides' ruling today is a tricky business indeed! Consider that many gun buyers will argue that they need guns for defensive purposes, but then might use the weapon offensively, for example, in a marital dispute."

dant of converts, one must not say to him, "Remember the deeds of your forefathers" (Mishna, *Bava Mezia* 4:10).

The Talmud, commenting on this Mishnaic passage, adds more examples:

> If a person was a convert and came to study Torah, one must not say to him, "Shall the mouth that ate unclean and forbidden food …come to study the Torah that was uttered by the Almighty?" If sufferings came upon a person, if he was afflicted with disease, or has buried his children, one must not say to him as Job's friends said to him, "…Think now, what innocent man ever perished?" (Job 4:7; Babylonian Talmud, *Bava Mezia* 58b).

Why is it particularly evil to remind a penitent sinner of his or her earlier offenses?

People often repent because they want to acquire a good name, and to be accepted back into the society of good people. But if you remind a penitent of his or her former evil deeds, you send a very demoralizing message both to the penitent and to others who wish to rectify past misdeeds: No matter how much good he might do now, no matter how much charity and hard work he might donate to a good cause, he will always be associated with the worst act of his life. Wouldn't that alone make a person feel that there is little point in changing his or her ways?

It is striking that two of the four examples cited above deal with verbal injury to converts. While it is commonly believed that conversions to Judaism were rare throughout history, the Talmud's citing of two examples of verbal mistreatment of converts indicates both how evil it regarded such behavior to be, and that conversions to Judaism must have been more common than is imagined; otherwise, why focus on this subject?

The ultimate cruelty may be telling parents who have buried a child that he or she deserved to die. Yet, unbelievably, that is exactly what Job's friends suggested to him.

The Book of Job's opening chapter tells of a series of calamities that befell its prosperous protagonist, a particularly righteous man, who had ten children. First, Job lost his wealth, then, almost immediately thereafter, all ten of his children died when a building collapsed on them. While he was mourning his children, his friends arrived and, after a few days spent grieving with him, uttered the terrible words: "Think now, what innocent man ever perished?"

How could otherwise decent people say such a cruel thing? Job's friends were probably terrified by the fate that had befallen him, and wished to believe in his guilt and that of his children; otherwise they too might be in danger of their lives.

But readers of the Book of Job know how faulty their reasoning was, for its opening chapter makes it clear that Job's sufferings were not imposed because of his sins. Unfortunately, as the text makes clear, God has structured the world so that evil sometimes has temporary dominion.

Remember these talmudic admonitions the next time you are tempted to use information you have about another to hurt him or her. You know how wrong it would be if someone did this to you. It is equally wrong when you do it to somebody else.

Penitents, converts, and people who have suffered deaths in their families need friends. Real friends. Not friends like the accusers who visited Job.

DAY

361    WEDNESDAY
_____

## The Telephone as an Instrument for Good

As has been noted repeatedly, Judaism regards transmitting *lashon hara*, talk that lowers the status of the person being discussed, as a particularly serious moral offense (see, for example, Day 43). No invention has so facilitated the spreading of *lashon hara* as the telephone (and, more recently, e-mail). An embarrassing episode that happens to a person can now become known to many others in a matter of hours, even to those in far-off cities or countries.*

There are Orthodox Jews who keep a picture of the Chaffetz Chayyim, the famous scholar who devoted much of his life to discouraging the speaking of *lashon hara,* above their telephones. Just seeing his visage reminds them not to say anything that defames another.

The telephone can, however, also be an instrument for great good. Throughout history, Jews who wished to fulfill the command of *bikur cholim* (visiting the sick) either had to live near the sick person or had to exert strenuous efforts to make a visit. Generally, those who lived at a great distance from the patient could only write a letter. The telephone enables one to "drop in" on a sick person (obviously, in the case of one who is very close to you, you should visit in person). And although it is still preferable to make a bedside visit to one who is ill, if you find that, good intentions aside, you are not doing so, how much better it is to pick up the telephone and call than to do nothing.

Telephoning also enables one who has already made a visit or two to a sick person to stay in touch. When you telephone, the one who is sick can still hear your voice, and feel and know that he or she is cared for.

I particularly urge you to make telephone calls to people who do not have large families or many friends. Pay special attention to those who otherwise might be ignored.

Does using the telephone to help those in need seem self-evident? Of course. Nonetheless, I am sure that there are many readers who, like me, utilize the phone often for business, personal matters, and even to gossip, yet frequently forget to utilize it in the performance of a mitzvah.

While you're at it, look through your personal telephone book periodically, see if you stumble across the name of someone with whom you have not spoken in a long time, and give him or her a call. Obvious advice, but if you follow it, you might find yourself reestablishing a connection that should never have been broken.

---

*Television and radio can, of course, make the matter known more quickly to millions of people, but electronic media generally report embarrassing and humiliating details only about people who are famous.

# Torah Study and the Importance of Review

The writer and editor Clifton Fadiman once observed, "When you reread a classic you do not see more in the book than you did before; you see more in you than there was before." Such reasoning is perhaps part of the logic behind the Jewish tradition's emphasis on systematically reviewing Judaism's classic religious texts. Thus, a portion of the Torah is read each Shabbat, so that the Torah in its entirety is completed during the course of the year. Many Jews also study the Torah portion at home during the week preceding its public reading in the synagogue. Although I have now read through the Torah many times, I am amazed each year at how my own life experiences cause me to perceive things within it that I had not previously noticed.

So committed is the Talmud to the significance of review that the Rabbis write (with perhaps only a touch of exaggeration): "He who repeats what he has learned one hundred times cannot be compared to one who repeats it a hundred and one times" (*Hagigah* 9b). They also note, "Words of Torah are forgotten only through inattention" (*Ta'anit* 7b).

A friend of mine periodically makes note cards of insightful quotations from Jewish sources, carries them around with him, and systematically reviews them. Similarly, I suggest that you consider using this book for a second year, for with the passage of time, many of the lessons might be forgotten.

A first-century rabbi with the unlikely name of Ben-Bag-Bag taught, "Turn it over and over again, for one can find everything in it" (that is, the Torah and other religious texts; *Ethics of the Fathers* 5:22). But in order to extract the gems of Judaism—or of anything that you study— you have to go over it, again and again.

# A Week of Kindness, a Week of Gemilut Chesed

Jack Doueck's book, *The Hesed Boomerang*, is based on the talmudic proposition that acts of kindness (in Hebrew, *gemilut chesed*) are rewarded not only in the World-to-Come but in this world as well (*Shabbat* 127a; see Days 115–17). Unhappy that the word *boomerang* has a negative connotation ("I'm afraid it will boomerang"), Doueck cites scientific data documenting the medical advantages of doing kind deeds. He refers to a controlled study of 2,754 people initiated at the University of Michigan between 1967 and 1969, following which the subjects chosen were closely monitored for twelve years. The investigators discovered that those people who did not engage in volunteer work at least once a week were *two and a half times* more likely to have died than those who did participate in such activities. These results were independent of the subjects' gender, health, and age. As Doueck concludes, "If it were a new drug [that had led to so dramatic a diminution in deaths], it would have been hailed as a revolutionary advance in modern medicine."

In citing such data, it is clear that Doueck does not want to inspire people to act kindly solely because of selfish motivations ("I'll do some kind acts, and then I'll live longer"). Rather, he is relying on a well-known Talmudic dictum that advises people to do the right thing even if their motivation is impure: the regular process of doing good, even if for ulterior motives, will eventually cause them to do it for its own sake (*Pesachim* 50b).

Doueck provides numerous examples of daily kindnesses that we can all start to perform immediately, activities that do not require our joining a volunteer organization. I cite some of his suggestions as motivators for us, both for this weekend and over the coming weeks:

- At the supermarket, put your shopping cart back when you're finished with it.
- Write a thank-you card to someone who doesn't expect it.
- Take someone's picture with a Polaroid camera and give it to him or her as a gift.
- Call someone just to say "I miss you."
- Pick up trash from the sidewalk and put it where it belongs.
- Give your waiter an extra-generous tip.
- Get up and give your seat to a woman or elderly person on the train or bus.
- Help someone walk across the street (the blind, seniors, kids).
- Allow another driver to merge into your lane on the highway.
- Send a bouquet of flowers to someone as a surprise.
- Pay the toll for the car behind you at the tollbooth.
- Make an anonymous donation to a local charity.
- Sit with a homeless person on the street and listen to him or her.
- Gather all of your old clothes and give them directly to homeless people.
- Spend an hour in a hospice or hospital visiting the sick.
- Bring your secretary a cup of coffee.
- Find someone doing something right, and praise him or her.
- Encourage your children to donate their old toys to children who might need and appreciate them most.
- Be the first to greet everyone today.
- Hold the door open for someone.
- Call your mayor's action volunteer line and find out places to offer your services.
- Hold back on your criticisms and tolerate other people's weaknesses.*

May you have a Shabbat Shalom!

---

*Doueck, *The Hesed Boomerang*, 30–31 and 116–17. The Michigan study was reported in *Reversing Heart Disease* by Dr. Dean Ornish, 215.

## 364     S H A B B A T

During the course of this Shabbat, try to review the material from the preceding six days, and use some of the texts studied as the basis for discussion during the Shabbat meals:

Day 358. Unfair Competition
Day 359. Would Jewish Ethics Permit a Jew to Own a Gun Store?
Day 360. Wronging with Words
Day 361. The Telephone as an Instrument for Good.
Day 362. Torah Study and the Importance of Review
Day 363. A Week of Kindness, a Week of *Gemilut Chesed*

Shabbat Shalom!

## 365     S U N D A Y

# *Your First Check for the New Year*

Several years ago, a friend, finding himself inundated with bills that he had delayed paying, sat down on New Year's Day to start writing checks. He looked through his bills and grew discouraged. Then he came across an envelope from City Harvest, a New York–based organization that provides food to the homeless and other poor people. He promptly wrote out a check, his first for the year, and sent it to the organization.

He confided to me that writing that check, starting out his year with an act of *tzedaka*, charity, somehow made paying the other bills seem less irksome. Now he makes sure each year that the first check he writes is for charity.

So now, as one year ends and a new one begins, let the first check you write this year be to a charitable organization. And maybe let your last one for this year be to a charity as well. End one year with kindness, then start the new one the same way.

And may I wish you a *shana tova,* a year of goodness and sweetness.

# A Topical Index

❦

Rferences refer to the day of the entry, not to the page on which the entry appears (for example, on "Intellectual honesty," see Day 65, "Cite Your Sources"). Some entries cover more than one topic, and are listed in different categories (such as Day 146, "Don't Embarrass Your Guest, Don't Embarrass Your Children," which is listed under both "Hospitality" and "Between parents and children").

**Abortion**   179, 180

**Aged, treatment of the**   199, 200

**Anger, controlling**   22, 23, 87, 125, 156, 157

**Animals, treatment of**   94, 95, 171, 172, 173, 227, 228

**Arguing fairly**   51

**Bar mitzvah and bat mitzvah**   54, 212, 274

**Between children and parents**   127, 128, 132, 164, 165, 242, 243

**Between employers and employees**   109, 122, 123, 158, 191, 195, 201

**Between husbands and wives**   17, 18, 148, 149, 157, 165, 202, 246, 247, 251, 283, 352, 353

**Between parents and children**   10, 11, 13, 80, 81, 100, 101, 134, 135, 139, 146, 166, 185, 186, 197, 215, 234, 235, 249, 250, 253, 271, 272, 284, 298, 299, 311, 312, 314, 320, 330, 339, 340, 346, 355

*Bikur cholim* (see "Visiting the sick")

**Building character**   82, 150, 198, 201, 239, 240, 244, 254, 258, 281, 282, 297, 324, 333

**Business ethics**   2, 3, 6, 60, 113, 114, 194, 201, 260, 261, 309, 351, 358, 359

**Celebrating**   274

**Changing oneself**   27, 150

**Charity**   8, 9, 37, 38, 50, 169, 170, 174, 188, 236, 274, 275, 279, 293, 302, 303, 307, 345, 365

**Cheerfulness**   39

**Child abuse**   86

**Comforting mourners**   136, 137, 255, 326

**Commonsense living**   15, 16, 66, 93, 202, 286, 316

**Communication**   20, 29, 255, 291

**Complaining**   74, 214

**Confronting others**   46, 263

**Criticism, accepting it, and how to criticize others**   211, 218, 263

**Cruelty**   237

**Death**   289, 290, 354

*Derech eretz* (see "Good Manners")

**Divorce**   283, 318, 319

Empathy   244, 299

Enemy, treatment of one's   88, 97, 228, 267

Envy   323

Ethical living   55, 92, 207, 332

Ethical speaking   43, 44, 48, 52, 53, 96, 153, 204, 205, 209, 265, 318, 321, 328, 331, 334, 335, 337, 338, 344, 360, 361

Ethical will   197

Fear of God   162, 163, 264

Forgiveness   187, 269, 270, 276, 277, 285, 339

Friendship   202, 211

*Gemilut chesed* (see "Kindness")

God   100, 138, 162, 163, 285

Good manners   40, 102, 226, 310

Goodness   55, 111, 184, 216, 223, 233, 235, 295

Gratitude   61, 64, 65, 69, 164, 167, 213, 268, 297, 300, 325, 326

*Hachnasat orchim* (see "Hospitality")

Hatred   45

Health, guarding one's   36, 41

Hospitality   129, 145, 146, 159, 160, 216

Humiliating others, importance of not   271, 278, 284

Humility   248

In-laws   19

Intellectual honesty   65

Interest, not charging   78

Joy   79, 356

Judaism's essence   120, 152, 221

Judging people fairly   24, 25, 219, 220, 223, 306

Justice, fighting for   12, 59, 121, 304

*Kiddush Hashem* (see "Sanctifying, and not desecrating, God's name")

Kindness, acts of   4, 5, 62, 83, 109, 111, 115, 116, 117, 118, 142, 151, 155, 183, 184, 188, 225, 233, 268, 313, 349, 356, 361, 363

Love your neighbor   1, 99, 241, 257

Loving oneself   230, 321

Moral imagination   62

*Nichum aveilim* (see "Comforting mourners")

Non-Jews   141, 194, 288

Peace   229

Pious fool, don't be a   143

Pleasure   67

Prayer   1, 75, 99, 213

Privacy   215, 253

Professional ethics   33, 178

Racism   296, 328

Repentance   106, 107, 108, 110, 192, 193, 289, 327

Responsibility   232, 304, 305, 341

Returning lost objects   26, 341

Revenge and grudges   205, 257

Rituals   262, 314

Sanctifying, and not desecrating, God's name   103, 104, 194, 195

Saving lives   85, 86, 90, 148, 149, 305

Self-defense   222

Self-esteem   130, 230

Self-sacrifice   208

Sharing helpful news   34

Siblings   124

Society's vulnerable members   47, 57, 58, 60, 76, 113, 190

Teaching   292

Temptation   281, 282

*Teshuva* (see "Repentance")

Tolerance   131, 256

Torah study   292, 342, 347, 348, 362

Truth and lies   68, 71, 72, 73, 89, 263, 298, 309

*Tzedaka* (see "Charity")

Visiting the sick   31, 32, 176, 177, 181, 233

Wealth, true   66

Who is wise   30, 144

# Glossary of Hebrew Texts Cited

❧

**Ethics of the Fathers**   see Mishna.

*Kitzur Shulchan Aruch*   Rabbi Shlomo Ganzfried's nineteenth-century Abridged Code of Jewish law.

*Mechilta*   Rabbinic insights and commentaries on Exodus.

*Midrash Rabbah*   A collection of rabbinic commentaries, parables, and reflections on the five books of the Torah, as well the scrolls (Song of Songs, Ruth, Lamentations, Ecclesiastes, and Esther). Individual books are called *Rabbah:* for example, *Genesis Rabbah, Song of Songs Rabbah.*

**Mishna**   Law code compiled by Rabbi Judah the Prince in Israel around 200 of the Common Era. The Mishna classifies Jewish law into sixty-three discrete, short books, known as tractates. For example, the tractate of *Kiddushin* explains the procedures in getting married, and *Gittin,* in getting divorced. The best-known book in the Mishna, *Ethics of the Fathers (Pirkei Avot)*, contains the favorite maxims and teachings of different rabbis over a period of many generations.

*Mishneh Torah*   Moses Maimonides' twelfth-century all-encompassing fourteen-volume summary and codification of Jewish law, perhaps the most influential book published in Jewish law subsequent to the Talmud.

*Shulchan Aruch*   Rabbi Joseph Karo's sixteenth-century code of Jewish law, a knowledge of which is required for those seeking rabbinical ordination.

*Sifra*   Rabbinic insights and commentaries on Leviticus from the early centuries of the Common Era.

*Sifre*   Rabbinic insights and commentaries from the School of Rabbi Ishmael on Numbers, and from the School of Rabbi Akiva on Deuteronomy.

**Talmud**   There are two editions of the Talmud, the first set down in final form by the Rabbis of Palestine around 400 of the Common Era, the second by the Rabbis of Babylon about a century later. They are known respectively as the *Yerushalmi* (after Jerusalem; it is also known as the Palestinian Talmud) and the *Bavli* (Hebrew for Babylon; it is known as the Babylonian Talmud). The Babylonian Talmud is the more extensive and authoritative of the two, and is also more widely used (if someone tells you he is studying the Talmud, it is almost invariably the Babylonian Talmud he is studying). Unless otherwise noted, the citations in this book derive from the Babylonian Talmud. All printed editions of the Babylonian Talmud adhere to the same pagination (if a quote is identified as appearing in *Bava Mezia* 32b, you can find it in that volume on page 32, side two).

**Tosefta** A sort of enormous appendix to the Mishna, the *Tosefta* consists of rabbinic statements dating from the same period during which the Mishna was composed (the first centuries of the Common Era), but which were not included in the Mishna.

# Bibliography

❦

A NOTE ON CITATIONS FROM JUDAISM'S CLASSIC TEXTS

When citing verses from the Hebrew Bible, I have generally followed the translation of the Jewish Publication Society (Philadelphia, 1985), a highly readable and accurate rendering of the Bible into contemporary English. I have, however, sometimes translated the verses myself, or cited other translations that seemed to me preferable for a specific verse.

In quoting from the Talmud (when the word "Talmud" is used, it refers to the Babylonian Talmud only, and does not include the less authoritative Palestinian Talmud), I have often relied on the accurate and very literal translation of the Soncino Press (London, 1935), the only complete translation of the Babylonian Talmud into English. Currently, however, two other translations of the Talmud into English are being published. Random House is publishing a translation of large sections of the Talmud into English, following the Hebrew translation and commentary of Rabbi Adin Steinsaltz; and ArtScroll, a large Jewish publishing house in Brooklyn, is bringing out an English translation of, and commentary on, the Talmud, and plans to have the entire Talmud completed within the next few years. So far, both of these translation have been excellent, and I have occasionally consulted them both. However, I have translated many of the talmudic texts cited in this book from the original. Where I have utilized translations that have appeared in other books (such as William Braude's translation of *The Book of Legends*), I have acknowledged the source within.

There are several English translations of the Mishna, among them one by Herbert Danby (Oxford, England: Clarendon Press, 1933), and one by Jacob Neusner, *The Mishnah* (New Haven: Yale University Press, 1988).

Over several decades, Yale University Press has also published translations of all fourteen volumes of Maimonides' *Mishneh Torah*, under the title *The Code of Maimonides.* Currently, Moznaim Publishing in Brooklyn is bringing out a translation and commentary, *Maimonides Mishneh Torah,* by Rabbi Eliyahu Touger. Unfortunately the *Shulchan Aruch,* the sixteenth-century code of Jewish law, has not, with the exception of a few small sections, been systematically translated into English. But Rabbi Shlomo Ganzfried's nineteenth-century legal code, *Kitzur Shulchon Aruch: The Classic Guide to the Everyday Observance of Jewish Law,* has been translated by Rabbi Eliyahu Touger and published by Moznaim (Brooklyn, 1991).

In quoting from the *Midrash Rabbah,* I have generally followed the ten-volume Soncino translation (London, 1983), although I have checked all translations against the original, and have often made some alterations. The *Mechilta* was translated by Jacob Lauterbach and published and in a three-volume set by the Jewish Publication Society (Philadelphia, 1933).

## Books and Articles Cited

Amsel, Nachum. *The Jewish Encyclopedia of Moral and Ethical Issues.* Northvale, N.J.: Jason Aronson, 1994.

Artson, Bradley Shavit. *It's a Mitzvah! Step-by-Step to Jewish Living.* West Orange, N.J.: Behrman House and Rabbinical Assembly, 1995.

Augustine, Saint. "On Lying," in R. J. Defarrari, ed., *Treatises on Various Subjects,* vol. 14. New York: Catholic University of America Press, 1952.

Bialik, Hayim Nahman, and Yehoshua Hana Ravnitzky. *The Book of Legends: Legends from the Talmud and Midrash* (translated from the Hebrew *Sefer Ha-Aggadah* by William Braude). New York: Schocken Books, 1992.

Blech, Benjamin. *Understanding Judaism: The Basics of Deed and Creed.* Northvale, N.J.: Jason Aronson, 1992.

Bleich, J. David. *Judaism and Healing.* New York: Ktav, 1981.

Blue, Lionel, and Jonathan Magonet. *Kindred Spirits: A Year of Readings.* London: HarperCollins, 1995.

Bok, Sissela. *Lying: Moral Choice in Public and Private Life.* New York: Vintage Books, 1989.

Brawarsky, Sandee, and Deborah Mark, eds. *Two Jews, Three Opinions: A Collection of Twentieth-Century American Jewish Quotations.* New York: Perigee Books, 1998.

Buber, Martin. *Tales of the Hasidim, Book One: The Early Masters,* and *Book Two: The Later Masters.* New York: Schocken, 1975.

Chipman, Jonathan. "Hevra Kadisha," in Sharon and Michael Strassfeld, *The Third Jewish Catalog.* Philadelphia: Jewish Publication Society, 1980, 136–39.

Cohen, Rabbi Alfred S., ed. *Halacha and Contemporary Society.* New York: Ktav, 1983.

David, Jay, ed. *Growing Up Jewish.* New York: Aron Books, 1997.

Domb, Cyril, ed. *Maaser Kesafim: Giving a Tenth to Charity.* Jerusalem and New York: Feldheim Publishers, 1980.

Doueck, Jack. *The Hesed Boomerang: How Acts of Kindness Can Enrich Our Lives.* Deal, N.J.: Yagdiyl Torah Publications, 1998.

Douglas, Kirk. *Climbing the Mountain: My Search for Meaning.* New York: Simon and Schuster, 1997.

Eliach, Yaffa. *Hasidic Tales of the Holocaust.* New York: Oxford University Press, 1982.

Etkes, Immanuel. *Rabbi Israel Salanter and the Mussar Movement.* Philadelphia: Jewish Publication Society, 1993.

Feldman, David. *Birth Control in Jewish Law: Marital Relations, Contraception and Abortion as Set Forth in the Classic Texts of Jewish Law.* New York: New York University Press, 1968.

Fox, Marvin, ed. *Modern Jewish Ethics: Theory and Practice.* Columbus: Ohio State University Press, 1975.

Frank, Anne. *The Diary of a Young Girl.* Garden City, N.Y.: Doubleday, 1952; New York: Pocket Books, 1963, 1974.

Freehof, Solomon. *The Responsa Literature and a Treasury of Responsa* (two volumes in one). New York: Ktav Publishing, 1973.

Friedman, Dayle. "The Crown of Glory: Aging in the Jewish Tradition," in Rela M. Geffen, ed., *Celebration and Renewal: Rites of Passage in Judaism.* Philadelphia: Jewish Publication Society, 1993, 202–25.

Glendon, Mary Ann. *Rights Talk: The Impoverishment of Political Discourse.* New York: Free Press, 1991.

Gold, Michael. *God, Love, Sex, and Family.* Northvale, N.J.: Jason Aronson, 1998.

Goodwin, Doris Kearns. *No Ordinary Time: Franklin and Eleanor Roosevelt: The Home Front in World War II.* New York: Simon and Schuster, 1994.

Greenberg, Blu. *How to Run a Traditional Jewish Household.* New York: Fireside Books, 1985.

Herring, Basil. *Jewish Ethics and Halakhah for Our Time: Sources and Commentary.* New York: Stave and Yeshiva University Press, 1984.

Hertz, Dr. J. H. *The Pentateuch and Haftorahs.* London: Soncino Press, 1980.

Himelstein, Shmuel. *Words of Wisdom, Words of Wit.* Brooklyn, N.Y.: Mesorah, 1993.

Isaacs, Ronald H. *The Jewish Book of Etiquette.* Northvale, N.J.: Jason Aronson, 1998.

Jacobs, Louis. *Jewish Law.* New York: Behrman House, 1968.

———. *Jewish Personal and Social Ethics.* West Orange, N.J.: Behrman House, 1990.

———. *Religion and the Individual: A Jewish Perspective.* Cambridge, England: Cambridge University Press, 1992.

Kant, Immanuel. "On a Supposed Right to Lie from Benevolent Motives," in *The Critique of Practical Reason,* translated and edited by Lewis White Beck. Chicago: University of Chicago Press, 1994, 346–50.

Katz, Dov. *T'nuat Ha-Mussar (The Mussar Movement).* 5 volumes. Tel Aviv, 1945–52.

Katz, Michael, and Gershon Schwartz. *Swimming in the Sea of the Talmud.* Philadelphia: Jewish Publication Society, 1998.

Kirschenbaum, Aaron. *Equity in Jewish Law: Halakhic Perspectives in Law: Formalism and Flexibility in Jewish Civil Law.* Hoboken, N.J.: Ktav, 1991.

———. "The Good Samaritan in Jewish Law," in Ze'ev Falk and Aaron Kirschenbaum, eds. *Dine Israel: An Annual of Jewish Law and Israeli Family Law.* Tel Aviv: Tel Aviv University, Faculty of Law Press, 1976, 7–8.

Klagsbrun, Francine. *Voices of Wisdom: Jewish Ideals and Ethics for Everyday Living.* New York: Pantheon, 1980.

Koch, Edward, with Daniel Paisner. *Citizen Koch: An Autobiography.* New York: St. Martin's Press, 1992.

Kurshan, Neil. *Raising Your Child to Be a Mensch.* New York: Atheneum, 1987.

Kushner, Lawrence. *Invisible Lines of Connection: Sacred Stories of the Ordinary.* Woodstock, Vt.: Jewish Lights Publishing, 1996.

Lamm, Maurice. *The Jewish Way in Death and Mourning.* New York: Jonathan David Publishing, 1969.

Lamm, Norman, ed. *The Good Society: Jewish Ethics in Action.* New York: Viking Press, 1974.

Leibowitz, Nehama. *Studies in Shemot: The Book of Exodus.* Jerusalem: The World Zionist Organization, Department for Torah Education and Culture in the Diaspora, 1976.

Levine, Rabbi Aaron. *How to Perform the Great Mitzvah of Bikur Cholim—Visiting the Sick.* Willowdale, Ontario: Zichron Meir Publications, 1987.

Luzzatto, Moshe Chaim. *The Path of the Just (Mesillat Yesharim),* translated, with commentary, by Yaakov Feldman. Northvale, N.J.: Jason Aronson, 1996.

Maimonides, Moses. *The Guide of the Perplexed,* translated, with introduction, by Shlomo Pines. Chicago: University of Chicago Press, 1963.

Mandelbaum, Yitta Halberstam. *Holy Brother: Inspiring Stories and Enchanted Tales About Rabbi Shlomo Carlebach.* Northvale, N.J.: Jason Aronson, 1997.

Nachmanides, Moses. *A Letter for the Ages,* translated by Rabbi Avrohom Chaim Feuer. Brooklyn, N.Y.: Mesorah Publications, 1989.

Newman, Louis. *Past Imperatives: Studies in the History and Theory of Jewish Ethics.* Albany: State University of New York Press, 1998.

Noveck, Simon, ed. *Great Jewish Personalities in Modern Times.* Washington, D.C.: B'nai Brith Department of Adult Jewish Education, 1960.

*Orchot Tzaddikim (The Ways of the Tzaddikim).* Anonymous; newly prepared and completely corrected Hebrew text edited by Rabbi Gavriel Zaloshinsky; English translation by Rabbi Shraga Silverstein. Nanuet, N.Y.: Feldheim, 1995.

Ornish, Dean. *Reversing Heart Disease.* New York: Random House, 1984.

Plaut, W. Gunther, and Mark Washofsky. *Teshuvot for the Nineties: Reform Judaism's Answers for Today's Dilemmas.* New York: Central Conference of American Rabbis, 1997.

Pliskin, Zelig. *Love Your Neighbor: You and Your Fellow Man in the Light of Torah.* Brooklyn, N.Y.: Aish HaTorah Publications, 1977.

Prager, Dennis. *Happiness Is a Serious Problem: A Human Nature Repair Manual.* New York: Regan Books, 1998.

———. *Think a Second Time.* New York: Regan Books, 1995.

Prager, Kenneth. "For Everything a Blessing," *Journal of the AMA,* May 28, 1997, 1589.

Raz, Simcha. *A Tzaddik in Our Time: The Life of Rabbi Aryeh Levin,* translated from the Hebrew, revised and expanded by Charles Wengrow. Jerusalem and New York: Feldheim Publishers, 1976.

*Resource Guide for Rabbis: On Domestic Violence.* No author or editor listed. Washington, D.C.: Jewish Women International, 1996.

Riemer, Jack, ed. *Jewish Insights on Death and Mourning.* New York: Schocken, 1995.

———, ed. *The World of the High Holy Days.* Miami, Fla.: Bernie Books, no date.

Riemer, Jack, and Nathaniel Stampfer, eds. *So That Your Values Live On: Ethical Wills and How to Prepare Them.* Woodstock, Vt.: Jewish Lights Publishing, 1991.

Rosner, Fred. *Modern Medicine and Jewish Ethics.* Hoboken, N.J.: Ktav and Yeshiva University Press (2nd revised edition), 1991.

Salkin, Rabbi Jeffrey. *Being God's Partner: How to Find the Hidden Link Between Spirituality and Your Work.* Woodstock, Vt.: Jewish Lights Publishing, 1994.

———. *For Kids; Putting God on Your Guest List: How to Claim the Spiritual Meaning of Your Bar or Bat Mitzvah.* Woodstock, Vt.: Jewish Lights Publishing, 1998.

Schimmel, Solomon. *The Seven Deadly Sins.* New York: Free Press, 1992.

Schwartz, Richard H. *Judaism and Vegetarianism.* Marblehead, Mass.: Micah Publications, 1988.

Shapiro, Rabbi Rami M. *Minyan: Ten Principles for Living a Life of Integrity.* New York: Bell Tower, 1997.

Sherwin, Byron, and Seymour Cohen. *How to Be a Jew: Ethical Teachings of Judaism.* Northvale, N.J.: Jason Aronson, 1992.

Siegel, Danny. *Family Reunion: Making Peace in the Jewish Community.* Spring Valley, N.Y.: The Town House Press, 1989.

Steinberg, Milton. *As a Driven Leaf.* West Orange, N.J.: Behrman House, 1996.

Tamari, Meir. *The Challenge of Wealth: A Jewish Perspective on Earning and Spending Money.* Northvale, N.J.: Jason Aronson, 1995.

Tavris, Carol. *Anger.* New York: Touchstone, 1989.

Teller, Hanoch. *And from Jerusalem, His Word: Stories and Insights of Rabbi Shlomo Zalman Auerbach zt'l.* New York: New York City Publishing Company, 1995.

Telushkin, Joseph. *Biblical Literacy: The Most Important People, Events and Ideas of the Hebrew Bible.* New York: William Morrow and Co., 1997.

———. *Jewish Literacy: The Most Important Things to Know About the Jewish Religion, Its People and Its History.* New York: William Morrow and Co., 1991.

———. *Words That Hurt, Words That Heal.* New York: William Morrow and Co., 1996.

Tucker, Gordon. "Jewish Business Ethics," in Joseph Lowin, ed., *Jewish Ethics: A Study Guide.* New York: Hadassah, 1986, 33–34.

Twerski, Rabbi Abraham J., M.D. *Do Unto Others: How Good Deeds Can Change Your Life.* Kansas City: Andrews McMeel, 1997.

Twerski, Rabbi Abraham J., M.D., and Ursula Schwartz, Ph.D. *Positive Parenting: Developing Your Child's Potential.* Brooklyn, N.Y.: Mesorah Publications, 1996.

Wein, Berel. *Second Thoughts: A Collection of Musings and Observations.* Brooklyn, N.Y.: Shaar Publications, 1997.

Weiss, Saul. *Insights: A Talmudic Treasury.* Jerusalem: Feldheim, 1990.

Wiener, Herbert. *9½ Mystics.* New York: Holt, Rinehart and Winston, 1969.

Wiesenthal, Simon. *The Sunflower: On the Possibilities and Limits of Forgiveness.* New York: Schocken, 1997.

Will, George. *The Morning After: American Successes and Excesses 1981–1986.* New York: Collier Books, 1986.

Winkler, Gershon, with Lakme Batya Elior. *The Place Where You Are Standing Is Holy: A Jewish Theology on Human Relationships.* Northvale, N.J.: Jason Aronson, 1994.

Wolfson, Dr. Ron. *A Time to Mourn, a Time to Comfort.* Woodstock, Vt.: Jewish Lights Publishing, 1996.

---

## *Permission Acknowledgments*

Grateful acknowledgment is made to the following for permission to reprint previously published material:

*Jason Aronson, Inc. and Yitta Halberstam Mandelbaum:* excerpts from *Holy Brother* by Yitta Halberstam Mandelbaum. Copyright © 1997 by Yitta Halberstam Mandelbaum. Reprinted by permission of Jason Aronson, Inc., Northvale, NJ, and the author. *ArtScroll/Shaar Press:* excerpt from *Second Thoughts* by Rabbi Berel Wein. Reprinted by permission of ArtScroll/Shaar Press. *Behrman House, Inc.:* excerpt from *It's a Mitzvah!* by Rabbi Bradley Artson. Published by Behrman House, Inc., 235 Watchung Avenue, West Orange, NJ 07052. Used with permission. *Jewish Lights Publishing:* excerpt from *So That Your Values Live On: Ethical Wills and How to Prepare Them,* copyright © 1991 by Jack Riemer and Nathaniel Stampfer. ($17.95 pb and $3.50 s/h); excerpt from *For Kids—Putting God on the Guest List: How to Claim the Spiritual Meaning of Your Bar or Bat Mitzvah,* copyright © 1998 by Jeffrey K. Salkin. ($14.95 pb and $3.50 s/h); excerpt from *Being God's Partner: How to Find the Hidden Link Between Spirituality and Your Work,* copyright © 1994 by Jeffrey K. Salkin. ($16.95 pb and $3.50 s/h) Woodstock, VT: Jewish Lights Publishing. Order by mail or call 1-800-962-4544. Permission granted by Jewish Lights Publishing, P.O. Box 237, Woodstock, VT 05091. Simcha Raz: excerpts from *A Tzaddik in Our Time* by Simcha Raz. Reprinted by permission of the author. *Schocken Books:* excerpt from *The Sunflower* by Simon Wiesenthal. Copyright © 1969, 1970 by Opera Mundi Paris. Copyright renewed 1997, 1998 by Simon Wiesenthal. Reprinted by permission of Schocken Books, a division of Random House, Inc. *Sterling Lord Literistic, Inc.:* "Maimonides, Art Buchwald and the Importance of Every Deed" by Art Buchwald. Copyright by Art Buchwald. Reprinted by permission of Sterling Lord Literistic, Inc.

# Index

Aberbach, Moses, 54
Abortion, 257–60
Abraham ibn Ezra, 444
Abuse, 15–17, 82–83, 122–24, 123, 210–14,
    351–52, 397–98
Accidents, 367–69
Adler, Dr. Joseph, 22
Adler, Rabbi Joseph, 115
Adopted children, 440
Adultery, 17
Advice, 157–58
Aged. *See* Elderly
Akiva, Rabbi, 1, 44–45, 56–57, 115,
    298–99, 473
Alcohol use, 61–63, 159, 206–7, 285–86
Alpert, Merrill, 155
Amsel, Nachum, 246–47, 464, 468
Anger, controlling, 31–34, 124–26, 178–79,
    216, 222–25, 286, 361–62, 408–9
Animals, treatment of, 133–36, 243–47,
    323–26
Apologizing, 464–65
Appreciation, expressing, 153–54
Arguing fairly, 76–77
Arrogance, antidote to, 340–41
Artson, Bradley, 45–47, 247, 267–68
Auerbach, Shlomo Zalman, 109–10, 250–51,
    257, 322, 360–61
Augustine, Saint, 100
Autopsies, 405

Baal Shem Tov, Israel, 10–11, 328, 430, 479
Bahya ibn Pakuda, 340–41
Bar mitzvah and bat mitzvah, 80–82, 141,
    302–3, 386
Beggars, 11–13, 393

Behavior
    changing negative, 215–16
    considerate, 429
    judging favorably, 34–35
    self-destructive, 115–16, 204–5
Beltzer, John, 156
Ben-Bag-Bag, Rabbi, 497
Ben Sira, 128
Ben Zoma, 95, 237–38
Berger, Michael, 80n
Berman, Herman, 156
Berman-Potash, Nancy, 156
Bialik, Hayyim Nachman, 488
*Bikur cholim. See* Sick, visiting the
*Bittul Torah. See* Time, not wasting
Blech, Benjamin, 204
Bleich, J. David, 252–53
Blessing of children, 18–20, 433–34
Blind people, 86–87
Body, rights to, 260
Bribes, lifesaving, 115–16
Buber, Martin, 407
Buchwald, Art, 376–78
Bunam, Simcha, 185
Business ethics
    consumers' obligations, 88–89, 160–62
    defrauding equated with stealing, 481
    honest vs. dishonest, 4–7, 97, 145–46,
        157–59, 278–79
    legal not equal to moral, 454–55
    misleading, 427–29
    temptation to cheat, 10–11
    unfair competition, 491–92
    verbal commitments, 458n
    of weapons sales, 492–93
    *See also* Employer-employee relations

Camus, Albert, 129
Carlebach, Shlomo, 59–60, 147, 168–69,
    202–3, 238–39, 402–3, 410
Chaffetz Chayyim. *See* Kagan, Israel Meir
    Ha-Cohen
Chaim of Sanz, 13
Changing oneself, 39, 154–55, 215–16
Character, 341–42
    three traits of, 285–86
Charity
    accepting, 420–21
    acts of kindness as, 8–9
    anonymous, 421–22, 472–74
    to beggars, 11–13, 393
    at celebratory times, 81–82, 141, 385–87
    degrees of, 54–57, 248–49, 271–72,
        336–37
    income percentage, 75–76
    lack seen as idolatry, 409–10, 426
    on New Year's Day, 500–501
    significance of, 74–76
    as steadily repeated act, 241–42
    training child to give, 140–41
    while traveling, 240–41
Chayyim of Volozhin, Rabbi, 466
Cheating, 10–11, 388, 481
Cheerfulness, 57–58
Children. *See* Parent-child relations
Cohen, Hermann, 85
Competition, unfair, 491–92
Complaining, 106–7, 305–6
Compliments, 237–39, 453–54
Confronting others, 68–70, 370–72
Consideration of others, 9–10, 143–44
Courtesy, 89–90
Cremation, 260
Criticism, 219–20, 301–2, 309–11
Cruelty, 338–39, 471–72, 487–88
Curiosity, personal, 127–28
Custody, child, 438–39

Dating, 462–64
Deaf people, 86–87
Death and dying, 252–55, 260, 403–7,
    432–33, 447–48, 484–86
Debts, 173–74
Demands of others, 131–32
*Derech eretz. See* Manners
Disabilities, 86–87, 109–10, 273–74
Dishonesty. *See* Honesty; Lies

Disraeli, Benjamin, 29
Divorce, 152–53, 397–98, 437–38
Dole, Bob, 50
Doueck, Jack, 498–99
Douglas, Kirk, 133
Dov Baer, 328
Drazin, Nathan, 54
Drugs, illegal, 115–16, 260

Earliness vs. promptness, 322–23
Education, Jewish, 266–68, 475
Eideles, Solomon Elazar, 242
Eiger, Akiva, 208
Elazar, Rabbi, 437, 458–59
Elderly, 82, 286–89
Eliach, Yaffa, 60
Elijah, Rabbi (Gaon of Vilna), 466
Elior, Lakme Batya, 346n
Elisha ben Abuyah, 362–63
Elitism, 352–54
Embarrassing others, 208–9
Emden, Jacob, 52
Empathy, 347–48, 416–17
Employer-employee relations, 88–89,
    173–76, 225–26, 274–75, 280–81,
    289–90, 461–62
Enemies, treatment of, 126–27, 137–38,
    325–26, 375–76
Engelhart, Donni, 156
Envy, 443–45
Epstein, Mendel, 467
Ethical wills, 177–78, 282–85
Evil urges, 455–57
Exaggerations, 97

Falsehoods. *See* Lies
Fasting, 242
Favoritism, avoiding, 14–15
Fear of household head, 15–17, 82
Feinstein, Moshe, 52–53, 75n, 115
Feldman, Leonid, 98–99
Feuds, 103–4, 327
Feuerstein, Aaron, 280–81
Fifth Commandment, 383–84
Forgiveness, 270–71, 289–90, 378–82,
    388–91, 400–401, 464–65, 469–70
Frank, Anne, 12
Frankl, Viktor, 218
Freund, Kathy, 156
Friendship, 291–92, 301–2, 343–44

Funerals, 432–33, 484–86
Fur, wearing of, 246–47

Gamliel, Rabbi, 274–75, 302
Gandhi, Mahatma, 42–43, 318n
Ganzfried, Shlomo, 182
Garfein, Stanley, 406
*Gemilut chesed. See* Kindness, acts of
Generosity, 286, 359–61
Gershom, Rabbenu, 358
Ginsberg, Victoria, 156
God
    fear of, 230–32, 372–73
    forgiveness by, 400–401
    not using name in vain, 197–98
    as owner of human's body, 260
    primary concerns of, 170–71
    sanctifying, 145–48, 278–81
Gold, Michael, 177, 178, 439
Golden Rule, 5, 64–65, 219, 295
Gompers, Samuel, 89
Good deeds. *See* Kindness, acts of
Good intentions, 401
Goodness, 82–83, 142–43, 155–56, 265–66,
    318–22, 331–33, 334–35, 455–57
Gossip, 64–65, 72–73, 435–36
Graham, Billy, 205
Grandparents, 82, 475
Gratitude
    beginning day with, 303–4
    expressing, 233–34, 237–39, 376–78,
        418–19
    for life's good things, 98–99, 446–48
    for parents, 233–34
    saying "thank you," 89–90
    for teachers, 92–93
    tipping as, 153–54
Greetings, 59–61
Grudges, 295–96, 363–65, 380–82
Guests. *See* Hospitality
Guilt, recognizing, 151–53
Gun sales, 492–93
Gur Aryeh ha-Levi, 347

*Hachnasat orchim. See* Hospitality
*Hakarat hatov. See* Gratitude
Halevi, Haim David, 53–54
Half-truths, 97, 427–29
Happiness, marital, 356–57
Hatred, groundless, 67–68

Health, 51–54, 61–63, 260
Hebrew names, 82, 114–16
Heine, Heinrich, 134
Helpful information-sharing, 49–50
Henkin, Joseph, 176
Heroism, 365–66
Hertz, Joseph, 226, 413–14
Heschel, Abraham Joshua, 194–95, 199–200,
    383–84, 389–91
Heschel, Susannah, 199–200
Hillel, Rabbi, 186–87, 218–19, 478
Hirsch, Samson Raphael, 96
Honesty
    in business, 4–7, 97, 145–46, 157–59,
        278–79, 427–29
    with dying person, 252–55
    in friendship, 301–2
    intellectual, 93–94
    interpersonal, 4–6
    nonconstructive, 65–67
    without oath-taking, 457–58
    with powerful people, 370–72
    teaching children, 414–15
    vs. tact, 41–42
    *See also* Lies
Honoring parents, 163, 164, 165, 167,
    180–82, 189, 345–46, 383–84
Hospitality, 105, 163, 164, 167, 184, 206–9,
    226–29, 307–8
Humiliation, 137–38, 382–83, 391–92,
    398–99, 435–36
Humility, 104–5
Hunting, 133–34
Hurtful speech, 65–67, 103, 299–300, 436–37,
    493–95
    cruel nicknames as, 471–72
    as damaging reputation, 78, 293–94, 437
    negative comments as, 64–65, 136, 294–95,
        461–64
    rumors as, 78–79
    about spouse, 27
    stereotyping as, 450–51
    *See also* Gossip
Husbands. *See* Spouse

Idolatry, 409–10
Immortality, 321–22
Indifference, 467–48
Ingratitude, 413–14
Inheritances, 474–75

In-laws, 27–28, 234–35
Insincerity, 40–41
Insults, 458–60
Interest charges, 111–12
Invitations, genuine, 40–42
Isserles, Moses, 123

Jacobs, Louis, 426
Joshua, Rabbi, 274–75
Joshua ben Korcha, 199
Judah the Chasid, Rabbi, 127, 430–31
Judah the Prince, Rabbi, 324, 352–53
Judaism
    child's education in, 266–68, 475
    essence of, 170–71, 218–19, 315–17
Judging people fairly, 34–37, 311–14, 318–20
Justice, fighting for, 17–18, 87–88, 172–73,
    422

Kagan, Israel Meir Ha-Cohen (Chaffetz
    Chayyim), 44, 117, 203, 441, 462–64
Kamenetzky, Jacob, 90
Kant, Immanuel, 100–101
Karelitz, Abraham, 144
Karo, Joseph, 123, 420n
Kashrut. See Kosher laws
Katz, Michael, 311–12
Kelman, Wolfe, 360
Kiddush Hashem. See God, sanctifying
Kielburger, Craig, 156
Kindness, acts of, 90–91, 113–14, 118–19,
    130–31, 163–69, 271–72
    as charity, 8–9
    consideration as, 9–10
    daily, 203–4, 221–22, 498–99
    for the dead, 432–33
    examples of, 155–56, 221–22
    helping others as, 264–65
    immortality from, 321–22
    impulsive, 265–66
    as lifelong obligation, 217–18
    toward non-Jews, 201–3
    random, 479–80
    removing stumbling blocks, 297
    telephoning as, 495–96
    tipping as, 153–54
    See also Charity; Sick, visiting the
Klagsbrun, Samuel, 254–55
Koch, Ed, 486
Koidonover, Tzvi Hirsch, 6

Kook, Abraham Isaac, 68, 364
Kosher laws, 133–34, 244–46
Kreiser, Aaron, 67
Kula, Irwin, 14–15, 48, 102–3n, 141n, 200n,
    337n
Kurshan, Neil, 208–9
Kurzweil, Dana, 141n
Kushner, Lawrence, 128–29

Landau, Ezekiel, 133–34
Lashon hara. See Speech, ethics of
Laughter, 113–14, 489–90
Laziness, 9–10
Learning from others, 362–63
Lebovics, Shirley, 210, 213–14
Leibowitz, Nechama, 443
Letter of the law, going beyond the,
    289–90
Levine, Aryeh, 90–91, 184, 241, 257, 261–63,
    364, 387
Levine, Raphael Benjamin, 90
Liability, 367–69
Lichtenstein, Aharon, 10
Lies
    half-truths as, 97, 427–28
    instances of permissible, 100–105
    keeping away from, 97–98
    not forcing others into, 127–28
    parent-child relations and, 97–98, 183
    See also Honesty
Lifesaving actions, 100–102, 115–16, 120–24,
    128–29, 210–14, 405–7, 423–24
Listening, 407
Lost objects, returning, 37–39, 467–68
Love
    anger as killer of, 124–26
    for neighbor, 3–4, 343–44, 363–65
    nurturing child's capacity for, 452
    of oneself, 328
    parental, 14–15, 430–31
    for stranger, 84–85
Luzzatto, Moshe Chayyim, 176, 428

Maimonides, Moses, 7, 12, 31, 38, 53, 54–55,
    70–71, 96, 175, 215–16, 244, 265, 273,
    287–88, 305, 347, 369, 376, 400, 436,
    440, 449, 486–88, 492–93
Malbim, 29
Mandelbaum, Yitta Halberstam, 59, 147, 168,
    201

Manners, 59–61, 89–90, 116–17, 143–44, 361–62
Marmer, Stephen, 86n, 132, 371–72
Marriage. *See* Spouse
McCormack, Thomas, 454
Meir, Rabbi, 362–63, 401
Meir, Golda, 466
Meiri, Menachem, 178
Mercifulness, 289–90
Money
    bequests to children, 474–75
    generosity toward parents, 189
    lending of, 111–12
    not selecting mate based on, 354–55
Moral obligations, 120–24, 422
Motives, actions and, 455–57
Mourners, comforting, 81, 193–97, 361–62, 401, 447–48
Murder, 317–18, 487

Nachman, Rabbi, 2, 150, 490
Naming children, 82, 114–16
Neighbor
    choosing wisely, 23–24
    loving, 3–4, 343–44, 363–65
    protecting, 120–21
Newman, Louis, 379n
*Nichum aveilim. See* Mourners, comforting
Nicknames, cruel, 471–72
Nobel, Alfred, 154–55
Non-Jews, treatment of, 111, 201–3, 278–79, 402–3

Oath-taking, 457–58
Obligations, 120–24
Organ donations, 405–7
Orphans, treatment of, 70–71, 440

Parent-child relations
    abuse of child, 15–17, 122–24
    adopted child, 440
    apologizing to child, 464–65
    appreciating child's gifts, 236–37
    avoiding favoritism, 14–15
    avoiding in-law conflicts, 234–35
    avoiding physical punishment, 192–93, 487–88
    bequests, 474–75
    custody of child, 438–39
    ethical will, 177–78, 282–85
    exceptions to obeying parents, 182–83
    expressing gratitude to parents, 233–34
    expressing love for child, 14–15, 430–31
    expressing respect for parents, 188–89
    father's financial responsibilities, 399
    honoring parents, 163, 164, 165, 167, 180–82, 189, 345–46, 383–84
    lifesaving contracts with child, 115–16
    obligations to senile parents, 346–47
    overseeing child's moral development, 97–98, 140–43, 183, 268–70, 334–35, 354–56, 382–83, 414–17
    playfulness with child, 199–200
    providing Jewish education, 266–68, 475
    raising child to love self and others, 452
    respecting child's privacy, 306–7, 358–59
    sensitivity to child's feelings, 208–9
    Shabbat blessing of child, 18–20, 433–34
    spending time with child, 466–67
    talking about child's namesake, 114–16
    teaching survival skills, 431–32
    teaching work skills, 333–34
    treating each child uniquely, 190–91
Peace, 163, 165, 167, 327
Perilman, Yehuda, 259n
Pets, treatment of, 135–35
Pious fool, 204–6
Pious platitudes, 373–74, 426
Plagiarism, 93–94
Plaut, W. Gunther, 54
Pleasure, 95–96
Pliskin, Zelig, 35
Political asylum, 17–18
Power
    generous use of, 259–61
    misuse of, 15–17, 82–83
Prager, Dennis, 26, 37, 58, 76, 95, 106, 142–43, 160–62, 197, 268–70, 305, 335, 367
Prager, Kenneth, 107–8
Praise, 436–37
Prayer
    after bathroom use, 107–8
    bedtime, 380–82
    confessional, 403–5
    daily morning, 303–4
    meaning of, 163, 164, 167
    for others, 3–4, 139–40
    with sick people, 46, 47
Pride, excessive, 420–21

Privacy, 46, 104–5, 306–7, 358–59
Professional ethics, 48–49, 255–57, 454–55
Punishment, physical, 192–93, 487–88

Racism, 412–13
Rathenau, Walter, 277
Rava, Rabbi, 41–42, 48n
Reinhart, Harold, 445
Repentance, 149–53, 154–55, 275–78, 403–5,
    448–49
Reputation, damaging, 78, 293–94, 437.
    See also Gossip
Respect for others, 26–28, 48–49, 82, 92–93,
    109–10, 189, 225–26, 288–89, 371
Responsibility, 151–52, 329–31, 370–72, 422,
    467–68
Retarded people, 109–10
Revenge, 137–38, 363–65
Reynolds, David, 305–6
Riemer, Jack, 114–15, 177, 194, 282–85, 321,
    376, 418–19
Riskin, Shlomo, 19n
Rituals, 369–70, 433–34
Roosevelt, Eleanor, 460
Rosenthal, A. M., 85
Rosner, Fred, 54, 259n
Rudeness, 116–17
Rumors, 78–80

Safra, Rabbi, 41–42, 130–31
Salanter, Israel, 1, 39, 106, 113, 205, 217,
    220, 342, 369–70, 420, 478, 483–84,
    489–90
Salkin, Jeffrey, 81, 255–56
Sarnoff, David, 491
Schachter-Shalomi, Zalman, 3
Schacter, Jacob J., 139
Schindler, Oskar, 36
Schneersohn, Menachem Mendel, 251
Schwartz, Gershon, 311–12
Self-defense, 317–18
Self-destructive behavior, 115–16, 204–5
Self-esteem, 185, 328
Self-image, 452
Self-importance, 429
Self-sacrifice, limits of, 298–99
Senility, 346–47
Shabbat, 18–20, 61–62, 433–34
Shame, sparing others from, 271–72
Shammai, Rabbi, 186–87, 218–19

Shapiro, Rami, 305
Shaw, George Bernard, 412
Shimon ben Lakish, Rabbi, 476–77
Shimon bar Yochai, Rabbi, 310
Shiva, 447–48
Shlomo Shwadron, 373–74
Shlomo Zalman.
    See Auerbach, Shlomo Zalman
Shmelke, Rabbi, 480
Siblings, 14–15, 177–78
Sick, visiting the, 44–47, 81, 163, 164, 167,
    250–51, 261–63, 331–33
Siegel, Danny, 155, 156
Siegel, Morton, 87
Singer, Isaac Bashevis, 172n
Slander, 65, 103
Slavery, 17–18
Smith, Al, 435
Smoking, 51–54, 115–16, 260
Soloveitchik, Joseph Dov, 172, 248
Soul, 484
Speech, ethics of, 64–67, 441–42, 495–96
    gossip avoidance, 64–65, 72–73,
        435–36
    importance of listening, 407
    sharing helpful news, 49–50
    times to remain silent, 29–30, 40–42,
        219–20, 361–62, 435–36
    See also Honesty; Hurtful speech; Lies
Spouse
    abuse of, 15–17, 123, 210–14, 351–52,
        397–98
    anger at, 124–26, 224–25
    consulting with, 291–92
    desirable traits in, 25–26
    guest invitations and, 207–8
    helping others to find, 264–65
    husband's obligations to, 482–83
    in-law conflicts and, 234–35
    kindness toward, 349–51, 483–84
    playfulness with, 356–57
    selection of, 183, 354–55
    speaking critically about, 26–27
    See also Divorce
Stampfer, Nathaniel, 283–84
Stealing. See Theft
Steinsaltz, Adin, 409
Stereotyping, 450–51
Sternhull, Mendel, 238–39
Stinginess, 286

Suffering
  learning from, 82–83
  sensitivity to, 445–46
Suicide, 260
Survival skills, teaching, 431–32

Tact, honesty vs., 41–42
Tamari, Meir, 159
Tardiness, 143–44
Tarfon, Rabbi, 94–95
Tattoos, 260
Taub, Daniel, 16, 87, 354n
Tavris, Carol, 69
Teachers, 92–93, 371–72, 408–9
Teasing, 382–83
Techow, Ernst Werner, 277
Telephone calls, 495–96
Telushkin, Helen, 13
Telushkin, Nissen, 49, 449
Temper. *See* Anger, controlling
Temptation, resisting, 365–66, 394–96
*Teshuva. See* Repentance
Theft, 6–7, 38–39, 97
  of another's ideas, 93–94
  defrauding as, 481
Threats, 192–93
Time, not wasting, 21–22, 143–44, 322–23
Tipping, 153–54
Tobacco. *See* Smoking
Tolerance, 186–87, 362–63
Torah law, secular fulfillment of, 411–12
Truth. *See* Lies; Honesty
Twain, Mark, 66
Twerski, Abraham, 62–63, 72–73, 296,
  331–33, 370, 385–86, 434
*Tzedaka. See* Charity

Ungar, André, 445

Vegetarianism, 133, 323–25

Waldenberg, Eliezer, 54
Washofsky, Mark, 54
Wealth, true, 94–95
Weddings, 163, 164, 167, 385–86
Wein, Berel, 90, 207
Weiss, Saul, 453
White lies, 102–4
Widows, treatment of, 70–71, 440
Wiener, Herbert, 19
Wiesel, Elie, 85, 231n
Wills, 177–78, 282–85, 474–75
Wine, 61–63
Winkler, Gershon, 346n
Wisdom, 42–43
Wise, Stephen S., 445
Wives. *See* Spouse
Wolfson, Ron, 196, 406
Woman's rights, 257–60
Work
  helping others find, 264–65, 273–74
  sacredness of, 255–57
  teaching child about, 333–34
  *See also* Business ethics; Professional
    ethics
Wouk, Herman, 22
Woznica, David, 135, 198n

Yitzchak, Levi, 150
Yochanan ben Zakkai, Rabbi, 76–77, 372–73,
  435, 476–77
Yom Kippur, charity and, 242
Yossi, Rabbi, 5, 437–38

Zalman, Reb. *See* Schacter-Shalomi, Zalman
Ziv, Simcha Zissel, 217
Zutra, Mar, 105

# About the Author

❦

Rabbi Joseph Telushkin, spiritual leader and scholar, is the author of *Jewish Literacy*, the most widely read book on Judaism of the past two decades. Another of his books, *Words That Hurt, Words That Heal*, was the motivating force behind Senators Joseph Lieberman and Connie Mack's 1996 Senate Resolution 151 to establish a "National Speak No Evil Day" throughout the United States. Rabbi Telushkin serves as an associate of CLAL, the National Jewish Center for Learning and Leadership, and has been the rabbi of the Los Angeles–based Synagogue for the Performing Arts. He has been hailed by *Talk* magazine as one of the fifty best speakers in the United States. He lives with his family in New York City, and lectures regularly throughout the United States.